# Military Helicopters
# of the World

# Military Helicopters of the World

Military Rotary-Wing Aircraft Since 1917

By Norman Polmar and
Floyd D. Kennedy, Jr.

**Naval Institute Press**
Annapolis, Maryland

Library of Congress Cataloging in Publication Data

Polmar, Norman.
　Military helicopters of the world.

　Includes index.
　1. Military helicopters.　I. Kennedy, Floyd D.
II. Title.
UG1230.P64　　　623.74′6047　　　80-84060
ISBN 0-87021-383-0　　　　　AACR2

Front endpaper photograph: A Piasecki HRP-1, Sikorsky HO3S-1, and Bell HTL-1, all U.S. Navy helicopters, with a blimp at the Naval Air Station, Lakehurst, New Jersey, in 1948. (U.S. Navy)

Back endpaper photograph: Nine U.S. Army H-21s from the 93rd Transportation Company land after an assault in Kien Giang province in southwestern Vietnam in the early 1960s. Behind them are six HU-1B Huey troop carriers from the 114th Air Mobile Company and six armed UH-1B Hueys from the Utility Tactical Transport Company. (U.S. Army)

# Foreword

*Military Helicopters* is an outstanding example of research and documentation on a subject of increasing importance in aviation literature. In reviewing this book, one is amazed at the amount of information presented regarding the early experiments in a great many countries to solve the challenge of vertical takeoff and landing.

It is interesting that experimentation started very soon after the Wright Brothers first flew but did not result in practical helicopters until the mid-1930s with the pioneering work of Louis Bréguet in France, Professor Henrich Focke in Germany, and Igor Sikorsky in the United States. It is also interesting to note how early the helicopter was put into production as a military machine for observation and light transport. However, it was always a great source of satisfaction to my father that these earliest machines quickly became very versatile and useful tools of mankind. Indeed, the lifesaving role of the helicopter has been one of the most satisfying aspects of the story of the development of helicopters. To date, it is conservatively estimated that the helicopter has saved over one million lives in its relatively short existence.

From the earliest sketches of Leonardo da Vinci in 1483 to the advanced helicopters of the 1980s, it is a long and fascinating story. The intensity of the effort is brilliantly catalogued in this book. It deserves a place of honor in every aviation historian's library. I congratulate the authors and collaborators on having produced what may well become a textbook against which all future efforts will be measured.

Sergei Sikorsky

# Acknowledgments

The authors of this book are in debt to many individuals and organizations for their assistance in producing this book, especially Harold Andrews, engineer, Naval Air Systems Command, and naval historian; Lt. Col. Nick P. Apple, public affairs, U.S. Air Force; Charles Brown, head, aviation analysis, Headquarters, U.S. Marine Corps; Thomas E.G. Bucksey, public relations, Ministry of Defence (Great Britain); Miss Madelyn Bush, public relations, Boeing Vertol; C.F. Bushey, manager, product information, aircraft equipment division, General Electric; Robert A. Carlisle, head, photojournalism branch, Office of Information, U.S. Navy; Robert G.H. Carroll, III, director of public relations, Sikorsky Aircraft; Miss Kathy Cassity, researcher, Air Force Museum, Wright-Patterson Air Force Base; Jean Labayle Couhat, editor, *Flottes de Combat*; Cdr. Ronald Despard, Information Spectrum, Inc.; Miss Evelyn Jutte, photojournalism branch, Office of Information, U.S. Navy; William Green, managing editor, *Air International*, and author; Mrs. Roxie Gresham, librarian, BDM Corp.; Khoji Ishiwata, editor, *Ships of the World*; Hal Klopper, public affairs, Hughes Helicopters; Mrs. Patty Maddocks, photographic librarian, U.S. Naval Institute; Bob Merzoian, Jr., public relations manager, Hiller Aviation; Ed Michalski, public affairs directorate, Department of Defense; Lt. (jg) Russell Miller, formerly intelligence staff, Helicopter ASW Wing 1; Capt. Gordon Murray, office of the Deputy Chief of Naval Operations (Air Warfare); Fred Rainbow, departments editor, U.S. Naval Institute *Proceedings*; G.S. Reed, public relations, Ministry of Defence (Great Britain); Theron Rinehart, public relations, Fairchild Republic; Dr. Robert L. Scheina, historian, U.S. Coast Guard; Fritz Schwartz, aviation enthusiast; Miss Betty Sprigg, public affairs directorate, Department of Defense; Gordon Swanborough, editor, *Air International* and author; John W.R. Taylor, editor, *Jane's All the World's Aircraft* and author; Dr. Milan Vego, military historian; Anthony J. Watts, editor, *Navy International*; and Mrs. Vicki Wolcott, librarian, BDM Corp.

The authors are also in debt to the staff of the Naval Institute Press who made this book possible: Thomas F. Epley, Deborah Guberti, and Beverly S. Baum. In addition, our wives, Beverly Polmar and Lynell Kennedy, spent considerable time working on this volume as well as tolerating us while we worked on it.

# Preface

This volume describes those rotary-wing aircraft developed for and flown by the world's armed forces. Included are the now-discarded autogiro and convertiplane types, as well as a few planned projects that were never completed. Current rotary-wing types, in addition to helicopters, include compound helicopters, which have forward flight propulsion systems as well as powered main rotors, and tilt-rotor aircraft. Figure 1 indicates the relationship of these aircraft to others that have vertical or short-runway operating characteristics. In the tilt-wing concept the entire wing pivots to change the angle of attack to shorten takeoff and landing runs; in lift-fan aircraft large fan-like devices, fixed or pivoting, provide lift; and in vectored-thrust aircraft the exhaust from the turbojet or turbofan engine is deflected downward to provide vertical lift. Generally, helicopter-type aircraft are described as low disc-loading.

Within this volume, rotary-wing aircraft are arranged first by nation of design origin and then by designer. The shifting of certain major rotary-wing aircraft designers from one institution or commercial firm to another, and the renaming of organizations makes this an imperfect arrangement. However, the reader will be assisted by the index, which contains both military designations and aircraft names. Also, because of the large number of aircraft types developed in the United States and the several military designation systems used since 1922, a full listing of military rotary-wing aircraft designations is provided at the start of the U.S. section.

Civil and military serials are indicated only for prototypes and certain significant aircraft. Several volumes that list military serials are described in the appendixes.

A number of one-man helicopters and rotary-wing devices have been developed since World War II, in part to provide the ultimate mobility for the individual soldier. Only those that received official military designations are described.

Finally, a large number of individuals and organizations have assisted the authors. They are acknowledged, with sincere appreciation, on the facing page. However, five individuals in particular are cited here: Mr. Sergei I. Sikorsky, who has assisted the authors and very kindly consented to write a foreword, and Messrs. William Green, Gordon Swanborough, and J.W.R. Taylor. In addition to their friendship and assistance, their innumerable writings in the aviation field have been a source of material and a standard of excellence. Also, Mr. Tommy Thomason has continually given answers to a multitude of questions.

Norman Polmar
Floyd D. Kennedy, Jr.

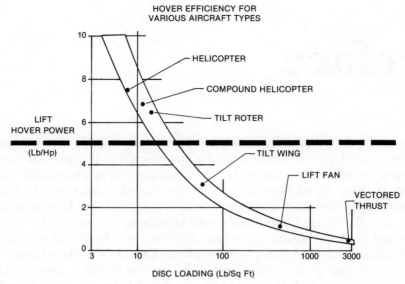

Figure 1.

# Glossary

| | |
|---|---|
| AAFSS | Advanced Aerial Fire Support System |
| AAH | Advanced Attack Helicopter |
| articulated | hinging of rotor blades at hub to permit upward and downward motion of rotor blades relative to the hub during flight |
| ASH | Advanced Scout Helicopter |
| ASW | Antisubmarine Warfare |
| collective pitch | changing of angle of incidence of all rotor blades simultaneously to improve lift and reduce drag |
| critical components | helicopter equipment and systems that if destroyed or severely damaged would prevent completion of the aircraft's mission; includes dynamic components |
| cyclic pitch | changing of angle of incidence of individual rotor blades as they rotate to give maximum angle for lift and minimum angle for drag |
| DASH | Drone Antisubmarine Helicopter |
| dynamic components | helicopter engine, rotor, transmission, and related components |
| FLIR | Forward-Looking Infrared |
| Hellfire | Helicopter Fire-and-forget missile |
| HLH | Heavy Lift Helicopter |
| HOT | Haut subsonique Optiquement Teleguide (high subsonic optically guided missile) |
| IFR | Instrument Flight Rules |
| IGE | In-Ground Effect |
| IR | Infrared |
| LAMPS | Light Airborne Multi-Purpose System |
| length | fuselage length |
| loaded | gross takeoff weight |
| LOH | Light Observation Helicopter |
| MAD | Magnetic Anomaly Detector |
| MG | machine gun |
| NASA | National Aeronautics and Space Administration (U.S.) |
| off-load (rotor) | use of fixed wings on helicopter to generate additional lift in forward flight to permit rotor energy to be applied to forward thrust rather than lift |
| OGE | Out-of-Ground Effect |
| RAF | Royal Air Force (Britain) |
| rotor diameter | main rotor diameter |
| SAR | Search and Rescue |
| semi-monocoque | fuselage structure providing structural strength without bracing and with minimal stiffeners |
| SOTAS | Stand-Off Target Acquisition System |

| | |
|---|---|
| stabilator | tail surface that serves as a stabilizer and elevator surface |
| STOL | Short Takeoff and Landing |
| T/O | Takeoff |
| TOW | Tube-launched, Optically tracked, Wire-guided missile |
| USAF | U.S. Air Force (from 1947) |
| USAAF | U.S. Army Air Forces (1941 to 1947) |
| UTTAS | Utility Tactical Transport Aircraft System |
| VIP | Very Important Person (modification for carrying senior government or military officials) |
| VSTOL | Vertical/Short Takeoff and Landing |
| VTOL | Vertical Takeoff and Landing |

# Contents

# Military Helicopters
# of the World

# Perspective

"Adoption by the Army of the airmobile concept—however imperfectly it may be described and justified by this report—is necessary and desirable. In some respects the transition is inevitable, just as was that from animal mobility to motor." That single conclusion of the U.S. Army's Howze Board in 1962 was a most farsighted view of the future of military helicopters. Rotary-wing aircraft have become as much a part of virtually all military activities as motorized vehicles have of ground forces. Indeed, it is difficult to find an aspect of military activity, at least in the armed forces of the major nations of the world, that have not been affected by the helicopter. Even the U.S. Strategic Air Command and the Soviet Strategic Rocket Forces rely upon helicopters for ICBM site inspection and security. Helicopters, of course, are fully integrated into the ground, naval, and air forces of most nations, as well as such quasi-military forces as the Soviet KGB and MVD internal security forces.

The earliest design of a rotary-wing machine is generally attributed to Leonardo da Vinci who, in 1483, sketched an "air gyroscope." He wrote: "I find that if this instrument with a screw be well made—that is to say, made of linen of which the pores be stopped up with starch—and be turned quickly, the said screw will make its spiral in the air and it will rise high." Da Vinci had his spiral rotary wing held in place by iron wire, with a small platform on which a man could stand and turn the screw-like wing. While the Italian master may not have described his device in military terms, his penchant for weapons and warfare make it obvious that had his air gyroscope been built it would have been considered in a military context.

Almost 200 years passed before the next significant event in rotary-wing development was recorded, when Mikhail V. Lomonosov, the "father of Russian science," in 1754 demonstrated a self-propelled model of a lifting airscrew to the Russian Academy of Science. Lomonosov intended his spring-powered device to lift instruments into the air. The Academy described his invention in these words: "The honorable Advisor Lomonosov demonstrated his invention called *Aerodynamic* to be used for the purpose of depressing the air by means of wings rotated horizontally in the opposite directions by the agency of a spring of the type used in clocks in order to lift the machine into the upper layers of the air."

In 1768 the French mathematician J.P. Paucton published a treatise, *Theorie de la vis d'Archimedes*, wherein he described a man-powered flying machine with two airscrews, one to support the machine in flight and one to provide forward propulsion. Although his design was impractical, Paucton led a number of Europeans in the discussion and construction of models of flying machines that could take off and land vertically, some of which might have hovered in flight. Again, however, these machines proved impractical.

Igor I. Sikorsky, a graduate of the Russian Naval Academy at Petrograd, left the Navy in 1906 to devote his energies to aviation and by 1908—at age nineteen—began the design and construction of helicopters. His first two rotary-wing machines, powered by gasoline motors and designed to carry an operator, were not successful and he turned his talents to more conventional aircraft. He built the

1

largest aircraft of the World War I era, which were successfully employed against the Germans as "strategic bombers."

At the same time, in France, Louis Bréguet built what was in many respects the first successful helicopter. In 1907, only four years after the Wright Brothers had flown at Kitty Hawk, North Carolina, Bréguet's machine managed to lift a man off the ground (albeit steadied by men with long poles).

Many more persons demonstrated an interest in rotary-wing aircraft as part of the massive thrust into the century of manned flight. These pioneer efforts are not discussed in this volume, which concentrates on military rotary-wing aircraft with a few significant exceptions. The Focke Fa 61 of Nazi Germany and Sikorsky VS-300 in the United States were undertaken with keen military interest and had a profound influence on senior officers who witnessed their trials. Thus they warrant a place in a volume about military rotary-wing aircraft.

When World War II erupted in Europe in September 1939, there were several rotary-wing aircraft under development. These were both helicopters and autogiros, the latter having an unpowered rotor which rotates from the movement of the aircraft through the air to serve as a lifting surface (i.e., wing).* There were also "mid-way" convertiplanes between the two types of rotary-wing aircraft.

Between the World Wars there was some limited interest in the military potential of these aircraft, especially in the United States. In particular, the U.S. Navy acquired three Pitcairn autogiros in 1931 (designated OP-1) and the U.S. Army bought a similar machine in 1936 (YG-2). The Navy machines undertook what were the first carrier evaluation and first combat area evaluation of rotary-wing aircraft. In 1931 the Navy flew trials with one of the autogiros from the pioneer carrier *Langley*, and the following year the Marine Corps flew one during counterguerrilla operations. Of special interest in this respect, the U.S. Marine Corps is the only such service of any nation to have a significant integral air arm.

There was extensive interest in autogiro development in the 1930s, all based on the work of La Cierva except for some indigenous Soviet efforts. Some 500 La Cierva-type autogiros were produced in a number of countries. The autogiro concept, however, was soon overtaken by that of the helicopter, and development of the autogiro essentially halted with the death of La Cierva in a commercial air crash in December 1936 in England.

During World War II, the Soviet Union, Third Reich, Japan, and the United States used rotary-wing aircraft on an operational basis. Soviet autogiros were employed in 1941 for reconnaissance and dropping propaganda leaflets. The Germans used helicopters for a number of logistic missions and at sea for antisubmarine operations, while the Japanese used autogiros flown from an aircraft carrier to hunt submarines. The Germans also flew a tethered, unpowered helicopter from U-boats. The U.S. Army Air Forces flew Sikorsky VS-316As (military R-4s) almost exclusively for search and rescue.† However, in 1944 an R-4 was used to fly a secret agent of the OSS (Office of Strategic Services, predecessor of the Central Intelligence Agency) into the Balkans on a clandestine mission.

---

*The term Autogiro was coined by Juan de la Cierva. Other terms for this type of aircraft include "autogyro," "giro," "giroplane," and "rotorplane." Unless some power can be briefly diverted to the rotor for a "jump start," an autogiro is actually a short takeoff and landing aircraft.

†U.S. Army Aviation was established in 1907 as a branch of the Signal Corps and in 1918 became the Air Service. In 1926 it was renamed Air Corps, and in 1941 the Air Forces, all part of the Army. In 1947 the U.S. Air Force was established as a separate service.

The U.S. and British navies, with the cooperation of their air forces, also flew trials from merchant ships to test the suitability of the VS-316A (naval designation HNS) for antisubmarine surveillance. The U.S. Coast Guard, a part of the Navy during the war, was placed in charge of U.S. naval helicopter development and also flew an HNS from a large cutter. Tests were also conducted during the war of a helicopter using a "dipping" sonar that was lowered into the water while the aircraft was in a hover mode.

After the war, U.S. military helicopter activity blossomed forth in terms of numbers of aircraft, types, and missions. Helicopters were evaluated in such roles as rescue at sea (including plane-crash guard for aircraft carriers), transport, casualty evacuation, wire laying, reconnaissance and surveillance, and ship-to-shore (amphibious) assault. At sea, helicopters replaced the floatplanes previously carried for reconnaissance and rescue aboard battleships and cruisers.

The Korean War (1950-1953) gave the U.S. armed forces extensive experience in helicopter operations in a wartime environment. The first U.S. military helicopters in Korea were four Sikorsky HO3S-1s that arrived with a Marine squadron during the desperate battle for the Pusan perimeter in August 1950. The Marine Corps led in the deployment of helicopters to Korea, followed by smaller numbers of Army machines. In November 1951, General Matthew B. Ridgway, the American commander in Korea, asked the Department of the Army to provide him with four helicopter transport battalions, each with 280 helicopters.

Used mainly for evacuation, observation, and liaison, hundreds of such machines were provided by the vast industrial capability of the United States for Army, Navy, Air Force, and Marine Corps use. Lieutenant General Maxwell Taylor, commander of the Eighth Army in Korea after February 1953, and a veteran airborne commander, observed, "The cargo helicopter, employed in mass, can extend the tactical mobility of the Army far beyond its normal capability. I hope that the United States Army will make ample provisions for the full exploitation of the helicopter in the future." The extensive employment of sea mines by the navy-less North Koreans led to a rejuvenation of U.S. minesweeping forces including extensive experimentation with helicopters for this role.

American helicopter operations in Korea were in stark contrast to the simultaneous French experience in Indochina. With perhaps a half dozen Sikorsky machines and a pair of Hiller 360 helicopters, the contribution of helicopters to the French forces in Indochina was minimal. But the French Army rapidly came to understand the significance of helicopters. Noted authority on unconventional war Bernard B. Fall wrote in his classic *Street Without Joy* that: "The French . . . used them in Algeria with a vengeance. In fact," he could write in the early 1960s, "no nation today can claim even remotely to have as much combat experience with helicopters as the French acquired in Algeria—although the French, for understandable reasons, keep that fact out of the news. By the time of the Algerian cease-fire in 1962, the French had concentrated no less than *six hundred* helicopters in that country: 380 troop-carrying craft of the H-34 and Vertol H-21 type; 25 medium craft of the S-55 and H-19 type, and about 200 light helicopters mainly of the 'Alouette' type." The French Army also experimented with arming these helicopters with a variety of guns and rockets.

But, according to Fall, "In spite of the fact that the barren hills of Algeria made aerial surveillance a great deal easier than the jungle-covered terrain of Viet-Nam, the results of 'heliborne' operations were not overly successful. The Alge-

The U.S. Navy's first experience with rotary-wing aircraft was this XOP-1 autogiro, shown here during trials aboard the pioneer carrier *Langley* (CV-1) in 1931. (U.S. Navy)

Autogiros were evaluated extensively for naval use in the 1930s. This is a privately owned Avro/La Cierva C 30A during evaluation aboard the Italian cruiser *Fume* in 1935. (Italian Navy)

Although little publicized in the West, during World War II the Germans used helicopters for antisubmarine operations at sea while the Japanese used ASW autogiros at sea. This is the highly successful German F1 282 Kolibi. (Imperial War Museum)

The first Allied helicopter to go to sea was the U.S. R-4, designated HNS-1 by the Navy. Here a YR-4B sits on the deck of the merchant ship *Daghestan* during Anglo-American trials in January 1944. A Royal Navy Swordfish biplane passes overhead. (U.S. Coast Guard)

The U.S. Marine Corps conducted extensive experiments in vertical assault operations during the late 1940s. These HRP-1 helicopters are demonstrating landing techniques at Quantico, Va., in November 1948. (U.S. Marine Corps)

U.S. Marines ride a flight-deck elevator up to the deck of an escort carrier during an amphibious exercise in 1952. Marine HRS troop helicopters stand ready on the flight deck. (U.S. Marine Corps)

Search-and-rescue has been a key role for helicopters since their introduction. This U.S. Navy HUP Hupmobile (officially named Retriever) is picking up the pilot of an AF Guardian ASW aircraft that crashed after taking off from the escort carrier *Block Island* (CVE-106). (U.S. Navy)

British naval helicopters and marines found themselves far from the sea during the Borneo campaign of the 1960s as they were used against Indonesian-supported guerrillas. This Wessex from the *Albion* is working with Gurkha troops in the jungles of Borneo. (Royal Navy)

rian nationalists soon learned about the foibles of the lumbering and noisy craft and quickly developed effective techniques for helicopter-baiting and trapping."

In this period the French began a strong domestic helicopter industry. However, British development of a viable helicopter industry lagged in the 1950s and early 1960s despite some highly innovative designs and prototypes. Instead, Britain produced mostly Sikorsky-developed machines under license in addition to large purchases from the United States. (Since the early 1960s there have been several joint Anglo-French helicopter production programs.)

The U.S. Marine Corps had conducted the first "vertical assault" exercises using helicopters to land troops ashore as early as 1948. But it was British carriers that launched the first helicopter assault into combat at Suez in November 1956. As part of the Anglo-French attempt to seize the Suez Canal, the British light carriers *Ocean* and *Theseus* used sixteen Whirlwind and six Sycamore helicopters to lift 415 British marines and twenty-three tons of ammunition and equipment ashore in just eighty-nine minutes.

The British subsequently made extensive use of helicopters in their numerous "police" and "caretaker" operations in Africa and Asia. Helicopters carried marines ashore from British aircraft carriers off Kuwait in 1961 and Tanganyika in 1964. During counter-guerrilla operations in Malaysia, Sarawak, Sabah, and Borneo, helicopters became a common sight as they supported British and allied ground troops. Their bases were often clearings in the jungles and, in some terrain, bamboo mats.

The true military transition to helicopters had to come about in the U.S. armed forces, as America is the only nation with sufficient industrial capacity to produce all of the helicopters desired by the military (and approved by the civilian-controlled defense establishment). The transition came about because of the Vietnam War.

On 11 December 1961, the escort carrier *Card* docked in Saigon, South Vietnam, and unloaded thirty-two U.S. Army H-21 helicopters. In his excellent study *Airmobility 1961-1971*, Lieutenant General John J. Tolson observed: "This event had a two-fold significance: it was the first major symbol of United States combat power in Vietnam; and, it was the beginning of a new era of airmobility in the United States Army." Twelve days later these helicopters were committed to the first airmobile combat action in Vietnam, Operation Chopper. Approximately 1,000 Vietnamese paratroopers were airlifted into a suspected Viet Cong complex ten miles from Saigon. The paratroopers met only slight resistance from the surprised enemy.

Two more Army helicopter companies were soon dispatched to South Vietnam and on 9 April 1962, the helicopter carrier *Princeton* stood offshore and launched a Marine helicopter squadron of UH-34s. The massive buildup of U.S. ground, air, and naval forces in Vietnam that followed the initial advisors "in country" was accompanied by a massive influx of helicopters. The number of helicopters in South Vietnam by the late 1960s was several thousand—Army, Navy, Air Force, and Marine, plus a number under CIA sponsorship.

The U.S. Army had assigned helicopters to ground divisions since the 1950s with a 1960 infantry division having a single aviation company with a score of helicopters and light aircraft. In late 1961, Secretary of Defense Robert S. McNamara ordered an extensive Army study of its aviation requirements. Lieutenant General Hamilton H. Howze, who had been the first director of Army Aviation, was placed in charge of the project. The so-called Howze Board actually had troop and aviation units assigned for field experimentation to support the group's analysis. The board's final report, submitted in August 1962, led to establishment of the Army's 1st Air Cavalry Division (Airmobile). This division, which deployed to Vietnam in the summer of 1965, had 434 aircraft assigned, all but 6 of which were helicopters. The 16,000-man unit became the most tactically mobile division in military history.

Significantly, several other Army units in Vietnam had comparable helicopter capability, while the Marine Corps similarly operated large numbers of helicopters. Beyond troop carriers, helicopters were used for casualty evacuation, surveillance, fire support (called "gunships"), and heavy lift ("flying cranes"). The gunships, initially standard troop helicopters carrying machine guns to lay down covering fire for their troops, led to the development of specialized gunships. The intensity of operations "in country" during the Vietnam War could be seen when, for example, in 1968 there were 42,000 medical evacuation ("medevac") missions flown by helicopters, carrying some 67,000 wounded U.S. troops and South Vietnamese civilians.

The Navy formed a helicopter attack squadron with twenty-four heavily armed UH-1B Hueys in 1966-1967 to provide close support for the large "brown-water" naval operations in the Mekong Delta (Operation Game Warden). These helicopters were based aboard amphibious ships and various floating craft.

Offshore, Navy helicopters provided search and rescue, at-sea replenishment of warships, oceanographic survey, and other support to the massive naval forces supporting U.S. involvement in Vietnam. Separate and apart from the Vietnam requirement, the Navy had also developed helicopter units for antisubmarine and mine countermeasure operations.

The American aerospace industry expanded apace to produce these helicopters. In their peak years during the Vietnam War, Boeing's Vertol Division built 398 CH-46s and CH-47s, the Hughes Tool Company's Aircraft Division delivered 1,129 OH-6s and TH-55s, while Bell Helicopter built 2,485 helicopters in one year—UH-1s, AH-1s, and TH-13s. In addition, these firms were producing helicopters for civil use and foreign military services. (The maximum production year for the Sikorsky Aircraft Division of United Aircraft was 467 helicopters in 1957—H-19s, CH-37s, and CH-34s. During the Vietnam War period, Sikorsky produced fewer but larger machines, including the CH-53 and CH-54.)

The large-scale helicopter operations were not without cost. From 1961 to the end of 1970 the U.S. armed forces lost 4,112 helicopters in Vietnam (compared to 3,217 fixed-wing aircraft). These losses were both while airborne and on the ground, the latter casualties occurring from Viet Cong mortars, rockets, and satchel charges, and included operational (non-combat) losses. Their use as aerial observation posts and to transport VIPs was indicated by the fact that five of the eight U.S. generals killed in Vietnam died while in helicopters.

Two other nations have used helicopters extensively in combat, Israel and the Soviet Union. The Israelis acquired their first helicopter during the October 1956 war. Their helicopter force grew slowly, mostly with U.S. and French machines. They were used extensively in the 1967 war, on both the Syrian and Egyptian fronts. Used primarily to carry troops into combat, they generally returned to base carrying wounded soldiers. One Israeli CH-34 was attacked by two Egyptian MiG-21 fighters. Because of the condition of the wounded, the Israeli pilot was

The U.S. Navy and Royal Navy both developed specialized aircraft carriers for the amphibious assault role. Here, Royal Marines rush to board Wessex HU 5 helicopters aboard the commando ship *Albion*. (Royal Navy)

Soldiers climb aboard U.S. Army UH-1D Huey helicopters for a search-and-destroy mission in Vietnam. Note the machine guns in the helicopter door openings. (U.S. Army)

U.S. Marine UH-1E Huey helicopters touch down with ammunition for Marine 105-mm howitzers at a fire support base in Vietnam. (U.S. Marine Corps)

A Marine CH-53 Sea Stallion lifts a howitzer during the relocation of an artillery battery during the Vietnam War. Helicopters gave U.S. troops unprecedented tactical mobility in that conflict. (U.S. Marine Corps)

An Army UH-1D Huey lands aboard a 56-foot landing craft modified for riverine operations in the Vietnam War. This was a joint Army-Navy operation in the Mekong Delta. (U.S. Navy)

Military helicopters are used for resupply at sea as well as on land. Here a Navy UH-56 Sea Knight carries aircraft fuel tanks to the carrier *Hancock* (CVA-19) while the flattop refuels from an oiler in the Gulf of Tonkin. (U.S. Navy)

A U.S. Navy CH-53 Sea Stallion prepares to lift an Mk-105 mine countermeasures sled from an amphibious assault ship. (U.S. Navy)

severely limited in the evasive action he could take but succeeded in evading the Soviet-built MiG-21s for several minutes before landing in a grove of palm trees which hid his helicopter. (During World War II the German air force had tested the ability of a helicopter to survive attacks by high-performance piston fighters.) Helicopters continue to play a major role in Israeli military activities. They have been used to steal an Egyptian radar, and more recently the Israelis have begun fitting their relatively small missile ships with helicopter platforms. The Israelis were also probably the first to employ helicopters in the electronic-jamming role in direct support of ground troops, using jammers to blank out enemy radars in support of their own operations. Subsequently, U.S. Army helicopters have been configured for radar surveillance of enemy ground positions and movements, while U.S. and Soviet helicopters as well as probably Israeli ones have been fitted to intercept enemy tactical communications.

The Soviet Union is the world's largest operator of helicopters after the United States. Soviet helicopters in military markings are used in a variety of roles. While Soviet-supplied helicopters have been used in combat by the North Vietnamese, Egyptians, Iraqis, and other Third World nations, probably the first major Soviet use of helicopters came in the late-1979 invasion of Afghanistan. A large number of troop-carrying helicopters as well as the multi-purpose Mi-24 Hind gunship have been seen in that conflict, the Soviet Union's first direct use of helicopters in combat. In early 1981, U.S. Defense officials estimated more than 200 helicopters were with the Soviet forces in Afghanistan.

The following table shows the approximate current helicopter strengths of the Soviet and U.S. armed forces.

In general, Soviet helicopter development has been less innovative than that of the United States. However, the Soviet helicopter efforts have demonstrated leadership in two areas: helicopter gunships and heavy-lift helicopters. The U.S. Army pioneered the use of gunships in the Vietnam War, from simply mounting a pair of flexible machine guns in the door openings of troop carriers, to the "Go-Go Birds" of the 1st Air Cavalry Division. The latter were four CH-47s which were armed with two 20-mm multi-barrel Gatling guns, 40-mm grenade launchers, and .50-caliber machine guns. These "flying battleships" were not successful; more so were the AH-1 Cobra and SeaCobra series gunships, and the more specialized gunship designs. But the Soviets have flown more heavily armed helicopters in the form of modified Mi-8 Hip and some variants of the Mi-24 helicopters. Not until the AH-64 being developed by Hughes is operational in numbers in the mid-1980s will the United States match the firepower of the existing Soviet gunship helicopters.

The Soviet Union has also developed an impressive array of heavy-lift helicopters. The Mi-10 Harke can lift over sixteen tons and the Mi-6 Hook and Mi-26 Halo can carry almost ten tons of cargo. (The larger Mi-12 Homer was flown in only small numbers and is no longer operational.) The largest helicopter in U.S. service, which will reach operational squadrons in the early 1980s, is the Sikorsky CH-53E, with a sixteen-ton lift. The U.S. Army's Boeing Vertol CH-47 can lift fourteen tons, while the Sikorsky CH-54—dubbed Skycrane—which is flown by Army reserve units can lift ten tons.

The Soviet armed forces appear to be developing advanced concepts for using helicopters as tactical Command Posts (CP). In the oft-used Soviet style of attributing new developments to foreign armies, a 1981 issue of the *Soviet Military Review* describes advanced helicopter CPs: "Besides the commander, they carry a group of staff officers of different specialities, who collect data on enemy and friendly forces, control artillery fire and guide aircraft to enemy targets, bring new combat missions to the notice of the forces in good time, and maintain uninterrupted communications between them and their neighbours.

"Plans are being drawn up to create air CPs fit for use by control bodies both in flight and after landing. One foreign variant of such an air CP envisages the use of a helicopter with a specifically designed container attached underneath and provided with ventilation and illumination [lighting] systems, and with wheels to move on land.

"To ensure reliable and flexible troop control, it is considered essential to provide helicopters with TV, radar, relay and other special equipment, which will make it possible to transfer immediately to the CP or artillery fire positions images of the battlefield, results of using this or that type of weapons, troops' actions, newly detected targets, and other installations."

Recent Soviet writings have also stressed the role of the armed helicopter in air-to-ground operations and in the antihelicopter mission. According to some Soviet writers, the armed Mi-8 Hip and Mi-24 Hind are the best weapons for countering Western antitank helicopters. Innovative Soviet tactics and doctrine for the use of helicopters, the continued development of advanced types, and a high production rate—over 1,000 per year of all types, military and civil—insure that these aircraft will play an increasing role in the armed forces of the Soviet Union.

Similarly, Western military helicopter development, especially in the United States, France, and Italy, plus significant production in Great Britain and West Germany, indicate a continued growth in the West's use of military helicopters. However, as these words were being written, the appearance of the latest models of the Mi-24 Hind, the improved Mi-17 configuration of the widely used Mi-8 Hip, and the powerful new Mi-26 Halo, combined with Soviet production rates, tend to indicate a new level of Soviet military competition with the West.

**Table 1. Military Helicopters, Early 1981**

**Soviet Union**

| Air Forces* | Naval Aviation |
|---|---|
| 300 {Mi-1 Hare / Mi-2 Hoplite | 180 Ka-25 Hormone |
| 170 Mi-4 Hound | few Mi-8 Hip |
| 360 Mi-6 Hook | 70 Mi-14 Haze |
| 2,500 + Mi-8 Hip | |
| 10 Mi-10 Harke | |
| 1,200 + Mi-24 Hind | |
| few Mi-26 Halo | |
| (~5,000) | (~250) |

**United States**

| Army | Army Reserve | Army National Guard |
|---|---|---|
| 900 AH-1 HueyCobra | 280 UH-1 Huey | 16 AH-1 HueyCobra |
| 9 EH-1 Huey | 53 CH-47 Chinook | 1,350 UH-1 Huey |
| 1,960 UH-1 Huey | 94 OH-58 Kiowa | 385 OH-6 Cayuse |
| 16 OH-6 Cayuse | | 59 CH-47 Chinook |

330 CH-47 Chinook
2 CH-54 Tarhe
100 TH-55 Osage
1,385 OH-58 Kiowa
100 UH-60 Blackhawk
(~4,700)

(427)

70 CH-54 Tarhe
510 OH-58 Kiowa
7 TH-1 Huey

(~2,400)

*Navy*
6 AH-1 SeaCobra
28 TH-1 Huey
78 UH-1 Huey
70 SH-2 LAMPS
120 SH-3 Sea King
90 HH/UH-46 Sea Knight
21 CH/RH-53 Sea Stallion
35 TH-57 SeaRanger
(~450)

*Naval Reserve*
8 HH-1 Huey
6 HH-3 Sea King
28 SH-3 Sea King

(42)

*Marine Corps*
84 AH-1 SeaCobra
84 UH-1 Huey
few VH-3 Sea King
200 CH-46 Sea Knight
134 CH-53 Sea Stallion
few CH-53E Super Stallion
(~510)

*Marine Corps Reserve*
8 AH-1 SeaCobra
36 UH-1 Huey
18 CH-46 Sea Knight
18 CH-53 Sea Stallion

(80)

*Air Force*
24 HH-1 Huey
19 TH-1 Huey
110 UH-1 Huey
38 CH-3 Sea King
21 HH-3 Jolly Green Giant
38 HH-53 Super Jolly
(250)

*Air Force Reserve*
5 HH-1 Huey
5 UH-1 Huey
7 CH-3 Sea King
7 HH-3 Jolly Green Giant

(24)

*Air National Guard*
11 HH-3 Jolly Green Giant

(11)

*Coast Guard*
37 HH-3F Pelican
70 HH-52A Sea Guard
(107)

---

*The Soviet Air Forces provide helicopters to all of the other Soviet armed services except the Navy, which has its own integral air arm. The other services are Ground Forces (Army), Strategic Rocket Forces, and National Air Defense Forces. The para-military KGB security service and MVD boarder troops also operate large numbers of helicopters.

A Bell Huey carrying a mine-dispensing cannister sowing 2,200 mini land mines over an area some 160 feet wide and 3,280 feet in length (50 m × 1 km). (Valsella SpA)

U.S. Navy RH-53D Sea Stallion and Soviet Mi-8 Hip helicopters were used to sweep the Suez Canal in the 1974 mine-clearing operation. (U.S. Navy)

The Bell Huey (Iroquois) series has been produced in greater numbers than any other helicopter design in history with some 12,300 of the Huey types and 1,700 of the Cobra types having been built through 1980. This is a view of the Huey production line at Fort Worth, Texas. (Bell)

This ominous-looking helicopter is a Soviet Mi-24 Hind-A carrying four rocket pods. The improved Hind-D is more heavily armed, while the most heavily armed helicopters now flying are Mi-8 Hips.

The Soviet Mi-12 Homer has a greater lift capability than any other helicopter, being able to carry some 27½ tons of cargo for vertical takeoff and 33 tons with a short-run takeoff.

The British-built Wasp is a small antisubmarine helicopter for use aboard frigates and other small warships. This moving deck structure was developed for research and to help train Wasp pilots. (Royal Navy)

A U.S. Navy SH-3 Sea King helicopter lowers its dipping sonar during an ASW exercise in the Western Pacific. (U.S. Navy)

Allies at sea: A British Sea King antisubmarine helicopter from the carrier *Ark Royal* hovers above a U.S. nuclear-propelled attack submarine. (Royal Navy)

South Vietnamese marines prepare to board U.S. Marine CH-46 Sea Knight helicopters. The massive U.S. helicopter force greatly increased the effectiveness of Allied forces in the Vietnam War. (U.S. Marine Corps)

# ARGENTINA

# Cicaré Aeronautica

CH-III Colibri
C.K. 1

The Cicaré Colibri is a small training helicopter currently under development for the Argentine Air Force. Originally designated the CH-III, this 1973 design was extensively modified during construction of the first prototype so that in the 1975-1976 period its designation was changed to C.K. 1. First flight of the C.K. 1 prototype took place in September 1976, and construction of a pre-series batch of five Colibris was initiated in 1978 for evaluation by the Argentine military.

The Colibri is a two- or three-place light helicopter with a four-bladed, rigid main rotor and a two-bladed anti-torque tail rotor driven by a 190-hp Lycoming flat-four cylinder engine. The fuselage is of steel tube construction with a fiberglass cabin and aluminum tailboom. The rotors are also of fiberglass construction. Landing gear is a pair of tubular skids, and the cabin accommodates either two (in the training version) or three (in the utility version) in side-by-side seats. There is additional space for up to 100 pounds of baggage.

The Argentine Air Force intends to use production C.K. 1s for training helicopter pilots, and an additional market is perceived to exist throughout Latin America for C.K. 1 use as a light utility/agricultural aircraft.

First flight: September 1976
Service introduction: 1981 (?)
Users: Argentina

**Characteristics**

Crew: 1 pilot, 1 copilot/student
Engine: 1 Lycoming HIO-360-D1A piston 190 hp
Dimensions: length 28 ft (8.53 m); height 8 ft 1¼ in (2.47 m); rotor diameter 24 ft 11¼ in (7.6 m)
Weight: empty 1,034 lbs (469 kg); loaded 1,764 lbs (800 kg)
Speed: cruise 74.5 mph (120 km/h); maximum 101 mph (163 km/h)
Range: 298 miles (480 km)
Ceiling: hover OGE 5,575 ft (1,700 m); service 12,800 ft (3,900 m)
Climb: 1,180 ft/min (360 m/min)
Payload: 1 or 2 troops (total capacity 3 persons)

# AUSTRO-HUNGARY

The two World War I-era helicopters described on the following pages were designated Schraubenfesselflieger or "propeller-driven captive aircraft" in Austro-Hungarian records of the time. However, they were informally known as the PKZ 1 and PKZ 2, the designation derived from their designers' names.

## Petróczy-Kármán-Zurovec

### PKZ 1

This early effort at developing a rotary-wing machine for military observation was undertaken by three Austro-Hungarians: Lieutenant Stefan Petróczy, chief instructor for balloon crews in the Austro-Hungarian Ministry of War; Dr. Theodore von Kármán, director of the research group at Fischamend airfield; and Ensign Wilhelm Zurovec, an engineer at Fischamend. As early as February 1916, Petróczy, a pre-war aviator, proposed a captive helicopter-like device that would be tethered to the ground. Driven by an electric motor, this device could replace the vulnerable hydrogen-filled balloons then used for observation at the battlefront. He was able to obtain some funding from the Austro-Hungarian War Ministry, with even the Austro-Hungarian Navy expressing interest. Tentatively, specifications for the machine included an operational altitude of some 2,000 feet, the ability to be towed by a ship steaming at 30 knots, and the ability to be rapidly winched down onto the ship. This harbinger of the modern military helicopter (and especially the German Fa 330 automotive kite of World War II) led Petróczy to engage the help of several military and civilian experts. His efforts were facilitated by his advances in the Army, and several designs for a captive helicopter were developed. The aircraft would carry one observer, a machine gun, camera, and telephone and would be connected to the ground (or ship) through the tethering cable. In April of 1917, von Kármán and Zurovec were assigned to assist in constructing the actual helicopter. Several models were built and tested prior to a man-carrying helicopter being ordered on 21 August 1917.

The Hungarian General Engine Works (Allgemeine Maschinen Fabrik) or MAG in Budapest constructed this first helicopter. The aircraft's frame consisted of open steel tubing, with an observer's station in the center. The electric motor was fitted under the observer. The motor, which weighed 430 pounds, produced 190 hp, significantly less than the 250-hp goal for the Austro-Daimler motor. Reduction gears and right-angle transmissions drove the four four-bladed propellers, mounted in tandem on top of the airframe, two forward of the observer and two aft. The motor was powered with direct current generated by a gasoline-driven dynamo and transmitted up to the helicopter through an aluminum cable. A cable length of 2,625 feet was planned for operational use.

Assembly of the helicopter began on 18 October 1917 and it was completed the following March. During flight tests the helicopter was tethered by three cables and made four flights, carrying aloft three men on the second test. The cables limited the machine to an altitude of 20 feet. When the electric motor burned out during the fourth test the program ended as it was impossible to repair the motor. Plans were made to install an internal-combustion engine in the helicopter but this was not done.

First flight: March 1918 (tethered)
Service introduction: not operational

**Characteristics**

Crew: 1 pilot-observer
Engine: 1 Austro-Daimler electric motor 190 hp powered by a gasoline-driven dynamo
    with power transmitted through cable to the helicopter while hovering
Dimensions: length approximately 85 feet (25.9 m); rotor diameter 13 ft 9 in (4.2 m)
Weight: loaded 1,433 lbs (650 kg)
Speed: (tethered)
Range: (tethered)
Ceiling: approximately 2,000 ft (610 m) designed
Climb:

The PKZ 1 after being completed by the Hungarian General Engine Works in Budapest in March 1918. The Austro-Daimler electric motor, located below the cockpit, drove four contra-rotating propellers through a right-angle transmission system. Rubber air bags were fitted as an undercarriage during flight tests. (Courtesy Peter M. Grosz)

# Zurovec

## PKZ 2

After his participation in the PKZ 1 project, Zurovec began work on an improved helicopter of his own design in November 1917. Petróczy encouraged the project, but it was privately financed by a Hungarian bank without formal government support. Still, Petróczy's interest in the helicopter and an ill-fated demonstration for Austro-Hungarian military officers on 10 June 1918 led to its consideration in a military context.

The Zurovec helicopter had a simple, triangular metal frame that was modular in construction to facilitate being disassembled and transported, reflecting its intended role as a battlefield observation aircraft. Although tethered, the Zurovec machine was self-propelled with three 100-hp Gnome rotary engines being geared to drive two contra-rotating, wooden airscrew-rotors. The pilot-observer sat in a cockpit below the rotors, with the whole machine resting on one large and three smaller rubberized-fabric bags (that were kept inflated by an on-board compressor pump driven by the motors). After several successful test flights between 2-5 April 1918, during which the PKZ 2 reached a height of four feet, the original engines were replaced. Three 120-hp Le Rhône engines were installed and flight tests resumed on 17 May.

The PKZ 2 was built at the iron and steel works of Dr. Liptak & Co. AG in Pestszentlörincz, near Budapest. Over 30 successful flights were conducted during May and early June with the more powerful Le Rhône engines, with the PKZ 2 reaching a reported altitude of 164 feet (tethered) and remaining aloft for up to one-half hour. With the improved engines, Zurovec also fitted an observer's cockpit *above* the rotors. Fuel for one hour of flight could be carried. The 10 June demonstration of the PKZ 2 before Austro-Hungarian military officials ended in a crash when the engines began to lose power and the cable crew winching down the helicopter failed to use sufficient care. This marked the end of the Zurovec project, although he proposed replacing the air-cooled Le Rhône engines with water-cooled versions and certain other improvements. Much later von Kármán claimed that he had flown the PKZ 2 to an altitude of 984 feet and remained aloft for one hour, although this appears to have been unlikely.

First flight: 2 April 1918
Service introduction: not operational

**Characteristics**

Crew: 1 pilot-observer; a second observer could be carried after refitting with 120-hp
   engines
Engines: 3 Gnome rotary piston 100 hp each; replaced by 3 Le Rhône rotary piston
   120 hp each
Dimensions: rotor diameter 19 ft 8 in (6.0 m)
Weight: loaded 3,087 lbs (1,398 kg)
Speed: (tethered)
Range: (tethered)
Ceiling:
Climb:

*Left*: The PKZ 2 in flight at the Liptak & Co. factory on 5 April 1918. Wilhelm Zurovec, the designer, is reaching for one of the air bags of the aircraft's undercarriage. After this flight the 100-hp Gnome engines were replaced by more powerful Le Rhônes. (Courtesy Peter M. Grosz). *Right*: The PKZ 2 in flight at an altitude of 82 feet. Several other helicopter-type aircraft were proposed for the Austro-Hungarian Army during the 1914–1918 war. In the late 1920s, additional helicopters based on the PKZ 2 design were privately built. (Courtesy Peter M. Grosz).

The modified PKZ 2 after installation of the 120-hp Le Rhône engines and new air-bag cushions as well as an observer's cockpit. The man in the cockpit is probably Zurovec. There are reports of the PKZ 2 being seen in an Italian museum in 1935. After World War I, the Italians confiscated the Fischamend laboratory and may have transported the PKZ 2 to Italy. (Courtesy Peter M. Grosz)

# CZECHOSLOVAKIA
# Central Bohemian Machine Works

HC 2
HC 102

The HC 2 was the first helicopter to be produced in numbers in Czechoslovakia, with the Czech government stating that between 20 and 30 were built for both military and civil use. This helicopter was followed by the more powerful HC 102, again produced in a small series although the exact number has not been published. (In addition, the state-owned aircraft industry produced prototypes of larger HC 3 and HC 4 helicopters but they did not enter series production.)

The HC 2 and HC 102 resembled the smaller Hiller helicopter designs, with a small cabin with plexiglass covering, a long tailboom supporting an anti-torque rotor, and a skid landing gear. Two persons were seated side by side, with the right-hand seat and controls being removable so that a stretcher or cargo could fit in the cockpit. The HC 2 was powered by an 83-hp Praga DH engine while the HC 102 had a more powerful engine, giving increased performance. The later helicopter also had reinforced plastic parts.

In military service these helicopters were used for liaison, rescue, and casualty evacuation. They are no longer believed to be in Czech military service.

First flight: HC 2 1953
Service introduction:
Users: Czechoslovakia

**Characteristics**

Crew: 1 pilot, 1 observer
Engine: 1 M110H radial piston 115 hp
Dimensions: length 27 ft 7¾ in (8.4 m); rotor diameter 28 ft 10 in (8.78 m)
Weight: loaded 1,500 lbs (681 kg)
Speed: cruise 75 mph (120.75 km)
Range: 109 miles (175 km)
Ceiling:
Climb:

The Czechoslovak armed forces have used Soviet-designed helicopters almost exclusively with a small number of Czech-built HC 2 and HC 102 helicopters being employed in military roles.

# FRANCE

The helicopters listed here were all developed by the government-owned aerospace industry, which has undergone several reorganizations since the late 1940s when the first military programs were initiated. Accordingly, these helicopters are listed in chronological order. Details of the reorganizations are provided in Appendix A.

In addition to the joint Anglo-French helicopter projects described under the French listings, the Westland-Aérospatiale Lynx is described under the listings for Great Britain. Also mentioned under Great Britain (Westland) is the aborted WG 34, which was to have been a collaborative effort of Westland, Aérospatiale, and Agusta. That project was dropped in favor of a joint Anglo-Italian helicopter being developed by EHI Ltd. (see page 80).

# Sud-Ouest

SO 1220                     Djinn
SO 1221                     HO-1

The Djinn was designed by Sud-Ouest as a two-seat utility helicopter using a unique propulsion system (described below) that had been pioneered in the Sud-Ouest SO 1110 Ariel II and SO 1120 Ariel III helicopters. The prototype SO 1221 flew in late 1953, followed by the pre-production Djinn on 23 September 1954, and the first production machine on 5 January 1956. One hundred seventy-nine Djinns were built before production terminated in the early 1960s. The main customer for the SO 1221 was the French armed forces, which received over 100 of the type. Civilian customers were located in the United States, Argentina, Switzerland, and seven other countries. Examples were evaluated for military use in the United States and West Germany.

The Djinn used a "cold-jet" propulsion system wherein a 240-hp Turboméca turbogenerator mounted aft of the cabin supplied compressed air through the rotor shaft and twin rotor blades to rotor-tip ejectors, creating nearly a ramjet effect without the bulky combustion chambers necessitated by the latter system at the rotor tips. Directional stability was provided by a cantilever monoplane-type tail unit with two fins mounted at the ends of the horizontal stabilizer and a large central rudder positioned in the engine exhaust. The fuselage was a welded steel-tube structure surrounding an extensively glazed cabin with accommodations for a pilot and one passenger. A skid-type landing gear was fitted; instrumentation was minimal.

The principal operator of the Djinn was the French Army, which used the SO 1221 for observation, liaison, training, and casualty evacuation. One French machine was used in the launching trials of the Nord SS 10 wire-guided, antitank missile, but no armament was fitted to operational helicopters. The U.S. Army evaluated three with the designation YHO-1 and the Federal German Army conducted trials with six. Most Djinns were withdrawn from French front-line service in the late 1960s.

First flight: SO 1220 2 January 1953, SO 1221 16 December 1953
Service introduction: 1956
Users: France (evaluated by West Germany and United States)

**Variants**

SO 1220  single-seat, open-framework propulsion system test bed; 2 built.

SO 1221  utility and liaison helicopter for military and civilian use; total production
         consisted of 5 prototypes, 22 preproduction, and 150 production units.

YHO-1    U.S. Army designation for 3 evaluation aircraft (assigned serial 57-6104/106);
         sold to French Army after U.S. trials.

**Characteristics**

Crew: 1 pilot

Engine: 1 Turboméca Palouste IV turbogenerator 240 shp

Dimensions: length 17 ft 4 in (5.3 m); height 8 ft 5 in (2.6 m); rotor diameter 36 ft 1 in
     (11.0 m)

Weight: empty 794 lbs (360 kg); loaded 1,764 lbs (800 kg)

Speed: cruise 65 mph (105 km/h); maximum 80.5 mph (130 km/h)

Range: 118 miles (190 km)

Ceiling: hover IGE 5,904 ft (1,800 m)

Climb:

Payload: 1 passenger

The Djinn was used by the French armed forces as a two-place utility helicopter and was
evaluated by the U.S. and West German armies. During the U.S. evaluation of three
aircraft, the first of which is shown here, they were designated YHO-1. (U.S. Army)

# Sud-Est

SE 3130                          Alouette II
SA 313B                          Alouette II Astazou
SA 318C

The original Alouette (Lark) was a three-seat, general-purpose helicopter developed by Sud-Est for agricultural duties. When Sud-Est's sister company, Sud-Ouest, successfully used the gas turbine engine in the SO 1221 Djinn, Sud-Est fitted the same type of engine to the basic Alouette airframe, creating the highly successful SE 3130 Alouette II. The subsequent provision of an improved power plant led to the redesignation of the helicopter as Alouette II Astazou. The Alouette II series, in production through 1975, was used widely for military (including naval) and civilian activities by 46 nations. Several world helicopter flight records fell to this helicopter.

The Alouette II series has a "wasp's head" cockpit, extensively glazed with a light metal frame and a tailboom of steel-tube framework. The engine is mounted aft of the cockpit with a three-bladed, all-metal main rotor. The anti-torque tail rotor is at the right-hand extremity of the tailboom. The cockpit seats a pilot and four passengers. Either a quadracycle landing gear or skids with retractable wheels for ground maneuvering are fitted.

As listed below, a large number of military services have used Alouette IIs for a variety of missions, among them ASW, observation, casualty evacuation, rescue, transport, liaison, close air support, and flying crane duties. Total production—for military and civil use—came to over 900 SE 3130/SA 313B and over 400 SA 318C variants when production ended in 1975. The British Army acquired two Alouette IIs in 1958 for trials (assigned serials XN 132/133).

An Aéronavale Alouette II on skids. (French Armed Forces)

First flight: SE 3130 12 March 1955
Service introduction: 1957
Users: Algeria, Belgium, Cameroun, Central African Republic, Chad, Dominican Repub-
lic, Finland, France, West Germany, Great Britain, India, Indonesia, Israel, Ivory Coast,
Laos, Lebanon, Libya, Mexico, Morocco, Netherlands, Nigeria, Peru, Portugal, South
Africa, Sweden, Switzerland, Tunisia

**Variants**

SE 3130  prototype and production Alouette II. Prototype had Turboméca Artouste I
             turboshaft 360-shp engine; changed in production aircraft (see below).
SA 313B redesignation of SE 3130 in 1957.
SA 318C production Alouette II with improved engine.

**Characteristics**

Crew: 1 pilot
Engine: SE 3130 1 Turboméca Artouste IIC6 turboshaft 530 shp derated to 360 shp
      SA 318C 1 Turboméca Astazou IIA turboshaft 530 shp derated to 360 shp
Dimensions: length 31 ft 10 in (9.7 m); height 9 ft (2.75 m); rotor diameter 33 ft 5⅝
      in (10.2 m)
Weight: SE 3130 empty 1,973 lbs (895 kg); loaded 3,527 lbs (1,600 kg) SA 318C emp-
      ty 1,929 lbs (875 kg); loaded 3,630 lbs (1,650 kg)
Speed: SE 3130 cruise 102 mph (165 km/h); maximum 115 mph (185 km/h) SA 318C
      cruise 105 mph (170 km/h); maximum 127 mph (205 km/h)
Range: SE 3130 350 miles (565 km) SA 318C 446 miles (720 km)
Ceiling: SE 3130 hover OGE 3,018 ft (920 m); hover IGE 5,412 ft (1,650 m); service
      7,050 ft (2,150 m) SA 318C hover OGE 3,115 ft (950 m); hover IGE 4,985 ft
      (1,520 m); service 10,824 ft (3,300 m)
Climb: SE 3130 1,000 ft/min (300 m/min); SA 318C 1,300 ft/min (396 m/min)
Payload: 4 troops or 2 ASW homing torpedoes in ASW variants

A French Alouette II fires an SS-11 antitank missile.

An Alouette II of France's Aéronavale takes off from the aircraft carrier *Arromanches*. The aircraft is fitted with a quadracycle landing gear, more useful than skids when manually moving aircraft on a flight deck or to and from hangars. (French Armed Forces)

An Israeli-flown Alouette II rests atop an outcropping in the Sinai desert. The Israeli Air Force (Heyl Ha'Avir) has used helicopters extensively in combat, in both conventional and unconventional operations. The latter includes tactical electronic jamming, raids across borders, and stealing a Soviet radar installed in Egypt. (Israeli Air Force)

# Sud-Est

SE 3160                                    Alouette III
SA 316B                                   Alouette III Astazou
SA 319B

The Alouette III is a seven-seat derivative of the earlier five-place Alouette II. It was designed by the Sud-Est organization and was successively produced, as the result of corporate mergers, by Sud-Aviation, beginning in 1956, and by Aérospatiale from 1970. The original Sud-Est designation SE 3160 was used for all Artouste-engined Alouette IIIs delivered through 1969. Upon takeover of the Alouette III production line by Aérospatiale on 1 January 1970, the designation of all subsequent Artouste-powered Alouette IIIs became SA 316B. The Sud-Aviation designation SA 319B was applied to the Astazou-powered variant of the Alouette III from its inception in the mid-1960s. The SA 319B differs from the SA 316B only in engine type and resulting weight and performance figures.

The SA 316B has an 870-shp Turboméca Artouste IIIB turboshaft engine, derated to 570 shp; the SA 319B has the Turboméca Astazou turboshaft engine, also 870 shp but derated to 600 shp. All variants of the Alouette III have a three-bladed main rotor and a boom-mounted anti-torque tail rotor. The fuselage is constructed of welded-steel tubes with a semi-monocoque tail section and is completely enclosed in contrast to the open fuselage of the Alouette II. The skids of the Alouette II are replaced with tricycle landing gear on the Alouette III, with optional skis or pontoons available. Armament on the military versions varies with mission, ranging from a 7.62-mm machine gun firing from the starboard side of the fuselage to AS 11 or AS 12 antitank missiles on jettisonable launching rails. A naval version of the SA 319B carries one Mk-46 ASW homing torpedo and MAD gear or two Mk-46 torpedoes.

Even more popular than the Alouette II, the Alouette III has been sold to military and civilian operators in 73 countries. Over 1,400 Alouette III helicopters of both the SA 316B and SA 319B variants have been built, and production continued into 1980. India, Romania, and Switzerland negotiated licenses with Sud-Aviation to build the Alouette III, with production runs having been completed in India and Switzerland but continuing in Romania.

First flight: Alouette III 28 February 1959; Alouette III Astazou 1967
Service introduction: Alouette III 1960; Alouette III Astazou 1969
Users: Abu Dhabi, Angola, Argentina, Australia, Austria, Bangladesh, Belgium, Burma, Burundi, Cambodia, Cameroun, Congo Republic, Denmark, Dominican Republic, Ecuador, Eire, Ethiopia, France, Gabon, Ghana, India, Indonesia, Iraq, Israel, Ivory Coast, Jordan, Laos, Lebanon, Libya, Malaysia, Mexico, Nepal, Netherlands, Pakistan, Peru, Portugal, Rhodesia, Romania, Rwanda, Saudi Arabia, Singapore, South Africa, Switzerland, Tunisia, Venezuela, Vietnam, Yugoslavia, Zaire, Zambia

**Variants**

SE 3160  original Sud-Est designation for Artouste-powered Alouette IIIs through 1969. Military versions carry 7.62-mm MG or 20-mm gun in remote-control mount or two wire-guided AS 12 antitank missiles or four AS 11 missiles or two 68-mm multiple rocket pods.
SA 316B  redesignation of SE 3160 on 1 January 1970.
SA 319B  Astazou-powered Alouette III; naval aircraft have ASW capability; SAR aircraft fitted with rescue hoist on the left side of fuselage.

## Characteristics

Crew: 1 pilot

Engine: SA 316B 1 Turboméca Artouste IIIB turboshaft 870 shp derated to 570 shp
SA 319B 1 Turboméca Astazou XIV turboshaft 870 shp derated to 600 shp

Dimensions: length 35 ft 10¾ in (10.0 m); height 9 ft 10 in (3.0 m); rotor diameter 36
ft 1¾ in (11.0 m)

Weight: SA 316B empty 2,474 lbs (1,122 kg); loaded 4,850 lbs (2,200 kg) SA 319B
empty 2,443 lbs (1,108 kg); loaded 4,960 lbs (2,250 kg)

Speed: SA 316B cruise 115 mph (185 km/h); maximum 130 mph (210 km/h) SA 319B
cruise 122 mph (197 km/h); maximum 136 mph (220 km/h)

Range: SA 316B 298 miles (480 km) SA 319B 375 miles (605 km)

Ceiling: SA 316B hover IGE 9,450 ft (2,880 m); hover OGE 5,000 ft (1,520 m); service
10,500 ft (3,200 m) SA 319B hover IGE 10,170 ft (3,100 m); hover OGE 5,575 ft
(1,700 m)

Climb: SA 319B 885 ft/min (270 m/min)

Payload: 6 troops or various combinations of weapons (see text)

The Alouette III can be easily distinguished from the Alouette II by the covered tailboom
and tricycle landing gear. This French Aéronavale helicopter has the French Navy's
roundel with anchor superimposed on the insignia. There is a rescue hoist on the other side
of the cabin. (French Armed Forces)

A French Army Alouette III; note the tail configuration with twin endplates. (French
Armed Forces)

# Aérospatiale

SA 321                              Super Frelon

The Super Frelon (Hornet) is a large helicopter developed by Sud-Aviation for troop assault and ASW. It is based on the prototype Frelon (SA 3200), only two examples of which were built. The Super Frelon is in first-line military use in several nations and is based aboard aircraft carriers in the French Navy.

The prototype Frelon, which flew for the first time on 10 June 1959, was powered by three 750-800-shp Turboméca Turmo IIIB turboshaft engines, two mounted side by side forward of the rotor shaft and the third mounted aft. The Super Frelon retains the same engine layout but replaced the Turmo IIIB engines with three 1,320-shp Turmo IIICs. Sikorsky assisted in the redesign of the Frelon's rotor systems, and the manufacture of the main gearcase and transmission box was subcontracted to Fiat. The first Super Frelon flew in late 1962. The SA 321 has a watertight fuselage for amphibious operations, non-retractable tricycle landing gear, and a six-bladed main rotor with an anti-torque tail rotor. The power plant used in the later versions of the aircraft is the 1,550-shp Turboméca Turmo $IIIC_6$ turboshaft. The fuselage has a rear loading ramp and on the ASW variant (SA 321G) the tailboom folds forward to facilitate shipboard handling.

Variants of the Super Frelon are flown by several air forces as well as the French Navy. Israel's Super Frelons have been used extensively for a variety of combat operations in the Middle East. Through 1980 some 200 SA 321s of all types had been delivered including the SA 321F, SA 321J, and 321K civil helicopters carrying 27-34 passengers in various configurations.

First flight: SA 3210 7 December 1962
Service introduction: 1966
Users: China, France, Iran, Israel, Libya, Malta, South Africa, Syria

**Variants**

SE 3200    Frelon prototype with 3 750-800-shp Turboméca Turmo IIIB turboshaft engines; first flight 1959; 2 built.

SA 3210    Super Frelon prototype with 3 1,320-shp Turmo $IIIC_2$ turboshaft engines; first was in troop assault configuration and second aircraft represented the naval ASW version; 2 built.

SA 321    pre-production aircraft; 4 built.

SA 321G    production ASW helicopter for French Navy; fitted with radar, dipping sonar, and provision for 4 ASW torpedoes; first flight 30 November 1965; 24 built.

SA 321H    French Army and Air Force variant with Turmo $IIIE_6$ engine.

SA 321J    civil and military utility variant with internal cargo of 8,818 lbs or 27 passengers; external sling load of 11,023 lbs; first flight 6 July 1967; 13 SA 321Ja built for China.

SA 321K    modified SA 321Ja; 9 built for Israel.

SA 321L    modified SA 321Ja; 15 built for South Africa.

SA 321M    SAR-configured helicopter; 9 built for Libya with 1 retransferred to Malta in 1978.

**Characteristics (SA 321)**

Crew: 1 pilot, 1 copilot, 1 crewman
Engines: 3 Turboméca Turmo $IIIC_6$ turboshaft 1,550 shp each

Dimensions: length 63 ft 7¾ in (19.4 m); height 21 ft 10¼ in (6.66 m); rotor diameter
    62 ft (18.9 m)
Weight: SA 321G empty 15,130 lbs (6,863 kg); loaded 28,660 lbs (13,000 kg) SA 321Ja
    empty 15,141 lbs (6,868 kg); loaded 28,660 lbs (13,000 kg)
Speed: cruise 155 mph (250 km/h); maximum 170.5 mph (275 km/h)
Range: 508 miles (820 km)
Ceiling: hover IGE 7,120 ft (2,170 m); service 10,325 ft (3,150 m)
Climb: 1,312 ft/min (400 m/min)
Payload: SA 321G 4 ASW homing torpedoes + 2 Exocet antiship missiles; SA 321Ja
    27 troops

An Aéronavale Super Frelon banks to starboard, preparing to land aboard an aircraft carrier of the *Clemenceau* class. Note the landing gear extending from the sponsons which, like those in the Sea King and Sea Guard, serve as stabilizing floats for amphibious operations. The nose wheel retracts into the forward, boat-like hull of the helicopter. (French Armed Forces)

Paratroops scramble from an Israeli Super Frelon during an exercise. The Israelis used primarily French aircraft through the 1967 (Six-Day) War. Subsequently, the Israelis have been supplementing their remaining Super Frelons in the heavy-lift role by the United States's CH-53 Sea Stallion. (Israeli Defense Force)

# Sud-Aviation
SA 330                          Puma
SA 332


The SA 330 Puma was designed by Sud-Aviation to meet a 1962 French Army requirement for a medium-sized, all-weather, transport helicopter. In June 1963, the French War Ministry allocated funds for the production of eight prototype and pre-production versions of the Puma, the first of which flew in the spring of 1965. The first production aircraft flew in September 1968. In 1967, the SA 330 was also selected by the Royal Air Force for its tactical transport requirement, and an initial order for 48 machines was placed with Sud-Aviation. As part of the RAF package, the Puma was included in the joint production agreement between Sud-Aviation (later Aérospatiale) and Westland, an arrangement that led to the joint development of the Gazelle and Lynx.

All Pumas are equipped with four-bladed main rotors and five-bladed tail rotors of all-metal construction, with a manual folding capability for the main rotor. Power plants vary as the initial military version was delivered with two 1,300-shp Turboméca Turmo $IIIC_4$ turboshafts, but these later yielded to the 1,575-shp Turmo IVC engines. The latter power plant is also installed in the latest civilian variant, the SA 330G. The fuselage is of conventional all-metal, semi-monocoque construction, with a monocoque tailboom supporting a horizontal stabilizer to the left side and tail rotor to the right side. The tricycle landing gear is semi-retractable, and deployable emergency flotation devices can be fitted to the rear landing gear fairings and forward fuselage. The crew can vary from one to three, depending upon the mission, and the cabin can accommodate up to 20 troops, or 6 stretchers with an additional 6 seated patients or attendants, or 5,500 pounds of internal cargo. A trap door in the cabin floor directly under the rotor hub gives access to an internally mounted cargo sling which can carry external cargo up to 7,055 pounds. Full IFR instrumentation is installed in most versions, and search and rescue variants also have search radar and navigation systems. A variety of armament can be installed, including rockets, air-to-surface missiles, 20-mm cannon, and 7.62-mm machine guns.

SA 330 sales totalled over 600 units by 1980, with production for civil and military use continuing at the rate of 8 per month. Military and civil operators are found in almost 40 nations (military users are listed below). Civil variants are SA 300F/G/J. Pumas are also produced in Indonesia under license.


First flight: 15 April 1965
Service introduction: 1969
Users: Algeria, Belgium, Cameroun, Chad, Chile, Ecuador, Ethiopia, France, Gabon, Great Britain, Indonesia, Iraq, Ivory Coast, Kenya, Kuwait, Morocco, Nepal, Nigeria, Pakistan, Portugal, South Africa, Sudan, Togo, United Arab Emirates, Zaïre

**Variants**

SA 330A    2 prototype and 6 pre-production aircraft with 1,300-shp Turmo $IIIC_4$ turboshaft engines.

SA 330B    production helicopter for French Army and Air Force with Turmo $IIIC_4$ engines; first flight January 1969; service introduction June 1970; approximately 130 built.

SA 330C     military export helicopter with Turmo IIIC$_4$ engines; first flight September 1968.

SA 330E     RAF variant designated Puma HC 1 with Turmo IIIC$_4$ engines; first flight November 1970; 48 built.

SA 330H/L Military export helicopter with Turmo IVC engines.

SA 332B     Super Puma with Turboméca Makila 1,800-shp turboshaft engines; 16,756 lbs loaded; "kneeling" undercarriage; improved avionics; ASW configuration provides radar, dipping sonar, doppler navigation, 2 ASW homing torpedoes, 2 Exocet antiship missiles; first flight AS 331 experimental prototype 5 September 1977; AS 332 prototype 13 September 1978. (AS 332A is civil version)

**Characteristics (330 L)**

Crew: 1 pilot, 1 copilot

Engines: 2 Turboméca Turmo IVC turboshaft 1,575 shp each

Dimensions: length 46 ft 1½ in (14.1 m); height 16 ft 10½ in (5.1 m); rotor diameter 49 ft 2½ in (15.0 m)

Weight: empty 7,970 lbs (3,615 kg); loaded 16,315 lbs (7,400 kg)

Speed: cruise 168 mph (271 km/h); maximum 182 mph (294 km/h)

Range: 341 miles (550 km)

Ceiling: hover OGE 13,940 ft (4,250 m); hover IGE 14,435 ft (4,400 m); service 19,680 ft (6,000 m)

Climb: 1,400 ft/min (426 m/min)

Payload: 16-20 troops; various combinations of 20-mm cannon, 7.62-mm machine guns, missiles, and rockets can be fitted

The Puma is one of several helicopters produced jointly by the Westland/Aérospatiale organizations. This is an RAF Puma HC 1 on a test flight from Westland Helicopters, where it was built. Note the large horizontal tail surface mounted opposite the anti-torque tail rotor. The other Anglo-French helicopter programs are the Gazelle and Lynx. (Westland)

Another Puma in flight. Although Britain, West Germany, and Italy are major producers of helicopters, the French aerospace industry probably has the best design, development, and production capability in this field outside of the United States. (Westland)

# Sud-Aviation

SA 315B                                    Lama
                                           Cheetah

The SA 315B Lama is a hybrid of the Aérospatiale Alouette II and III, having the same general airframe as the former with the engine and dynamic components of the latter. It was designed in 1968-1969 in response to an Indian Army requirement for a powerful, lightweight utility helicopter capable of taking off and landing in the rarefied atmosphere of the Himalayas. Named Cheetah by the Indian Army, the helicopter's capability in this environment was demonstrated in 1969 when a prototype made the highest takeoffs and landings ever recorded—24,600 feet. Three years later another record was set by a production SA 315B, which achieved an absolute helicopter altitude flight of 40,820 feet.

Like the Alouette III, the Lama has a three-bladed, all-metal main rotor turned by an 870-shp Turboméca Artouste IIIB turboshaft derated to 550 shp. The fuselage is of light metal with extensive plexiglass, a tailboom supporting the right-side anti-torque rotor. The boom is exposed metal framework. There is accommodation in the cabin for a pilot and four passengers or a pilot, medical attendant, and two stretchers. An external sling can carry loads up to 2,200 pounds. The Lama shares the Alouette II's skid landing gear with provision for floats for water operation.

The SA 315B is manufactured under license in India by Hindustan Aeronautics Ltd. (HAL) as the Cheetah and in Brazil by the Franco-Brazilian firm of Helibras. In 1980 the total SA 315B production was approximately 2½ units per month with more than 250 having already been delivered for military and civil use.

First flight: 17 March 1969
Service introduction:
Users: Argentina, Bolivia, Chile, Columbia, Ecuador, El Salvador, India

**Characteristics**

Crew: 1 pilot
Engines: 1 Turboméca Artouste IIIB turboshaft 870 shp derated to 550 shp
Dimensions: length 33 ft 8 in (10.3 m); height 10 ft 1¾ in (3.1 m); rotor diameter 36
    ft 1¾ in (11.0 m)
Weight: empty 2,235 lbs (1,014 kg); loaded 5,070 lbs (2,300 kg)
Speed: cruise 119 mph (192 km/h); maximum 130 mph (210 km/h)
Range: 320 miles (516 km)
Ceiling: hover 18,370 ft (5,600 m); service 20,670 ft (6,300m)
Climb: 768 ft/min (234 m/min)
Payload: 4 troops or 2,200 lbs (1,000 kg) on external sling

An SA 315B Lama is largely a hybrid of the Alouette II and III helicopters. This is a French civil version (serial F-BMRF) supporting the installation of communication lines in a mountainous region. (Aérospatiale)

# Aérospatiale
SA 340                          Gazelle
SA 341
SA 342

Intended as the successor to the popular Alouette II/III series of Aérospatiale helicopters, the Gazelle is a five-place, light observation helicopter capable of performing a multitude of civilian and military missions. As a result of the January 1967 agreement between the French and British governments, the Gazelle is jointly produced by Westland and Aérospatiale, as are the Puma and the Lynx.

Equipped with a standard three-bladed, all-metal main rotor, the Gazelle departs from helicopter tradition with a shrouded, 13-bladed *fenestron*, or fan-in-fin, anti-torque tail rotor. All versions are powered by variants of the Turboméca Astazou turboshaft engine, although the models differ with the variants. The fuselage is divided into three sections, the forward segment being a welded alloy frame for the windows and doors resting atop a semi-monocoque bottom structure. The center section supports the main gearbox and houses the cargo compartment and fuel tank and is constructed of light alloy honeycomb sandwich panels. Honeycomb sandwich panels also support the engine and the tailboom in the after fuselage. Horizontal stabilizers are fitted to both sides of the tail fin. The landing gear is of the skid type, with provision for either floats or skis. A variety of avionics can be fitted, including a total "blind flying" system. Armament options are combinations of four AS 11 or two AS 12 missiles, two pods of 2.75-inch or 68-mm rockets, four or six HOT wire-guided missiles, or two 7.62-mm machine guns.

Following six prototypes and pre-production aircraft, the first French-assembled production machine flew on 6 August 1971, and the Westland assembly line began completing Gazelles in 1972. Total Gazelle orders as of 1980 were approximately 800, with production continuing in Britain and France and under license in Yugoslavia. Over 115 military and civilian operators in some 30 countries operate the Gazelle in both its production configurations (SA 341 and 342). The designation X300 was used in the design stage; civil variants are the SA 341G and SA 342J.

First flight: SA 340 7 April 1967, SA 341 2 August 1968
Service introduction:
Users: Egypt, France, Great Britain, Iraq, Kuwait, Libya, Malaysia, Morocco, Qatar, Senegal, Syria, Yugoslavia

**Variants**

SA 340      prototype with Turboméca Astazou II N2 360-shp turboshaft; 2 built.
SA 341      pre-production aircraft; 4 built.
SA 341B     production helicopter for British Army with Astazou IIIN turboshaft; designated Gazelle AH 1.
SA 341C     training aircraft for Royal Navy; designated Gazelle HT 2.
SA 341D     training aircraft for RAF; designated Gazelle HT 3.
SA 341E     communications helicopter for RAF; designated Gazelle HT 4.
SA 341F     production variant for French Army with Astazou IIIC turboshaft; 166 built.
SA 341H     military export version with Astazou IIIB engine.

SA 342K    military variant for Iraq and Kuwait with Astazou XIVH 870-shp turboshaft.
SA 342L    military export variant with improved fenestron.
SA 342M    variant for French Army armed with 6 HOT antitank missiles; reduced infrared signature.
SA 349-A   experimental configuration with auxiliary wing.

### Characteristics (SA 341H)

Crew: 1 pilot
Engines: 1 Turboméca Astazou IIIB turboshaft 590 shp
Dimensions: length 31 ft 3 $^3/_{16}$ in (9.5 m); height 10 ft 2⅝ in (3.2 m); rotor diameter 34 ft 5½ in (10.5 m)
Weight: empty 2,002 lbs (908 kg); loaded 3,970 lbs (1,800 kg)
Speed: cruise 164 mph (264 km/h); maximum 192 mph (310 km/h)
Range: 415 miles (670 km)
Ceiling: hover OGE 6,560 ft (2,000 m); hover IGE 9,350 ft (2,850 m); service 16,400 ft (5,000 m)
Climb: 1,770 ft/min (540 m/min)
Payload: 4 troops or various combinations of weapons (see text)

Six Royal Navy Gazelles piloted by instructors from the Royal Naval Air Station Culdrose form "The Sharks," a helicopter display-demonstration team. Westland produces the Aérospatiale-designed Gazelle for the Royal Navy and RAF. (Royal Navy)

# Aérospatiale

SA 361                    Dauphin
SA 365                    H-65 Dolphin
SA 366

The Dauphin was initially developed as a replacement for the highly successful Alouette III in the civilian market, but the helicopter was subsequently directed at military markets in several countries, including the United States. The standard Dauphin is a ten-place utility helicopter, the prototype of which first flew on 2 June 1972. This single-engine civil SA 360 was certified by the French authorities in 1975 and in the United States in 1976. Successive models include the SA 361H general purpose military version and the twin-engined SA 365 Dauphin 2. A specially redesigned version of the SA 365 was chosen by the U.S. Coast Guard in 1979 to fulfill the requirement for a Short Range Rescue (SRR) aircraft.

All Dauphins have a four-bladed, semi-articulated main rotor and a 13-bladed "fan-in-fin" or *fenestron* tail rotor. In the SA 360 these are powered by a single Turboméca Astazou XVIIIA turboshaft delivering 1,050 shp for takeoff. The SA 361H replaces this engine with the 1,400-shp Astazou XXB turboshaft, and the SA 365N has two 650-shp Turboméca Ariel turboshafts. The three versions are virtually identical in other respects. The cabin is a standard assembly of frame and plexiglass built atop a strong box structure with a semi-monocoque tailboom attached, complete with a horizontal stabilizer just forward of the *fenestron*. Two types of landing gear are available, one being the skid type used in the Alouette II and Gazelle, and the other being a three-wheel arrangement, with two main wheels forward and a free-castoring tail wheel attached to the tail fin. The cabin provides accommodations for 10 in the standard configuration, 14 in the high-density version, or 4 stretchers and an attendant plus crew in the air ambulance. The military variant may be armed with eight HOT missile launchers or a combination of rockets, cannon, and machine guns.

All three versions continued in production in 1980, although demand was lower than anticipated by Aérospatiale. Total orders for the Dauphin in 1980 numbered less than 1,000, the majority of which were for civil operation. The basic SA 360 configuration carrying ten passengers was used for the two prototypes plus production for civil operation; the SA 365C with twin engines is also a major civil variant, used extensively to support offshore drilling operations. The U.S. Coast Guard variant marks the first U.S. government purchase of a foreign helicopter for service use. On 2 July 1980, China signed an agreement with France to build the SA 375N variant under license with the 670-hp Turboméca Ariel 1-C turboshaft.

First flight: SA 360 2 June 1972, SA 365 24 January 1975
Service introduction: SA 360 1975, SA 365 1978
Users: China (from 1982), Dominican Republic, Saudi Arabia (from 1982), Sri Lanka, United States (from 1982)

**Variants**

SA 361H  military variant with Astazou XXB 1,400-shp turboshaft; armament options include 8 HOT antitank missiles or 20-mm cannon, 7.62-mm machine guns, rockets.

SA 365F    production aircraft for Saudi Arabia, armed with 15TT missile; 25 ordered in
           1980.
SA 365N    Dauphin 2 for shipboard use; ASW variant with towed MAD and ASW homing
           torpedoes or antiship variant with AS 15 antiship missiles.
SA 366G    SAR variant for U.S. Coast Guard with 2 Avco Lycoming LTS-101-750A-1 680
           hp turboshaft engines; 3 crew + 3 passengers and rescue equipment; 8,400 lbs
           loaded; U.S. designation HH-65A Dolphin; first flight 23 July 1980; 90 on order
           for delivery 1982-1985.

**Characteristics (SA 365)**

Crew: 1 pilot, 1 copilot
Engines: 2 Turboméca Ariel turboshaft 650 shp each
Dimensions: length 36 ft (11.0 m); height 11 ft 6 in (3.5 m); rotor diameter 38 ft 4 in
    (11.7 m)
Weight: empty 3,946 lbs (1,790 kg); loaded 7,495 lbs (3,400 kg)
Speed: cruise 158 mph (255 km/h); maximum 195 mph (315 km/h)
Range: 288 miles (465 km)
Ceiling: hover OGE 8,530 ft (2,600 m); hover IGE 11,000 ft (3,350 m); service 19,680
    ft (6,000 m)
Climb: 1,810 ft/min (522 m/min)
Payload: 8 troops or various ASW stores or weapons (see text) or 2,865 lbs (1,300 kg)
    external cargo

This is an Aérospatiale SA 366 during evaluation for use by the U.S. Coast Guard for
the Short Range Rescue (SRR) role. In U.S. service the helicopter is designated HH–65A
Dolphin. It does not have standard U.S. Coast Guard markings.

# GERMANY (THIRD REICH)

# Doblhoff
WNF                                          Wn 342

The Wn 342 was a small observation helicopter, designed to meet a German Navy requirement for operation from submarines as well as surface ASW ships. It introduced the use of blade-tip jets to drive the rotor. Although extensive trials were flown with four prototypes, the helicopter did not enter production or operational service.

The Wn 342 had a highly innovative rotor drive in which a centrifugal supercharger fed a fuel-air mixture through the three hollow rotor blades to small jets at each tip. The high fuel consumption of the tip jets in the prototypes V1 and V2 led to the tip-drive being retained only for takeoff, hovering, and landing in the V3 and V4, with a selective clutch enabling the radial engine to drive either the air compressor for lift or a conventional pusher propeller for forward flight while the rotor blades rotated freely. The helicopter fuselage was a fabric-covered tube structure with twin tailbooms. The advantage of the Wn 342 was that it did not need an anti-torque rotor or transmission.

Von Doblhoff initially built a test rig to demonstrate the feasibility of rotor-tip jets. After these successful tests, four prototypes were built and flown, incorporating major improvements. At the end of World War II, the V4, having completed 25 hours of testing, was captured by the Americans. Accompanied by von Doblhoff, it was taken to the United States for further tests.

First flight: 1943
Service introduction: not operational

**Variants (also see Characteristics)**
V1 prototype with twin tail fins.
V2 prototype with single large tail fin.
V3 prototype with twin oval tail fins; destroyed in test program.
V4 prototype with single tail fin.

**Characteristics**
Crew: 1 in V1-3; 2 in V-4
Engine: V1 1 Walter Mikron II radial piston 60 hp
          V2 1 Walter Mikron II radial piston 90 hp
          V3-4 1 BMW Bramo Sh-14A radial piston 140 hp
Dimensions: length 16 ft 7½ in (5.1 m); height 7 ft 10½ in (2.4 m); rotor diameter 32
     ft 8½ in (10.0 m)
Weight: loaded V1 794 lbs (360.5 kg)
          loaded V2 1,014 lbs (460.0 kg)
          loaded V3 1,208 lbs (548.0 kg)
          loaded V4 1,411 lbs (640.6 kg)
Speed: maximum 25 mph (40 km/hr)
Range:
Ceiling:
Climb:

The V3 prototype of the Wn 342 in flight during World War II. The prototypes differed in several respects, with the V3 having distinctive twin oval tail fins. The V1 was an open-frame aircraft with similar but more rounded tail fins. (*Air International*)

The Wn 342 V4 prototype being readied for a flight at the USAAF's Wright Field test center after World War II. In this particular view, one of the rotor-tip jets was malfunctioning, and the aircraft did not leave the ground. (U.S. Army/National Air and Space Museum)

# Flettner

## Fl 184

This aircraft—often labeled a giroplane—was similar to an autogiro but had *part* of the available power applied to the rotor during normal flight. It was also the first autogiro to employ cyclic pitch to control the rotor. The German Navy planned to evaluate the Fl 184 for possible shipboard application, but the prototype caught fire in the air and was completely destroyed in 1936, before the naval trials could begin.

The aircraft had a two-bladed wooden propeller and a single three-bladed rotor.

The lone prototype was given the registration D-EDVE.

First flight: November 1936
Service introduction: not operational

### Characteristics

Crew: 1 pilot, 1 observer
Engine: 1 BMW Bramo Sh. 14 radial piston 140 hp
Dimensions: rotor diameter 39 ft 4½ in (12.0 m)
Weight:
Speed:
Range:
Ceiling:
Climb:

The Flettner Fl 184 with civil registration D-EDVE evoked interest from the German Navy for possible shipboard use but was destroyed shortly after its first flight. The aircraft was an improved autogiro design often referred to as a giroplane. Because of the loss of German aviation records during World War II there is little technical data about the Flettner machines available. (*Air International*)

# Flettner

## Fl 185

Following the ill-fated Fl 184, Flettner developed a true helicopter in his Fl 185. This aircraft had a single rotor in which the torque was counteracted by the unusual method of mounting two variable-pitch propellers on lateral outriggers, one with thrust directed forward and the other backward.

The three-bladed wooden rotor and two airscrews permitted the Fl 185 to function as an autogiro or helicopter. In addition, there was a small, three-bladed frontal cooling fan for the single radial engine. The starboard anti-torque propeller faced forward and the port propeller faced aft to counteract torque. The aircraft had a fixed tricycle landing gear.

Flettner conducted only limited testing with the single Fl 185 (registration D-EFLT) before abandoning the design in favor of twin intermeshing rotors. The latter configuration would become Flettner's hallmark.

First flight: 1936
Service introduction: not operational

### Characteristics

Crew: 1 pilot
Engine: 1 BMW Bramo Sh. 14A radial piston 140 hp
Dimensions: rotor diameter 39 ft 4½ in (12.0 m)
Weight: loaded 1,984 lbs (900 kg)
Speed:
Range:
Ceiling:
Climb:

The first in the Flettner series of helicopters was the Fl 185, the only helicopter developed by Anton Flettner with a single main rotor. Note the outrigger forward of the cockpit for the left-side anti-torque rotor. (*Air International*)

# Flettner

## Fl 201

The Fl 201 "heligiro" was an enlarged development of the Fl 185 with twin rotors, power to be applied to the rotors only in vertical and hovering flight. During forward flight, twin turboprop engines would provide propulsion. The aircraft did not progress beyond the design stage.

This was to have been a large aircraft capable of carrying some 30-40 passengers. Twin three-bladed rotors were to have been fitted.

First flight: not completed

### Characteristics

Crew: 2-4
Engines: 2 gas turbines
Dimensions: rotor diameter 80-90 ft (24.4-27.4 m)
Weight:                                    Ceiling:
Speed: 140 mph (225 km/h)                  Climb:
Range:                                     Payload: 30-40 troops

# Flettner

## Fl 265

This was the first Flettner helicopter to incorporate his distinctive and highly successful system of intermeshing rotors. The Fl 265 was one of several German helicopters intended for ASW and had the distinction of being the first military helicopter to be ordered into production. Prototypes were successfully tested aboard surface warships and a submarine (although one aircraft was lost after being launched without refueling). Some saw limited operational service at sea. The Army also evaluated the Fl 265, especially to assist in river crossings; one Fl 265 recovered an engine from a fighter that had crashed in remote territory, and on another flight a cannon carriage weighing 496 pounds was suspended beneath the aircraft. During flight tests a Bf 109 and an Fw 190 maneuvered with an Fl 265 for 20 minutes with gun camera film indicating that neither one of the fighters was able to gain a firing position on the helicopter!

The Fl 265 had a fuselage and tail configuration similar to the previous Fl 185. The design provided twin intermeshing two-bladed rotors with hubs close together, angled slightly outward and rotating in opposite directions, alleviating the need for an anti-torque tail rotor or outriggers for rotors. This was the first helicopter to have automatic pitch change to permit autorotation and safe landing in the event of power failure.

Six prototypes for service evaluation were ordered by the German Navy in 1938. A production order was given in 1940 by the Navy but then deferred in favor of the two-seat Fl 282.

First flight: May 1939                 Service introduction: not operational

## Variants

V1    registration D-EFLV; anti-torque trim surface on rudder; crashed during tests when
      rotor blades struck each other while in flight.
V2    modified rudder; conducted shipboard trials.
V3-6  prototypes for trials and evaluation.

## Characteristics

Crew: 1 pilot
Engine: 1 BMW Bramo Sh. 14A radial piston 140 hp
Dimensions: rotor diameter 40 ft 4½ in (12.3 m)
Weight: empty 1,764 lbs (800 kg); loaded 2,205 lbs (1,000 kg)
Speed: maximum 99 mph (160 km/h)
Range:
Ceiling:
Climb:

The German Navy used helicopters operationally from surface ships and rotary kites from
submarines during World War II. Here an Fl 265 takes off from a platform mounted over
one of the after triple 5.9-inch gun turrets of the light cruiser *Köln*. The aftermost 5.9-inch
turret, in foreground, is trained forward. (Courtesy Heinz J. Nowarra)

Flettner's Fl 265 had a fuselage and tail surfaces similar to his previous Fl 184 but was
highly innovative with twin intermeshing two-bladed rotors and automatic blade pitch
control for autorotation in the event of power failure, enhancing the possibility of safe
landing. TK-AN were the military markings of the second Fl 265. (*Air International*)

# Flettner

### F1 282 Kolibi (Humming Bird)

The F1 282 was probably the most capable helicopter developed during World War II. An advanced version of the F1 265 designed specifically for Anti-submarine Warfare (ASW), it was reliable and highly maneuverable. After trials, which included operations from the cruiser *Köln* during heavy seas in the Baltic, the F1 282 was ordered into mass production for the German Navy. Although only 22 aircraft were actually completed, it became the first helicopter in operational military service with any nation.

The F1 282 had twin two-bladed intermeshing rotors in the Flettner style, with the hubs two feet apart and inclined to the right and left by 12 degrees and forward by 6 degrees. Longitudinal and lateral control were achieved by the unusual method of changing the pitch of both rotors in the corresponding plane; the turn was then produced by the differing torque of the two rotors. Of steel tube construction with plywood covering, the rotors were removable so that the helicopter could be stowed in a pressurized container on a submarine deck (although this scheme was probably never tested). The fuselage was a steel tube construction with light metal covering. The later models discarded the glass-bubble cockpit cover of the early prototypes. Fuel capacity was 27.8 U.S. gallons when one pilot only was carried but was limited to 17.2 U.S. gallons when an observer or passenger was also embarked. The Fl 282 demonstrated reliability during an endurance test when it flew for 95 hours without necessitating any repairs or replacements. The aircraft was sufficiently stable for hands-off flight for sustained periods. A mooring cable device was fitted to the helicopter which could be lowered to a ship for winching down the aircraft.

The German Navy ordered 30 prototypes of the F1 282, followed in 1944 by orders for 1,000(!) of the helicopters for use by the Navy and Air Force. The Luftwaffe planned to use the F1 282 in liaison and communication roles. Mass production was begun by Bayerische Motorenwerke of Munich at the firm's Eisenach plant. However, allied bombings soon halted the program. The Navy used the completed prototypes for ASW operations from ships in the Baltic, Aegean, and Mediterranean. They were used for submarine search only, having no attack capability. One landing on the deck of a moving, surfaced submarine was reported. Three aircraft survived the war; prototypes V15 and V23 were taken to the United States and a third aircraft to the Soviet Union.

First flight: 1940
Service introduction: 1942
Users: Germany

**Variants**

F1 282A V1/2   2 prototypes with single-seat plexiglass cockpit.
F1 282B V3/24   operational prototype aircraft; only 29 are believed to have been completed; some were F1 282B-1 variants, a lightweight aircraft intended to carry bombs or rubber boat, and F1 282B-2 variants, a planned 2-seat aircraft for Army use.

**Characteristics**

Crew: 1 pilot, 1 observer

Engine: 1 BMW Bramo Sh. 14A radial piston 140 hp

Dimensions: length 21 ft 6¼ in (6.56 m); height 7 ft 2⅝ in (2.2 m); rotor diameter 39 ft 2⅞ in (11.96 m)

Weight: empty 1,410 lbs (640 kg); loaded 2,205 lbs (1,000 kg)

Speed: cruise 68 mph (109 km/h); maximum 93 mph (150 km/h)

Range: 106 miles (170 km) with 2 crew; 186 miles (300 km) with pilot only

Ceiling: hover ~ 1,000 ft (305 m); service 13,450 ft (4,100 m) maximum, 10,800 ft (3,292 m) with 2 crew

Climb: 300 ft/min (91 m/min) with 2 crew

The Flettner Fl 282 was the first helicopter of any nation to enter operational military service and the first to be ordered into mass production. Although orders for the Luftwaffe and Kriegsmarine totaled 1,000, just over a score were completed because of Allied bombings and a German change in priorities. Note the horizontal tail surfaces with their outer panels angled upward. (U.S. Air Force)

Mechanics prepare an Fl 282 for flight. (U.S. Air Force/National Archives)

The F1 282 V21 in flight with two passengers in the after cockpit; the forward cockpit in this later Kolibi is open. The close-set rotor hubs appear as a single rotor mounting in this photograph. (Courtesy Heinz J. Nowarra)

A later F1 282 hovers near a Fieseler Storch (Stork). The Storch was the outstanding light liaison aircraft of World War II, with some 2,700 being built for German and Italian use. This Storch is an improved, five-seat Fi 256. The original Fi 156 beat out the Focke-Wulf Fw 186 in a 1935 competition. (Courtesy Heinz J. Nowarra)

# Flettner

## Fl 285

This helicopter, under development when World War II ended, was intended to be used for shipboard observation and reconnaissance. It was designed to carry two small bombs with a mission endurance of two hours.

First flight: not flown

**Characteristics**

Engine: 1 Argus As 10C radial piston


# Flettner

## Fl 339

This was to have been an Army cooperation helicopter to provide liaison, observation, and communication functions for German ground troops.

Although an extremely small machine, the Fl 339 was to have had inter-meshing rotors, with twin two-bladed rotors. The two-man crew was to have been seated back to back with excellent visibility through a glazed cockpit. A four-seat variant was also planned.

The project was cancelled before the first machine had flown.

First flight: not flown

**Characteristics**

Crew: 1 pilot, 1 observer
Engine: 1 Argus As 10C radial piston 240 hp
Dimensions: rotor diameter 43 ft 3¾ in (13.2 m)
Weight: empty 2,095 lbs (951 kg); loaded 2,866 lbs (1,300 kg)
Speed:
Range:
Ceiling:
Climb:

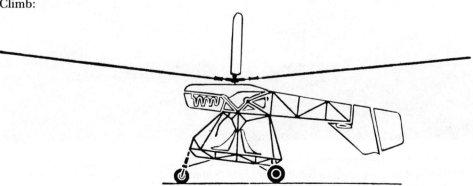

# Focke-Achgelis

## Fa 61

This machine is often credited with being the world's first practical helicopter, although it was preceded by the French machine of Louis Bréguet. The Fa 61 was developed by Professor-Dr. Henrich K. J. Focke with government support, and military interest was significant. Its agility was demonstrated when flown inside a 100-by-300-foot exhibition hall in Berlin by aviatrix Hanna Reitsch for 14 successive evenings in February 1938.

The Fa 61 used the fuselage of an Fw 44 biplane trainer with the two main rotors mounted on side-by-side outriggers. The rotors each had three articulated blades. A small wooden propeller was fitted for engine cooling. A T-tail was provided with a tricycle landing gear, with both a nose wheel and tail wheel being fitted. This design was subsequently scaled up for the Fa 223/266 helicopters.

This was the first helicopter of any nation to be formally registered, the prototypes being assigned German registrations D-EBVU and D-EKRA. In 1937-1939 the Fa 61 established several helicopter flight records, among them a speed of 77 mph, distance of 143 miles, altitude of 11,243.5 feet.

First flight: 26 June 1936
Service introduction: not operational

**Characteristics**

Crew: 1 pilot
Engine: 1 BMW Bramo Sh. 14A radial piston 160 hp
Dimensions: rotor diameter 23 ft (7.0 m)
Weight: empty 1,764 lbs (800 kg); loaded 2,100 lbs (953 kg)
Speed: cruise 62 mph (100 km/h); maximum 77 mph (124 km/h)
Range: 143 miles (230 km)
Ceiling: service 7,900 ft (2,410 m)
Climb: 710 ft/min (215 m/min) as helicopter; 266 ft/min (81 m/min) as autogiro

The first Fa 61 being prepared for flight. It has civil registration D-EBVU, the D for Deutschland being the international prefix for German aircraft. Note the wide separation of motors compared to the close, intermeshing rotors of the Flettner designs. German rotary-wing aircraft of this period were in advance of other nations' efforts. (National Air and Space Museum)

Aviatrix Hanna Reitsch hovers a Fa 61 while General Ernst Udet holds onto the tail wheel in a demonstration of the helicopter's stability. As head of the Luftwaffe technical office and later chief of supply, Udet was largely responsible for German aviation technical developments before he committed suicide in November 1941. (National Air and Space Museum)

Aviatrix Hanna Reitsch pilots the second Fa 61 (D-EKRA) inside the Deutschlandhalle in Berlin during one of her successive demonstrations during a two-week period in February 1938. This dramatic demonstration of the aircraft's agility greatly impressed Germany's leadership of the helicopter's potential. (Courtesy Heinz J. Nowarra)

# Focke-Achgelis

Fa 223 Drache (Dragon)
Fa 266 Hornisse (Hornet)

The Fa 266 was the world's first transport helicopter and was ordered by Lufthansa in 1938 for commercial service. However, before the prototype flew, the project was taken over by the Luftwaffe. Redesignated Fa 223, the aircraft was used operationally during the war, the largest helicopter to be put into production during these years.

A scaled-up Fa 61, the Fa 223/226 was distinguished by its twin three-bladed rotors on outriggers (non-intermeshing) and a T-tail configuration. Having its engine in the fuselage made possible the improved location of the crew cabin in the helicopter's nose section. Overall width over both rotors was 80 feet 4¾ inches. An MG15 machine gun was fitted in the nose of some units for self-defense. The helicopter featured excellent control and stability. Up to 2,000 pounds could be lifted by cable sling. A rescue capsule could be attached to the sling and lowered to a man below, and then winched up directly into the helicopter. Other special equipment in the Fa 223 included a four-man rubber raft, extensive instrumentation, and a landing light. If oil pressure dropped (i.e., there was engine failure) the rotor blades automatically changed pitch and the clutch disengaged for autorotation. The helicopter demonstrated some instability at speeds below about 60 mph.

The Luftwaffe used the Fa 223 in transport, supply, casualty evacuation, and reconnaissance roles. Production was ordered with a goal of 400 units per month. Allied bombings stopped production with only 10 having flown. Of the 3 Fa 223s known to have survived the war, one was taken by the British to become the first helicopter to fly the English Channel in September 1945. Two Fa 223s were completed by Zavody in Czechoslovakia in 1945-1946 from captured German components, and a third by SNCA du Sud-Est in France in 1947-1948 (designated SE 3000). The following data are based on available records; Professor-Dr. Focke reportedly claimed a rate of climb of 1,728 feet per minute and a ceiling of 23,000 feet, with an endurance of 3 hours 42 minutes when fitted with an auxiliary fuel tank. An enlarged, twin-engined version, under development at the end of the war and having a loaded weight of 37,500 pounds, was designated Fa 264.

First flight: August 1940
Service introduction: 1942
Users: Germany

**Characteristics**

Crew: 2 pilots
Engine: 1 BMW Bramo Fafnir 323Q-3 (later redesignated 301R) radial piston 1,000 hp
Dimensions: length 40 ft 2¼ in (12.26 m); height 14 ft 3⅝ in (4.36 m); rotor diameter 39 ft 1 in (11.9 m)
Weight: empty 7,055 lbs (3,200 kg); loaded 9,502 lbs (4,310 kg); maximum overload in tests 11,020 lbs (5,000 kg);
Speed: cruise 75 mph (120 km/h); maximum 115 mph (185 km/h)
Range: 200 miles (320 km); with auxiliary tank 435 miles (700 km)
Ceiling: hover 6,500 ft (1,980 m); service 16,000 ft (4,880 m)
Climb: 720 ft/min (219 m/min)
Payload: 4 troops or 2,000 lbs (908 kg) cargo on external sling

The Focke-Achgelis Fa 223 was one of the several advanced helicopters flown by the German armed forces in World War II. Note the similarity in design to the earlier and much smaller Focke designs. (Imperial War Museum)

A Luftwaffe Fa 223 sits on a mountain top during a World War II rescue operation. The helicopter was fitted with a sophisticated internal rescue hoist that could lower a rescue capsule through the fuselage floor. (Bibliothek für Zeitgeschichte)

# Focke-Achgelis

## Fa 225

The Fa 225 was an attempt to improve the landing characteristics of the German DFS 230 assault glider by replacing the aircraft's conventional wing with a single rotor from an Fa 223 helicopter. The conventional DFS 230 required about 200 feet of runout upon landing with a full load. In 1942 a single DFS 230 was modified to the rotary-wing configuration. This concept was successful, and the Fa 225 could land with a runout of only 60 feet after an almost vertical descent. However, the rotary-wing glider could only be towed at a speed of some 120 mph behind a Ju 52 transport compared to 130 mph for a conventional glider. Apparently only one glider was so modified, and the concept was never used operationally as German airborne assaults essentially ceased after the successful (and costly) seizure of Crete in 1941.

The large, almost 40-foot diameter rotor from the Fa 223 was mounted above the glider's fuselage, just aft of the cockpit. The wings were removed but the conventional tail and landing gear were retained.

First flight: 1942
Service introduction: not operational

**Characteristics**

Crew: 1 pilot
Engine: none
Dimensions: length 36 ft 10½ in (11.2 m); rotor diameter 39 ft 4⅛ in (12.0 m)
Weight: empty 2,000 lbs (905 kg); loaded approx. 4,600 lbs (2,088 kg)
Speed: 120 mph (192 km/m)
Range:                                          Climb:
Ceiling:                                        Payload: 8 troops

This photo shows the lone Fa 225 in flight being towed by a Ju 52-3m tri-motor transport. Note the height of the pylon assembly above the fuselage, the landing gear, and horizontal tail surface. The Fa 225 was a unique merger of the helicopter and glider concepts, both of which had their combat debut in World War II. (Courtesy Heinz J. Nowarra)

There was a single Fa 225 modified by the Luftwaffe from a DFS 230 glider. The standard DFS 230s were in combat from the assault on Belgium in May 1940 onward. The standard DFS 230 had a jettisonable undercarriage that was dropped after takeoff with the glider landing on skids mounted under the forward fuselage (not fitted in the Fa 225). The rotary-wing glider was not used operationally. (Courtesy Heinz J. Nowarra)

# Focke-Achgelis

## Fa 284

This was the largest helicopter designed during World War II, being developed to lift a payload of almost eight tons. Initially, the aircraft was to have been powered by two 1,600-hp engines and been able to lift two tons. An improved variant with 2,000-hp engines was to have lifted almost eight tons. However, the prototype of this ambitious project was never completed.

The Fa 284 design featured a lattice forward section with side-by-side, three-bladed rotors on supports extending from the fuselage, giving the helicopter a span of over 100 feet. An enclosed cockpit was provided aft, with cargo to be carried on an external sling arrangement. The purpose of this "flying crane" was to airlift outsize cargo, armored vehicles, and trucks. All drawings were destroyed in allied bombings during the war.

Considerable design work and some fabrication took place on the Fa 284 prototype, with part of the work being undertaken by the French helicopter firm of Bréguet during the German occupation.

First flight: not flown

### Charactersitics

Crew: 1 pilot, 1 crewman
Engines: 2 BMW 801 radial piston 1,600 hp each
Dimensions: length 45 ft (13.72 m); rotor diameter 59 ft ⅝ in (18.0 m)
Weight: empty 18,000 lbs (8,165 kg); loaded 26,400 lbs (12,000 kg)
Speed: 130 mph (208 km/h)
Range: 248 miles (400 km)
Ceiling: service 20,800 ft (6,340 m)
Climb:

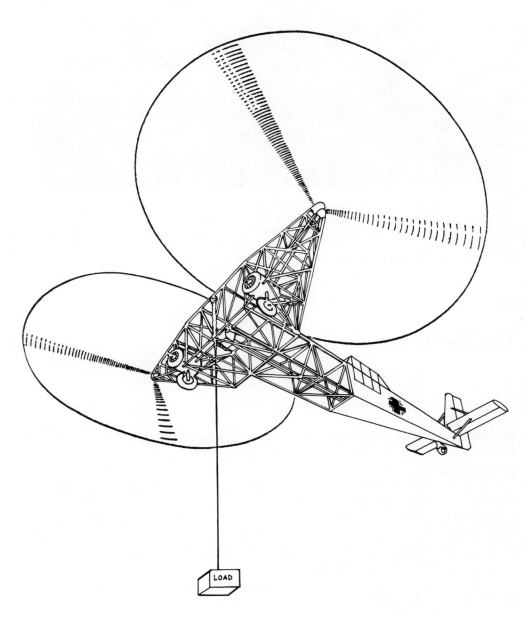

# Focke-Achgelis

## Fa 330

The Fa 330 was a unique "automotive kite," developed to be towed by a surfaced submarine to increase observation range. It was not self-propelled, although there were proposals to fit it with a small engine. For convenience, it is addressed in this volume as a "helicopter."

The helicopter had a steel tubular construction with a conventional tail assembly that could be folded and disassembled and stowed in the submarine. Launching required a 17-mph airspeed (i.e., submarine speed plus wind). Some 200 to 500 feet of steel cable were usually winched out for operation, a telephone line being imbedded in the cable for communication with the submarine. In an emergency the cable could be released by the helicopter, and the pilot could escape by a parachute system that safely released him from the helicopter. The kite controls consisted of a conventional stick and rudder pedals. In flight the three-bladed, 24-foot rotor typically rotated at 205 rpm.

Approximately 200 Fa 330s were built by Weser Flugzeugwerke at Delmenhorst, near Bremen, with some being used operationally from U-boats. Generally, the pilots were enlisted submarine personnel who trained in a wind tunnel at Chalais-Meudon, France. Some helicopters were fitted with simple wheeled undercarriages and a tail skid so that they could be towed behind Storch observation planes for in-flight training. Professor-Dr. Focke proposed a powered model with a 60-hp engine, but apparently none was built.

First flight:
Service introduction:
Users: Germany

### Characteristics

Crew: 1 pilot
Engine: none
Dimensions: rotor diameter 24 ft (7.3 m); 28 ft (8.5 m) on some later kites
Weight: empty 180 lbs (82 kg)

| | |
|---|---|
| Speed: cruising 25 mph (40 km/h) | Ceiling: approximately 328 ft (100 m) |
| Range: | Climb: |

A Fa 330 in flight during postwar trials. The helicopter is being towed by a truck and has been fitted with wheels. (U.S. Air Force)

A Focke-Achgelis unpowered "automotive kite" on the conning tower of a U-boat. The one-man aircraft could be quickly disassembled and stowed below. These craft were used operationally during World War II. (National Air and Space Museum)

A German sailor sits apprehensively on his Fa 330 aboard a U-boat at sea during World War II. He may be holding the craft's rotor blade to stop it from windmilling. He wears a flight cap, goggles, and life vest. (U.S. Air Force Museum)

# Focke-Wulf

## Fw 186

The Fw 186 was designed as a giroplane for a battlefield observation and communications role in competition with the fixed-wing Fi 156 Storch. The project ended when Professor-Dr. Focke left the Focke-Wulf firm in 1937 to concentrate on rotary-wing aircraft (as Focke-Achgelis). The single Fw 186 was tested as a private venture after the military leadership determined that there were too many disadvantages to rotary-wing aircraft at the time.

The aircraft had a conventional autogiro configuration with the rotor mounted on a streamlined pylon forward of the two open cockpits.

First flight: 1935
Service introduction: not operational

### Characteristics

Crew: 1 pilot, 1 observer
Engine: 1 Argus As 10C piston 240 hp
Dimensions:
Weight:
Speed: 112 mph (180 km/h)
Range:
Ceiling:
Climb:

The Focke-Wulf Fw 186 was proposed as a light Army observation and communications aircraft in place of the widely used Storch. (Air International)

# WEST GERMANY
# Messerschmitt-Bölkow-Blohm

Bö 105
PAH-1
VBH

The MBB Bö 105 was the first significant German helicopter of postwar design intended for military service. It is a four-to-six-place multi-mission helicopter, which has in turn led to the specialized PAH-1 antitank helicopter and the VBH liaison-observation machine. The MBB series began with the Bö 102, a non-flying trainer machine for the West German Army Air Force, followed by the Bö 103 which reached prototype flight stage, and the cancelled Bö 104, a two-seat military helicopter. Subsequently, the Bö 105 was developed and, following a long gestation period, was produced in large numbers for the West German Army and several other nations.

The helicopter has a four-bladed main rotor above the fuselage, with rigid, fiberglass-reinforced blades, and a tailboom supporting an anti-torque rotor on the left side. The fuselage is a conventional semi-monocoque pod. A horizontal stabilizer is fitted on the tailboom; a Bö 105HGH experimental aircraft has been flown with stub wings (exceeding 250 mph in a shallow dive). The aircraft was designed with Allison 250-C18 engines. Twin MAN 6022-A3 turboshaft engines were tested in the third prototype but discarded in the fourth aircraft in favor of two Allison 250-C20 turboshafts which became the standard for production helicopters. The PAH-1 and VBH have Allison T63 engines built under license. The cabin can accommodate three passengers behind the pilot and copilot or two stretchers in the evacuation configuration. A tubular skid landing gear is provided on all variants. A variety of avionics have been fitted to these helicopters for different roles by the various users. The PAH-1 has been strengthened for mounting weapons and in the antitank role carries six HOT missiles and has an APX M397 stabilized daylight sight mounted in the cabin roof and a doppler navigation system (AN/ASN-128).

The prototype aircraft (V1) was destroyed during ground tests with the first flight by the V2 aircraft not occurring until early 1967. The primary success of the Bö 105 from its first flight in 1967 through 1975 was in the civilian market, with few military orders forthcoming. In 1976 the West German government authorized the purchase of 227 Bö 105s for the German Army and subsequently authorized 212 of the PAH-1 and 160 of the VBH variants. By 1980 MBB was producing 12 helicopters per month to meet the German Army orders plus another 5 or 6 per month for civil and foreign markets. In addition, licensing arrangements have been made with Boeing Vertol in the United States and with the Indonesian and Philippine governments. The aircraft (modified by Boeing Vertol) was a competitor in the U.S. Navy's LAMPS III evaluation of potential shipboard ASW helicopters. (That aircraft was lost in a 1970 crash.) There are several Bö 105 civil variants as well as the Bö 106 (stretched fuselage with seven seats).

First flight: Bö 105 V2 16 February 1967
Service introduction:
Users: West Germany, Indonesia, Netherlands, Nigeria, Philippines, Sudan

**Variants**

Bö 105V1/V3   prototype aircraft 375-shp engines with Allison 250-C18 turboshaft with 3-bladed Westland Scout main rotor; destroyed during ground tests.

Bö 105V4/V7   preproduction aircraft with Allison 250-C18 engine

Bö 105A       planned production aircraft with Allison 250-C18 engine; deferred in favor of updated 250-C20 engine; none built.

Bö 105B       planned production variant with MAN-Turbo 6022-A3 turboshaft engines; none built.

Bö 105C       initial production helicopter with twin Allison 250-C20 400-shp turboshaft engines.

Bö 105HGH     Bö 105V4 modified with auxiliary wings for high-speed flight tests.

Bö 105M       military variant of commercial Bö 105CB helicopter; Allison 250-C20B turboshaft engines; variety of armament can be fitted including six HOT missiles, rocket pods, or 20-mm cannon.

Bö 115        early designation for PAH-1.

PAH-1         Bö 105M configured for German Army; 212 ordered; first delivery 4 December 1980.

VBH           Bö 105M for military liaison and communications duties; 227 ordered; first delivery 1980.

**Characteristics (Bö 105M)**

Crew: 1 pilot, 1 copilot
Engines: 2 Allison 250-C20B turboshaft 420 shp each
Dimensions: length 28 ft 1 in (8.56 m); height 9 ft 9½ in (3.0 m); rotor diameter 32 ft 2½ in (9.8 m)
Weight: empty 2,469 lbs (1,120 kg); loaded 5,070 lbs (2,300 kg)
Speed: cruise 144 mph (232 km/h); maximum 167 mph (270 km/h)
Range: 407 miles (656 km)
Ceiling: hover 8,922 ft (2,720 m); service 17,000 ft (5,180 m)
Climb: 1,320 ft/min (402 m/min)
Payload: 3 troops or 2 stretchers or 6 HOT missiles or 6 TOW missiles

A PAH-1 variant of the MBB Bö 105 carrying six HOT antitank missiles. The daylight missile-sighting device is visible above the left side of the cockpit in this view.

A German PAH-1 helicopter fires one of six HOT antitank missiles. Produced jointly by MBB of Germany and Aérospatiale of France, the HOT is similar to the American wire-guided TOW missile. Helicopters are viewed in the West as a counter to the superior Soviet tank forces arrayed in Eastern Europe. (MBB)

A German PAH-1 hovers above a Marder armored personnel carrier during winter exercises in West Germany. The German Army—like most other modern ground forces— uses a large number of helicopters for command and control, troop lift, antitank, fire support, medical evacuation, engineering support, and other missions. (MBB)

# Messerschmitt-Bölkow-Blohm/Aérospatiale

PAH-2
HAC

The PAH-2 was to be a night-capable, specialized antitank helicopter under joint international development by Messerschmitt-Bölkow-Blohm of West Germany and Aérospatiale of France. The governmental memorandum of understanding signed by Germany and France to cover the developmental stage of the helicopter stated that MBB would be prime contractor and Aérospatiale would cooperate in the development and eventual manufacture of the PAH-2. PAH-2 was the acronym for Panzerabwehr Hubschrauber 2, the German designation, while the French term for the project was Helicoptere Anti-Char (HAC). The project was cancelled early in 1981 because of West Germany's defense spending cutback.

The basic configuration under consideration by the two companies was a standard attack helicopter with a narrow fuselage and twin seats in tandem, powered by twin MTU/Turboméca turboshafts generating 1,000 shp and driving a four-bladed main rotor and *fenestron* (fan-in-fin) tail rotor. Landing gear was to consist of twin-wheeled main gear and a tail wheel, and the tail fin topped with a horizontal stabilizer, creating a readily identifiable T-tail. Armament was expected to be either eight HOT antitank missiles in containers on hard points under the stub wings or a 30-mm antitank cannon under the forward fuselage.

**Characteristics**

Crew: 1 pilot, 1 gunner
Engine: 2 MTU/Turboméca turboshafts 1,000 shp each
Dimensions: main rotor diameter 41 ft (12.5 m)
Weight: loaded 8,818 to 9,920 lbs (4,000 to 4,500 kg)
Speed:
Range:
Ceiling:
Climb:

# GREAT BRITAIN
# Avro

C 30A                                    Rota

The Rota autogiro was the British military version of the La Cierva machine produced under license by Avro (A. V. Roe). The prototype was built in 1934 from C 19 autogiro components in the workshops of National Flying Services, Ltd., in Hanworth, England. After successful trials the Air Ministry ordered the aircraft into production.

The Rota had a conventional aircraft fuselage and non-retracting landing gear with an air-cooled engine. The prototype C 30A had an Armstrong Siddeley Genet Major I engine rated at 100 hp; the production aircraft had the Genet Major IA developing 140 hp. The three-bladed rotor had a direct control head, meaning that it was able to tilt in all directions and give fore and aft control as well as lateral control in flight. No stub wings were fitted.

Avro produced 66 of the C 30A autogiros in England for private and foreign military use. In addition, the RAF took delivery of 12 machines designated Rota Mk I in 1934-1935. Twin floats were fitted to some of the aircraft. An RAF officer landed a private C 30A on the Italian cruiser *Fume* in 1935, and a short time later one flew from the British aircraft carrier *Courageous*. La Cierva autogiros were flown by the RAF through World War II, being used mainly as radar calibration targets. Fifteen privately owned C 30A and other La Cierva autogiros were taken over by the RAF during the 1930s for trials and wartime use. Several C 30 autogiros were also produced for the French Navy by Lioré et Olivier.

First flight: 1934        Service introduction: 1934        Users: France/Great Britain

### Variants

Mk I RAF variant; 12 built (serial K 4230/239, 4296, 4775); K 4775 was experimentally fitted with a Civet Major engine in 1935.

A C 30A Rota autogiro is prepared for takeoff from an RAF station during World War II. These aircraft—both original RAF purchases and civilian machines taken when the 1939 war started—were used for liaison and radar calibration. (Imperial War Museum)

**Characteristics**

Crew: 1 pilot, 1 observer
Engine: 1 Armstrong Siddeley Genet Major IA radial piston 140 hp
Dimensions: length 19 ft 8½ in (6.0 m); rotor diameter 37 ft (11.3 m)
Weight: loaded 1,900 lbs (862.6 kg)
Speed: maximum 100 mph (161 km/h)          Ceiling: 8,000 ft (2,438 m)
Range: 250 miles (402.5 km)                Climb: 700 ft/min (213 m/min)

# Brennan

Louis Brennan, who had worked extensively in the development of gyrostabilization, especially for naval torpedoes, designed a helicopter at the Royal Aircraft Establishment's Farnborough test center in the 1920s. The aircraft had a four-bladed, 60-foot diameter rotor which was driven by small propellers mounted on the tips of two of the rotor blades. Thus, power shafts ran the length of the two blades, connected through a gearbox to a 230-hp Bentley BR-2 rotary engine. Several configurations were tested.

The helicopter had adequate lift and easily achieved almost 80 takeoffs. However, stability and control were so poor that the maximum height reached was only about 8 feet and the longest controlled flight in a straight line was about 600 feet. Work halted after a crash in 1926.

First flight: tethered 1924, free May 1925          Service introduction: not operational

**Characteristics**

Crew: 1 pilot
Engine: 1 Bentley BR 2 rotary piston 230 hp
Dimensions: rotor diameter 60 ft (18.29 m)
Weight: empty 3,000 lbs (1,362 kg)
Speed:              Range:              Ceiling:              Climb:
Payload: 4 passengers (designed with 1-hr endurance)

The Brennan helicopter in flight at Jersey Brow in May 1925. At this stage the helicopter had small auxiliary "wings" fitted to improve stability as well as a shock-absorbing undercarriage and partially enclosed cockpit. (Royal Aircraft Establishment)

Louis Brennan's helicopter is shown suspended in a hangar at the Royal Aircraft Establishment in Farnborough, England. The tubular cockpit below the engine mounting was partially covered during later flights. During hover trials within the hangar the helicopter reached a height of 20 feet. (Royal Aircraft Establishment)

# Bristol

171                                Sycamore

The Bristol Type 171 Sycamore was the first post-World War II helicopter to be built in Great Britain. The Royal Air Force was its principal customer with West Germany being the largest foreign purchaser. The helicopter was one of the first to be used operationally in combat in the post-World War II era.

The Sycamore was a four- to five-place aircraft with a three-bladed main rotor and anti-torque tail rotor powered by a single piston engine. The fuselage was constructed in three sections, the nose being a metal monocoque cabin with windscreen, the center a welded tubular frame with metal skin housing the engine, and the tailboom a metal monocoque. It had large cabin doors on both sides and a tricycle landing gear.

The helicopter was flown in several roles by the RAF and in limited numbers by the British Army and Royal Navy as well as military services in several other countries. Sycamores were in combat bearing the Belgian insignia during operations in the Congo, and with British roundels in Aden, Kenya, and Malaya. All have been withdrawn from military service. Several Sycamores were flown in civil service, with some military variants being developed from civil marks.

First flight: 24 July 1947
Service introduction: September 1951
Users: Australia, Belgium, West Germany, Great Britain

**Variants***

| | |
|---|---|
| Type 171 Mk I | prototype built to Ministry of Supply specification E.20/45; 450-hp Pratt & Whitney R-985 Wasp Junior engine; 2 built (serial VL 958, 963; latter initially had civil registration G-ALOU). |
| Type 171 Mk II | prototype aircraft built to Ministry of Supply specification E.34/46; 570-hp Alvis Leonides 71 engine; pilot + 3 passengers; 1 built. |
| Type 171 Mk III | production helicopter based on Mk II; 550-hp Alvis Leonides engine; military marks 10-13 built to this design. |
| Type 171 Mk IV | final production variant with 550-hp Alvis Leonides 73 engine; military marks 14, 50-52 built to this design. |
| HC 10 | evacuation helicopter with space for 2 stretchers and attendant; for Army evaluation; 1 built. |
| HC 11 | evacuation and transport helicopter; hard points for external loads of 1,600 lbs; for British Army; first flight 13 August 1950; 4 built. |
| HR 12 | SAR helicopter for RAF Coastal Command; 4 built. |
| HR 13 | SAR helicopter for RAF Fighter Command; 2 built. |
| HR 14 | major production variant; configured for evacuation, SAR, and transport; for RAF, Australian, and Belgian air forces; 86 built. |
| HR 50 | SAR-configured helicopter for Royal Navy evaluation; 3 built. |
| HR 51 | SAR helicopter for Royal Navy; 7 built. |
| HR 52 | SAR and transport helicopter for West Germany; 50 built (4 operated by Navy and 46 by Army). |

---

*Type 171 marks are Bristol designations.

A Sycamore HR 52 flown by the German Air Force is tuned up in preparation for a flight. (*Soldat und Technik*)

**Characteristics (HR 14)**

Crew: 1 pilot

Engine: 1 Alvis Leonides Mk 73 radial air-cooled piston 550 hp

Dimensions: length 46 ft 2 in (14.1 m); height 12 ft 2 in (3.7 m); rotor diameter 48 ft 7 in (14.8 m)

Weight: empty 3,810 lbs (1,730 kg); loaded 5,600 lbs (2,542 kg)

Speed: cruise 105 mph (169 km/h); maximum 127 mph (204 km/h)

Range: 300 miles (483 km)

Ceiling: hover OGE 4,000 ft (1,200 m); service 15,500 ft (4,724 m)

Climb: 1,300 ft/min (396 m/min)

Payload: 4 troops or 2 stretchers

An RAF Sycamore HR 14 (serial XD 196). This helicopter was widely used by the RAF and by the German Air Force during the 1950s.

# Bristol

173                              Belvedere
191
192

The Bristol Type 173 was Great Britain's first multi-engine helicopter, designed in the late 1940s and first flown in January 1952. Royal Navy trials with the first three prototypes led to the selection of a derivative of the Type 173 as an Antisubmarine Warfare (ASW) helicopter (Type 191). Prototype sea trials were conducted aboard the aircraft carrier *Eagle*. However, the British defence policy of 1957 caused a drastic reassessment of naval requirements, and the Type 191 never entered production. Instead, additional prototypes were completed in support of the Type 192, a configuration for the Royal Air Force. Only 26 were subsequently built for RAF service by Westland, which took over the Bristol helicopter production in 1960.

The first two Type 173 prototypes were equipped with two 500-520-hp Alvis Leonides radial engines driving a pair of tandem, wooden, four-bladed rotors. Three more prototypes were ordered by the British government with two 850-hp Alvis Leonides radials and metal rotor blades. Four Type 191 prototypes were completed for the Royal Navy, two with the radial engine and two with two 1,650-shp Napier Gazelle free-turbine engines. Production Type 192 Belvederes had two metal, four-bladed main rotors, mounted atop the power plants at the front and rear of the Belvedere's main cabin. These engines were free turbines, each developing 1,650 shp. The fuselage was an aluminum alloy stressed-skin structure with an inverted-V horizontal stabilizer beneath the aft rotor. The landing gear was a non-retractable, quadricycle type, with the front wheels fully castoring. Up to 30 passengers could be carried in an emergency or 6,000 pounds of internal or external cargo. Avionics included full instrumentation for either day or night flying and provision for an automatic pilot.

A total of five prototypes and 26 production aircraft were built. The second prototype was delivered to British European Airways for airline trials in July 1956 but was later taken out of service as the result of an accident. No other Belvederes entered commercial service. The RAF's 26 Belvederes saw combat service during the Indonesian confrontation of the mid-1960s and were withdrawn from active service shortly thereafter. Only the Type 192 production models were technically Belvederes.

First flight: 3 January 1952
Service introduction: September 1962
Users: Great Britain

**Variants**

| | |
|---|---|
| Type 173 | prototype for Type 191/192 series; 2 helicopters with 2 500-520-hp radial engines and 3 aircraft with 2 850-hp radials; 5 built. |
| Type 191 | ASW variant; 2 with radial engines, 2 with Napier Gazelle free-turbine engines; with shorter fuselage, folding rotors, ASW sensors, 68 ordered but production cancelled in 1957 and 4 prototypes completed as part of Type 192 program. |
| Type 192/Belvedere HC 1 | Belvedere production aircraft with 2 1,650-shp Napier Gazelle free-turbine engines; 26 built. |

**Characteristics (HC 1)**

Crew: 1 pilot, 1 copilot
Engines: 2 Rolls-Royce Napier Gazelle NGa 2 free turbine 1,650 shp each
Dimensions: length 54 ft 4 in (16.56 m); height 17 ft 3 in (5.25 m); rotor diameter 48 ft 8 in (14.83 m)
Weight: empty 11,634 lbs (5,278 kg); loaded 20,000 lbs (9,072 kg)
Speed: cruise 115 mph (185 km/h); maximum 138 mph (222 km/h)
Range: 437 miles (715 km)
Ceiling: hover OGE 6,000 ft (1,830 m); service 17,300 ft (5,273 m)
Climb: 1,350 ft/min (411 m/min)
Payload: 19 troops or 12 stretchers + 3 attendants or 6,000 lbs (2,720 kg) cargo internal or external sling

A Belvedere HC 1 takes off during a demonstration. Note the crew chief standing in the open doorway, the quadracycle landing gear, and tail surfaces. Although only 26 production aircraft were built for the RAF, they were extremely useful. (Imperial War Museum)

This Bristol 173 was used for naval trials in 1953, including flights from a British fleet carrier. The aircraft has military serial XF 785 but was also assigned civil registration G-ALBN. The tail surfaces, landing gear, and details differ from the production Belvedere. (U.S. Air Force)

# Cierva
W 9

The W 9 was an experimental helicopter using jet thrust for torque compensation instead of a conventional tail rotor or a combination of main rotors. The design was begun in 1944 as a joint effort of the Cierva company and G. & J. Weir, Ltd., responding to the Air Ministry specification E.16/43. Only one was built.

The W 9 fuselage had a tapered cylindrical form, with a steel-tube cabin structure at the forward end. The plexiglass-covered cabin could accommodate two persons. A six-cylinder piston engine behind the cabin turned the three-bladed rotor. A multi-bladed fan with variable-pitch blades was used to cool the engine. Air from the fan was ducted aft through the fuselage, heated with exhaust gases from the engine, and ejected from the left side of the fuselage to counter rotor torque. Shutters controlled exhaust flow. There were no wings or tail control surfaces. A tail-wheel landing gear was fitted.

The single W 9 was completed in 1947 (serial PX 203). No further development of this concept was undertaken.

First flight: 1947
Service introduction: not operational

**Characteristics**

Crew: 1 pilot, 1 observer
Engine: 1 de Havilland Gipsy 6 Series III piston 200 hp
Dimensions:
Weight:
Speed:
Range:
Ceiling:

The Cierva/Weir W 9 used jet exhaust instead of an anti-torque rotor to counter the effects of the main rotor. Only one experimental aircraft of this type was flown. (Charles E. Brown)

# Cierva

W 11                          Air Horse
W 12

The Air Horse was conceived in 1944-1945, in part by former members of the Weir firm. Designed on the basis that scaling up in size reduced the cost per pound, making large helicopter procurement and operation economically feasible, the Air Horse was to have had three main rotors, the only helicopter to be so built. Early support for the project was elicited from the Ministry of Agriculture and Fisheries and the Agricultural Research Council. Such a large helicopter would carry some three tons of insecticide and be dubbed "Spraying Mantis." Civil Aviation Requirement 3/46 was written around this project (later specification E19/46) and a contract was issued with the military serial VZ 724. (Civil registration G-ALCV was also assigned.) A second prototype W 11 was ordered before the first had flown (serial WA 555; civil registration G-AKTV was allocated but never used). The largest helicopter in existence when it began flight trials in late 1948, the first prototype flew successfully until mid-1950. About to begin RAF evaluation, on 13 June 1950 the aircraft was destroyed in a crash that killed the three men on board. The second Air Horse was examined extensively and, with Mr. James Weir withdrawing financial backing for the project, the aircraft flew only tethered tests and was then used as a ground test rig until dismantled in early 1954.

The Air Horse had a unique triple-rotor configuration with all three rotors mounted on outriggers, one forward of the nose and two amidships. The three wooden rotors were driven in the same direction through transmission drive from a single distributor gearbox powered by a single engine. The Rolls-Royce Merlin 24 was a 12-cylinder, V-type, liquid-cooled engine. The semi-monocoque fuselage had a rectangular cross-section with clamshell doors in the rear to facilitate loading. The landing gear was a fixed, tricycle type with oleo-pneumatic shock struts with a vertical travel of 5 feet. The tail consisted of a horizontal stabilizer with large endplates. The freight compartment was 19 feet long, 7½ feet wide, and 5¾ feet high; span over rotors was 95 feet.

Several variants of the Air Horse were proposed for commercial and military operation. The most developed design was the W 11T, which was to have twin 1,435-hp Rolls-Royce Merlin 502 engines on stub wings, the option of auxiliary propellers for forward flight, and a capacity of 36 passengers who could be carried at a maximum speed of 137 mph. The W 12 and W 12A were intended to have improved rotor boom layouts and other aerodynamic improvements.

Design characteristics are listed below. Maximum permitted ceiling was 12,000 feet because the forward door had to be left open to help cool the engine; speed was limited to 80 mph because of rotor vibration problems.

First flight: 8 December 1948
Service introduction: not operational

**Characteristics**

Crew: 1 pilot, 2 copilots, 2 crewmen
Engine: 1 Rolls-Royce Merlin 24 liquid-cooled piston 1,620 hp T/O; 1,290 hp continuous
Dimensions: length 52 ft (15.85 m); height 17 ft 9 in (5.4 m); rotor diameter 47 ft (14.3 m)

Weight: empty 12,136 lbs (5,505 kg); loaded 17,498 lbs (7,937 kg)
Speed: maximum 140 mph (225 km/h)
Range: 330 miles (531 km)
Ceiling: service 23,300 ft (7,100 m)
Climb: 1,210 ft/min (369 m/min)
Payload: 24 troops

The Cierva W 11 Air Horse was the result of an attempt to reduce unit costs by building the largest possible rotary-wing aircraft. The Air Horse is believed to have been the only helicopter with three main rotors. Two prototypes were built but only the first, the VZ 724 shown here, flew untethered tests. Further development of this type ended when the aircraft crashed. (Charles E. Brown)

The second prototype of the large Air Horse (WA 555) in tethered flight. Note the length of the landing gear and position of the cockpit. This aircraft did not have the clamshell rear doors of the first prototype. (British Hovercraft)

# Cierva

## Skeeter

The Skeeter was designed and originally built by the Cierva Autogiro Company as a two-seat private helicopter. The first prototype flew in 1948. When Cierva was taken over by Saunders-Roe in 1951, the latter company continued development of the basic Cierva design under a British Ministry of Supply contract for a lightweight utility helicopter. Production models of the Skeeter entered service with the British Army and the Royal Air Force beginning in 1957, and the type continued in production through the 1959 takeover of Saunders-Roe by Westland. The last Skeeter rolled off the Westland production line in 1960. Although conceived, designed, and developed by Cierva as a commercial aircraft, the Skeeter never received any non-government orders and thus all production was of the military variants.

The Skeeter was equipped with a three-bladed main rotor and a two-bladed anti-torque and steering tail rotor. The main rotor blades were constructed of steel spars, wood ribs, and wood and fabric skin; the tail rotor was solid wood. The fuselage had a forward section fabricated of sheet metal, a steel tubular frame center section, and a monocoque tailboom. All production models were equipped with tricycle landing gear, although experiments were run with landing skids. The cabin seated two.

A total of 77 aircraft were built for the British Army, Royal Air Force, and West German Army and Navy. Ten German Skeeters were transferred to the Portuguese Air Force in 1961. All Skeeters had been withdrawn from active service by the early 1970s. Mk 1 to 8 were company designations, with the last being a commercial variant of the Mk 7 (3 built).

First flight: 8 October 1948      Users: Great Britain, West Germany, Portugal
Service introduction: 1957

**Variants**

Mk 1     original prototype development by Cierva Autogiro with 106-hp Jameson flat-four cylinder engine; 1 built.

Mk 2     slightly larger than original prototype with 145-hp de Havilland Gipsy Major 10 air-cooled engine; first flight 20 October 1949; 1 built.

Mk 3     prototypes completed for evaluation by British government; originally with same power plant as Mk 2; refitted with 180-hp Blackburn Cirrus Bombardier engine; 2 built.

Mk 4     Mk 3 completed as naval variant; 1 built.

Mk 5     private venture prototypes with Cirrus Bombardier engines; 2 built.

Mk 6     military prototype with 200-hp de Havilland Gipsy Major 200 engine; first flight 29 August 1954; served as prototype for military production run; 3 built.

AOP 10   Air Observation Post variant for British Army; factory designation Mk 6A.

T 11     trainer version of AOP Mk 10 for Royal Air Force; factory designation Mk 6B.

AOP 12   similar to AOP Mk 10 with 215-hp de Havilland Gipsy Major 215 inverted air-cooled engine; factory designation Mk 7A; 1 experimentally fitted with 220-hp Gipsy Major engine, and 1 fitted with 400-shp turbine derated to 250 shp.

T 13     Training version of AOP Mk 12; factory Mk 7B.

Mk 50    similar to AOP Mk 12 for West German Army; 11 built.

Mk 51    similar to AOP Mk 12 for West German Navy; 4 built (both Mk 50 and 51 were factory-designated Mk 7).

**Characteristics**

Crew: 1 pilot, 1 copilot

Engine: 1 de Havilland Gipsy Major piston 215 hp

Dimensions: length 26 ft 6 in (8.1 m); height 7 ft 6 in (2.29 m); rotor diameter 32 ft (9.76 m)

Weight: empty 1,720 lbs (780 kg); loaded 2,293 lbs (1,040 kg)

Speed: cruise 101 mph (163 km/h); maximum 103.5 mph (167 km/h)

Range: 212 miles (342 km)

Ceiling: hover OGE 2,500 ft (762 m); hover IGE 5,500 ft (1,680 m); service 12,800 ft (3,900 m)

Climb:

The Skeeter utility helicopter, shown here in German markings over the Saunders-Roe plant with two more Skeeters on the ground, was begun as a private venture. It was subsequently produced under contract to the British and German armed forces and used as a flying "jeep." (Saunders-Roe)

# EHI

EH 101

A joint company formed by Westland and the Italian firm Agusta, EHI was established to develop an advanced ASW helicopter to replace the Sikorsky S-61 Sea King currently in use in the two countries' navies. The London-based Westland seeks to produce a helicopter superior to the previously planned Westland WG 34 (*q.v.*). The Royal Navy will require a replacement for the Sea King starting in 1987 and the Italian Navy from about 1990 on. The project designation for the new helicopter is EH 101.

The EH 101 is expected to be smaller than both the Sea King and the Sikorsky S-70, being produced for the U.S. Navy as the SH-60B in its antisubmarine configuration. This implies that the EH 101 will be approximately 20,000 pounds loaded.

The Royal Navy has a requirement for about 60 of these helicopters and the Italian Navy for a smaller number. EHI believes that there would be a much larger market for a civil version of the helicopter as well as interest from foreign military users, with a total market of some 1,000 helicopters projected by the year 2000.

An artist's concept of the Westland-Agusta EH 101 ship-based helicopter. The British and Italian flags adorn the tail of the helicopter, planned for use in the ASW and other ship-based roles. (Westland)

# Fairey

FB-1                              Gyrodyne
                                  Jet Gyrodyne

This was the first rotary-wing aircraft developed by the Fairey Aviation Company, which had been founded in World War I. Predecessor to the large Rotodyne (*q.v.*), the Gyrodyne was a compound helicopter completed in 1947. The first of two prototypes subsequently crashed during flight, after which the second aircraft was grounded but rebuilt into the Jet Gyrodyne some four years later. The term Gyrodyne was a contraction of *gyratory* and *aerodyne*, while FB indicated Fairey and designer Dr. A. J. Bennett.

As originally built, the single-rotor Gyrodyne had stub wings with tractor airscrews driven by a shaft and gears mounted outboard on wing-tip pods. The single 525-hp Alvis Leonides nine-cylinder radial engine was fitted in the fuselage, aft of the cabin, which had extensive plexiglass covering and accommodations for a crew of two plus two or three passengers in bench-type seating. The fuselage was welded steel tubing covered with detachable metal alloy panels. The three-bladed rotor was mounted atop a streamlined pylon and in forward flight was powered. The stub wings (span 15 feet 8 inches) helped to offload the rotor, and a single propeller on the starboard wing countered torque and gave additional forward thrust. A twin-tail configuration and fixed tricycle landing gear were provided. The second prototype flew for the first time in January 1950 but was grounded and then rebuilt to the Jet Gyrodyne configuration. In the later configuration this aircraft retained the basic arrangement of the earlier design, but a larger, two-bladed, 59-foot-diameter rotor was fitted with rotor-tip jets that were fed compressed air produced by a Rolls-Royce centrifugal compressor in the fuselage. The compressed air was carried through tubes in the rotor blades. Twin pusher-type propellers were also mounted at the extremities of both stub wings. In this configuration the piston engine was apparently uprated to 550 hp.

The first prototype (military serial VX 591 and civil registration G-AIKF) was the first British-built helicopter to capture a major performance record, reaching 124.3 mph over a three-kilometer course in 1948. That aircraft crashed on 17

April 1949, killing both men on board. The second prototype was initially given the military serial XD 759 (civil G-AJJP), but it was later noted that this military serial had been given previously to a North American Sabre supplied to the RAF under U.S. defense aid, and the Jet Gyrodyne was reassigned serial XJ 389. The Jet Gyrodyne concept, sponsored by the Ministry of Supply, was found to be too complicated and the test aircraft was underpowered. This program was terminated after flight tests.

First flight: 7 December 1947
Service introduction: not operational

### Characteristics (Gyrodyne)

Crew: 1 pilot, 1 copilot
Engine: 1 Alvis Leonides radial piston 525 hp
Dimensions: length 25 ft (7.62 m); height 10 ft 2 in (3.1 m); rotor diameter 51 ft 9 in (15.77 m)
Weight: empty 3,600 lbs (1,633 kg); loaded 4,800 lbs (2,177 kg)
Speed: cruise 110 mph (177.5 km/h); maximum 171 mph (275 km/h)
Range: 250 miles (400 km)
Ceiling:
Climb: 1,300 ft/min (390 m/min)
Payload: 2-3 passengers

The second Gyrodyne prototype in flight as the Jet Gyrodyne with the incorrectly assigned British military serial XD 759 (it was later given the number XJ 389). This was the Fairey Aviation Company's first rotary-wing aircraft. Like the two others that reached the flight stage, it did not enter production. Note the wing-tip pusher propeller and twin tail fins. (Fairey)

The first Gyrodyne with civil registration G-AIKF. The aircraft was also assigned British military serial VX 591. The original design, as shown here, had only a single tractor propeller on a right-side pod mounting. (Fairey/Westland)

Another view of the Jet Gyrodyne in flight, with its enlarged rotor and twin pusher-type propellers clearly visible. The strong helicopter program that Britain developed after World War II dissipated rapidly because of the economic situation and poor government policies. (Westland)

# Fairey/Westland

### Rotodyne

The Rotodyne was conceived as a large transport type aircraft capable of vertical takeoff and landing. Design of the convertiplane began in 1947 with a variety of engine, wing, and fuselage configurations being considered. The first formal design—submitted to the government in January 1949—called for a 20-seat aircraft with a single four-bladed rotor powered by two turboprop engines. Subsequent designs were larger, and when completed in 1957 the prototype was the largest helicopter of its day. Larger versions were contemplated—carrying up to 66 passengers in the civil configuration or 75 troops in military service—but the project was cancelled in 1962, two years after the takeover of Fairey interests by Westland.

The single aircraft completed (serial XE 521) had one four-bladed, all-metal (mainly stainless steel) rotor mounted on a large pylon above the large, semi-monocoque fuselage. A high wing with a span of 46 feet 6 inches carried the turboprop engines in underslung nacelles. The tail had two fins and after 1960 three fins. The fuselage, with a rectangular cross section, had clamshell loading doors at the rear and could accommodate 40 passengers. A fully retracting, tricycle landing gear was provided. The Rotodyne could be flown as a helicopter, with rotor-tip jets and propellers providing zero thrust, or as an autogiro, with engine power being delivered only to the propellers, the rotor being in autorotation.

Original support for the Rotodyne came from British military and civil interests, with the considerable foreign interests including Kaman in the United States. Following successful prototype flights, the British government appeared ready to order 18 aircraft—12 for the RAF and 6 for civilian operation. Then, in a sudden turnaround, official funding for the Rotodyne was halted on 26 February 1962 and the project died. The prototype established a world speed record for rotorcraft of 191 mph in 1959.

First flight: 6 November 1957
Service introduction: not operational

**Variants**

Y  later designation for prototype; 1 built.
Z  proposed production aircraft with 2 5,250-shp Rolls-Royce Tyne turbine engines; length 64 ft 6 in; rotor diameter 104 ft; 54 passengers or 70 troops; none built.

**Characteristics (Rotodyne Y)**

Crew: 1 pilot, 1 copilot
Engines: 2 Napier Eland NEL 3 turboprop 3,000 ehp each
Dimensions: length 58 ft 8 in (17.9 m); height 22 ft 2 in (6.8 m); rotor diameter 90 ft (27.4 m)
Weight: loaded 32,998 lbs (14,968 kg) maximum weight flown; design military configuration loaded 60,053 lbs (27,240 kg)
Speed: cruise 185 mph (298 km/h); maximum 191 mph (307 km/h)
Range: 450 miles (724 km); radius with 17,015 lbs (7,718 kg) 230 miles (368 km)
Ceiling:
Climb:
Payload: 40 troops

The Fairey/Westland Rotodyne represented another postwar British effort to develop a very large helicopter. The British government's periodic turnarounds on various advanced aircraft projects helped to kill this most promising helicopter design. The single prototype Rotodyne was one of the few helicopters to have turboprop engines.

The prototype Rotodyne in commercial colors (although its military serial XE 521 is on its tail fins) during a lower-level flight with landing gear fully retracted. The aircraft held promise for both military and civil operations. (Fairey)

An underside view of the Rotodyne in flight. (U.S. Air Force)

# Fairey

### Ultra-light Helicopter

The Ultra-light Helicopter was the result of specification H 144T issued in 1953 by the War Office, Air Ministry, and Ministry of Supply to provide the Army with a light observation helicopter. Four prototypes were ordered from Fairey in July 1954. The prototypes developed by Fairey were evaluated by the Army and, subsequently, by the Royal Navy, and Fairey attempted to sell a civil version. However, in 1956, the government halted support of the project for reasons of economy. Fairey continued to develop and evaluate the Ultra-light Helicopter as a military machine as well as to try to market civil models of it until 1958.

The diminutive Ultra-light Helicopter was a simple, lightweight construction, with a lower metal shell supporting a plexiglass cockpit, the tail structure supported by a short boom, and the turbine engine mounted under the boom. A French engine was adopted as the most suitable, and a large centrifugal compressor provided power to the rotor-tip jets. The tail assembly normally consisted of a horizontal surface with endplates plus a ventral fin. A skid landing gear was included. There were provisions for a two-man crew, with the observer facing to the rear in the Army observation configuration. The left-hand seat could be removed and, with a modified door, a stretcher could be accommodated.

Four military prototypes were built (serial XJ 924, 928, 930, 936), with the first one flying a year after contract award. Fairey also produced two Ultra-light Helicopters for civil evaluation. Military trials were continued after withdrawal of government support in 1956, with one unit conducting flight trials from a British frigate in 1957. Despite efforts to market civil models in the United States (under license to Piasecki) and Canada as well as in Great Britain, no helicopters were produced beyond the six prototypes.

A Fairey Ultra-light helicopter taking off during the September 1955 air show at the Farnborough Royal Aircraft Establishment. Like several American helicopters developed in the same period, the Ultra-light was intended to provide ground troops with a very small, easily handled and supported utility helicopter. Note the all-around visibility. (U.S. Air Force)

First flight: 14 August 1955
Service introduction: not operational

**Characteristics**

Crew: 1 pilot, 1 observer
Engine: 1 Turboméca Palouste BnPe 2 turbine 250 hp
Dimensions: length 15 ft (4.57 m); height 8 ft 2 in (2.49 m); rotor diameter 28 ft 3½ in (8.61 m)
Weight: loaded 1,800 lbs (817 kg)
Speed: cruise 95 mph (153 km/h)
Range: 180 miles (290 km)
Ceiling: hover OGE 4,800 ft (1,463 m); hover IGE 10,200 ft (3,109 m)
Climb: 950 ft/min (290 m/min)
Payload: 1 stretcher in place of observer

# Hafner

## Rotabuggy

The Rotabuggy was the Rotachute (*q.v.*) configured for use with a jeep-type light truck. A rotor device and tail assembly could be attached to a jeep which would then be towed behind an aircraft tug and released near the objective area. The concept was also dubbed Rotajeep.

Various fuselage fairings and tail fin combinations were tried in the Rotabuggy project. A "hanging" control stick was suspended into the jeep from the rotorhead. The vehicle was a Willys 4 × 4 truck weighing 2,125 pounds empty. The rotor and tail unit weighed 550 pounds.

Development of the Rotabuggy was assigned to the M. L. Aviation Company at White Waltham in 1942. One prototype was completed. After flight trials of varying success the project was dropped because of the availability of large vehicle-carrying gliders.

(A similar flying jeep or "fleep" project, with a rotary-wing device being added to a standard 4 × 4 vehicle, was undertaken in Australia by the Army Inventions Directorate in 1943. This effort, totally independent of the Hafner project, used specially fabricated 37-foot diameter rotor blades and components from three grounded C 30A autogiros. Given the code name Skywards, the project was discontinued before any flights had taken place.)

First flight: 1943
Service introduction: not operational

**Characteristics**

Crew: 2 pilots + paratroopers (in jeep)
Engine: none
Dimensions: rotor diameter 46 ft 8 in (12.4 m)
Weight: loaded 3,110 lbs (1,411 kg)
Speed: 150 mph (241 km/m)
Range:
Ceiling:
Climb:

# Hafner

### Rotachute

The Rotachute was developed by Raoul Hafner when director of the Airborne Forces Experimental Establishment in England during World War II. The Rotachute was one of a series of unpowered devices intended to move more men and vehicles behind enemy lines than possible with parachutes. Work began on the Rotachute on 3 October 1940, and practical tests of experimental devices were started only eight days later.

A one-man, rotary-wing glider, the Rotachute consisted of a steel tube frame to seat the pilot-paratrooper, a free-moving two-bladed rotor, and a tail fairing, which was to be made of rubberized fabric without framework to minimize stowage space in a transport aircraft. The Rotachutes were to be carried on an overhead rail inside of such a transport, from which they would be launched at the rate of one every 15 seconds. The basic Rotachute was to carry about 240 pounds—pilot, parachute, Bren machine gun, and 300 rounds of ammunition. Several different Rotachute configurations were developed. The original landing skids were replaced by wheels after tethered (truck-pulled) trials. When the aircraft was towed, its average takeoff run was 300 feet and its landing run 0 to 50 feet, depending upon the wind force and direction.

Production of Rotachutes was assigned to F. Hills and Sons of Manchester and the Airwork General Trading Company of Hounslow. Flight tests ended in October 1943 when it was decided that there was no longer an operational need for the Rotachute.

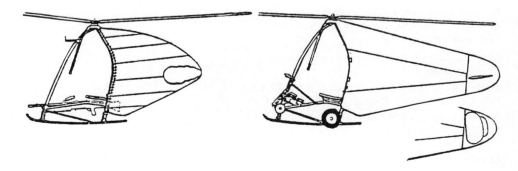

First flight: first free flight from ground vehicle 29 May 1942; first free flight from aircraft
    17 June 1942
Service introduction: not operational

**Characteristics**

Crew: 1 pilot-paratrooper
Engine: none
Dimensions: rotor diameter 15 ft (4.6 m)
Weight: empty 50 lbs (22.7 kg); loaded 290 lbs (131.7 kg)
Speed: 93 mph (150 km/h)
Range:
Ceiling:
Climb:

A Hafner Rotachute awaiting its pilot-paratrooper. This prototype (as indicated by the P on
the "tail" structure) was a later version having wheeled landing gear in place of the original
skids. The Rotachute was formally known as a "controllable rotary-wing parachute."

A Hafner Rotachute with pilot mounted on the back of a truck during a test run. (*Air
International*)

# Hafner

Rotatank

The ultimate Rotachute (*q.v.*) developed by the Airborne Forces Experimental Establishment in England, this device was intended to permit a 16-ton Valentine tank to be towed by an aircraft tug and then safely landed by rotary wing.

A giant 155-foot rotor for use with a 16-ton Valentine tank was fabricated but never tested.

# Westland

P 531                                   Wasp
                                        Scout

The development of the P 531 was begun by Saunders-Roe as a general purpose, five- to six-seat sequel to their two-place Skeeter, which had entered military service in 1957. Design work on what was to become the Wasp in its naval version and the Scout in its army variant began in November 1957. These aircraft incorporated several features of the earlier Skeeter, including the rotor blades, tailboom, and wheeled landing gear. Two prototype P 531s had flown when Westland acquired Saunders-Roe in 1959. The design was improved and new prototypes constructed, these having skid landing gear and more powerful engines. Three of these prototypes were evaluated by the Royal Navy. The first production batch was ordered by the British Army and became the Scout AH 1; the first naval variant was the Wasp HAS 1. Both series of helicopters have enjoyed widespread use.

Both the Scout and the Wasp have a four-bladed, all-metal main rotor and an anti-torque tail rotor powered by a 1,050-shp Bristol turboshaft engine, derated to yield 685 shp in the Scout and 710 shp in the Wasp. The all-metal fuselage in both helicopters is of semi-monocoque construction, with a horizontal stabilizer under the tailboom on the Scout and opposite the tail rotor on the Wasp. There is space for the pilot plus four or five passengers, or the pilot and two stretchers. The Scout has a tubular steel skid landing gear while the ship-based Wasp is equipped with a quadricycle, wheeled undercarriage. Both variants can be armed, the Scout with machine guns and air-to-surface missiles, and the Wasp with two Mk-44 ASW homing torpedoes or depth bombs. Blind-flying instrumentation is standard.

Production of the Scout terminated in 1970 and that of the Wasp in 1974. Some 200 Scouts and Wasps were built by Westland before the production lines were closed, the primary customers being the British Army and the Royal Navy. The Wasp is flown from frigates in the British, Brazilian, Dutch, New Zealand, and South African navies as a weapon (torpedo) delivery vehicle. The helicopter relies completely upon the surface ship for detection of the submarine and guidance to the torpedo release point.

First flight: P531 prototype 20 July 1958
Service introduction: 1963
Users: Australia, Bahrain, Brazil, Great Britain, Jordan, Netherlands, New Zealand, South Africa, Uganda

## Variants

Wasp

| | |
|---|---|
| P 531-0 | Saunders-Roe prototypes with Skeeter components; powered by 400-shp Turboméca Turmo turboshaft derated to 325 shp; tricycle wheeled landing gear; first flight 20 July 1958; 2 built. |
| P 531-ON | Westland development of the P 531; fitted with Nimbus turboshaft engine derated to 635 shp or Gnome H.1000 turboshaft derated to 685 shp; skid landing gear; 3 built. |
| P 531-2 | pre-production helicopter for British Army with Bristol Siddeley Nimbus 1,050-shp turboshaft derated to 650 shp. |
| HAS 1 | production ASW variant of Wasp P 531-2 for Royal Navy; no sensors; torpedo or depth bombs carried externally; first flight 28 October 1962; entered service in late 1963. |
| Scout AH 1 | production variant of P 531-2 for army liaison with Bristol Nimbus 101 turboshaft engine; first flight 4 August 1960; entered service in early 1963. |

## Characteristics (HAS 1)

Crew: 1 pilot, 1 observer

Engine: 1 Bristol (Rolls-Royce) Nimbus 503 turboshaft derated to 710 shp

Dimensions: length 30 ft 4 in (9.2 m); height 8 ft 11 in (2.7 m); rotor diameter 32 ft 3 in (9.9 m)

Weight: empty 3,452 lbs (1,566 kg); loaded 5,500 lbs (2,495 kg)

Speed: cruise 110 mph (178 km/h); maximum 120 mph (193 km/h)

Range: 303 miles (488 km)

Ceiling: hover OGE 8,800 ft (2,682 m); hover IGE 12,500 ft (3,810 m); service 12,200 ft (3,720 m)

Climb: 1,440 ft/min (439 m/min)

Payload: 3-4 troops or 2 Mk-44 ASW homing torpedoes or depth bombs or 1,500 lbs (680 kg) cargo

A Royal Navy Wasp HAS 1 hovers over a frigate in preparation for landing aboard. Note the angle of the wheels to reduce movement once the helicopter touches down on the deck. A rescue hoist is mounted aft and above the cockpit, attesting to the versatility of this aircraft, designed to carry torpedoes for attacking submarines detected by shipboard sonar. (Royal Navy)

A Wasp HAS 1 of the Brazilian Navy hovers over the U.S. missile destroyer *Mahan* (DDG-42) during exercises off the Pacific coast of South America. When this photograph was taken the helicopter was delivering a passenger to the warship. (U.S. Navy)

# Westland

WG 13                         Lynx
WG 30                         H-14


The Lynx is based on a twin-engined, multi-purpose helicopter designed by Westland but is actually produced under the Westland-Aérospatiale collaboration agreement of 1967. Approximately 70 percent of Lynx production is performed by Westland and 30 percent by Aérospatiale. Thus far the British government has acquired two versions of the Lynx, the AH 1 for its ground forces and the HAS 2 for the Royal Navy, while France has acquired only a naval version. Export orders have been received from several nations. Under the 1967 Anglo-French Agreement, naval variants of the WG 13 were to be developed for both navies, a utility variant for the British Army, and an armed reconnaissance helicopter for the French Army. These requirements were later modified and there are currently two naval variants, one British, one French, and one British army variant.

Westland originally conceived the Lynx to be a replacement for the Whirlwind and Scout then in Royal Navy and British Army service. This paper design included proven components: two 720-shp PT6A turboshafts, Westland Whirlwind (Sikorsky S-55) dynamic components, and a modified Belvedere rotor. This design evolved into the WG 13 in 1963 with a newly designed, semi-rigid rotor and experimental Bristol Siddeley 900-shp turboshafts. The two Rolls-Royce BS 360-07-26 Gem turboshafts of production Lynxes drive a single four-bladed, semi-rigid main rotor and a four-bladed tail rotor. In lieu of hinges at the rotor hub, the WG 13's blades are attached by means of titanium plates and a flexible arm, thereby stiffening the rotor system to allow for greater maneuverability and performance. Unfortunately, this also stiffens the ride, and the Lynx is prone to more vibration than a helicopter with a fully articulated rotor system. The fuselage is a semi-monocoque pod-and-boom structure, with the power plants placed side by side atop the after cabin, just behind the rotor hub assembly. The tailboom is a monocoque structure ending in a swept-back vertical stabilizer, with the tail rotor mounted to port. The cabin can accommodate a pilot and up to ten troops, but normal operations in the British Army and Navy versions use only a pilot and observer or gunner, while the French naval version also carries systems operators. All naval versions are equipped with a wheeled tricycle undercarriage, while the British Army's AH 1 has skids.

A slightly modified Lynx was offered to the U.S. Navy by Sikorsky for the LAMPS II antisubmarine helicopter before that program was cancelled. Westland offered an improved Lynx to the U.S. Navy in competition with Sikorsky and Boeing Vertol for the LAMPS III competition but lost to Sikorsky. The Lynx remains in production with orders having totaled over 300 by mid-1980.

First flight: 21 March 1971
Service introduction: December 1977
Users: Argentina, Brazil, Denmark, France, West Germany, Great Britain, Netherlands, Norway, Qatar

**Variants**

AH 1              utility and antitank variant for British Army; armed with 8 TOW missiles

|              |                                                                                                   |
|--------------|---------------------------------------------------------------------------------------------------|
|              | in launchers plus 8 reloads in cabin; no guns provided; 114 ordered through 1980.                 |
| HAS 2        | specialized antiship ASW variant for Royal Navy; fitted with radar, electronic countermeasures, navigation computer, 4 Sea Skua antiship missiles; 80 ordered as of late 1980. |
| Lynx (French Navy) | specialized ASW antiship variant for French Navy; similar to HAS 2 with dipping sonar, AS 12 wire-guided missiles; first delivered September 1978; 40 ordered as of mid-1980. |
| Sea Lynx     | similar to HAS 2 for West German Navy with dipping sonar; 12 ordered for delivery in 1981. |
| UH-14A       | similar to AH 1 for SAR duties with Netherlands Navy; 6 built. |
| SH-14B       | similar to French naval Lynx for Netherlands Navy with Alcatel dipping sonar; 10 built. |
| SH-14C       | similar to HAS 2 for Netherlands Navy with MAD gear; 8 built. |
| WG 30        | privately funded Lynx development for civil and military use; enlarged cabin capable of carrying 14-22 troops; horizontal tail surface with small endplates; retractable landing gear; rotor diameter 43 ft 8 in; weight loaded 11,750 lbs; first flight 10 April 1979; 2 prototypes built. |

**Characteristics (AH 1)**

Crew: 1 pilot, 1 copilot/observer/gunner
Engines: 2 Rolls-Royce BS 360-07-26 Gem turboshafts 900 shp each.
Dimensions: length 49 ft 9 in (15.163 m); height 12 ft (3.66 m); rotor diameter 42 ft (12.802 m)
Weight: empty 5,847 lbs (2,658 kg); loaded 10,478.6 lbs (4,763 kg)
Speed: cruise 81 mph (130 km/h); maximum 175 mph (282 km/h)
Range: 336 miles (540 km)
Ceiling: hover OGE 9,580 ft (2,920 m)
Climb: 2,180 ft/min (664 m/min)
Payload: 10 troops or 16 TOW missiles (8 ready to fire plus 8 reloads)

A Royal Navy Lynx HAS 2 in flight with four Sea Skua antiship missiles. This concept gives small surface warships increased antiship missile capability, supplementing ship-launched missiles. Note the wheeled undercarriage of this naval Lynx; Army helicopters have skid-type landing gear for field operations. (Westland)

A Lynx AH 1 flown by the British Army. Note the camouflage paint scheme, intended to help the helicopter survive while on the ground in Europe. The helicopter's Army markings and serial number (XX 907) are in low-visibility paint, but Lynx on the nose, the British roundel, and the danger warning for the tail rotor are in standard paint. (Westland)

An Aéronavale Lynx with landing gear extended comes in for a landing. (French Armed Forces)

# Westland
WG 34

This helicopter was planned by the British Ministry of Defense as a replacement for the Royal Navy's Sea King HAS 2 helicopter, to enter service in 1987. The aircraft was to have been smaller than the Sea King but with increased payload. Westland had sought collaboration in the WG 34 effort with Aérospatiale and Agusta. However, the program was reconsidered in favor of a joint Anglo-Italian helicopter to be developed by the new company EHI Ltd.

The WG 34 was to have been a three- or four-seat aircraft with a conventional semi-monocoque fuselage. Two or three turboshaft engines would have been fitted with intakes facing sideways to assist deicing. The landing gear was to have been fully retractable, with a sealed hull for emergency water landings. Planned ASW equipment was listed as surface search radar, advanced navigation and electronic warfare systems, data links (to surface ships and other aircraft), towed Magnetic Anomaly Detector (MAD), expendable sonobuoys, and an internal weapons bay for ASW homing torpedoes. The following characteristics were tentative and approximate.

**Characteristics**

Crew: 1 pilot, 1 observer, 1 sensor operator; possibly 1 copilot
Engines: 2 or 3 turboshaft
Dimensions: length 56 ft 9 in (17.3 m); height 13 ft 6 in (4.11 m); rotor diameter 55 ft 6 in (16.92 m)
Weight: loaded 24,000 lbs (10,886 kg)
Speed:
Range:
Ceiling:
Climb:
Payload: ASW homing torpedoes

An artist's concept of the abortive Westland WG 34 helicopter, intended as a successor to the Sikorsky-Westland Sea Kings in Royal Navy service. Several of the WG 34 features have been incorporated into its replacement, the EH 101. (Westland)

# ITALY

## Agusta
A 101G

The A 101G was the first indigenously designed Italian helicopter to come off the drawing boards of the Costruzioni Aeronautiche Giovanni Agusta SpA, although it was not the first to fly. That honor belongs to the smaller A 103. Nevertheless, the A 101G was, in 1979, the largest helicopter ever designed in Italy. It was a three-engined, heavy transport helicopter designed for the Italian armed services; however, the A 101G never entered production.

The A 101G had a five-bladed main rotor and a six-bladed anti-torque tail rotor mounted on the left side of the tailboom. Power was provided by three Rolls-Royce 1,400-shp turboshafts mounted above the main cabin. The fuselage was of the conventional semi-monocoque pod-and-boom type, with a vertical stabilizer and starboard-mounted horizontal stabilizer. Two crew members could be accommodated on the flight deck and 36 passengers could be carried in the main cabin, with alternative loadings of 18 stretchers and 5 attendants or 11,025 pounds of cargo. The undercarriage was a non-retractable tricycle type. All prototypes were equipped for IFR flight. Three prototypes of the A 101G were built and tested by the Italian Air Force.

First flight: 19 October 1964
Service introduction: not operational

An Augusta A 101G in flight. The helicopter is one of the largest of indigenous European construction and one of the few three-engine helicopters. Although designed primarily to meet Italian Air Force specifications, no production orders were forthcoming and only three prototypes were built. (*Jane's All the World's Aircraft*)

**Characteristics**

Crew: 1 pilot, 1 copilot
Engines: 3 Rolls-Royce Bristol Gnome H 1400 turboshaft 1,400 shp each
Dimensions: length 66 ft 3 in (20.15 m); height 21 ft 6¼ in (6.56 m); rotor diameter 66 ft 11 in (20.4 m)
Weight: empty 15,100 lbs (6,855 kg); loaded 28,465 lbs (12,912 kg)
Speed: cruise 134.5 mph (217 km/h); maximum 149.5 mph (241 km/h)
Range: 250 miles (402 km)
Ceiling: hover OGE 9,184 ft (2,800 m); hover IGE 11,316 ft (3,450 m); service 15,088 ft (4,600 m)
Climb: 2,860 ft/min (872 m/min)
Payload: 36 troops or 11,023 lbs (5,000 kg) internal cargo

# Agusta
A 106

The A 106 was a single-seat light ASW helicopter which was produced in small numbers for the Italian Navy. An original Agusta design, the A 106 took many design features from earlier Agusta experimental helicopters, the piston-engined A 103 and A 104, and the turboshaft-powered A 105. Efforts to market the A 106 for a variety of military uses met with no success, and the 23 ASW variants built for the Italian Navy marked the limit of the production run. The Agusta-Bell AB 204 replaced most A 106s only a few years after the latter entered service in 1969.

One of the very few single-seat helicopters to enter military service, the A 106 had two-bladed aluminum main and tail rotors, turned by a Turboméca-Agusta TAA 230 turboshaft derated to 330 shp. The fuselage was of conventional semi-monocoque construction, with a tailboom that was hinged just forward of the tail rotor for shipboard stowage. The main rotor also folded to facilitate stowage. ASW gear included Julie active sonobuoys, all-weather avionics, and two Mk-44 torpedoes.

First flight: November 1965
Service introduction: 1969
Users: Italy

**Characteristics**

Crew: 1 pilot
Engine: 1 Turboméca-Agusta TAA 230 turboshaft 330 shp
Dimensions: length 36 ft (10.97 m); height 8 ft 2½ in (2.5 m); rotor diameter 31 ft 2 in (9.5 m)
Weight: empty 1,300 lbs (590 kg); loaded 3,000 lbs (1,360 kg)
Speed: cruise 115 mph (185 km/h); maximum 124 mph (200 km/h)
Range: 174 miles (280 km)
Ceiling: hover OGE 6,560 ft (2,000 m); hover IGE 10,500 ft (3,200 m)
Climb: 1,220 ft/min (372 m/min)
Payload: 2 Mk-44 ASW homing torpedoes

Probably the lightest manned ASW helicopter, the Agusta A 106 reacts to submarine targets detected by shipboard sonar or other means to deliver two Mk-44 homing torpedoes. It can carry alternative weapons, cargo on an under-fuselage hook, or two external stretcher pods. (*Jane's All the World's Aircraft*)

A diminutive Agusta A 106 with rotor blades folded. (Agusta)

# Agusta
A 109                                    Hirundo

The A 109 Hirundo is perhaps one of the most asthetically pleasing helicopters to be produced. Seating eight, this high-performance, twin-engined helicopter is the culmination of years of independent design efforts as well as over two decades of license production of both Bell and Sikorsky designs. The result is a high-speed competitor with the most advanced modern American helicopters. The A 109s have been completed in the standard commercial configuration as well as experimental military and naval variants for evaluation by the Italian armed forces.

The A 109 has a fully articulated four-bladed main rotor and a semi-rigid tail rotor driven by two 420-shp Allison turboshaft engines. These are mounted side by side above the after section of the cabin and behind the main rotor and are separated from the main cabin by stainless steel firewalls. The fuselage is a combination of honeycomb panel and semi-monocoque construction, broken down into a standard pod-and-boom configuration. A pair of swept-back vertical stabilizers are installed above and below the tailboom, and the anti-torque tail rotor is mounted on the port side of the tailboom. Dual horizontal stabilizers are fitted just forward of the tail rotor. The various versions have different seating accommodations, the standard commercial configuration providing for a pilot and seven passengers. An ambulance version has room for two crew, two stretchers, and two attendants, while the military versions can carry either seven troops or the same number of stretchers as the civilian variant. The naval version provides for a crew of four, plus the specialized naval sensor fits. All variants have retractable tricycle landing gear, but avionics depend on the user and the helicopter's mission; commercial variants have been delivered with as little as a basic VFR instrument panel, while sophisticated electronic warfare suites are available for installation in the military versions. Available weapons systems include HOT or TOW antitank missiles, 7.62-mm machine guns, rocket launchers, and mini-guns.

Production of the A 109 began in 1975 and worked up to 12 per month in 1979. Military buyers thus far include only Italy and Argentina, but there are several other potential customers.

First flight: 4 August 1971
Service introduction: 1976
Users: Argentina, Italy

**Variants**

military  A 109 ordered by Italian Army for evaluation; 5 built for evaluation; (3 with TOW missiles and 2 for transport/liaison); subsequently entered series production.

naval     offered by Agusta, no firm orders; all-weather avionics; ASW or antiship weapons to order, including homing torpedoes, MAD, radar, AS 12 or AM 10 antiship missiles.

**Characteristics**

Crew: 1 pilot, 1 copilot; 1 or 2 systems operators in naval version
Engines: 2 Allison 250-C20B turboshaft 420 shp each
Dimensions: length 42 ft 10 in (13.05 m); height 10 ft 10 in (3.3 m); rotor diameter 36 ft 1 in (11 m)
Weight: empty 3,120 lbs (1,415 kg); loaded 5,400 lbs (2,450 kg)

Speed: cruise 143 mph (231 km/h); maximum 193 mph (311 km/h)
Range: 351 miles (565 km)
Ceiling: service 16,300 ft (4,968 m)
Climb: 1,620 ft/min (493 m/min)
Payload: 6 troops or 2 7.62-mm machine guns + 2 XM-157 rocket launchers or HOT
or TOW antitank missiles or Mk-46 ASW homing torpedoes

An Agusta A 109 for the Argentine Army with two rocket launchers and two machine-gun
pods. Note the tail configuration and fully retracting landing gear of this streamlined
helicopter. (*Jane's All the World's Aircraft*)

An Agusta A 109 in the naval configuration. This variant, with a crew of three or four, is
intended to be fitted with various ASW sensors and carry antiship missiles or ASW homing
torpedoes. (*Jane's All the World's Aircraft*)

# Agusta
A 129                                    Mangusta (Mongoose)

Derived from the earlier A 109A Hirundo, and using most of its dynamic components, the A 129 Mongoose is a light antitank helicopter that is planned for quantity production for the Italian Army. Five prototypes were ordered in 1979, and early estimated requirements were for 60 production units, possibly increasing to 100 by the late 1980s. Agusta estimates a worldwide requirement for 1,000 light attack helicopters and is gearing up a marketing effort to ensure that the Mongoose represents a significant portion of the 1,000. First flight of the A 129 was expected in 1981 with squadron delivery in 1984.

The fuselage is narrow (measuring the new standard 37.5 inches), with two seats in tandem, the gunner in front and the pilot in the rear. Two stub wings each have two stores stations for eight HOT or TOW antitank missiles, rockets, or miniguns. The rotor system is based on that of the A 109, but it is considerably improved and will keep functioning 1½ hours after the loss of all lubrication. The Mongoose has a four-bladed main rotor and two-bladed tail rotor, a wheeled undercarriage, and horizontal stabilizers just forward of the tail fin.

First flight: 1981 (est.)     Service introduction: 1984 (est.)     Users: Italy

**Characteristics**

Crew: 1 pilot, 1 gunner
Engines: 2 Rolls-Royce Gem-2 turboshaft
Dimensions: length 41 ft (12.5 m); height 10 ft 6 in (3.2 m); rotor diameter 39 ft ½ in (11.9 m)
Weight: empty 4,976 lbs (2,257 kg); loaded 7,826 lbs (3,550 kg)
Speed: maximum 202 mph (325 km/h)
Range: 391 miles (629 km)
Ceiling: hover OGE 8,860 ft (2,700 m); hover IGE 11,155 ft (3,400 m)
Climb: 1,970 ft/min (600 m/min)
Payload: 8 HOT or TOW antitank missiles; rocket pods; 7.62-mm or 12.7-mm gun pods

This is a model of the A 129 Mangusta (Mongoose), developed for the Italian Army by Agusta. The gunner and pilot are seated in tandem to reduce the aircraft's cross section. Like other attack helicopters, it is specifically designed to survive small-arms fire while carrying heavy armament. (*Jane's All the World's Aircraft*)

# JAPAN

## Kayaba

Ka-1
Ka-2

This autogiro was flown by the Japanese Army for observation and antisubmarine warfare during World War II. It was based on the Kellett KD-1A (designated YG-1 by the U.S. Army). One KD-1A was imported by the Japanese Army in 1939 for tests in the artillery spotting role. It crashed during trials and the severely damaged wreck was given to the Kayaba Industrial Company for duplication. The Kayaba firm had been involved in producing specialized aircraft parts. Some design changes were made and the resultant Ka-1 proved to be a highly maneuverable autogiro that was used for artillery spotting, liaison, and ASW. Those Ka-1s with ASW duties flew from land bases and from a small aircraft carrier, the *Akitsu Maru*, which was converted from a merchant ship in 1941. She was operated by the Japanese Army until sunk by a U.S. submarine in November 1944.

The Ka-1 had a standard autogiro configuration with seating for two, although only the pilot could be carried when the machine was armed with depth charges. No wings were provided; twin elliptical fins were fitted to the horizontal tail surface. The crewmen sat in open cockpits. Normally the rotor was rotating at 160 revolutions per minute at takeoff with a run of 100 feet required in no-wind conditions. The Ka-1 KAI variant was tested with powder rockets on the rotor tips in an effort to increase load-carrying capability. A three-bladed rotor was standard and could be folded back to facilitate ground handling.

About 240 Ka-1s were produced for the Japanese Army through the end of the war at the Kayaba plant in Sendai, northern Japan. One machine was fitted with a Jacobs engine and designated Ka-2.

First flight: 26 May 1941    Service introduction: 1941    Users: Japan

A Kayaba Ka-1 in flight during World War II. In a little-known operation, the Japanese Army flew this helicopter from a small aircraft carrier in the ASW role. Note the aircraft's similarity to American Kellett autogiros upon which its design was based. (*Ships of the World*)

**Variants**

Ka-1 production aircraft; approximately 240 built.
Ka-2 aircraft fitted with Jacobs L-4MA-7 radial piston 240 hp; 1 built.

**Characteristics**

Crew: 1 pilot, 1 observer
Engine: 1 Kobe Argus As 10C radial piston 240 hp
Dimensions: length 30 ft 2¼ in (9.2 m); rotor diameter 40 ft ¼ in (12.2 m)
Weight: empty 1,709 lbs (776 kg); loaded 2,579 lbs (1,171 kg)
Speed: cruise 71.5 mph (115 km/h); maximum 102.5 mph (165 km/h)
Range: 174 miles (280 km)
Ceiling: service 11,485 ft (3,500 m)
Climb: 994 ft/min (303 m/min)
Payload: 2 × 132-lb (60-kg) depth charges

One Ka-2 autogiro with rotor-tip powder rockets was built. It also had a Jacobs engine with different engine cowling than the standard Ka-1. (*Ships of the World*)

# SPAIN

## Aerotecnica

AC-12                           EC-XZ-2

This helicopter was developed by the French engineer Cantinieau working in Spain with the firm Aerotecnica SA. The Spanish Air Force sponsored two prototypes as well as a production run of 12 helicopters which entered service with the designation EC-XZ-2.

The AC series of helicopters had a distinctive arrangement: the Lycoming or Turboméca engine was mounted atop the cabin, and the transmission and reduction gear were based on commercial automobile equipment. The fuselage, mounted on a skid-type landing gear, had two seats with dual controls. A three-bladed anti-torque rotor supported by the boom was fitted on the right side. The main three-bladed rotor had duralumin spars, ribs, and trailing edges, with a compound filling and fiberglass covering. The engine was fan cooled.

The AC-12 saw service only with the Spanish Air Force. Development of a turbine-powered variant of the AC-12 was halted when the Aerotecnica firm was dissolved in 1962.

First flight: 20 July 1956     Service introduction:

**Characteristics**

Crew: 1 pilot, 1 copilot/student/observer
Engine: 1 Lycoming O-360-B2A piston 168 hp
Dimensions: length 24 ft 9 in (7.55 m); height 9 ft (2.75 m); rotor diameter 27 ft 10 in (8.5 m)
Weight: empty 1,102 lbs (500 kg); loaded 1,808 lbs (820 kg)
Speed: cruise 71.5 mph (115 km/h); maximum 87 mph (140 km/h)
Range: 140 miles (230 km); with auxiliary tanks 280 miles (460 km)
Ceiling: hover IGE 7,875 ft (2,400 m); service 13,100 ft (4,000 m)
Climb: 985 ft/min (300 m/min)

A Spanish EX-XZ-2 in flight. Note the unusual configuration with the engine mounted above the bubble cockpit. The helicopter saw military service only with the Spanish Air Force. (Aerotecnica)

# Aerotecnica

AC-14                                        EC-XZ-4

This was an improved version of the same firm's AC-12 training-utility helicopter, but with a shaft-turbine engine. The AC-14 was developed from two AC-13 prototypes built under contract by Nord in France. Subsequently, ten production helicopters were ordered by the Spanish Air Force with the designation EC-XZ-4.

As in the AC-12, the engine was mounted above the cabin, with accommodations for a single pilot plus four passengers in two pairs of seats. Instead of an anti-torque rotor, the AC-14 had controlled gas deflection in low-speed flight and twin control rudders mounted on the tailboom for high-speed flight. The skid-type landing gear was retained.

Larger helicopters based on this design were proposed, but no work was undertaken prior to the firm's dissolution.

First flight: AC-13 16 July 1957
Service introduction:

**Characteristics**

Crew: 1 pilot
Engine: 1 Turboméca Artouste IIB1 shaft-turbine 400 shp
Dimensions: length 26 ft 8 in (8.13 m); height 10 ft 2 in (3.1 m); rotor diameter 31 ft
    8 in (9.65 m)
Weight: empty 1,433 lbs (650 kg); loaded 2,975 lbs (1,350 kg)
Speed: cruise 93 mph (150 km/h); maximum 112 mph (180 km/h)
Range: 185 miles (300 km); with auxiliary tanks 400 miles (640 km)
Ceiling: hover IGE 16,075 ft (4,900 m); service 22,300 ft (6,800 m)
Climb: 1,375 ft/min (420 m/min)
Payload: 4 troops

An Aerotecnica AC-14 hovering at low altitude. The craft could be distinguished by the tail fins and absence of an anti-torque tail rotor. (*Air International*)

# UNION OF SOVIET SOCIALIST REPUBLICS

## Bratukhin

Omega I
Omega II
G-3
G-4

The Omega series of helicopters was developed by the OKB-3 experimental design bureau set up in January 1940, initially under B. N. Yuryev, but from March of that year under I. P. Bratukhin. The latter had made an extensive study of foreign helicopter developments and had been greatly impressed by Focke's successful twin-rotor designs. This concept of side-by-side rotors became evident in Bratukhin helicopter designs, beginning with the Omega I. The Omega was formally approved for development on 27 July 1940.

The basic Omega I and the G-4 derivative had a metal-tube fuselage covered with fabric, a high-mounted cockpit with 360-degree visibility, and a large, conventional tail fin with rudder in a T-tail arrangement. The twin engines were mounted on open lattice outriggers with the three-bladed rotor hubs extending up from the nacelles. The main landing gear, consisting of both nose and tail wheels, extended down from the nacelles. These three Bratukhin helicopters differed principally in their engines. The distance between rotor hubs on the Omega II was 23 feet 7 inches, with maximum span over both rotors approximately 46½ feet.

The Omega I was completed in August 1941. Tethered tests revealed some difficulties, but the evacuation of OKB-3 from Moscow delayed modifications. Free flight tests began in early 1943 and later that year the Omega II, having more powerful engines, was initiated. This helicopter was completed in September 1944 and, after flight trials ended in January 1945, was used to train helicopter pilots. The Omega II was publicly demonstrated at the Tushino aviation display on 18 August 1944. Two G-3 prototypes, with improved engines and transmissions plus other changes, were completed in early 1945, followed by five more G-3 variants. The G-3 was exhibited in the first postwar display of Soviet aircraft at Tushino (Moscow) in August 1946. The first G-4, which started flight trials in October 1947, crashed on 28 January 1948 as a result of pilot error. At least two additional G-4s were completed before the project ended in late 1948. These aircraft demonstrated the ability to sustain flight with only one engine and provided useful data for subsequent Soviet helicopter development.

First flight: Omega I August 1941 (tethered), Omega II 1944, G-3 1945, G-4 1947
Service introduction: not operational

**Variants (see below)**

**Characteristics (Omega II except as indicated)**
Crew: 1 pilot, 1 observer
Engines: Omega I   2 MV-6 air-cooled radial piston 220 hp each
        Omega II 2 MG-31F air-cooled radial piston 330 hp each T/O; 350 hp continuous

G-3    2 Pratt & Whitney R-985-AN-1 radial piston 450 hp T/O; 370 hp
       continuous
G-4    2 Ivchenko AI-26GR(f) radial piston 500 hp

Dimensions: length 26 ft 11 in (8.2 m); height 10 ft 7½ in (3.24 m); rotor diameter 23
    ft (7.0 m)

|  |  | *empty* | *loaded* |
|---|---|---|---|
| Weight: | Omega I | 3,800 lbs (1,760 kg) | 4,519 lbs (2,050 kg) |
|  | Omega II | 4,144.5 lbs (1,880 kg) | 5,070.5 lbs (2,300 kg) |
|  | G-3 | 4,839 lbs (2,195 kg) | 5,732 lbs (2,600 kg) |
|  | G-4 | 5,211.5 lbs (2,364 kg) | 6,614 lbs (3,000 kg) |
| Speed: | Omega I | 115 mph (186 km/h) |  |
|  | Omega II | 93 mph (150 km/h) |  |
|  | G-3 | 105 mph (170 km/h) |  |
|  | G-4 | 92 mph (148 km/h) |  |
| Range: | Omega I | 155 miles (250 km) |  |
|  | G-4 | 144 miles (233 km) |  |
|  |  | *hover* | *service* |
| Ceiling: | Omega I | 9,512 ft (2,900 m) | 19,680 ft (6,000 m) |
|  | Omega II |  | 9,840 ft (3,000 m) |
|  | G-3 | 3,608 ft (1,100 m) | 8,200 ft (2,500 m) |
|  | G-4 | 7,872 ft (2,400 m) | 7,872 ft (2,400 m) |
| Climb: | Omega II | 1,200 ft/min (366 m/min) |  |

In a stability test, the Omega II hovers low to the ground with a man holding onto one of its
wheels. Development of Bratukhin's helicopter began in 1939 but was slowed during
World War II, with only the initial prototypes being flown before the war ended in the
spring of 1945.

The Omega helicopter design was begun by I.P. Bratukhin in 1939 following his participation in autogiro development at the Central Aero-Hydrodynamic Institute (TsAGI), which directed Soviet aviation development. Note the Omega II's conventional fuselage, with T-shaped tail and contra-rotating rotors on outriggers, in the style of the German Focke designs.

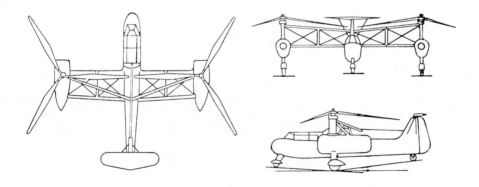

# Bratukhin

| | |
|---|---|
| B-5 | B-10 |
| B-9 | B-11 |

These helicopters, successors to the Omega series, were similar in design but had better aerodynamic characteristics and could carry more personnel or cargo. The designation prefix B indicated the Bratukhin OKB. Design of this B-series began in early 1945.

The B-5 was a refined G-3/G-4 design with the maximum power of the Ivchenko engines boosted for takeoff, and the engines mounted on wings rather than outriggers. The latter feature off-loaded the rotors by about 25 percent at cruising speed. The B-5 introduced a nose cockpit for two pilots, aft of which there was space for five-six passengers. The B-9 had a redesigned fuselage with space for four stretchers and one attendant in the passenger compartment. The design was further refined in the B-10 to include two struts placed on each side of the fuselage running from its bottom to the wing and above the wing to the base of the rotor hubs (to change vibration characteristics). The B-10 also had a plexiglass nose, a turret dome above the cockpit, and twin tail fins. This variant was designed for military reconnaissance and had provisions for cameras in the passenger compartment and an observer's station. The final Bratukhin helicopter was the B-11, which was fitted for night flying. With a clearer aerodynamic shape than the B-10, it returned to the T-tail of the B-5/B-9 and had a large cargo compartment with outsize door.

The B-5 was completed in 1947 and flew at low altitudes during its year of ground tests; full testing was not conducted. The B-9, completed in the same year, encountered technical problems. Soviet sources cite the B-9 as having been "entirely successful" while some Western authorities question if it ever flew at all, with the latter being more probable. The B-10 was also completed in 1947 and was apparently flight tested before the project was halted. Work on the B-11, with instrumentation for night/all-weather flight, began in 1947 and two aircraft were completed in early 1948. Flight tests started in June of that year with the helicopters suffering from excessive vibration. One B-11 demonstrated successful single-engine flight for 47 minutes. The second B-11 prototype crashed during a test flight on 13 December 1948, killing both crewmen. Tests and modifications of the surviving B-11 continued until May 1950 with the Bratukhin OKB being disbanded the following year.

First flight: B-5 1947 (low altitude tests only), B-9 1947–1948(?), B-10 1948, B-11 June 1948
Service introduction: not operational

### Characteristics

Crew: 1 pilot, 1 copilot, with 1 observer in B-10
Engines: B-5 and B-9 2 Ivchenko AN-26-GR radial piston 550 hp each T/O; 420 hp continuous

        B-10 2 Ivchenko AN-26-GR(f) radial piston 575 hp each T/O; 400 hp continuous

        B-11 2 Ivchenko AN-26-GR(f) radial piston 550 hp each T/O; 420 hp continuous

Dimensions: rotor diameter 32 ft 10 in (10.0 m)

| Weight: | | *empty* | *loaded* |
|---|---|---|---|
| | B-5 | 6,464 lbs (2,932 kg) | 8,889 lbs (4,032 kg) |
| | B-9 | (not calculated) | (not calculated) |
| | B-10 | 6,656 lbs (3,019 kg) | 8,598 lbs (3,900 kg) |
| | B-11 | 7,491 lbs (3,398 kg) | 9,149 lbs (4,150 kg) |
| | | *maximum* | |
| Speed: | B-5 | 146 mph (236 km/h) | |
| | B-9 | (not calculated) | |
| | B-10 | 135 mph (218 km/h) | |
| | B-11 | 96 mph (155 km/h) | |
| Range: | B-5 | 369 miles (595 km) | |
| | B-9 | (not calculated) | |
| | B-10 | 273 miles (440 km) | |
| | B-11 | 203 miles (328 km) | |
| | | *hover* | *service* |
| Ceiling: | B-5 | 7,478 ft (2,280 m) | 20,992 ft (6,400 m) |
| | B-9 | (not calculated) | |
| | B-10 | 7,216 ft (2,200 m) | 21,484 ft (6,550 m) |
| | B-11 | | 8,364 ft (2,550 m) |

Climb:
Payload: B-5 5-6 troops, B-9 4 stretchers + attendant, B-10 2-3 troops

The Bratukhin B-10 in this heavily retouched photograph shows the continued refinement of the original Omega. The B-10 had an observation dome above the cockpit, twin tail fins, and special provisions for cameras. By the time of the B-10's first flight, however, senior Soviet aviation authorities were already losing interest in this type of helicopter. (*Air International*)

The B-11 was the final Bratukhin helicopter design. Modifications lowered its performance over that of its predecessors. The period in which Bratukhin dominated Soviet helicopter development ended as new design concepts were sought from Kamov, Mil', and Yakovlev. (*Air International*)

# Kamov

Ka-8
Ka-10 Hat

Nikolai I. Kamov, one of the Soviet Union's most distinguished rotary-wing aircraft designers, experimented with a series of one-man craft in an effort to produce a *vozdushny mototsikl* or "flying motorcycle." The Ka-10, given the NATO code name Hat, was his final effort in this field and was designed with a minimum of mechanical complexity to permit its use in Red Army units as an observation and communications machine. According to some reports, it was also to be used as a ship-based helicopter for spotting submarines. Although several prototypes of two versions were built, the Ka-10 was not used by the Army or Navy.

In the Kamov style, the Ka-8 had coaxial contra-rotating rotors, alleviating the need for a tail assembly to carry an anti-torque rotor. These rotors were three-bladed and powered by an M-76 two-cylinder motorcycle engine that produced

44.8 hp. Insufficient for the task, the M-76 engine was replaced in the Ka-10 by a more powerful, 55-hp Ivchenko AI-4V four-cylinder engine, although the Ka-10 was still considered underpowered. Its basic design included a single seat just behind the rotor mast, with the fuel tank and engine in front of the mast. Twin floats permitted operation from ashore, water, and ships. The Ka-10M had a modified rotor system, twin elliptical tail fins in place of the previous single fin, lengthened floats, and other changes to improve performance.

Three prototypes of the Ka-8 were built, followed by four Ka-10 prototypes and then eight pre-production Ka-10M variants. Although these helicopters were tested extensively, no production followed.

First flight: Ka-8 1947, Ka-10 September 1949
Service introduction: not operational

### Characteristics

Crew: 1 pilot
Engine: Ka-8 1 M-76 piston 44.8 hp
       Ka-10 1 Ivchenko AI-4V radial piston 55 hp

|  |  | Ka-8 | Ka-10 |
|---|---|---|---|
| Dimension: | rotor | 18 ft 4½ in (5.6 m) | 20 ft 1 in (6.1 m) |
| Weight: | empty | 403 lbs (183 kg) | 516 lbs (234 kg) |
|  | loaded | 606 lbs (275 kg) | 827 lbs (375 kg) |
| Speed: | maximum |  | 56 mph (90 km/h) |
| Range: |  |  | 93 miles (150 km) |
| Ceiling: | hover |  | 1,640 ft (500 m) |
|  | service |  | 6,500 ft (1,980 m) |
| Climb: |  |  |  |

Kamov's Ka-10 represented an effort to develop a one-man helicopter for use as an Army observation and communications aircraft. Although widely displayed and touted as bringing a new dimension to battlefield mobility, the helicopter was not produced in significant numbers. (*Air International*)

# Kamov

## Ka-15 Hen

The Ka-15, assigned the NATO code name Hen, was the first helicopter designed by N.I. Kamov to enter mass production. The Ka-15 was a light, two-place utility helicopter extensively flown by the Soviet Navy. The inherent stability and small rotor span achieved by the Kamov contra-rotating rotor design appealed to the Navy for shipboard operation. The Hen has been replaced in Soviet naval service by the Ka-25 Hormone. A number of helicopters of this design were also used in the civil role by Aeroflot (with the designation Ka-15M).

The Hen's two three-bladed rotors were constructed of wood and foam plastic filler and were powered by one 275-hp nine-cylinder radial engine. The fuselage was a metal frame covered with plywood with a large transparent nose section and accommodations for two in side-by-side seats. Also typical of Kamov designs was the large tail plane with vertical stabilizers at each end. The aircraft was supported on the ground with a quadricycle landing gear. Two stretchers could be mounted externally on the ambulance version.

Although the helicopter had limited ASW capabilities, it was used in that role by the Soviet Navy as well as for general communication and liaison both afloat and ashore. A rack for depth bombs could be attached to each side of the fuselage. Production ceased in the early 1960s. The subsequent Ka-18 (NATO Hog) had the same power plant and rotor system but with a larger cabin and a loading door in the nose. This helicopter apparently was not flown by the Soviet armed forces.

First flight: 1952    Service introduction: 1955    Users: USSR

The Ka-15 was the first Kamov helicopter to be used widely by the Soviet armed forces. Kamov's helicopters are distinguished by their contra-rotating main rotors. The Kamov and Mil' bureaus are today the only designers of Soviet military helicopters. (*Air International*)

The Soviet Air Forces evaluated the Ka-18 Hog but it was apparently flown only by Aeroflot in operational service. Note the streamlined shape refined from the Ka-15 Hen. The early Ka-18s had their predecessors' engine but subsequently the AI-14VF with 275 hp was fitted, permitting a maximum weight of 3,307 pounds. The Ka-18 also had deicing equipment and all-weather instrumentation.

## Characteristics

Crew: 1 pilot, 1 observer
Engine: 1 Ivchenko AI-14V radial piston 275 hp
Dimensions: length 21 ft 6 in (6.6 m); rotor diameter 32 ft 8½ in (9.96 m)
Weight: loaded 2,850 lbs (1,293 kg)
Speed: cruise 77.5 mph (125 km/h); maximum 93 mph (150 km/h)
Range: 298 miles (480 km)
Ceiling: hover IGE 2,230 ft (680 m); service 9,842 ft (3,000 m)
Climb:
Payload: small depth bombs when configured for ASW

# Kamov

Ka-20 Harp
Ka-25 Hormone

The Ka-20 Harp was the prototype for the Ka-25 Hormone, a widely used ASW and missile-targeting helicopter which has been the principal ship-based helicopter of the Soviet Navy since the late 1960s. The Harp was first publicly displayed at the July 1961 Aviation Day flyover at Moscow's Tushino airport. The aircraft had a chin-mounted radome, additional antennas projecting from the nose, and—significantly—two dummy missiles, one mounted on either side of the fuselage. However, the subsequent Ka-25 Hormone has never been identified carrying missiles.

The Harp/Hormone retains the standard configuration of previous Kamov helicopter designs: dual three-bladed, contra-rotating rotors, a boxy fuselage with tailboom supporting a multi-fin empennage, and quadricycle landing gear. The rotors are driven by a pair of Glushenkov turboshaft engines mounted side by side above the fuselage. Some ship-based helicopters have flotation bags attached to the landing gear that can be inflated if the helicopter has to come down at sea. The Hormone-A ASW configuration has surface search radar, expendable sonobuoys, dipping sonar that can be lowered while the helicopter is in hover, and internal weapons bay for ASW homing torpedoes or depth charges, and probably an electro-optical sensor. The Hormone-B has additional electronics for targeting hostile warships at sea and for providing data-link representation to the missile-launching ship. Some A models have been refitted with an external container for long torpedoes and external wire-guidance equipment.

The first Soviet warships to deploy with the Hormone were the *Kresta*-class cruisers and the *Moskva*-class helicopter cruisers of 1967. Since 1976, the Hormone has also gone to sea in the larger *Kiev*-class aircraft carriers. These helicopters have operated from shore bases as well. Approximately 160 Hormones were operational in Soviet Naval Aviation during the late 1970s. Production appeared to have ended at that time with no successor ship-based ASW/targeting helicopter having been identified. There is a "flying crane" civil version of this helicopter designated Ka-25K with a removable cargo gondola. The civil Ka-25 can carry 12 passengers or two tons of cargo internally.

First flight:
Service introduction: 1965-1966
Users: India, Syria, USSR, Vietnam, Yugoslavia

**Variants**

| | |
|---|---|
| Ka-20 | NATO Harp; prototype aircraft. |
| Ka-25 | Hormone-A ASW configuration. |
| | Hormone-B missile-targeting configuration. |
| | Hormone-C vertical replenishment configuration. |

**Characteristics***

Crew: 1 pilot, 1 copilot, 2-3 sensor operators
Engines: 2 Glushenkov GTD-3F turboshaft 900 shp each

*Dimensions and weight are for Ka-25K; naval version believed similar.

Dimensions: length 32 ft 3 in (9.8 m); height 17 ft 7½ in (5.4 m); rotor diameter 51 ft 8 in
    (15.74 m)
Weight: empty 9,700 lbs (4.400 kg); loaded 16, 100 lbs (7,300 kg)
Speed: cruise 120 mph (193 km/h); maximum 136 mph (220 km/h)
Range: 403 miles (650 km)
Ceiling: service 11,500 ft (3,500 m)
Climb:
Payload: 2 ASW torpedoes

The Ka-25 Hormone is the only ship-based helicopter of the Soviet Navy, being flown
primarily in the ASW and over-the-horizon targeting roles. For the latter role, the Hormone-B has a data link for transmitting its radarscope views to missile-armed submarines
and surface ships. (U.S. Navy)

The Hormone—unlike Western ASW helicopters—has an internal weapons bay for depth
charges and ASW homing torpedoes. This Ka-25 has been modified with an external casing
for carrying longer torpedoes than can be accommodated internally. Just behind the
cockpit on the side of the fuselage is a reel cannister for use with wire-guided torpedoes.
(U.S. Navy)

A Hormone aboard the Soviet missile cruiser *Admiral Isachekov*. The contra-rotating rotors of the Hormone can be folded back for shipboard stowage. Note the unusual method for opening the hangar, and the adjacent wind sock and mini control tower. (Royal Navy courtesy *Navy International*)

# Kamov

### Ka-22 Hoop

Only one example of the Ka-22 *Vintokryl* (Screw wing)–NATO code name Hoop–has ever been seen by Western observers, when it was flown in the 1961 Soviet Aviation Day display. It would appear that the Ka-22 and the later Mi-12 Homer were designed to the same approximate specifications, although the former, with its two four-bladed propellers in addition to its rotors, is a convertiplane, whereas the Homer is a true helicopter.

The fuselage of the Hoop is of the same general size as that of the four-engined Antonov An-12 transport (which resembles the American C-130), permitting it to carry up to 100 passengers if so configured, or 35,250 pounds of vehicles or cargo, loaded through a ramp beneath the upswept tail. The two four-bladed rotors are mounted atop engine pods which, in turn, are fitted at the tips of a high-mounted cantilever wing, spanning approximately 92 feet. The rotors apparently autorotate during forward flight when the two turbines mounted on the wing tips drive the forward-facing propellers. During takeoff, landing, and hovering, the turbines are connected to the rotors, which are of the same general size and configuration as the main rotor of the Mi-8 Hip helicopter.

In October-November of 1961, the Hoop established a world convertiplane speed record of 227.4 mph and several payload-to-altitude records. The aircraft never entered production. It is considered unlikely that more than the one prototype was built.

First flight:
Service introduction: not operational

**Characteristics**

Crew: 1 pilot, 1 copilot, 2 crewmen
Engines: 2 Soloviev TB-2 turboshaft 5,622 shp each
Dimensions: length 75 ft (23.0 m); height 27 ft (8.25 m); rotor diameter 69 ft (21.0 m)
Weight: empty 29,762 lbs (13,500 kg); loaded 66,138 lbs (30,000 kg)
Speed: cruise 186 mph (300 km/h); maximum 217 mph (350 km/h)
Range:
Ceiling:
Climb:
Payload: 36,376 lbs (16,500 kg) internal cargo capacity

The Ka-22 Hoop was the Kamov design bureau's effort to design a heavy-lift helicopter. Only the right-side rotor is visible in this view while both propellers can be seen. This convertiplane lost in the apparent competition for the heavy-lift role to the later Mi-12 Homer, a true helicopter (i.e., no conventional propellers). (*Air Force* magazine)

# Kamov

### Ka-26 Hoodlum

The Ka-26 Hoodlum is a light utility helicopter designed by Kamov to replace the earlier Ka-18 Hog utility helicopter. First flying in 1965, the Hoodlum entered civil service with Aeroflot as a cropduster in the late 1960s. The large number of Aeroflot Hoodlums would of course come under Soviet military control in the event of a war.

Using the standard Kamov rotor configuration of two contra-rotating, three-bladed rotors, the Ka-26 powers them with two 325-hp air-cooled radial engines vice the turboshafts found in the other modern Kamov designs. The multiple tail unit is similar to other contemporary Kamovs, but it is mounted at the end of a dual tailboom rather than the more common single boom. The quadricycle landing gear is similar to that of the rest of the Ka-15/18/20/25 series. Avionics give the aircraft an all-weather capability. The Ka-26 is an extremely versatile aircraft with a variety of interchangeable pods that fit just aft of the pilot's cabin and beneath the rotor assembly. A passenger pod seating six, an agricultural hopper for cropdusting, a cargo pod for 1,985 pounds of freight, and an ambulance pod for two stretcher patients or two ambulatory patients and an attendant are available. Alternatively, the aircraft can be operated without a pod, using either an open platform for freight or a hook for slung cargo.

Hoodlums have been used at sea from Soviet fishing ships to scout for schools of fish (in this role, pontoons are fitted to give them an amphibious capability), and ashore in aerial photography, fire fighting, ice scouting, and geophysical survey. The Ka-26 is operated by the military forces of some client states, and civil variants are used commercially in several countries, both in and out of the Warsaw Pact nations.

First flight: 1965
Service introduction: 1969
Users: Hungary, Sri Lanka

### Characteristics

Crew: 1 pilot
Engines: 2 Vedeneev M-14V-26 radial piston 325 hp each
Dimensions: length 25 ft 5 in (7.75 m); height 13 ft 3½ in (4.0 m); rotor diameter 42 ft 8 in (13.0 m)
Weight: empty 4,300 lbs (1,950 kg); loaded 7,165 lbs (3,250 kg)
Speed: cruise 93 mph (150 km/h); maximum 105 mph (170 km/h)
Range: 248 miles (400 km); with external tanks 745 miles (1,200 km)
Ceiling: hover OGE 2,625 ft (800 m); hover IGE 4,265 ft (1,300 m); service 9,840 ft (3,000 m)
Climb:
Payload: 7 troops or 2,425 lbs (1,100 kg) external load

Employed for geophysical survey, this Kamov coaxial-rotor Ka-26 Hoodlum has a large, circular antenna to generate an electromagnetic pulse, bringing to mind similar devices installed on fixed-wing aircraft during World War II to explode magnetic mines. Small, special-mission pods can be fitted to the after end of the fuselage. Note the twin booms and multiple tail arrangement. (Stephen P. Peltz courtesy *Air International*)

# Kamov-Skrzhinsky

KaSkr-1
KaSkr-2

The first of a series of autogiros produced in the Soviet Union was the result of a design by N. I. Kamov and N. K. Skrzhinsky. Their efforts were apparently not based on the work of La Cierva, making the USSR the only nation to have developed autogiros independently.

The KaSkr-1 used the fuselage of a U-1 monoplane, which was actually a British Avro 504 built under license. The aircraft was modified extensively, and a four-bladed rotor was fitted forward of the single open cockpit. The KaSkr-1 had a 110-hp rotary engine which was insufficient for the aircraft. Numerous difficulties were encountered during ground tests, which began on 1 September 1929, and prior to its first takeoff the autogiro capsized and was seriously damaged.

In 1930 the aircraft was rebuilt with a more powerful 225-hp engine as well as other modifications. With the designation KaSkr-2, the autogiro made 90 flights, the most extensive lasting for 28 minutes.

First Flight: KaSkr-2 1930
Service introduction: not operational

**Variants**

KaSkr-1 original configuration with M-2 120-hp rotary engine.
KaSkr-2 rebuilt autogiro with 225-hp engine and other modifications.

**Characteristics (KaSkr-2)**

Crew: 1 pilot
Engine: Gnome-Le Rhône-Titan radial piston 225-hp
Dimensions: length 29 ft 6 in (9.0 m); rotor diameter 39 ft 4 in (12.0 m)
Weight: empty 1,907 lbs (865 kg); loaded 2,425 lbs (1,100 kg)
Speed: 68 mph (110 km/h)
Range:
Ceiling: 1,475 ft (450 m)
Climb:

# Mil'

Mi-1 Hare
SM-1
SM-2

The Mi-1—NATO code name Hare—was the first production design from the bureau of Mikhail L. Mil'. The Hare is a general utility helicopter that enjoyed a very long production run in both the Soviet Union and Poland. Designed in 1947-1948, this long-lived helicopter served in military and civil capacities in most Communist bloc nations.

The helicopter has a conventional design, with a three-bladed main rotor and a long tailboom supporting an anti-torque tail rotor. The Hare established the general configuration that would be the trademark of almost all Mil' designs in the next three decades with the notable exception of the giant Mi-12 Homer. All versions of the helicopter are fitted with the 575-hp AI-26V seven-cylinder, fan-cooled radial engine; the Polish Wytwornia Sprzetu Komunikacyjnego (WSK) SM-1 and SM-2 variants have the LiT-3 license-built version of the AI-26V. The Soviet-built and early Polish-built helicopters had composite wood-metal rotor blades, but later production models from Poland have all-metal blades. The main fuselage is constructed of tubular steel with metal covering while the tailboom is semi-monocoque. The standard tricycle landing gear was replaced on some coastal patrol models with landing gear extensions to give additional clearance for four floats.

Three Mi-1 prototypes were followed by initial production orders in September 1949. Variants of the Mi-1 have been built or modified for the roles of ambulance, transport, postal delivery, crop dusting, pilot training, coastal patrol, observation, and military liaison. In the late 1950s the Hare established several distance and speed records for helicopters. Production terminated in the mid-1960s. Hares remain in service in many nations in both military and civil service, the latter variants including the Mi-1NKh, SM-1Z, and SM-2 which are fitted for agricultural roles, especially crop dusting.

First flight: September 1948
Service introduction: 1951
Users: Bulgaria, China, Cuba, Czechoslovakia, Egypt, East Germany, Hungary, India, Indonesia, Iraq, Mongolia, Poland, USSR, Yugoslavia

**Variants**

Mi-1      Soviet-built utility helicopter; pilot + 3 passengers in early aircraft; subsequently pilot + 2 passengers.
Mi-1T     Soviet-built utility helicopter with additional operational equipment; small horizontal stabilizers near tail rotor.
Mi-1U     Soviet-built dual-control trainer.
Mi-3      *erroneous* designation used in West to identify an Mi-1 experimentally fitted with four-bladed main rotor and other improved features.
SM-1      Polish-built helicopter; first flight in early 1956.
SM-1W     improved helicopter with metal rotor blades; pilot + 3 passengers.
SM-1WS    ambulance variant with 2 stretcher pods external to the fuselage (accessible from cabin).
SM-1SZ    Polish-built dual-control trainer.
SM-2      Polish development of SM-1 with redesigned forward fuselage for pilot + 4 passengers; structural improvements permit 15% increase in payload; military and civil variants built; first flight mid-1960.

**Characteristics (SM-1W)**

Crew: 1 pilot
Engine: 1 Ivchenko AI-26V radial piston 575 hp
Dimensions: length 39 ft 4¾ in (12.1 m); height 10 ft 10 in (3.3 m); rotor diameter 47 ft (14.35 m)
Weight: empty 4,142 lbs (1,880 kg); loaded 5,300 lbs (2,404 kg)
Speed: cruise 87 mph (140 km/h); maximum 105 mph (170 km/h)
Range: 360 miles (580 km)
Ceiling: service 9,840 ft (3,000 m)
Climb: 886 ft/min (270 m/min)
Payload: 3 troops

The Mi-1 Hare was the first of a long line of helicopter designs from the Mil' OKB to enter production. Several hundred were produced for the Soviet armed forces, plus a large number for foreign military clients and civil users. (*Air International*)

# Mil'

## Mi-2 Hoplite

The Mi-2, assigned the NATO code name Hoplite, is a turboshaft-powered derivative of the Mi-1 Hare. After completion and trials of the prototype by the Mil' bureau in the Soviet Union, the Mi-2 went into large-scale production at Poland's Wytwornia Sprzetu Komunikacyjnego (WSK) Swidnik plant. In turn, the Soviet Union has been the principal Mi-2 customer.

The Mi-2 retains the basic configuration of the Hare, but replaces the earlier helicopter's single radial engine with two turboshaft engines mounted side by side atop the fuselage. The Mi-2 has an all-metal, three-bladed main rotor and an anti-torque tail rotor powered by two 400- or 450-shp Isotov GTD-350 turboshaft engines built in Poland. The fuselage is of semi-monocoque construction and accommodates a pilot and up to eight passengers. Alternatively, the cabin can be configured for up to 1,550 pounds of cargo or, as an ambulance, four stretchers and a medical attendant. The landing gear is very similar to that of the earlier Hare: a non-retractable tricycle type with dual-wheeled nose gear and single-wheeled main gear. Polish Air Force Hoplites have been observed with air-to-surface rocket pods mounted on the fuselage.

Production began in Poland in 1966 and continued for more than a decade. Several different versions of the Mi-2 have been completed for military and civil customers worldwide, including passenger-only, convertible passenger-cargo, cargo-only (with external hoist), search and rescue, ambulance, crop-duster, and trainer. Mi-2R ambulance and Mi-2M civil versions with enlarged fuselages have also been produced. The Hoplite is gradually replacing the Hare in the inventories of the Warsaw Pact countries. Over 3,000 of these helicopters had been produced by early 1980.

First flight: 1961
Service introduction: USSR 1964
Users: Bulgaria, Czechoslovakia, East Germany, Hungary, Poland, Romania, Syria, USSR

**Characteristics**

Crew: 1 pilot

Engines: 2 Isotov GTD-350 turboshaft 450-shp each

Dimensions: length 37 ft 4¾ in (11.4 m); height 12 ft 3½ in (3.75 m); rotor diameter 47 ft 6¾ in (14.5 m)

Weight: empty 5,180 lbs (2,350 kg); loaded 8,157 lbs (3,700 kg)

Speed: cruise 124 mph (200 km/h); maximum 130 mph (210 km/h)

Range: 360 miles (580 km)

Ceiling: hover OGE 3,275 ft (1,000 m); hover IGE 6,550 ft (2,000 m); service 13,776 ft (4,200 m)

Climb: 885 ft/min (270 m/min)

Payload: 6-8 troops

Although Mil' designed, the Mi-2 Hoplite was produced entirely by the Polish WSK-Swidnik works with a long production run. This Mi-2 is wearing the markings of the Polish armed forces which fly Soviet-designed and Polish- or Soviet-built helicopters almost exclusively, as do other members of the Warsaw Pact. (*Air International*)

# Mil'

## Mi-4 Hound

The Mi-4 has probably been produced in larger numbers than any other Soviet helicopter. It was developed during the early 1950s as a medium-lift transport helicopter and is believed to have entered series production by 1952. While a contemporary of and greatly resembling the Sikorsky S-55 (military H-19), the Hound (NATO's code name) has a maximum takeoff weight twice that of the Sikorsky helicopter and a 40 percent greater load. The Hound also had a considerably longer production period than the H-19, with several thousand Mi-4s having been turned out in the Soviet Union and in China during the 15 years that the helicopter was produced.

The Hound has a single 18-cylinder radial engine rated at 1,700 hp which drives a four-bladed main rotor constructed of plywood over steel spars, and a three-bladed tail rotor. Like its Sikorsky counterpart, the Mi-4 has its engine fitted in the nose, leaving the after portion of the fuselage free for cargo, troops, or ASW equipment. Clamshell doors under the tailboom give ready access to the cabin, which has space for 14 troops or 3,500 pounds of cargo, including small vehicles or weapons. The helicopter is supported when on the ground by a quadricycle landing gear, with most of the weight being borne by the after pair of wheels. Civilian versions accommodate 8 to 11 passengers in addition to the 2-man crew situated on a flight deck above and forward of the cabin.

The Mi-4 has been used in Soviet service primarily in Frontal Aviation (where it has since been replaced by the Mi-8 Hip), Military Transport Aviation (where most operational units remain), and Soviet Naval Aviation (as a shore-based ASW helicopter). Aeroflot has a large fleet of civil Hounds that would be made immediately available to the military should the need arise. Mi-4s have been exported to almost every country that has received military assistance from the Soviet Union, in addition, of course, to the Warsaw Pact nations. The navy-flown ASW helicopters can be identified easily by the under-nose search radar, sonobuoys stowed on the side of the fuselage; MAD equipment is also carried by the ASW version of the Mi-4. Within the constraints of external payload space, the ASW variant can carry small ASW homing torpedoes or depth bombs. The civil passenger variant is designated Mi-4P and the crop-dusting aircraft Mi-4S.

First flight: August 1952
Service introduction: 1953
Users: Afghanistan, Albania, Algeria, Bulgaria, China, Cuba, Czechoslovakia, Egypt, Finland, East Germany, Hungary, India, Indonesia, Iraq, North Korea, Mali, Mongolia, Poland, Romania, Somalia, Soviet Union, Syria, Vietnam, North Yemen, South Yemen, Yugoslavia

**Characteristics**

Crew: 1 pilot, 1 copilot except ASW variant also 2-3 systems operators
Engine: 1 Shvestov ASh 82V radial piston 1,700 hp
Dimensions: length 55 ft 1 in (16. 8 m); height 17 ft (5.18 m); rotor diameter 68 ft 11 in (21.0 m)
Weight: empty 11,614 lbs (5,268 kg); loaded 17,196 lbs (7,800 kg)
Speed: cruise 99 mph (160 km/h); maximum 130 mph (210 km/h)
Range: 248 miles (400 km) with 11 troops; maximum 370 miles (595 km)
Ceiling: service 18,040 ft (5,500 m)
Climb:
Payload: 8 to 16 troops or rockets

The Mi-4 Hound is the only helicopter to have entered series production in China. In Chinese service the helicopter is designated H-5 (there were no aircraft designated H-1 through -4). Although replaced in Soviet service mainly by the Mi-8, the Mi-4 remains in wide use. (Chinese Armed Forces)

An Mi-4 Hound of Soviet Naval Aviation in flight. The ASW variant of the Hound was fitted with a nose-mounted radar and towed MAD device, shown here in the retracted position immediately behind the cabin. In addition, ASW weapons could be carried, as well as expendable sonobuoys on racks outside the cabin (next to the figure 5 in this view). (U.S. Navy)

An Mi-4 Hound of Soviet Naval Aviation hovers while transferring personnel to a "Whiskey"-class submarine. The German Navy carried unpowered Fa 330 rotary-wing kites aboard submarines, and the U.S. Navy experimented with carrying a Bell H-13 aboard the transport submarine *Perch* (APSS-313). However, several navies have used helicopters in the role shown here of carrying men and supplies to and from submarines.

A formation of Soviet Mi-4 Hound helicopters fly in loose formation during the June 1956 air show near Moscow. (U.S. Air Force)

# Mil'

## Mi-6 Hook

When it appeared in late 1957, the Mi-6 Hook was the largest operational helicopter in the world, and it retained that distinction for the next ten years. Five prototypes were constructed by Mil' for flight testing, and production was apparently initiated in 1960 to fulfill an initial order for 30 helicopters. Some 800 were subsequently completed for both civil and military roles before production terminated in the early 1970s. The first production units established several records in the early 1960s for payload and speed, one of which, a 62-mile closed-circuit speed of 183.54 knots, still stands in 1980.

Fitted with a five-bladed, all-metal main rotor and a four-bladed tail rotor, the Mi-6 is of the same general configuration as almost all other Mil' bureau designs. The fuselage is a semi-monocoque structure with auxiliary wings mounted high on the fuselage to off-load the rotor during cruising flight. The wings are removed when the Hook is being used as a flying crane. The vertical stabilizer mounts an anti-torque tail rotor on the starboard side, and a small horizontal stabilizer is fitted near the end of the tailboom. The tricycle landing gear is non-retractable. Two dorsal-mounted, 5,500-shp Soloviev D-25V turboshaft engines power the Mi-6 to a maximum level speed of 186 mph. The crew is seated forward of and on the same level as the main cabin. When equipped to carry passengers, the Hook can accommodate 65 persons. Alternatively, 41 stretchers can be carried with two medical attendants, or 26,450 pounds of cargo can be loaded through the large clamshell doors in the after part of the fuselage. Avionics include full all-weather instrumentation.

The Hook has been seen in civil fire-fighting, flying crane, passenger, and general heavy-lift cargo operations. Most have been retained for use in the Soviet Union although several have been exported.

First flight: 1957
Service introduction: 1960
Users: Egypt, Indonesia, Iraq, Peru, USSR, Vietnam

**Characteristics**

Crew: 1 pilot, 1 copilot, 3 crewmen

Engines: 2 Soloviev D-25V (TV-2BM) turboshaft 5,500 shp each

Dimensions: length 108 ft 10½ in (33.18 m); height 32 ft 4 in (9.86 m); rotor diameter 114 ft 10 in (35.0 m)

Weight: empty 60,053 lbs (27,240 kg); loaded 93,695 lbs (42,500 kg)

Speed: cruise 155 mph (250 km/h); maximum 186 mph (300 km/h)

Range: 385 miles (620 km); with external tanks 620 miles (1,000 km)

Ceiling: service 14,750 ft (4,500 m)

Climb:

Payload: 65 troops or 26,455 lbs (12,000 kg) internal cargo or 19,841 lbs (9,000 kg) external sling cargo

This is an early Mi-6 Hook, fitted with "pants" over its main landing gear and without wings to help off-load the rotor in forward flight. A heavy-lift aircraft, the Hook is used widely by the Soviet armed forces, with some units having a 23-mm cannon in the nose for suppressive fire. Auxiliary fuel tanks could also be fitted.

This Mi-6 Hook has Aeroflot markings. The Soviet airline serves as a ready reserve for the Soviet Air Forces, and these helicopters are used regularly in direct support of Soviet military operations. The civil registration SSSR 69318 is on the tailboom and wings, while H-836 is on the forward fuselage.

# Mil'

Mi-8 Hip
Mi-17

The Mi-8 Hip is the primary transport helicopter for Soviet armed forces and has been built in large quantities since entering production in the early 1960s. Originally based upon the Mi-4 Hound, the first prototype of the Hip used the Hound's rotors with one 2,700-shp turboshaft engine mounted above the cabin. Subsequent models increased the number of blades in the main rotor from four to five and replaced the single turboshaft engine with two 1,500-shp engines. This configuration has entered production and has been exported to over 25 Soviet client states, as well as to some countries which have traditionally purchased Western aircraft. Some 5,000 Hips were built through 1979 for both civil and military use.

The five-bladed main rotor and three-bladed tail rotor are of all-metal construction and are driven by two 1,500-shp Isotov TV2-117A turboshaft engines. The fuselage is the standard Mil' design: an all-metal, semi-monocoque pod and boom with the tail rotor mounted on the starboard side of a small vertical stabilizer and a small horizontal stabilizer at the end of the tailboom. Fixed tricycle landing gear is fitted. The crew consists of two pilots and a flight engineer, and 32 troops can be carried. The air ambulance conversion can accommodate 12 stretchers and a medical attendant. Clamshell doors at the rear of the cabin provide easy access for passengers or 8,820 pounds of internally carried cargo; alternatively, 6,614 pounds of cargo can be slung beneath the Hip. This helicopter is also relatively fast, having set a world speed record of 340 km/h in 1964. The Mi-17 is an improved Mi-8 first seen in 1981; it is powered by two TV3-117MT turboshafts rated at 1,900 shp each (with 2,200 shp available for takeoff).

The Mi-8 is the most numerous helicopter in Soviet Military Transport Aviation, and performs a variety of services for the armed forces. Fitted for assault duties, these helicoptors have been seen armed with rocket pods, bombs, and other ordnance, at times surpassing the weapons capabilities of the newer Mi-24 assault helicopter. An antisubmarine warfare derivative of the Hip has also been developed for the Soviet Navy, the Mi-14 Haze (see below). The basic Mi-8 in the civil configuration can carry 28 passengers and is convertible to an ambulance with 12 stretchers and one attendant. The Mi-8T convertible civil version can carry cargo or 24 passengers. Most or all civil versions have square windows. The Mi-8 Salon is a VIP aircraft having an elaborately furnished cabin for 11 passengers with toilet and wardrobe.

First flight: 1962          Service introduction: 1967
Users: Afghanistan, Algeria, Angola, Bangladesh, Bulgaria, Czechoslovakia, Egypt, Ethiopia, Finland, East Germany, Hungary, India, Iraq, Laos, Libya, Mozambique, North Korea, Pakistan, Peru, Poland, Romania, Somalia, Sudan, Syria, USSR, Vietnam, South Yemen, Yugoslavia

**Variants**

Hip-A   prototype helicopter with 1 Soloviev 2,700-shp turboshaft engine and 4-bladed main rotor.
Hip-B   prototype refitted with 5-bladed main rotor.
Hip-C   production military version with 2 Isotov 1,500-shp turboshaft engines; 3 crew + 24 troops; basis for Mi-14 Haze ASW helicopter.

Hip-E  assault helicopter with 2-6 Swatter antitank missiles or pods or 16 57-mm rockets + machine guns in addition to 3 crew + 14 troops.

Hip-F  assault helicopter with 6 Sagger antitank missiles or other weapons and troops.

**Characteristics**

Crew: 1 pilot, 1 copilot

Engines: 2 Isotov TV2-117A turboshaft 1,500 shp each

Dimensions: length 60 ft ¾ in (18.31 m); height 18 ft 6½ in (5.65 m); rotor diameter 68 ft 10½ in (21.0 m)

Weight: empty 15,026 lbs (6,816 kg); loaded 26,455 lbs (12,000 kg)

Speed: cruise 139.5 mph (225 km/h); maximum 161 mph (260 km/h)

Range: 298 miles (480 km)

Ceiling: hover OGE 2,625 ft (800 m); hover IGE 6,233 ft (1,900 m); service 14,760 ft (4,500 m)

Climb:

Payload: 24 troops or 12 stretchers + attendant; rockets, missiles, and guns on 8 external store stations; or 6,614 lbs (3,000 kg) external slung cargo

The Mi-8 Hip is the most widely used helicopter in the Soviet armed forces as well as in some two dozen other nations. This Hip is a troop carrier in Czechoslovak military service. The gunship version of the Hip is the most heavily armed helicopter of any nation.

An Aeroflot Mi-8 Hip in flight.

Mi-8 Hip helicopters support Soviet soldiers during an exercise. These Hips have air-to-ground missile racks on their fuselage and a small radome fitted under the tailboom. Other Hips have been modified for minesweeping, with some having been used from helicopter carriers to help clear the southern end of the Suez Canal after the 1973 war in the Middle East. (*Air International*)

# Mil'

### Mi-12 Homer

The Mi-12 remains the world's largest helicopter, having been designed to fulfill a Soviet requirement for a Vertical Takeoff and Landing (VTOL) aircraft to supplement the conventional An-22 cargo aircraft. In 1969 the Homer established and still holds several payload-to-height records previously held by its Mil' predecessors, the Mi-6 Hook and Mi-10K Harke. Although there is no evidence that the Homer has ever entered production, the three aircraft of this type known to have flown give the Soviet Union a unique heavy-lift capability which the West has never come close to matching. One prototype is thought to have crashed in 1969. The survivors have already been relegated to museums.

The Homer has two five-bladed rotors that rotate in opposite directions, thereby eliminating the need for an anti-torque tail rotor. Each rotor is mounted atop twin podded 6,500-shp Soloviev D-25VF turboshaft engines which in turn are fitted to the tips of shoulder-mounted, heavily braced wings. This power plant arrangement makes the Homer very distinctive and contributes to its massive appearance. The fuselage is of conventional semi-monocoque construction with clamshell doors at the rear providing access to the large, unobstructed cargo hold. This main cabin is 92⅓ feet in length, 14½ feet in height and width, and can carry up to 67,000 pounds of cargo. A flight deck above and forward of the main cabin can accommodate a six-man crew. The helicopter is supported on the ground by a non-retractable tricycle landing gear with two wheels on each unit of the gear. An airplane-type empennage having vertical and horizontal stabilizers with rudder and elevator controls is fitted. The span over rotors is 219 feet 10 inches!

Original plans called for both civil and military versions of the Homer to enter service in the early 1970s, but no production units have been identified.

First flight: 1967 (?)     Service introduction: not operational

### Characteristics

Crew: 1 pilot, 1 copilot, 1 flight engineer, 1 navigator, 1 radio operator, 1 electrician
Engines: 4 Soloviev D-25VF turboshaft 6,500 shp each
Dimensions: length 121 ft 4½ in (37.0 m); height 41 ft (12.5 m); rotor diameter 114 ft 10 in (35.0 m)
Weight: loaded 231,483 lbs (105,000 kg)
Speed: cruise 149 mph (240 km/h); maximum 161 mph (260 km/h)
Range: 310 miles (500 km)
Ceiling: service 11,480 ft (3,500 m)
Climb:
Payload: 50 troops or 55,049 lbs (24,970 kg) internal cargo or 76,070 lbs (34,505 kg) external slung cargo

The Mi-12 Homer remains the world's largest heavy-lift helicopter and the only four-engined helicopter. Its design was initiated in 1965 to meet a military requirement, but the aircraft has been used mainly in civil operations. This is one of the Mi-12 prototypes (civil registration SSSR 21142 with H-833 on the forward fuselage). The aircraft is particularly useful for supporting construction and oil and natural gas production in remote areas of Siberia.

Another view of the same Mi-12. Note the cockpit position and the chin radome. (Novosti Press)

# Mil'

## Mi-10 Harke

The Mi-10—NATO Harke—was developed from the Mi-6 Hook and shares virtually all of the latter's mechanical features. Although developed primarily as a heavy-lift flying crane, the Harke also has accommodations for 28 troops in its main cabin or can use that space for internal cargo. First displayed to the West at the 1961 Tushino Aviation Day display, it is estimated that the Mi-10 first flew the preceding year and entered limited production a short time later. The initial production line was terminated in the early 1970s, but was reopened in 1977.

The Harke uses the same five-bladed main rotor, four-bladed tail rotor, and twin 5,500-shp engine arrangement as the Mi-6. The most striking difference between these two Mil' helicopters is in the fuselage configurations; the Harke has a long, flat, high cabin supported by a stalky quadricycle undercarriage. This landing gear arrangement permits the Mi-10 to taxi over its load and lift it flush against the underside of its fuselage. Closed-circuit television monitors the load while in flight and facilitates cargo handling on the ground. Maximum slung payload is 17,635 pounds, while the maximum containerized payload in pods is 33,070 pounds. A further development of the Mi-10 is the Mi-10K, which has lowered the original undercarriage and replaced the television monitoring system with an underslung, rearward-facing gondola, complete with flying controls. This arrangement reduces the crew requirement from three to two. Maximum slung payload has been increased to 24,250 pounds.

First flight: 1960      Service introduction:      Users: USSR

The Mi-10 Harke, shown here lifting a prefabricated house during an air show, is also used in Soviet military and civilian service. The retractable observer's cockpit that could be lowered from the forward fuselage to direct cargo handling has been replaced by closed-circuit television. This Mi-10 is fitted with auxiliary fuel tanks on both sides of the fuselage. (*Air International*)

## Characteristics

Crew: 1 pilot, 1 copilot, 1 crewman
Engines: 2 Soloviev D-25V turboshaft 5,500 shp each
Dimensions: length 107 ft 9¾ in (32.86 m); height 32 ft 2 in (9.8 m); rotor diameter 114 ft 10 in (35.0 m)
Weight: empty 60,186 lbs (27,300 kg); loaded 96,341 lbs (43,700 kg)
Speed: cruise 111.5 mph (180 km/h); maximum 124 mph (200 km/h)
Range: 155 miles (250 km)
Ceiling: service 9,840 ft (3,000 m)
Climb:
Payload: 28 troops (in passenger pod); see text

A closeup view of an Mi-10 Harke heavy-lift helicopter. The wide-track quadricycle landing gear permits the lifting of large shapes as well as heavy loads. (Novsti Press)

This is the Mi-10K helicopter derived from the basic Mi-10 with a shorter, simpler undercarriage. The change limits the Harke's ability to lift large-size loads, but the reduction in landing gear weight permits heavier loads to be carried. The fuselage of the Mi-10 and -10K is similar with the latter helicopter having a rear-facing cargo handler's gondola under the nose. (Novsti Press)

# Mil'

## Mi-14 Haze

The Mi-14 Haze is a shore-based ASW derivative of the Mi-8 Hip-C. In service since 1975, the Haze has replaced the Mi-4 Hound as the Soviet Navy's land-based ASW helicopter. However, it is too large to operate from Soviet cruisers and aircraft carriers, whose elevators are not big enough to accommodate it, and thus has not replaced the ship-based Ka-25 Hormone. The Haze represents a significant increase in capability over the Hound, more than doubling the latter's payload for sensors and ordnance and increasing range/time-on-station performance by approximately 50 percent.

The power plant and dynamic components of the Haze are believed to be virtually identical to those of the Mi-8. The two aircraft differ primarily in the configuration of the fuselage and installed equipment. The Haze has a watertight amphibious hull with sponsons on each side to give stability when waterborne. A surface-search radar is fitted forward, with the dome projecting from the hull. The Haze also has towed Magnetic Anomaly Detection (MAD) gear, sonobuoys, and dipping sonar and can carry ASW homing torpedoes.

(See Mi-8 Hip listing for additional details.)

First flight: 1974 (?)
Service introduction: 1975                    Users: East Germany, Poland, USSR

**Characteristics**

Crew: 1 pilot, 1 copilot, several sensor operators
Engines: 2 Isotov TV2-117A turboshaft 1,500 shp each
Dimensions: length approximately 60 ft (18.0 m); rotor diameter approximately 70 feet
    (21.0 m)
Weight: loaded approximately 24,000 lbs (10,896 kg)
Speed: maximum 155 mph (250 km/h)
Range:
Ceiling:
Climb:
Payload: ASW homing torpedoes

The Mi-14 Haze is a land-based ASW variant of the Mi-8 Hip design, reconfigured to accommodate ASW sensors and weapons with an amphibious hull. Features evident in this photograph are the radome built into the boat hull, the MAD device aft of the cabin, a radome on the tailboom, and a float skid at the end of the boom. (U.S. Navy)

# Mil'

## Mi-24 Hind

The Mi-24 Hind was the first true assault helicopter to be produced in the Soviet Union. Unlike earlier Soviet helicopters, the Hind was designed from the outset to operate in a hostile environment, having considerable self-defense and close air support capabilities. Reportedly, the Mil' design bureau originally proposed a specialized gunship configuration to the Ministry of Defense. The MOD reaction was to demand that a troop-carrying capability be incorporated to avoid the costs of a new attack and troop-carrying helicopter. Six variants were identified through 1981, being given the NATO designations Hind-A through -F. The A and B, which actually developed in the reverse order, have limited gunship capabilities and appear to be primarily troop carriers. They differ in the configuration of their auxiliary wings and other minor features. The C is similar to the Hind-A but lacks its armament. The Hind-D was extensively redesigned to emphasize the gunship role, with the pilot and gunner in tandem, vertically staggered cockpits with individual canopies. The E variant is more heavily armed. The later Hind-E appears to be comparable to the U.S. Army-Hughes AH-64, which will not be available in significant numbers until the mid-1980s.

The Hind is of technologically advanced construction, with a five-bladed fiberglass main rotor, an anti-torque rotor mounted on the left side of the tail fin, an all-metal semi-monocoque fuselage, and a retractable tricycle landing gear. Auxiliary wings with a marked anhedral (downward angle) give additional lift while providing hard points for munitions. The empennage consists of a swept vertical fin and variable-incidence (moveable) horizontal stabilizer. Early models of the Hind had the tail rotor mounted on the right side of the fin. A tail skid protects the rotor. All variants have fuselage seating for eight to ten troops in addition to a crew of four. Armament of the Hind-A consists of a flexible 12.7-mm machine gun in the nose with six weapon stations on the wings for rockets or missiles. The B variant's wings have no anhedral and only four wing hard points (i.e., no wing-tip munition positions). The C is similar to the A but without nose gun or wing-tip weapon positions. The redesigned Hind-D has a four-barrel Gatling-gun (probably 12.7 mm) in a turret slung under the nose; there are six wing hard points for weapons, with the outer ones having double rails for antitank missiles (as in some Hind-A variants). Weapon-related sensors in the Hind-D include radar, Low-Light-Level Television (LLTV), and a laser range finder. The inner wing hard points can carry pods of 32 57-mm rockets, bombs, or other stores, while the wing-tip positions can accommodate Sagger, Swatter, or Spiral antitank missiles. Up to 2,800 pounds of ordnance can be carried (including gun armament).

The first operational Hind units, flying both A and B variants, were identified by Western intelligence with the Group of Soviet Forces in Germany in early 1973, only a year after probable introduction into Soviet service. By 1980 more than 1,000 units had been built with production continuing at a reported rate of 30 per month. Mi-24 Hinds were transferred in significant numbers to East Germany and a few went to Libya, as part of a transfer of advanced Soviet aircraft to that nation. Twelve Hinds were reportedly transferred to Afghanistan in early 1979 to help the Soviet-supported government curb Islamic uprisings; before the year was over Soviet troops invaded Afghanistan with Soviet Hinds being used extensively in the counter-guerrilla war that followed.

First flight: 1971
Service introduction: 1972
Users: Afghanistan, East Germany, Libya, USSR

**Variants**

Hind-A  assault transport helicopter; initial production model.
Hind-B  assault transport helicopter; modified wings; few produced.
Hind-C  similar to Hind-A without nose machine gun.
Hind-D  gunship-assault transport with redesigned forward fuselage; increased armament and sensors.
Hind-E  gunship with Spiral antitank missiles (vice Swatter).
Hind-F  reported gunship with improved weapons capability.

**Characteristics (Hind-A)**

Crew: 1 pilot, 1 copilot, 1 gunner-navigator, 1 observer-radar operator
Engines: 2 Isotov TV2-117A turboshaft 1,500 shp each
Dimensions: length 55 ft 9 in (17.0 m); height 14 ft (4.25 m); rotor diameter 12 ft 9½ in (3.9 m)
Weight: empty 10,360 lbs (4,700 kg); loaded 18,520 lbs (8,400 kg); Hind-D approximately 22,000 lbs (10,000 kg)
Speed: maximum 170-180 mph (273-290 km/h)
Range:
Ceiling:
Climb: approximately 3,000 ft/min (914 m/min)
Payload: 8-10 troops + 4 antitank missiles or rocket pods; Hind-D 8-10 troops + 4 antitank missiles + 4 rocket pods
Guns: 1 12.7-mm machine gun; Hind-D 1 4-barrel 12.7-mm Gatling-type machine gun

An Mi-24 Hind-A in flight, with four multiple rocket pods under its stub wings. The twin missile launchers on the end of each wing are empty. There is a single 12.7-mm machine gun in the nose, an armament judged too light for the Hind's gunship mission. Note that the landing gear is fully retracting, contributing to the helicopter's high performance. (*Air International*)

This view of a Hind-D shows the redesigned aircraft fuselage with nose gunner's cockpit and under-chin Gatling gun, optical (TV) viewing system, and laser range finder. The later Hind-F differs in part by having triple-rail missile racks at the ends of the stub wings. This Mi-24's landing gear is extended. (*Air International*)

The rear aspect of the Hind-A. The fuselage can accommodate 8 to 10 troops or reloads of rocket pods, ammunition, and missiles. Carrying the latter, the Hind can undertake a fire mission and come down in a safe spot to rearm itself, without having to return to base to rearm.

Hind-D assault helicopters during a break in maneuvers in the Carpathian Military District of the Soviet Union. These aircraft have a laser range finder on the inboard pylon of the port wing. The Soviet Air Forces provide helicopters for support of the Army, officially known as the Soviet Ground Forces. The Soviet Navy has its own helicopters. (*Air International*)

# Mil'
Mi-26
Halo

Halo is the NATO code name for a Soviet military helicopter expected to enter front-line service during the 1980s, apparently as a replacement for the Mi-6 Hook in the tactical troop and cargo-carrying role. In this role, it would supplement the lighter Mi-8 Hip and Mi-24 Hind. The Halo appears to be a scaled-up version of the Mi-8. It has an enormous fuselage that seems capable of carrying 100 troops. The Halo has an eight-bladed main rotor, two doors on the left side of the fuselage, and clamshell rear-loading doors. There is an internal sling hoist for cargo. Two very large turboshaft engines are mounted over the fuselage.

As the Halo is also to be used in support of resource exploitation in Siberia, reliability and maintainability have been emphasized in its design. The Halo set an unofficial record carrying a reported payload of 33,000 lbs to an altitude of 16,500 feet.

First flight: 14 December 1977     Service introduction: 1980 (?)     Users: USSR

**Characteristics**
Crew: (civil) 1 pilot, 1 copilot, 1 navigator, 1 flight engineer
Engines: 2 Lotarev D-136 turboshaft 11,400 shp each T/O
Dimensions: length 114 ft 10 in (35.0 m); rotor diameter 105 ft (32.0 m)
Weight: empty 62,040 lbs (28,200 kg); loaded 108,900 lbs (49,500 kg); maximum 123,200 lbs (56,000 kg)
Speed: cruise 158 mph (255 km/h); maximum 183 mph (295 km/h)
Range: 500 miles (800 km) with 44,100 lbs (20,000 kg) payload
Ceiling: hover OGE 5,904 ft (1,800 m); service 14,760 ft (4,500 m)
Climb:
Payload: 11,000 lbs (5,000 kg) or approximately 70–100 troops internal; 44,100 lbs (20,000 kg) external

Details of the large Mil' Mi-26, given the code name Halo in the West, were revealed when this machine appeared at the Paris air show in mid-1981. The Mi-26's conventional appearance belies its large size and carrying capacity. In addition to clamshell rear doors, there are two upward-hinging cabin doors to the left side and one on the right. (*Air International*)

# TsAGI

1-Э A
3-Э A

The 1-Э A was the first Soviet helicopter, built in 1929-1930 under the direction of B. N. Yuryev at the Central Aero-Hydrodynamic Institute (TsAGI) in Moscow. The 1-Э A and nearly identical 3-Э A were experimental machines, but ahead of their contemporaries in Western Europe and the United States.

The 1-Э A had a fuselage of welded steel tubes without covering and a seat for a single occupant just ahead of the engine and four-bladed rotor. The initial rotor blades were metal, but because of warping they were changed to duraluminum and plywood with canvas covering. An unusual feature was a small anti-torque rotor at each end of the fuselage turning in opposite directions.

The 1-Э A had several successful flights in 1930-1934 before crashing. On 14 August 1932 it set an altitude record of 1,985 feet and on 15 June 1933 it remained airborne for 14 minutes. The 3-Э A, built in 1933, was similar except that the tail wheel was replaced by a strut. The 3-Э A never made free flights but was used for tethered pilot training and ground testing.

First flight: 1-Э A 1930
Service introduction: not operational

**Characteristics**

Crew: 1 pilot
Engines: 2 M-2 rotary piston 120 hp each
Dimensions: rotor diameter 36 ft 1 in (11.0 m)
Weight: empty 2,160 lbs (982 kg); loaded 2,525 lbs (1,145.5 kg)
Speed:          Range:          Ceiling: 1,985 ft (605 m)          Climb:

The 1-ЭA was the first Soviet helicopter, constructed before the initial helicopter efforts in Germany or the United States. Anti-torque rotors were fitted to both the tail (left) and nose of the aircraft. The pilot sat just forward of the engine.

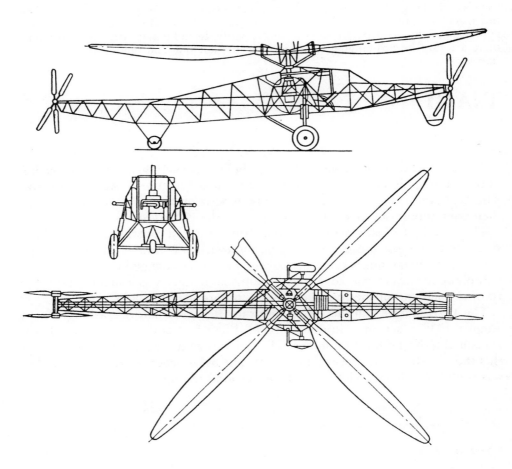

# TsAGI

## 2-ЭA

This autogiro design, by I. P. Bratukhin and V.A. Kuznetsov, was an experimental aircraft similar in design to La Cierva's C 19 autogiro. It was a highly successful design, and confidence was so great that prior to completion of the prototype a small series production was initiated with the designation A-4.

The 2-ЭA had a fuselage of welded steel tubing covered with canvas, and wooden wings. It had a four-bladed rotor and the engine drove a two-bladed propeller.

Completed in 1931, the aircraft made a number of flights, the longest being 105 minutes duration. After trials the aircraft was turned over to the Soviet Air Force in 1933 for propaganda duties with the "Maksim Gorkiy" squadron. It flew only until the motor wore out in 1934.

First flight: 17 November 1931
Service introduction: 1933
Users: USSR

### Characteristics

Crew: 1 pilot, 1 observer
Engine: 1 Gnome-Le Rhône radial piston 230 hp
Dimensions: length 21 ft 4 in ( 6.5 m); rotor diameter 39 ft 4 in (12.0 m)
Weight: empty 1,686 lbs (765 kg); loaded 2,275 lbs (1,032 kg)
Speed: 99 mph (160 km/h)
Range:
Ceiling: 13,775 ft (4,200 m)
Climb:

A trio of early Soviet rotary-wing aircraft: from left are the 2-ЭA autogiro designed by Bratukhin and Kuznetsov, the similar A-4 autogiro, and the improved A-6, an autogiro developed under the direction of Kuznetsov. The intensive Soviet aviation efforts from the late 1920s onward were initiated for both political and military reasons.

# TsAGI

This helicopter, designed by Bratukhin, was similar to previous Soviet efforts but had a unique rotor system of six blades with three long and three short blades fitted to the same rotor head. The larger blades gave lift while the smaller ones provided steering. The blades were constructed of wood and metal with fabric covering. There were small anti-torque rotors fore and aft.

The single 5-ЭA helicopter was completed in 1933 and was flown extensively in a research role until 1936. The longest duration flight was 13 minutes, accomplished in 1934.

First flight: 1933
Service introduction: not operational

**Characteristics**

Crew: 1 pilot
Engines: 2 M-2 rotary piston 120 hp each
Dimensions: rotor diameter: 3 x 39 ft 4 in (12.0 m) + 3 x 25 ft 6 in (7.8 m)
Weight: empty 2,308 lbs (1,047 kg); loaded 2,667 lbs (1,210 kg)
Speed: 12 mph (20 km/h)
Range:
Ceiling: 131 ft (40 m)
Climb:

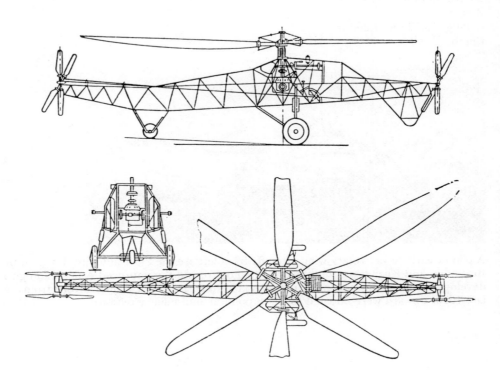

The Bratukhin-designed 5-϶A was an improved version of the earlier TsAGI helicopters, still with the unusual arrangement of anti-torque rotors at both ends. Note the pilot's position in front of the engine. This helicopter is reported to have made a 13-minute flight in 1934.

# TsAGI

## 11-϶A

This Bratukhin-designed helicopter was based on the experimental 5-϶A concept but was much larger, and only one significantly more powerful engine was required to drive both the main rotor and the three-bladed anti-torque propellers. Design began in 1934, and the 11-϶A would form the basis for the Omega series.

The helicopter had a conventional aircraft fuselage with the engine located forward. The engine drove the rotor with three large and three small blades plus the two anti-torque propellers positioned at the extremity of small wings. After extensive tethered tests in 1936-1938, the aircraft was greatly modified. Redesignated 11-϶A PV (Propulsion Variant), the 1938-1939 changes included replacing the original two propellers on stub wings with four propellers mounted on lattice outriggers. Tandem seating for pilot and observer was aft of the rotor bracing.

The 11-϶A PV flew successfully in 1939-1941 and was able to achieve sustained flight for almost one hour with two men on board. It was eventually grounded because of the engine and other components wearing out.

First flight: 11-϶A 1936 (tethered), 11-϶A PV 1939
Service introduction: not operational

**Characteristics**

Crew: 1 pilot, 1 observer
Engine: 1 Curtiss Conqueror water-cooled piston 630 hp
Dimensions: length 27 ft 10½ in (8.5 m); span 34 ft 9 in (10.6 m), increased in PV
    configuration to 36 ft 9 in (11.2 m); rotor diameter 3 x 50 ft 6¼ in (15.4 m) + 3
    x 30 ft 2¼ in (9.2 m)
Weight: loaded 5,732 lbs (2,600 kg); loaded as PV 4,960 lbs (2,250 kg)
Speed: 37 mph (60 km/h)   Range:   Ceiling: 164 ft (50 m)   Climb:

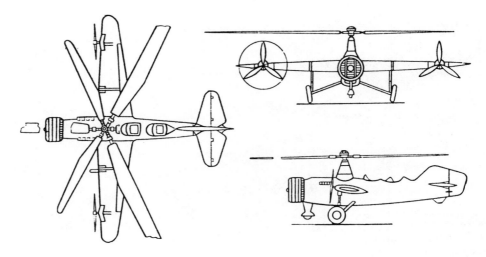

Further refining his 5-ЭA design, Bratukhin developed the 11-ЭA helicopter with two tractor propellers to give forward thrust and to counter torque from the main rotor. In these early helicopter designs, the wings were intended more for mounting propellers than for unloading the main rotor.

Bratukhin's modification of his 11-ЭA helicopter resulted in this improved design. The lattice outriggers each had a tractor and pusher propeller, and the main rotor had blades of two different lengths, demonstrating the vast number of design concepts evaluated in early helicopters.

# TsAGI

### A-4

The A-4 was a production version of a modified 2-϶A autogiro with a small number being produced for service use.

The aircraft differed from the 2-϶A in several details and had a more powerful engine.

All aircraft were tested successfully, but *all* crashed after being assigned to Soviet Air Force units that lacked specialized training in the operation of autogiros.

First flight: 1934     Service introduction: 1934     Users: USSR

**Characteristics**

Crew: 1 pilot, 1 observer
Engine: 1 M-26 radial piston 300 hp
Dimensions: length 23 ft 8¼ in (7.2 m); span 22 ft (6.7 m); height 13 ft 1½ in (4.0 m); rotor diameter 42 ft 7¾ in (13.0 m)
Weight: empty 2,348 lbs (1,065 kg); loaded 3,009 lbs (1,365 kg)
Speed: 109 mph (176 km/h)
Range: 115 miles (185 km)
Ceiling: 13,448 ft (4,100 m)
Climb:

# TsAGI

### A-6   A-13
### A-8   A-14

These autogiros, developed under the direction of Kuznetsov, were similar in design and relatively successful. None was produced in series.

Each aircraft introduced new features. They had aircraft-type fuselages and stub wings, with a three-bladed rotor and conventional propeller. The A-6 had folding wings and rotor blades to facilitate storage, a first among Soviet aircraft, and balloon-type wheels to alleviate the need for shock absorbers. After demonstrating excellent flight characteristics, the A-6 crashed in early 1934. The A-8 was similar to the A-6, but with hydraulic shock absorbers, the first Soviet aircraft with this feature. The A-13 was a two-seat aircraft while the A-14 dispensed with the stub wings of previous Soviet autogiros. Various improvements were made in these aircrafts' rotor systems and wing configurations.

Takeoff runs were around 135-160 feet except in the case of the A-13 whose larger rotor reduced this to 100-130 feet; essentially vertical landings could be made.

First flight: A-6 and A-8 1933; A-13 1934; A-14 1935
Service introduction: not operational

**Characteristics**

Crew: 1 pilot except A-13 1 pilot + 1 passenger
Engine: 1 M-11 radial piston 100 hp
Dimensions: length 20 ft 8 in (6.3 m) except A-13, 22 ft (6.7 m); height 10 ft 6 in (3.2 m); rotor diameter 36 ft (11.0 m) except A-13, 37 ft 9 in (11.5 m)

| Weight: | empty | loaded |
|---|---|---|
| A-6 | 1,239 lbs (562 kg) | 1,797 lbs (815 kg) |
| A-8 | 1,312 lbs (595 kg) | 1,845 lbs (837 kg) |
| A-13 | 1,190 lbs (540 kg) | 1,768 lbs (802 kg) |
| A-14 | 1,270 lbs (576 kg) | 1,797 lbs (815 kg) |

Speed: A-6 33 mph (53 km/h); others 28 mph (45 km/h)
Range:
Ceiling: A-6 6,560 ft (2,000 m); A-8 8,397 ft (2,560 m); A-13 9,840 ft (3,000 m)
Climb:

The A-8, shown here, was one of the series of relatively successful autogiros developed under the aegis of TsAGI during the early 1930s. V.A. Kuznetsov supervised several of these efforts but did not then move into helicopter development as did several of his contemporaries at TsAGI.

# TsAGI

## A-7

Design of the A-7 autogiro by N. I. Kamov began in 1931, and several were eventually produced. Setting a number of records in vertical flight, this aircraft established Kamov's credentials as a helicoptor designer. Prior to World War II, an A-7 was used for farm spraying while others were used in the battle of Smolensk (1941) for reconnaissance and dropping propaganda leaflets.

This was the first Soviet autogiro with a nose-wheel tricycle landing gear. The three-bladed rotor was mounted forward of the two open cockpits with the second and subsequent aircraft (A-7bis) having a solid pylon supporting the large rotor. The rotor blades and stub wings could be folded for storage. The takeoff run for the A-7bis was about 245 feet, its landing run about 65 feet.

First flight: 1934     Service introduction: 1936     Users: USSR

**Variants**

A-7     prototype aircraft; 2,866 lbs empty; 4,533 lbs loaded; 130 mph.
A-7bis  production prototype aircraft completed in 1936; production run in 1937-1938.

**Characteristics (A-7bis)**

Crew: 1 pilot, 1 observer-gunner
Engine: 1 M-22 radial piston 480 hp

Dimensions: rotor diameter 49 ft 10 in (15.2 m)
Weight: empty ~ 3,086 lbs (~ 1,400 kg); loaded 5,070 lbs (2,300 kg)
Speed: 120 mph (194 km/h)
Range: 370 miles (600 km)
Ceiling: 15,416 ft (4,700 m)
Climb:
Guns: 3 PB-1 machine guns

The Kamov-designed A-7 autogiro is believed to have been one of two autogiro types to be used in combat, flying operational missions during the July 1941 battle against the Germans at Smolensk, some 200 miles southwest of Moscow. Note the streamlined landing gear housings or "pants."

# TsAGI

## A-12

The A-12, designed by N. K. Skrzhinsky, was the first Soviet wingless autogiro, having been specifically designed for high-speed flight.

The aircraft used a Polikarpov I-16 fighter fuselage modified to incorporate a three-bladed rotor and a two-bladed propeller. It could take off with an 80-foot run and land in a space 16-33 feet long.

This experimental autogiro made 43 flights beginning in 1936. It crashed on 23 May 1937 when the rotor blades failed due to material fatigue. After the A-12 crash, the Skrzhinsky A-9N autogiro, the first designed with a two-bladed rotor, was not completed.

First flight: 1936
Service introduction: not operational

**Characteristics**
Crew: 1 pilot
Engine: 1 Wright Cyclone radial piston 670 hp
Dimensions: length 20 ft 8 in (6.3 m); height 13 ft 5½ in (4.1 m); rotor diameter 45 ft
     11 in (14.0 m)
Weight: empty 2,960 lbs (1,343 kg); loaded 3,719 lbs (1,687 kg)
Speed: 152 mph (245 km/h)
Range:
Ceiling: 18,270 ft (5,570 m)
Climb:

The TsAGI A-12 autogiro, designed by N.K. Skrzhinsky, marked another step in Soviet autogiro development, being the first built without wings. This aircraft was designed for high-speed flight and featured an enclosed cockpit.

# TsAGI

## A-15

This Kuznetsov-supervised autogiro was the largest such craft built by the Soviet Union, designed from the outset for artillery spotting and reconnaissance. M. L. Mil' did the design drawings for the A-15.

Conventional in design, without wings but with a large horizontal surface and three underside fins, this aircraft had a three-bladed rotor mounted on a pylon forward of the cockpit. Military features included a radio, three machine guns, and an aerial camera. Takeoff run was 115-200 feet and the A-15 could land vertically.

The aircraft flew for the first time in 1937, having been delayed because of problems related to the rotor system and the crash of the A-12.

The A-15 was the largest autogiro constructed, with special features for armed reconnaissance. No wings were fitted as the aircraft relied entirely upon the three-bladed rotor for lift.

First flight: 1937        Service introduction: not operational

**Characteristics**

Crew: 1 pilot, 1 gunner-observer
Engine: 1 M-25B radial piston 730 hp
Dimensions: length 28 ft 2½ in (8.6 m); height 13 ft 5½ in (4.1 m); rotor diameter 59
    ft (18.0 m)
Weight: empty 3,737 lbs (1,695 kg); loaded 5,644 lbs (2,560 kg)
Speed: 161 mph (260 km/h)
Range:
Ceiling: 20,922 ft (6,400 m)
Climb:
Guns: 3 ShKAS machine guns

# TsAGI

### AK

This was the last Soviet autogiro design, developed by Kamov with the help of
Mil'. However, the evacuation of TsAGI offices from Moscow in late 1941 ended
this effort.

The wingless AK autogiro was to have had enclosed, side-by-side seating for the
two crewmen. The design was begun in 1940.

First flight: not completed

**Characteristics**

Crew: 1 pilot, 1 passenger
Engine: 1 MB-6 radial piston 220 hp

# Yakovlev

### Yak-24 Horse

The Yak-24—NATO code name Horse—was the product of a determined
Soviet effort to develop a large transport helicopter within a 12-month period.
The effort was only partially successful. A.S. Yakovlev was given but 24 hours to
give his views on how to build such a helicopter and his design team, led by N.K.
Skrzhinsky of TsAGI, produced the basic Yak-24 concept within the stipulated
time. Twelve months later, four machines, two for ground tests and two for flight
tests, had been produced and the first one flown. Subsequently, the Yak-24
encountered serious resonance and vibration problems that were solved in 1953-
1956, after which limited production began. The aircraft set several lift records
and saw limited Soviet military and civil service. This was Yakovlev's sole production helicopter, his only other design to reach the flight test stage being the
Yak-100.

Making use of the Mi-4 Hound's rotor blades, rotor heads, and transmission,
the Yak-24 was fitted with twin engines, one to power each rotor and interconnected to permit single-engine operation in an emergency. The four-bladed
rotors were fabric covered in the early machines (as in the Mi-4) but changed to
tubular steel with metal covering in later units. The fuselage was also of tubular
steel construction; the early aircraft had the center fabric covered, but later units
were completely metal skinned. A high-dihedral tail plane was fitted to both sides

after fuselage. A quadricycle landing gear had fully castoring wheels. The basic Yak-24 cabin could accommodate up to 20 troops or three light trucks or various combinations of military equipment. The Yak-24U (*Usilenny*), with autopilot, autostabilization, larger rotor blades, and a wider fuselage, could accommodate 40 troops. Access to the fuselage was through a rear loading ramp as well as side doors, and cargo could be slung from a center hook.

The Horse was the only Soviet tandem-rotor helicopter to enter service and only 40 were produced for both military and civil operations, the latter being designated Yak-24A and Yak-24K. Never operational was the A-model (*Aeroflot-sky*), a 30-passenger transport, and the K-model (*Kupe*), a VIP aircraft for 9 passengers. A P-model (*Passazhersky*), having two 1,500-shp Izotov turbines and intended to carry 39 passengers, did not develop beyond the design stage.

First flight: Yak-24 3 July 1953, Yak-24U December 1957
Service introduction:
Users: USSR

**Variants**

Yak-24    4 prototype aircraft (2 for ground test and 2 for flight test) plus limited production run.

Yak-24U   improved production aircraft built from 1958 on.

The Yak-24 Horse was developed in record time but was not fully successful. It was used in limited numbers by both military and civilian organizations. Here a Yak-24 is photographed lifting roof trusses in Leningrad. Two braced tail fins are fitted. Some Yak-24s had only the horizontal surfaces with a marked upward dihedral.

**Characteristics**

Crew: 1 pilot, 1 copilot, 1 radio operator-navigator, 1 flight mechanic
Engines: Yak-24 2 Shvestov ASh 82V radial piston 1,430 hp each
   Yak-24U 2 Shvestov ASh 82V radial piston 1,700 hp each
Dimensions: length 80 ft (24.4 m): height 23 ft (7.0 m): rotor diameter Yak-24 68 ft
  11 in (21.0 m), Yak-24U 79 ft (24.0 m)
Weight: Yak-24 empty 23,384 lbs (10,607 kg); loaded 31,460 lbs (14,270 kg)
   Yak-24U empty 24,251 lbs (11,000 kg); loaded 34,899 lbs (15,830 kg)
Speed: cruise 126.5 mph (204 km/h); maximum 157.5 mph (254 km/h)
Range: 298 miles (480 km)
Ceiling: service 18,000 ft (5,500 m)
Climb:
Payload: Yak-24 20 troops or 18 stretchers or 3 light trucks
   Yak-24U 40 troops or 30+ stretchers or 3 light trucks

The same Yak-24 as above, showing the undercarriage with four wheels of the same
diameter. The main cabin, intended to carry troops and light vehicles, was 32 ft 9½ in long
and approximately 6 ft 6¾ in high and wide. The Yak-24U introduced an autopilot and
auto-stabilization to Soviet helicopters.

# Yakovlev

## Yak-100

The Yak-100 was the Yakovlev design bureau designation for a three-seat
utility helicopter that was developed to a military specification in competition with
the Mil' Mi-1. No military designation was assigned to the Yak-100, which was not
successful.

The Yak-100 project was initiated in 1947, the helicopter's design being based
largely on that of the Sikorsky S-51 (R-5/H-5). It had an Ivchenko 575-hp AI-
26GRFL engine, which drove a three-bladed main rotor and three-bladed anti-
torque tail rotor. All blades were fabricated of wood. A two-seat trainer variant
was also planned, and the first Yak-100 flew in November 1948 with the second
prototype beginning tests in July 1949. All tests were completed in June 1950 by
which time the decision had been made to abandon the project.

First flight: November 1948
Service introduction: not operational

**Characteristics**

Crew: 1 pilot
Engine: 1 Ivchenko AI-26GR(f) radial piston 575 hp TO; 420 hp continuous
Dimensions: rotor diameter 46 ft 7 in (14.5 m)
Weight: empty 3,979 lbs (1,805 kg); loaded 4,806 lbs (2,180 kg)
Speed: maximum 106 mph (170 km/h)
Range: 202 miles (325 km)
Ceiling: hover 9,578 ft (2,920 m); service 17,224 ft (5,250 m)
Climb:
Payload: 2 troops

This heavily retouched photograph shows the basic arrangement of the Yak-100 and similarity to contemporary Sikorsky S-51 design in the United States. The Yak-100 actually preceded the Yak-24, the former's number probably indicating the designation of the Yakovlev OKB, with Yak-24 being the military service designation of the later helicopter. Apparently only two Yak-100 prototypes were built. (*Air International*)

Another view of the Yak-100.

# UNITED STATES

The U.S. military services have used several different series of designations for rotary-wing aircraft. The following are lists of all designations used, arranged in chronological order by series and the numerical or alphabetical sequence. The dates indicate the period in which the particular series was in use. See Appendix B for additional information on U.S. military designations.

| *Designer* | *Designation* | *Notes* |
|---|---|---|
| **U.S. Navy Observation Aircraft (1922–1962)** | | |
| Pitcairn | OP | Army G-2 |
| Consolidated-Pennsylvania | OZ | modified N2Y |
| **U.S. Army Observation Aircraft (1924–1942)** | | |
| Kellett | O-60 | modified R-2 |
| Aga Aviation | O-61 | |
| **U.S. Army Giroplanes (1935–1939)** | | |
| Kellett | G-1 | |
| Pitcairn | G-2 | Navy OP |
| **U.S. Army Rotary-wing Aircraft (1941–1948)** | | |
| Platt LePage | R-1 | |
| Kellett | R-2 | YG-1 variant |
| Kellett | R-3 | YG-1 variant |
| Sikorsky | R-4 | Navy HNS |
| Sikorsky | R-5 | Navy HO2S/HO3S; to H-5 |
| Sikorsky | R-6 | Navy HOS; to H-6 |
| Sikorsky | R-7 | modified XR-6 |
| Kellett | R-8 | |
| Firestone | R-9 | to H-9 |
| Kellett | R-10 | to H-10 |
| Rotor-Craft | R-11 | to H-11 |
| Bell | R-12 | to H-12 |
| Bell | R-13 | Navy HTL/HUL; to H-13 |
| G&A (Firestone) | R-14 | |
| Bell | R-15 | to H-15 |
| Piasecki | R-16 | to H-16 |
| **U.S. Navy Helicopters (1942–1962)** | | |
| McDonnell | HCH | |
| McDonnell | HJD | to HJH |
| McDonnell | HJH | |
| Piasecki | HJP | to HUP; as H-25 |
| Sikorsky | HJS | |
| Sikorsky | HNS | Army R-4/H-4 |
| Hiller | HOE | Army H-32 |
| Hiller | HO2E | to ROE |
| Kaman | HOK | also TH-43E |

| Gyrodyne | HOG | to RON |
| Sikorsky | HOS | Army R-6/H-6 |
| Sikorsky | HO2S | Army R-5/H-5 |
| Sikorsky | HO3S | Army R-5/H-5 |
| Sikorsky | HO4S | also H-19 |
| Sikorsky | HO5S | also H-18 |
| Boeing Vertol | HRB | also H-46 |
| McDonnell | HRH | |
| Piasecki | HRP | also H-21 |
| Sikorsky | HRS | also H-19 |
| Sikorsky | HR2S | also H-37 |
| Sikorsky | HR3S | also H-3 |
| Bell | HSL | |
| Sikorsky | HSS-1 | also H-34 |
| Sikorsky | HSS-2 | also H-3 |
| Hiller | HTE | also H-12 |
| Kaman | HTK | also H-43 |
| Bell | HTL | also H-13 |
| McDonnell | HUD | |
| Kaman | HUK | also H-43 |
| Kaman | HU2K | also H-2 |
| Bell | HUL | also H-13 |
| McCulloch | HUM | also H-30 |
| Piasecki | HUP | also H-25 |
| Sikorsky | HUS | also H-34 |
| Sikorsky | HU2S | also H-52 |

## U.S. Army/Air Force Helicopters (1948–1962)

| Sikorsky | H-5 | former R-5; Navy HO2S/HO3S |
| Sikorsky | H-6 | former R-6; Navy HOS |
| | H-7 | not used |
| | H-8 | not used |
| Firestone | H-9 | former R-9 |
| Kellett | H-10 | former R-10 |
| Rotor-Craft | H-11 | former R-11 |
| Bell | H-12 | former R-12 |
| Bell | H-13 | former R-13; Navy HTL/HUL |
| | H-14 | not used |
| Bell | H-15 | former R-15 |
| Piasecki | H-16 | former R-16 |
| Hughes | H-17 | |
| Sikorsky | H-18 | Navy HO5S |
| Sikorsky | H-19 | Navy HO4S/HRS |
| McDonnell | H-20 | |
| Piasecki | H-21 | Navy HRP-2 |
| Kaman | H-22 | Navy HTK |
| Hiller | H-23 | Navy HTE |
| Seibel | H-24 | |
| Piasecki | H-25 | Navy HJP/HUP |
| American Helicopter | H-26 | |

| Piasecki | H-27 | modified H-16 |
|---|---|---|
| Hughes | H-28 | modified H-17 |
| McDonnell | H-29 | modified H-20 |
| McCulloch | H-30 | Navy HUM |
| Doman | H-31 | |
| Hiller | H-32 | Navy HOE |
| Bell | H-33 | to V-3 |
| Sikorsky | H-34 | Navy HSS-1/HUS |
| | H-36 | not used |
| McDonnell | H-35 | former L-25*; to V-1 |
| Sikorsky | H-37 | Navy HR2S |
| | H-38 | not used |
| Sikorsky | H-39 | modified H-18 |
| Bell | H-40 | to HU-1/UH-1 |
| Cessna | H-41 | |
| | H-42 | not used |
| Kaman | H-43 | Navy HOK |

### U.S. Air Force Special Research Aircraft (1948–1962)

| Curtiss-Wright | X-19 | |
|---|---|---|

### U.S. Air Force Convertiplane (1954–1962)

| McDonnell | V-1 | former L-25/H-35 |
|---|---|---|
| Sikorsky | V-2 | |
| Bell | V-3 | former H-33 |

### U.S. Navy Rotorcycle (1954–1959)

| Hiller | ROE | former HO2E |
|---|---|---|
| Gyrodyne | RON | former HOG |

### U.S. Army Cargo Helicopters (1956–1962)

| Boeing Vertol | HC-1A | to HRB/H-46 |
|---|---|---|
| Boeing Vertol | HC-1B | to H-47 |

### U.S. Army Observation Helicopters (1956–1962)

| Sud Aviation | HO-1 | to VZ-1** |
|---|---|---|
| Hughes | HO-2 | to H-55 |
| Brantley | HO-3 | |
| Bell | HO-4 | to H-4 |
| Fairchild Hiller | HO-5 | to H-5 |
| Hughes | HO-6 | to H-6 |

### U.S. Army Utility Helicopters (1956–1962)

| Bell | HU-1 | former H-40; to H-1 |
|---|---|---|

### U.S. Navy Drone Aircraft (1956–1962)

| Gyrodyne | DSN | to H-50 |
|---|---|---|

### U.S. Helicopters (1962–present)

| Bell | H-1 | former H-40/HU-1 |
|---|---|---|
| Bell | AH-1 | modified H-1 |
| Kaman | H-2 | former HU2K |

*The L designation, assigned briefly, indicated liaison aircraft.
**The VZ designation was used for Army vertical-lift research aircraft from 1958 to 1962.

| | | |
|---|---|---|
| Sikorsky | H-3 | former HSS-2/HR3S |
| Bell | H-4 | former HO-4 |
| Fairchild Hiller | H-5 | former HO-5 |
| Hughes | H-6 | former HO-6 |
| Boeing Vertol | H-46 | former HRB |
| Boeing Vertol | H-47 | former HC-1 |
| | H-48 | not used |
| | H-49 | not used |
| Gyrodyne | H-50 | former DSN |
| Lockheed | H-51 | |
| Sikorsky | H-52 | |
| Sikorsky | H-53 | |
| Sikorsky | H-54 | |
| Hughes | H-55 | former HO-2 |
| Lockheed | H-56 | |
| Bell | H-57 | |
| Bell | H-58 | |
| Sikorsky | H-59 | |
| Sikorsky | H-60 | |
| Boeing Vertol | H-61 | |
| Boeing Vertol | H-62 | |
| Bell | H-63 | |
| Hughes | H-64 | |
| Aérospatiale | H-65 | |

### U.S. VSTOL or STOL Aircraft (1962–present)

| | |
|---|---|
| Hughes | V-9 |
| Bell | V-15 |

# Aga Aviation

### O-61

The O-61 was an observation autogiro ordered by the U.S. Army in 1942 but cancelled the following year. The aircraft had a conventional autogiro configuration, similar to the Kellett O-60 design.

First flight: not flown

**Variants**

XO-61  prototype autogiro; 6 ordered; 5 changed to YO-61; none built.
YO-61  redesignation of 5 XO-61 autogiros.

**Characteristics**

Crew: 1 pilot, 1 observer
Engine: 1 Jacobs R-915-3 piston radial 300 hp
Dimensions:
Weight: loaded 3,038 lbs (1,379 kg)
Speed: maximum 103 mph (166 km/h)
Range:
Ceiling:
Climb:

# American

## H-26 Jet Jeep

The American Helicopter Company's XH-26 Jet Jeep was developed under the auspices of the U.S. Army and Air Force as a one-man, air-droppable, jet-powered rescue helicopter. It was the culmination of a design process that had begun in 1948 with a modification of a Sikorsky R-6 fuselage having a pulse-jet engine and designated the XA-5 Top Sergeant. The XA-6 Buck Private, a single-seat pulse-jet helicopter with a tubular frame, followed in 1951, the success of which led to the more refined H-26. The Jet Jeep could be broken down into a container that measured 5 × 5 × 14 feet, and assembled in less than 30 minutes. Its fuselage was pyramidal in shape, enclosing the pilot within a minimum of aluminum skin, with a pulse jet-powered rotor at the peak of the pyramidal structure. A short tailboom with a V-shaped horizontal stabilizer was attached to the after end of the fuselage. Five YH-26s were evaluated by the U.S. Army and Air Force between 1952 and 1954, but no production resulted.

First flight: June 1952
Service introduction: not operational

**Characteristics**

Crew: 1 pilot
Engines: 2 American AJ pulse jets 35-lbst each
Dimensions: height 6 ft (1.83 m); rotor diameter 27 ft (8.24 m)
Weight: empty 300 lbs (136 kg); loaded 875 lbs (397 kg)
Speed: cruise 70 mph (112 km/h); maximum 80 mph (129 km/h)
Range: 105 miles (168 km)
Ceiling: service 7,000 ft (2,134 m)
Climb:

The XH-26 Jet Jeep was evaluated by both the U.S. Army and Air Force but was not found suitable for military missions. The helicopter cabin had all-around visibility for the pilot. (U.S. Army)

# Bell
47                                      R-13
                                        H-13 Sioux
                                        HTL
                                        HUL
                                        Scout

The Bell 47, in widespread military use since 1946, has been produced in larger numbers than any other rotary-wing aircraft except for the later Bell 206 and Iroquois-Huey series. More than 6,000 have been built, most of these by Bell but also under license in Italy by Agusta, in Great Britain by Westland, and in Japan by Kawasaki. Their products have been flown by the armed forces of more than 30 nations plus innumerable civil organizations. In 1946 the Model 47 became the world's first helicopter certified for commercial operation. The H-13—to use the helicopter's principal U.S. military designation applied in 1948—is a two- to five-place utility, wire-laying, liaison, evacuation, and training helicopter, with Agusta also having produced an ASW variant. Although no longer flown by the U.S. armed forces, the Model 47 is still found in military and civil operation in several other nations.

The Model 47's simplified rotor system is based on that of the Model 30, the first Bell helicopter, which flew in 1943 (civil registration NX 41867). The two-bladed rotor has collective pitch controls, but the hub is not articulated and there are no flapping, drag, or other hinges. Instead, there is a stabilizer bar, normally some five feet long and weighted at both ends, mounted at a 90-degree angle to the rotor blades and attached to the hub. This design means simplified controls and maintenance and facilitates ground and shipboard handling. The helicopter was originally produced with an enclosed cabin, but was soon altered to the distinctive plexiglass bubble-type canopy by which the H-13 is easily identified. The open lattice tailboom, with an anti-torque rotor on the right side, became standard in 1949. Some variants have small horizontal stabilizers on the tailboom. A twin-skid landing gear with two retracting wheels for ground handling is standard; some naval variants were fitted with pontoons for shipboard and water operations. Two stretcher pods can be carried outside the cabin.

The U.S. Army, Navy, and Marine Corps made extensive use of the H-13 (HTL) in the Korean War, and the French Army used the Sioux in the Algerian conflict. The British armed forces flew 50 Agusta-produced variants before accepting 100 built by Westland (first flight 9 March 1965). Most of the British-flown Sioux were operated by the Army Air Corps. The Model 47 was in production longer than any other helicopter in history, with the last Bell and Agusta helicopters being completed in 1973. Prefix letter O (for Observation) added to Army H-13E/G/H and USAF H-13K in 1962; prefix U (for Utility) added to USAF H-13H/J. Later helicopters were ordered with O/T/U prefixes.

First flight: 8 December 1945
Service introduction: U.S. Army 1946, U.S. Navy 1947
Users: Argentina, Australia, Brazil, Burma, Colombia, Ecuador, France, Great Britain, Greece, Guinea, India, Italy, Japan, Kenya, Malaysia, Mexico, Morocco, New Zealand, Pakistan, Paraguay, Peru, Spain, Sri Lanka, Taiwan, Tanzania, Turkey, Uruguay, Venezuela, Zaïre, Zambia

**Variants**

| | |
|---|---|
| YR-13 | prototype for U.S. Army evacuation role with Franklin O-335-1 175-hp engine; enclosed cabin and tailboom; 18 built for U.S. Army and 10 for U.S. Navy (HTL-1); 2 modified to YR-13A configuration. |
| H-13B | production helicopter with 200-hp Franklin O-335-3 engine and bubble canopy; 65 built for Army with 16 converted to aerial ambulance (H-13C); 12 built for Navy (HTL-2). |
| H-13D | production helicopter with Franklin O-335-5 engine and open lattice tailboom; 87 built for Army. |
| H-13E/ OH-13E | production helicopter with Franlkin O-335-5 engine; similar to H-13D with dual controls; 490 built. |
| XH-13F | engine test helicopter with Continental XT15-T-3 Artouse turbine; 1 converted. |
| H-13G/ OH-13G | production helicopter similar to H-13E with Franklin O-335-3 engine; increased fuel capacity; controllable horizontal tail stabilizer; 1 crew + 3 passengers; 265 built for U.S. Army. |
| H-13H/ OH-13H/ UH-13H | production helicopter similar to OH-13G with 250-hp Lycoming 0-435-23 engine; all-metal rotor blades; weight loaded 2,700 lbs; 1 crew + 2 passengers; delivered from December 1965; 453 built for U.S. Army, 15 for foreign military service. |
| H-13J/ UH-13J | similar to OH-13H with enclosed cabin; 1 crew + 3 passengers; 2 built for USAF. |
| H-13K/ OH-13K | converted H-13H with 225-hp Franklin 6VS-O-335 engine for high-altitude flight; larger rotor; 2 converted. |
| TH-13L | dual-control trainer for Navy with 200-hp Aircooled Motors O-335-5 engine; 1 crew + 1 student; 46 delivered as HTL-4 in 1950-1951; 36 delivered as HTL-5 in 1951-1952. |
| TH-13M | dual-control trainer for Navy; similar to HTL-4/5; 48 delivered as HTL-6 in 1955-1956. |
| TH-13N | dual-control trainer for Navy with 250-hp Lycoming O-435-6/6A engine; all-weather instrumentation; 18 delivered as HTL-7 in 1958. |
| UH-13P | Navy utility helicopter with 250-hp Lycoming O-435-6 engine; 1 crew + 3 passengers; weight loaded 2,800 lbs; 28 delivered as HUL-1 in 1955-1956; 2 operated by Coast Guard (HUL-1G) and 2 converted to HUL-1M (see UH-13R). |
| HH-13Q | SAR-configured for Coast Guard; formerly HUL-1G; 2 transferred. |
| UH-13R | engine test aircraft with Allison YT63-A-3 turboshaft engine; formerly HUL-1M; 2 converted. |
| OH-13S | production helicopter based on OH-13H with 260-hp Lycoming O-435-25 engine with turbo supercharger; length 28 ft 6 in (tailboom lengthened); rotor diameter 36 ft; weight loaded 2,850 lbs; 1 pilot + 2 passengers; built for U.S. Army. |
| TH-13T | production instrument trainer; similar to OH-13S with 260-hp Lycoming TVO-435-B1A engine; cabin 8 in wider; tinted plexiglass bubble; 1 pilot + 1 student; built for U.S. Army. |
| HTL-3 | Navy training helicopter with 200-hp Franklin O-235 engine; 1 pilot + 1 student; 9 built for U.S. Navy, 3 for Brazil. |
| Scout | |
|   AH 1 | British variant. |
|   HT 2 | British trainer variant. |
| 47J-3 | Agusta-built ASW variant carrying 1 Mk-44 ASW homing torpedo. |

**Characteristics**

| | | H-13H | UH-13P/HUL-1 |
|---|---|---|---|
| Crew: | | 1 pilot | 1 pilot |
| Engine: | | 1 Lycoming VO-435 piston 200 hp | 1 Lycoming O-435-6 piston 240 hp T/O; 220 hp sustained |
| Dimensions: | length | 27 ft 4 in (8.33 m) | 32 ft 4 in (9.85 m) |
| | height | 9 ft 6 in (2.9 m) | 9 ft 6 in (2.9 m) |
| | rotor | 35 ft 1 in (10.69 m) | 37 ft 2 in (11.33) |
| Weight: | empty | 1,564 lbs (710 kg) | 1,652 lbs (750 kg) |
| | loaded | 2,450 lbs (1,112 kg) | 2,700 lbs (1,225.5 kg) |
| Speed: | cruise | 85 mph (137 km/h) | 78 mph (126 km/h) |
| | maximum | 100 mph (161 km/h) | 83 mph (134 km/h) |
| Range: | | 300 miles (483 km) | 200 miles (322 km) |
| Ceiling: | hover OGE | | 4,000 ft (1,219 m) |
| | hover IGE | | 6,600 ft (2,012 m) |
| | service | 13,200 ft (4,023 m) | 16,400 ft (4,999 m) |
| Climb: | | 770 ft/min (235 m/min) | 1,120 ft/min (341 m/min) |
| Payload: | | 2 troops | 3 troops |

The Bell H-13 series has been used by a large number of nations in a variety of military roles. This is a typical U.S. Army OH-13S with uncovered tailboom and skid landing gear. Two wheels could be lowered from the skids to facilitate ground handling. Note the guard for the anti-torque tail rotor. (U.S. Army)

This U.S. Navy HTL-3 has a covered tailboom and a four-wheel fixed landing gear. Despite its Navy markings, this helicopter was operating with the 1st Marine Division in the Korean War. The cabin side panels could be removed for photographic missions, and two stretcher pods could be carried. (U.S. Marine Corps)

A U.S. Navy HTL-4 flying off the coast of Greenland. This aircraft has pontoons fitted, indicating that it was based aboard a Navy icebreaker. The national insignia is displayed on metal plates attached to the open tailboom. The UR indicates Navy Helicopter Utility Squadron 2. (U.S. Navy)

# Bell

48                                    R-12
                                      H-12

The R-12 (redesignated H-12 in 1948) had the same rotor and other systems of the highly successful Bell R-13/H-13 Sioux helicopter with a larger cabin. The 13 helicopters of this design that were built were used mostly for research and development.

The R-13 had a fully enclosed, metal-clad structure with an enclosed boom to support the anti-torque tail rotor. Small stabilizing fins were fitted to the boom. The two-bladed main rotor was identical to that of the R-13. Either a quadracycle landing gear or twin pontoons were provided. The third prototype and subsequent machines had twice the capacity of the first two helicopters.

Thirteen R-12 utility helicopters were ordered in 1946. A production run of 34 of the larger variant, designated R-12A, was ordered and then cancelled in 1947.

First flight: XH-12B 21 November 1949
Service introduction: April 1950
Users: United States

**Variants**

XR-12    2 prototype aircraft; Pratt & Whitney R-1340 engine; 5,600 lbs loaded; 2 built (serials 46-214/215).
R-12A    34 planned production aircraft; cancelled in 1947.
XR-12B   enlarged prototype; 1 built.
YR-12B   evaluation aircraft; 10 built.

This YH-12B helicopter had the same rotor and other dynamic components of the highly successful H-13 series but had a larger cabin. The 13 completed H-12s were used for research and development and the design did not enter series production. Note the small horizontal stabilizer fin on the tailboom. (U.S. Air Force)

**Characteristics (YR-12B)**

Crew: 1 pilot, 1 crewman
Engine: 1 Pratt & Whitney R-1340-55 piston 600 hp T/O; 550 hp continuous
Dimensions: length 41 ft 7 in (12.68 m); height 14 ft 4 in (4.36 m); rotor diameter 47 ft 6 in (14.5 m)
Weight: empty 4,740 lbs (2,125 kg); combat 6,800 lbs (3,087 kg); loaded 7,200 lbs (3,269 kg)
Speed: cruise 85 mph (136 km/h); maximum 110 mph (176 km/h)
Range: 400 miles (640 km)
Ceiling: hover 6,800 ft (2,073 m); service 14,700 ft (4,480 m)
Climb: 1,225 ft/min (373 m/min)
Payload: 8-10 troops or 6 stretchers

An H-12 fitted with twin floats, a popular feature of helicopters of the period to permit operation from land, ships, ice, and swamps. The photograph was made prior to 1946, when this helicopter was designated XR-12. (U.S. Air Force)

# Bell

54                          R-15
                               H-15

Three Bell 54 helicopters were ordered as XR-15 (changed to XH-15 in 1948) for evaluation as a lightweight helicopter for observation, liaison, photographic, and line-cable inspection. The helicopter resembled a scaled-down Bell 48 (R-12/H-12). The Firestone R-14 was a competitive design.

The Model 54 had an all-metal, fully enclosed cabin and covered tailboom, with the distinctive Bell two-bladed main rotor and an anti-torque tail rotor at the right extremity of the boom. A tricycle landing gear was fitted. The two-man crew sat side by side in a monocoque fuselage.

Three prototypes were built (serial 46-530/532), but procurement was deferred in favor of the larger but more capable Bell 47 (R-13/H-13).

First flight: March 1948      Service introduction: not operational

**Characteristics**

Crew: 1 pilot, 1 observer
Engine: 1 Continental XO-470-5 radial piston 285 hp T/O; 250 hp sustained
Dimensions: length 25 ft 7 in (7.8 m); height 9 ft 2 in (2.79 m); rotor diameter 37 ft 4
    in (11.35 m)
Weight: empty 2,000 lbs (908 kg); loaded 2,777 lbs (1,261 kg)
Speed: cruise 80 mph (128 km/h)
Range: 201 miles (324 km)
Ceiling: hover 18,470 ft (5,630 m); service 27,000 ft (8,230 m)
Climb: 1,390 ft/min (424 m/min)

Another helicopter based on the initial Bell concepts was the XH-15, resembling the
unsuccessful H-12 more than the H-13. The tricycle landing gear of the three prototype
XH-15s easily distinguished them from the similar-looking XH-12. Note the restricted
cabin visibility as compared to that of the H-13 series. (U.S. Air Force)

# Bell

61                                             HSL

The HSL was the world's first helicopter designed from the outset for ASW.
Bell won the U.S. Navy's competition for an ASW helicopter in June 1950 (leading
to the firm's helicopter production being moved from Buffalo, New York, to a
new plant at Fort Worth, Texas). The HSL was produced in comparatively large
numbers but did not prove satisfactory in the ASW role. The helicopter was also
evaluated in the Mine Countermeasures (MCM), ship-towing, and troop-carrying
roles.

The HSL was the only tandem-rotor helicopter to be developed by Bell. It was
designed to carry dipping sonar and to attack submerged submarines with acoustic homing torpedoes as well as those caught on the surface with missiles (i.e., the
Fairchild Petrel). With a gross weight of 26,500 pounds, the HSL was the largest
helicopter produced in quantity up to its time, requiring a 1,900-hp engine, also
the largest used in a helicopter. The HSL was intended to operate in two-aircraft
"hunter-killer" teams: the hunter with a crew of three or four and AN/SQS-4A
dipping sonar, and the killer with a two-man crew carrying two Mk-43 torpedoes.
Any HSL was to be able to operate in either the hunter or killer mode (with the
latter retaining the AN/SQS-4A). However, trials revealed that helicopter noises

were too high for efficient sonar use, while the size of the HSL and manual rotor-folding made it too awkward for shipboard operation. The aircraft was fitted for night and instrument flight.

Three XHSL-1 prototypes were produced followed by an order for 96 HSL-1 helicopters for the U.S. Navy and 18 for the Royal Navy. The problems described above led to only 50 HSL-1s being built, with most being mothballed upon delivery. In mid-1954 work began on using the HSL in the MCM role, with subsequent tests demonstrating the helicopter's ability to pull a 310-ton barge at 18 knots. Six HSLs were modified for minesweeping and were employed in these experiments into 1960. Another HSL fuselage was stripped and suspended under a Sikorsky S-60 Skycrane in 1960 to test the feasibility of that helicopter for MCM operations. One HSL was evaluated by the Army in 1956 for use as a troop transport, lifting 5,000 pounds of ballast.

First flight: XHSL-1 3 March 1953
Service introduction: October 1953
Users: United States

**Variants**

XHSL-1   prototype; 3 completed 1953-1954 (Navy BuNo. 129133/135; fourth prototype cancelled).
HSL-1    production aircraft; 50 completed 1953-1956.

**Characteristics**

Crew: 1 pilot, 1 copilot, 2 sonar operators or 1 pilot, 1 sonar operator (with 2 torpe-does)
Engine: 1 Pratt & Whitney R-2800-50 Double Wasp radial piston 1,900 hp
Dimensions: length 39 ft 9 in (12.1 m); height 14 ft 6 in (4.4. m); rotor diameter 51 ft 6 in (15.7 m)
Weight: empty 12,450 lbs (5,652 kg)*; loaded 20,000 lbs (9,080 kg); maximum 26,500 lbs (12,031 kg)
Speed: cruise 98 mph (158 km/h); maximum 135 mph (217 km/h)
Range: 350 miles (563.5 km)
Ceiling: hover 9,900 ft (3,017.5 m); service 15,500 ft (4,724.5 m)
Climb: 1,140 ft/min (347.5 m/min)
Payload: 2 Mk-43 torpedoes or 1 Mk-24 mine (800 lbs) (with 2 crewmen)

---

*Empty weight includes 603-lb sonar in both hunter and killer configurations.

The first prototype XHSL-1 on its first flight. The forward rotor shaft and amidships R-2800 engine are visible. Note the single-wheel forward landing gear and twin-wheel after gear. No tail-fin plates are fitted. Despite a large production run for its time, the HSL was not successful. (Bell)

An HSL-1 demonstrates its submarine detection mode, hovering over Eagle Mountain Lake near Fort Worth, Texas, while lowering its AN/SQS-4A dipping sonar into the water. Operating noises prevented the helicopter's sonar operator from using the equipment effectively. (Bell)

Nose down to increase rotor thrust, an HSL-1 tows the Navy floating derrick YSD-51 to demonstrate its ability to tow minesweeping equipment. This test, off Corpus Christi, Texas, was part of a continuing U.S. Navy program that began during the Korean War to develop airborne mine countermeasure systems. (Bell)

# Bell

200

H-33
V-3

The XV-3 was an experimental tilt-rotor convertiplane developed jointly by the U.S. Army and Air Force beginning in 1951. The aircraft became the first in the world to fully tilt its rotor from the horizontal plane (i.e., that of a helicopter) to a vertical plane for conventional flight. After extensive flight tests into the mid-1960s, the concept was reinitiated a few years later with the Bell XV-15 tilt-rotor aircraft of significantly larger size and greater capability.

As built, the XV-3 had two three-bladed rotors that were articulated; from 1957 onward two-bladed semi-rigid rotors were mounted on the engine nacelles at the extremities of the stub wing. Electric motors in the nacelles tilted the rotors. The monocoque fuselage had a four-seat cabin forward with extensive plexiglass, a single radial engine mounted aft of the cabin, and a conventional tail. The second prototype also had a small lower fin. A helicopter-type skid landing gear was provided. Wingspan was 31 feet 3½ inches.

Two prototypes were ordered as XH-33 but were changed to XV-3 early in the program. The first prototype (serial 54-147) flew from 1955 to 1956, attaining 15 degrees in-flight conversion before being seriously damaged in a crash landing on 25 October 1956. The second prototype (54-148) was subjected to extensive wind-tunnel tests before flying and first achieved in-flight conversion from vertical to full horizontal flight on 18 December 1958. Flight tests continued and the aircraft was modified by the National Aeronautics and Space Administration (NASA) from 1962 to 1966, after which several successful tests were flown until the aircraft was damaged in 1966 wind tunnel tests. An improved XV-3A with a 600-shp Lycoming XT53 turbine engine was proposed but not built.

First flight: 23 August 1955     Service introduction: not operational

The second XV-3 prototype (54-148) is shown in flight having almost fully converted to a conventional aircraft configuration. The wing-tip rotor pods were fixed, and the rotor hubs rotated from the vertical to horizontal position. Like most prototype aircraft, the XV-3 went through several modifications. At one point a small ventral tail fin was fitted. (Bell)

**Characteristics**

Crew: 1 pilot
Engine: 1 Pratt & Whitney R-985 radial piston 450 hp
Dimensions: length 30 ft 3½ in (9.23 m); height 13 ft 6 in (4.11 m); rotor diameter 33
    ft (10.06 m)
Weight: empty 3,600 lbs (1,634 kg); loaded 4,800 lbs (2,179 kg)
Speed: maximum 181 mph (291 km/h)
Range: 255 miles (410.5 km)
Ceiling: hover OGE 4,700 ft (1,432 m); hover IGE 7,400 ft (2,256 m); service 15,000
    ft (4,572 m)
Climb: 550 ft/min (168 m/min)
Payload: 3 troops

The first XV-3 prototype (54-147) differed from the second in the configuration of the
fuselage section above the wing and in other minor points. Note the large rotor-blade
diameter, necessitating takeoff and landing in a helicopter or near-helicopter configuration. The XV-3 was the progenitor of the highly successful XV-15 technology-demonstration aircraft. (Bell)

# Bell

204
205

H-40 ⎱
HU-1 ⎬ Iroquois
H-1 ⎰

Far better known by its nickname "Huey," the ubiquitous UH-1 is a light utility helicopter used by a wide variety of military and commercial organizations world-wide. Almost 60 nations have operated Hueys of some variant in their armed services, and three nations produce or assemble UH-1s under license from the Bell Helicopter division of Textron, Inc. Two major versions of the UH-1 exist: the single-engined Bell Models 204/205 and the twin-engined Bell Models 212 and 412. (By virtue of their considerable differences in performance, they are treated as different aircraft and described separately herein.) The H-1 series of helicopters started life as the Bell XH-40, designed in 1955 to fulfill a U.S. Army requirement for a utility helicopter to be used for front-line evacuation of casual-ties, general utility missions, and as an instrument trainer. The first XH-40 flew in late 1956, and the first production variant, the HU-1A Iroquois, was delivered to the U.S. Army on 30 June 1959. In 1962 aircraft designations in the U.S. armed forces were standardized, and the Huey changed its designation one final time from the HU-1 series to the UH-1 series. Within that series, the Bell Model 204 has the model suffixes A/B/C/E/F/K/L/M/P, the Model 205 has the suffixes D/H, and the Model 212 (described separately) is designated UH-1N. The name Huey was derived from the pre-1962 designation HU.

The Model 204/205 variants of the UH-1 are single-engine, skid-equipped utility helicopters with a single two-bladed, all-metal main rotor and a two-bladed, all-metal, anti-torque tail rotor mounted on the left side of the tailboom. The fuselage is of all-metal semi-monocoque construction and accommodates two crewmen and seven passengers in the Model 204, and two crewmen and 11 passengers in the Model 205. Other differences between the two models include fuselage dimensions, rotor dimensions, power plant type, and performance. These differences are illustrated in the table below.

Well over 9,000 UH-1s of all types have been produced into 1981 by Bell at Fort Worth, Texas, and the plants of its licensees, Agusta in Italy, Mitsui/Fuji in Japan, and Aero Industry Development Center (AIDC) of the Chinese Nationalist Air Force in Taiwan. Hueys have seen combat in Southeast Asia, where they were the primary helicopters in use by both the United States and South Vietnamese armies, in the Arab-Israeli conflicts in the Middle East, in the Zimbabwe/Rhode-sian civil war, and in a variety of major military and police actions throughout the world. They have served in gunship, casualty evacuation, search and rescue, vertical envelopment/attack transport, antisubmarine warfare, and general utility roles in their 20-plus years of service, and are destined to remain in frontline service for many years to come.

First flight: 22 October 1956     Service introduction: HU-1 1958
Users: Argentina, Australia, Austria, Bolivia, Brazil, Brunei, Burma, Canada, Chile, Co-lombia, Dominican Republic, El Salvador (1981), Ethiopia, West Germany, Greece, Guate-mala, Indonesia, Iran, Israel, Italy, Japan, Kampuchea, South Korea, Kuwait, Mexico, Netherlands, New Zealand, Norway, Oman, Panama, Peru, Philippines, Saudi Arabia, Singapore, Somalia, Spain, Sweden, Taiwan, Thailand, Turkey, Uganda, United Arab Emirates, United States, Uruguay, Venezuela, North Yemen, Yugoslavia, Zambia, Zim-babwe (Rhodesia)

## Variants

| | |
|---|---|
| XH-40 | prototype powered by 825-shp Lycoming XT53 turboshaft engine; 3 built (serial 55-4459/461). |
| YH-40 | service test aircraft; 6 built. |
| HU-1 | pre-production aircraft with 700-shp T53-L-1A turboshaft; changed to UH-1 in 1962; 9 built. |
| HU-1A | initial production variant for U.S. Army with 860-shp T53-L-1A turboshaft derated to 770 shp; in Vietnam War some were modified to gunship configuration with 2.75-in rocket launchers and 2 .30-cal machine guns; first delivered June 1959; changed to UH-1A in 1962. |
| HU-1B | production helicopter with improved rotor system; first delivered with 960-shp T53-L-5 turboshaft; later changed to 1,100-shp T53-L-11 turboshaft; gunship version carried flexible-mount .50-cal machine guns and 40-mm grenade launcher; first delivered March 1961; changed to UH-1B in 1962. |
| YHU-1B | YH-40 modified; 2 modified. |
| UH-1C | UH-1B with modified rotor system. |
| UH-1D | major production aircraft with 1,100-shp T53-L-11 turboshaft; enlarged main rotor; longer fuselage; increased fuel capacity; 1 crew plus 12 troops, or 6 litters plus medical attendant; first flight August 1961; first delivered August 1963. |
| UH-1E | development of UH-1B for U.S. Marine Corps; additional USMC-required equipment including avionics, personnel hoist, rotor brake; armed with flexible-mount .50-cal machine guns, 2.75-in rocket pods. |
| TH-1F | training variant of UH-1F for USAF; flight instrument and hoist training. |
| UH-1F | UH-1B built for U.S. Air Force with 1,290-shp T58-G-3 turboshaft; 48-ft main rotor; first flight February 1964. |
| EH-1H | UH-1H modified with Army Security Agency electronic warfare equipment to intercept, locate, and jam enemy communications; Project Quick Fix. |
| HH-1H | UH-1H modified for local base rescue. |
| UH-1H | UH-1D with 1,400-shp T53-L-13 turboshaft. |
| HH-1K | UH-1E with 1,400-shp T53-L-13 turboshaft; built for U.S. Navy SAR operations. |
| TH-1L | training variant of UH-1L for U.S. Navy. |
| UH-1L | UH-1E with T53-L-13 turboshaft; armor and armament deleted; U.S. Navy general utility helicopter. |
| UH-1M | UH-1C uprated with T53-L-13 turboshaft |
| UH-1P | UH-1F modified by USAF to perform additional missions under adverse weather conditions. |
| CH-118 | UH-1H built for Mobile Command, Canadian Armed Forces. |
| AB 204AS | antisubmarine warfare variant of AB 204 built by Agusta with 1,290-shp T58-G-3 turboshaft; for Italian and Spanish navies; automatic stabilization equipment for sonar dipping operations; search radar; 2 Mk-44 torpedoes. |
| AB 204B | Agusta-manufactured UH-1B; versions completed with 44-ft or 48-ft rotors; Rolls-Royce Bristol Gnome, Lycoming T53, or General Electric T58 turboshafts; over 250 built. |
| AB 205 | Agusta-built version of UH-1D/H. |
| 204B-2 | Fuji-developed higher performance Bell Model 204B with 1,400-shp T5313B Lycoming turboshaft; anti-torque tail rotor mounted on right side of tailboom. (All other Fuji-built variants of H-1 series are identical to the Bell-built versions.) |
| 533 | Bell designation for YH-40/YUH-1B converted to high-speed research aircraft; 1 converted (serial 56-6723); listed separately. |

**Characteristics**

Crew: 1 pilot, 1 copilot
Engines: UH-1B 1 Lycoming T53-L-11 turboshaft 1,100 shp
      UH-1H 1 Lycoming T53-L-13 turboshaft 1,400 shp

|  |  | *UH-1B* | *UH-1H* |
|---|---|---|---|
| Dimensions: | length | 42 ft 7 in (12.98 m) | 44 ft 7 in (13.59 m) |
|  | height | 12 ft 8½ in (3.87 m) | 13 ft 5 in (4.08 m) |
|  | rotor | 44 ft (13.4 m) | 48 ft (14.63 m) |
| Weight: | empty | 4,519 lbs (2,050 kg) | 5,090 lbs (2,309 kg) |
|  | loaded | 8,500 lbs (3,856 kg) | 9,500 lbs (4,309 kg) |
| Speed: | cruise | 119.5 mph (193 km/h) | 126.5 mph (204 km/h) |
|  | maximum | 147 mph (238 km/h) | 130 mph (209 km/h) |
| Range: |  | 382 miles (615 km) | 357 miles (575 km) |
| Ceiling: | hover OGE | 10,000 ft (3,048 m) | 1,000 ft (305 m) |
|  | hover IGE | 10,600 ft (3,231 m) | 13,700 ft (4,176 m) |
|  | service | 11,500 ft (3,505 m) | 12,700 ft (3,871 m) |
| Climb: |  | 2,350 ft/min (716 m/min) | 1,600 ft/min (488 m/min) |
| Payload: |  | 7 troops + | 13 troops + |
|  |  | 2 .50-cal or 7.62-mm | 2 .50-cal or 7.62-mm |
|  |  | flexible MG | flexible MG |

The XH-40 began the ubiquitous Huey series, with the last of three prototypes (55-4461) shown here during flight tests. The right-angle stabilizing bars on the two-bladed rotor head are clearly visible in this photo. Radio antennas project from the nose of the craft. (Bell)

A Huey in war paint at war. This is a Navy UH-1B from Light Helicopter Attack Squadron (HAL) 3—the "Seawolfs"—over the Mekong Delta in South Vietnam during 1967. Twin machine guns and rocket pods are mounted on each side of the fuselage, and a door gunner holds an automatic rifle. (U.S. Navy)

Sailors from HAL-3 maintain UH-1B Hueys at a Mekong Delta base. During the Vietnam War these Hueys were based aboard landing ships and barges as well as ashore. Part of the nose structure is removed to reduce weight; sitting low on its skids, the Huey is easy to load, unload, and maintain. Most U.S. helicopters in Vietnam had low-visibility markings. (U.S. Navy)

The UH-1D Huey has a fuselage 3 feet 6 inches longer than earlier models, facilitating its use as an aerial ambulance, as shown here being loaded with wounded soldiers and sailors after a fire fight in the Mekong Delta in 1967. This Huey is sitting on the mini flight deck of a 56-foot riverine landing craft. (U.S. Navy)

This late-model, single-engine Huey is a TH-1L from Navy Helicopter Training Squadron (HT) 8. The last four digits of the bureau number (157812) are on the tail, as well as the letter E indicating Training Wing 5. The number 41 is the aircraft's tactical number within Wing 5. (U.S. Navy)

# Bell

533

This aircraft was a YH-40/YUH-1B Iroquois (Huey) converted to evaluate various high-speed configurations. Under U.S. Army sponsorship, successive modifications were made to the helicopter, which achieved a speed of 250 mph in April 1965 (its rotor tips reaching a speed of Mach 0.985). Although it was an Army test aircraft (serial 56-6723), it was assigned no military designation.

The initial changes to the basic Huey configuration were the addition of aerodynamic fairings on the fuselage, a vertical tail (cambered), and a tilting rotor mast inside a large fairing structure. Level flight in excess of 173 mph was recorded in this form, with a speed of 188 mph reached in shallow dives. The Lycoming 1,100-shp T53-L-9A turboshaft was then supplemented by two 920-lbst Continental J69-T-9 turbojet engines mounted in pods on the side of the fuselage. With this arrangement a speed of 210 mph was attained in level flight. Subsequently, two small, swept-back, low wings were fitted, changing the Model 533 to a compound helicopter. Thus configured, the aircraft achieved a speed of 222 mph on 11 May 1964. Other engine combinations were fitted, and, with two Lycoming T53-L-13 engines and two 3,300-lbst Pratt & Whitney JT12-A3 jet engines along with modified UH-1B rotor blades, the Model 533 attained 316 mph on 15 April 1969. A three-bladed and four-bladed rotor were also tested in addition to the basic two-bladed configuration.

First flight: Model 533 10 August 1962
Service introduction: not operational

The Bell 533 (56-6723) was a YH-40/YUH-1B extensively modified to evaluate various high-speed configurations. In this photo the aircraft has jet pods mounted on either side of the fuselage, thin, swept-back wings, and a standard two-bladed main rotor. Note the rotor housing pylon. (Bell)

**Characteristics**

Crew: 1 pilot, 1 copilot, 2 observers

Engines (see above discussion)

Dimensions: length 42 ft 7 in (12.98 m); height 12 ft 8½ in (3.87 m); rotor diameter 2
        × 44 ft (13.4 m), subsequently 3 × 42 ft (12.8 m)

Weight: normal for flight tests 8,500 lbs (3,859 kg)

Speed: maximum 250 mph (402.5 km)

Range: ⎫
Ceiling: ⎬ see UH-1B configuration for basic aircraft
Climb: ⎭

In this view the Bell 533 has a four-bladed rotor, jet pods fitted to stub wings, and a ventral
tail fin with additional horizontal stabilizers. The anti-torque tail rotor is on the left side of
the fin. The aircraft also flew with a two-bladed rotor in essentially the same configuration.
(Bell)

Still another Bell 533 configuration, this one having a shape much like that of the original
YH-40 with the addition of a rotor support pylon and jet pods mounted on the fuselage.
The streamlined rotor pylon reduced wind resistance. Again, sections of the nose structure
have been removed to reduce weight. (Bell)

# Bell
206

| | |
|---|---|
| HO-4 | H-58 Kiowa |
| OH-4 | CH-136 |
| H-57 SeaRanger | TexasRanger |

The Model 206 JetRanger was designed to compete in the 1961 U.S. Army light observation helicopter (LOH) program but lost that competition to the Hughes OH-6. The prototype Model 206 built for this competition against the OH-6 and Fairchild-Hiller OH-5 was designated OH-4 by the Army and first flew in late 1962, less than 13 months after it had been ordered. Despite its loss to the OH-6 for the LOH contract, the Model 206 became a significant commercial success for Bell. In 1968, the U.S. Navy ordered 40 slightly modified JetRangers for its basic helicopter flight instruction program, designating them TH-57A SeaRangers. Shortly thereafter the U.S. Army announced that the Model 206A had won the reopened LOH competition and, as the OH-58A Kiowa, an initial order for 2,200 aircraft was placed. The Model 206 has also been built under license in Italy and Australia.

All variants of the Model 206 are single-engined, general-purpose, light helicopters with landing skids, a two-bladed, semi-rigid main rotor and an anti-torque tail rotor mounted on the left side of the tailboom. The fuselage is made up of three sections, the nose, semi-monocoque center, and the tailboom, with accommodation for five in the cabin. The original Model 206 entered in the 1961 LOH competition was equipped with a 250-shp Allison T63 turboshaft engine, but this has grown to the current 317-shp of the uprated Allison T63. The U.S. Navy's TH-57As are equipped with dual controls and an electronics package modified to suit the Navy's needs. The U.S. Army's OH-58s have single controls, an extensive communications package, and can be equipped with the XM-27 armament kit that includes a 7.62-mm minigun. Late in 1980, Bell completed a 206L TexasRanger antitank variant designed to carry four TOW missiles or other weapons. The helicopter is also fitted with a roof sight, FLIR, and laser range finder/designator. Intended for multipurpose use, the aircraft has an Allison 250-C30 turboshaft engine.

The Model 206 and its variants have proved to be one of the most popular civilian and military helicopters in the world. Over 6,000 have been manufactured by Bell and its licensees in the past 15 years, and they are operated in most of the non-communist nations. Production continued in 1981 both by Bell in the United States and by Agusta in Italy.

First flight: 10 January 1966
Service introduction: TH-57A 1968
Users: Argentina, Australia, Austria, Brazil, Brunei, Canada, Chile, Finland, Guyana, Iran, Israel, Italy, Jamaica, Kuwait, Libya, Malaysia, Malta, Mexico, Morocco, Oman, Peru, Saudi Arabia, Spain, Sri Lanka, Sweden, Tanzania, Thailand, Turkey, Uganda, United Arab Emirates, United States, Venezuela, Vietnam

**Variants**

OH-4A     prototype Model 206 built for the U.S. Army's Light Observation Helicopter competition (original Bell designation D-250); original Army designation HO-4 changed to OH-4A in 1962; 250-shp Allison T-63 turboshaft; smaller 4-seat cabin than later models; 5 built (serial 62-4202/206).

TH-57A   U.S. Navy training helicopter; basic Model 206A with Navy instruments, com-
         munications, and flight control system; dual controls; 40 built and delivered in
         1968; 7 additional ordered in 1980.

OH-58A   modified Model 206A for U.S. Army's 1968 LOH competition; increased-
         diameter main rotor, 4-seat interior layout, Army electronics suite; tailboom
         lengthened by 10 in over Model 206A; 2,200 built.

OH-58C   OH-58A modified for reconnaissance, security, and target acquisition missions;
         420-shp Allison T63-8-720 turboshaft; 585 OH-58As scheduled for conversion
         by Bell.

CH-136   OH-58A for Canadian service; delivered from U.S. Army production line; 74
         built.

AB 206A  Model 206A produced under license by Agusta in Italy.

206B-1   OH-58A built for Australia; first 12 built by Bell, delivered in 1971-1972;
         remaining 44 units built by Commonwealth Aircraft Corporation in Australia.

206L     Company-sponsored antitank variant; see text.

**Characteristics (OH-58A)**

Crew: 1 pilot, 1 copilot
Engine: 1 Allison T63-A-700 turboshaft 317 shp
Dimensions: length 32 ft 7 in (9.93 m); height 9 ft 6½ in (2.91 m); rotor diameter 35
    ft 4 in (10.77 m)
Weight: empty 1,464 lbs (664 kg); loaded 3,000 lbs (1,362 kg)
Speed: cruise 117 mph (188 km/h); maximum 138 mph (222 km)
Range: 298 miles (481 km)
Ceiling: hover OGE 8,800 ft (2,682 m); hover IGE 13,600 ft (4,145 m); service 18,900
    ft (5,760 m)
Climb: 1,780 ft/min (543 m/min)
Payload: 2 troops

One of Bell's OH-4A entries in the U.S. Army's Light Observation Helicopter (LOH)
competition poses for the camera. Note the enlarged nose bubble compared to later
helicopters of this series. All Bell 206s had the distinctive tail fin shown here mounted on
the right side of the tailboom with the anti-torque rotor mounted on the left. (Bell)

# Bell

207                                    Sioux Scout

The Sioux Scout was built by Bell to demonstrate the firm's concepts in attack/gunship helicopters and in several respects was the progenitor of the AH-1 series of Cobra gunships. This helicopter incorporated a number of features found in subsequent armed attack helicopters and was used as a test bed for several advanced devices, such as a "hands-off" tracking gun sight whereby the guns could be directed through movement of the pilot's head.

Based on the highly successful H-13 Sioux, the Sioux Scout had the Lycoming TVO-435-B1A engine of the OH-13S with the tail rotor, transmission, center section, and tailboom of the commercial 47J-2 helicopter. The forward fuselage—only 39 inches wide—had the same box beam, honeycomb panel construction that would be used in the HueyCobra. A stepped, tandem seating arrangement placed the gunner ahead and below the pilot, directly over the TAT-101 turret carrying two 7.62-mm M60C machine guns. Stub wings were fitted high on the fuselage, aft of the cockpit, and a simple skid landing gear was provided.

The single Sioux Scout (civil serial N73927) first flew in July 1963 and during the following 16 months was demonstrated for Army commands throughout the United States.

First flight: July 1963
Service introduction: not operational

**Characteristics**

Crew: 1 pilot, 1 copilot/gunner
Engine: 1 Lycoming TVO-435-B1A piston 260 hp
Dimensions: rotor diameter 37 ft (11.28 m)
Weight:
Speed:
Range:
Ceiling:
Climb:
Payload: TAT-101 twin 7.62-mm turret

The Bell 207 was an early effort to develop a specialized attack/gunship helicopter, and several of its design concepts were used in the later AH-1 Cobra series. The pilot and copilot/gunner were seated in tandem. The "chin" turret housed twin 7.62-mm machine guns. Note that the aircraft had a civil registration number (N 73927). (Bell)

The Bell 207 Sioux Scout demonstrates its maneuverability during flight tests. The high stub wings of the aircraft were not suitable for carrying weapons as are the stub mid wings of the later AH-1 Cobra series of helicopter gunships. (Bell)

# Bell

209
249

AH-1 {HueyCobra
      {SeaCobra

Z 16

In 1962, the U.S. Army's Tactical Mobility Requirements Board issued a report that officially endorsed for the first time using armed helicopters in an escorting role. The war in Vietnam proved this concept valid, and armed Bell UH-1s were pressed into the gunship role. This was a stopgap measure at best, and the U.S. Army issued a requirement for an attack helicopter in 1964. The Bell D-262 was the resultant design but was too radical for the Department of Defense political situation at the time. Bell was eliminated from the competition in early 1965 but continued development of their attack helicopter as a private venture under the Bell model designation 209. It was resubmitted for Army evaluation in August 1965 when the Vietnamese War made it obvious that a radical attack helicopter was needed. The first prototype flew the following month and in December was turned over to the Army for trials. On 13 April 1966 the Army placed an initial order with Bell for 100 production AH-1s. Series production followed. In U.S. Army service the AH-1s are usually referred to as simply "Cobra" gunships.

The original HueyCobra is a heavily armed attack helicopter with a two-man crew seated in tandem in a streamlined fuselage and equipped with the engine, transmission, and the rotor systems of the Bell UH-1. The HueyCobra has been produced in both single-engined (AH-1G/Q/R/S) and twin-engined (AH-1J/T) versions. (The latter have "twin-pac" engines; see Bell 212/412 listing for description.) All share the same conventional, semi-monocoque, streamlined fuselage (lengthened slightly in the AH-1T) with a swept vertical tail fin and mid-mounted stub wings. The landing gear is a standard non-retractable H-1 tubular skid type. The armament packages vary widely from model to model, ranging from the early installation of twin 7.62-mm miniguns in an undernose turret and four underwing rocket launchers, each with 19 rockets, to the modern AH-1S equipped with a 20-mm cannon in the undernose turret plus eight TOW antitank missiles and rocket pods under the wings.

Over 1,800 AH-1s of all types have been built, with production continuing in 1981. The early AH-1Gs constructed for the U.S. Army are being upgraded to the AH-1S standard under a program that will continue into the mid-1980s. The U.S. Marine Corps is currently accepting the lengthened AH-1T with TOW missiles to improve its attack helicopter inventory. The Japanese Ground Self-Defense Force evaluated two AH-1S helicopters with tentative plans for procuring 54 more, of which 6 were to be built from Bell-supplied components and the remaining 48 produced in Japan. In March 1981, the Reagan Administration asked Congress for permission to transfer 24 AH-1S/TOW helicopters to Jordan.

First flight: 7 September 1965
Service introduction: AH-1G 1967
Users: Greece, Iran, Israel, Japan, Spain, United States

**Variants**

| | |
|---|---|
| D-262 | design designation for Bell entry in original U.S. Army attack helicopter competition; after Bell elimination from competition, design work continued under Bell Model 209 designation. |
| 209 | Bell privately funded prototype with T53-L-11 turboshaft and UH-1D rotor and transmission; retractable skid-type landing gear and ventral fin, 1 built. |
| AH-1G | initial production model with one T53-L-13 turboshaft derated to 1,100 shp; non-retractable skids; ventral fin removed; crew: co-pilot/gunner forward, pilot aft; initial armament of 2 7.62-mm miniguns in TAT-102A undernose turret; upgraded to 2 miniguns or 2 M-129 40-mm grenade launchers or 1 of each in M-28 undernose turret; 4 underwing hard points can accommodate 4 M-157 or M-159 rocket launchers or 2 M-18E1 minigun pods; 1,078 built including 38 to U.S. Marine Corps, 20 to Spain, 6 to Israel. |
| TH-1G | AH-1G modified to include instructor flight controls and instrument panel. |
| AH-1J | SeaCobra with T400-CP-400 coupled twin turboshaft engine (twin-pack) rated at 1,250 shp; undernose turret with M-197 3-barrel 20-mm cannon, same underwing stores as AH-1G; 69 built for U.S. Marine Corps with last two serving as AH-1T prototypes; 202 built for Imperial Iranian Army (62 equipped with TOW). |
| AH-1Q | AH-1G converted to fire TOW; 93 converted. |
| AH-1S (Modified) | AH-1G converted to fire TOW and upgraded with T53-L-703 turboshaft rated at 1,800 shp. |
| AH-1S (Production) | new production AH-1S to fire TOW with T53-L-703 engine; new instrument panels to facilitate nap-of-the-earth flying, and modified design cockpit canopy; 100 built. |
| AH-1S (ECAS) | new production AH-1S with Enhanced Cobra Armament System (ECAS) incorporated; universal chin-mounted turret with 20-mm cannon; underwing TOW (no rocket-firing capability); fiberglass main rotor blade; 98 built. |

AH-1S          AH-1G and AH-1S with fully upgraded weapon and sensor packages,
(Modernized)   including ECAS; laser range finder, ballistic computer, IR jammer, air
               data subsystem, 2.75-in rocket pods; 192 Modernized new-production
               AH-1S ordered; 372 AH-1Gs, 290 Modified AH-1Ss, and all new produc-
               tion AH-1Ss planned for upgrade to this standard by 1984.

YAH-1S         AH-1S demonstration aircraft with Bell Model 214 four-bladed rotor
               system (Bell 249).

AH-1T          improved SeaCobra with Bell Model 214 dynamic system, 2,050-shp
               T400-WV-402 twin-pac power plant; fuselage lengthened 1 ft, tailboom
               lengthened 2 ft 7 in; 57 ordered by USMC (23 with TOW).

Z 16           Spanish designation for AH-1G.

**Characteristics**

Crew: 1 pilot, 1 copilot/gunner
Engine: AH-1S 1 Lycoming T53-L-703 turboshaft 1,800 shp; AH-1T twin-pac Pratt &
       Whitney T400-WV-402 turboshaft 2,050 shp

|  |  | AH-1S | AH-1T |
|---|---|---|---|
| Dimensions: | length | 44 ft 7 in (13.59 m) | 48 ft 2 in (14.68) |
|  | height | 13 ft 6¼ in (4.12 m) | 13 ft 8 in (4.15 m) |
|  | rotor | 44 ft (13.41 m) | 48 ft (14.63 m) |
| Weight: | empty | 6,479 lbs (2,939 kg) | 8,014 lbs (3,635 kg) |
|  | loaded | 10,000 lbs (4,535 kg) | 14,000 lbs (6,350 kg) |
| Speed: | cruise | 1,230 ft/min (375 m/min) |  |
|  | maximum | 141.5 mph (228 km/h) | 207 mph (333 km/h) |
| Range: |  | 315 miles (507 km) | 358 miles (576 km) |
| Ceiling: | service | 12,200 ft (3,720 m) | 12,450 ft (3,794 m) |
| Climb: |  |  |  |
| Payload: |  | various guns, missiles, and rockets (see text) |  |

A German Army lieutenant (left) and a U.S. Army chief warrant officer climb into their
AH-1G HueyCobra during an exercise near Adelsheim, West Germany. The helicopter,
from the 2nd Armored Cavalry Regiment, was being used in a pilot exchange program.
There is a twin-weapon chin turret, and rocket pods are carried on the stub wings. (U.S.
Army)

This U.S. Marine Corps AH-1J SeaCobra has a three-barrel 20-mm Gatling gun forward and stub wings for carrying rockets, gun pods, and other stores. The AH-1Js provided to Iran can also carry wire-guided TOW antitank missiles. Note the twin engine "pac" above the fuselage. (Bell)

This AH-1J HueyCobra in Iranian colors has a laser range finder in a nose turret and four TOW missile launchers under each stub wing. Note that the pilot, seated to the rear of the gunner/copilot, is in an elevated position for improved visibility. (Bell)

This is the first AH-1S Modernized Cobra/TOW helicopter produced specifically for the U.S. Army National Guard. The M-197 Gatling gun has a 750-round magazine of 20-mm ammunition; eight TOW antitank missiles are carried on the stub wings. Eleven of these Cobras were to be delivered to the Army National Guard during 1981. (Bell)

# Bell

| | |
|---|---|
| 212 | H-1N Iroquois |
| 412 | CH-135 |

The UH-1N is a twin-engined version of the earlier UH-1 Huey series. It shares the fuselage of the UH-1H but few of its dynamic components. Bell began developing the aircraft in response to Canadian interest in a UH-1 powered by the Canadian Pratt & Whitney PT6T Twin-Pac. Canadian orders for 50 helicopters followed as well as U.S. government orders for an additional 141 aircraft. The U.S. helicopters were designated UH-1N, while the Canadian version was originally labelled CUH-1N. The first UH-1N entered U.S. service in 1970, and the first CUH-1N was delivered in the following year.

The main difference between the Model 212 and the earlier versions of the UH-1 is the power plant, which consists of two PT6 turboshaft engines coupled to a combining gearbox with a single output shaft. This PT6T-3 Turbo Twin-Pac produces 1,800 shp, derated to 1,250 shp for takeoff and 1,100 shp for continuous output. The Model 412 differs from the Model 212 in that the former is fitted with an improved four-bladed main rotor, replacing the two-bladed rotor standard on UH-1s since they were first produced. The four-bladed rotor can be retrofitted to all Model 212s to upgrade them to the 412 standard.

The Model 212 is produced under license in Italy by Agusta, which also holds licenses on the rest of the UH-1 model line. Agusta has marketed a naval version of the 212 for shipborne ASW missions as well as the standard transport version, also produced by Bell. The People's Republic of China has signed a memorandum of understanding with Bell for the license production of Model 212s and 412s at the Chinese helicopter factory in Harbin. When this book went to press, no production agreement had been reached.

First flight: 16 April 1969
Service introduction: 1970
Users: Argentina, Austria, Bangladesh, Brunei, Canada, China, Colombia, Ecuador, West Germany, Ghana, Greece, Guyana, Iran, Israel, Italy, Jamaica, South Korea, Lebanon, Libya, Malaysia, Mexico, Oman, Panama, Peru, Philippines, Saudi Arabia, Singapore, Spain, Syria, Turkey, United Arab Emerates, United States

**Variants**

| | |
|---|---|
| UH-1N | standard Model 212 transport with PT6T-3 Turbo Twin-Pac and UH-1H airframe; U.S. Marine Corps helicopters were being armed from 1981 onward with GAU-12B mini-gun and Mk-19 grenade launcher. |
| CH-135 | Canadian UH-1N; originally designated CUH-1N. |
| AB 212 | UH-1N produced under license by Agusta in Italy with PT6T-6 Turbo Twin-Pac producing 1,290 shp for takeoff. |
| AB 212 ASW | airframe and power plant identical to AB 212; extensive ASW electronics, including dipping sonar, automatic navigation system, automatic stabilization equipment, radar; carries 2 Mk-44 or Mk-46 ASW homing torpedoes or depth charges. |
| 412 | Model 212 with four-bladed main rotor. |

**Characteristics**

Crew: 1 pilot, 1 copilot, except AB 212 ASW 1 pilot, 1 copilot, 2 systems operators
Engine: 1 Pratt & Whitney of Canada PT6T-3 Turbo Twin-Pac 1,800 shp T/O; 1,100 shp continuous

Dimensions: length 57 ft 3¼ in (17.46 m); height 14 ft 4¾ in (4.39 m); rotor diameter
     48 ft 2¼ in (14.69 m)
Weight: empty 5,549 lbs (2,517 kg); loaded 11,200 lbs (5,085 kg)
Speed: maximum 126 mph (203 km/h)
Range: 273 miles (439 km)
Ceiling: service 17,400 ft (5,305 m)
Climb: 1,745 ft/min (532 m/min)
Passengers: 13 troops (transport version)

This UH-1N Huey is flown by the U.S. Air Force. The twin-pac engine exhausts are clearly
visible. This Huey has a camouflage paint scheme and low visibility markings on the tail fin.
A tail skid to protect the anti-torque rotor is visible under the tail. Large doors permit rapid
egress of troops and facilitate handling litters. (Bell)

Antarctic Development Squadron (VXE) 6 of the U.S. Navy operates aircraft in support of
U.S. Antarctic programs, military and civilian. This specially equipped UH-1N of VXE-6 is
painted in high-visibility orange. (U.S. Navy)

# Bell

214-Huey Plus                    Isfahan
214
214ST

The 214 series of Bell Huey-type helicopters was based on an improvement of the UH-1H capable of carrying 15 troops and—in the 214ST—18 troops. The only military user of this series is Iran,who had made plans prior to the fall of the Shah in 1979 for co-production by Bell and Iranian Helicopter Industry and subsequent large-scale production by IHI. Those production agreements were cancelled with the demise of the Shah's government, and only the 214A variants that were completed in 1975-1979 entered Iranian service.

The 214 design took the Bell 205/UH-1H helicopter and gave it an engine with higher power, larger rotor, improved rotor system that reduced noise and gave better performance at high speeds, strengthened airframe, and other features. A single 214-Huey Plus tested most of these changes with a 1,900-shp Lycoming T53-L-702 turboshaft engine and a gross takeoff weight of 11,000 pounds. Next, a similar 214A demonstration aircraft with a 2,050-shp T55-L-7C was built and flown to Iran. Based on this aircraft and Iranian requirements, the production 214A was specified. In time, Bell designed the 214ST specifically for production and service in Iran. The initials ST originally indicated Stretched Twin, to indicate the provision of two General Electric 1,625-shp turboshaft engines connected to a combining gearbox. Because the 214ST retained the basic UH-1H/205 configuration despite twin engines, it remained in the 214 series.

Following development of the 214-Huey Plus and the 214A demonstration aircraft, on 22 December 1972, Bell announced an Iranian order for 287 214A variants, to be contracted through the U.S. Army. Six more were ordered in March 1977, and 39 of the 214C variant configured for SAR were ordered for Iran in February 1976. Afterwards, Bell announced the co-production with IHI of 50 model 214A helicopters to be followed by 350 twin-engine 214ST variants entirely by IHI. Thus, a total of 732 214As of all variants were planned for the Iranian armed forces before the 1979 revolution. Actual deliveries were 296 A models and 39 C models. A military version of the 214A is also being built in Italy under license by Agusta. A 214B Biglifter, with a Lycoming T550-8D producing 2,930 shp, as well as the 214ST are also being offered for commercial service by Bell. Isfahan is the Iranian name for the helicopter.

First flight: 13 March 1974    Service introduction: 26 April 1975    Users: Iran

**Characteristics (214A)**

Crew: 1 pilot
Engine: 1 Lycoming LTC4B-8D turboshaft 2,930 shp
Dimensions: length 50 ft (15.24 m); height 15 ft 10½ in (4.84 m); rotor diameter 50 ft (15.24 m)
Weight: empty 7,450 lbs (3,382 kg); loaded 16,000 lbs (7,264 kg)
Speed: cruise 150 mph (241 km/h); maximum 161 mph (259 km/h)
Range: 299 miles (481 km)
Ceiling: hover OGE 13,000 ft (3,963 m); hover IGE 16,000 ft (4,877 m)
Climb: 1,720 ft/min (525 m/min)
Payload: 15 troops

An Iranian 214A improved Huey helicopter displays its desert camouflage paint scheme. Despite the cutback in production of this model after the fall of the Shah of Iran's government in 1979, total Huey-series production has been greater than that of any other helicopter. (Bell)

# Bell

409                                              H-63

In June 1973 the U.S. Army awarded Bell a contract to design and build two Advanced Attack Helicopter (AAH) prototypes to compete against the Hughes YAH-64 for the AAH award. Designated the YAH-63, the Bell AAH was based upon the company-funded Model 309 King Cobra, which embodies systems and performance characteristics closely approximating those required for the AAH. The first prototype YAH-63 flew in October 1975 but crashed on 4 June 1976, shortly before it was due to be handed over to the Army for evaluation. It was repaired and entered the competition in August. On 10 December 1976, the Army selected the Hughes YAH-64 for further development in the AAH program and the Bell Model 409 program was terminated.

The YAH-63 differed in many respects from the winning YAH-64 design, having a very wide chord, a two-bladed main rotor, and a two-bladed tail rotor, with tricycle wheeled landing gear and a T-shaped tail with no movable surfaces. A wing was provided with a span of 17 ft 2½ in. Unlike all other attack helicopters designed to date, the AH-63's pilot sat forward of the copilot/gunner to improve his visibility for Nap-Of-the-Earth (NOE) flying. Both the YAH-63 and -64 had the same armament (this was a requirement specified in the AAH competition): a 30-mm cannon turret positioned under the chin, 16 TOW or Hellfire missiles, or 4 pods of 19 2.75-inch rockets. Both shared the same power plant, the General Electric T700-GE-700 turboshaft, and both mounted the engines on the upper sides of the fuselage.

The two flying prototypes and one ground test vehicle were the only YAH-63s built. Bell did not continue to develop its losing entry and turn it ultimately into a success as it had following its unsuccessful entry in the Light Observation Helicopter Competition 13 years before (see OH-4/TH-57/OH-58 series).

First flight: 1 October 1975     Service introduction: not operational

**Characteristics**

Crew: 1 pilot, 1 copilot/gunner
Engines: 2 General Electric T700-GE-700 turboshafts 1,536 shp each
Dimensions: length 60 ft 9 in (18.51 m); height 12 ft 3 in (3.73 m); rotor diameter 51
    ft (15.54 m)
Weight: maximum 15,940 lbs (7,237 kg)
Speed: cruise 167 mph (269 km/h); maximum 202 mph (325 km/h)
Range:
Ceiling: hover OGE 6,500 ft (1,980 m)
Climb: 500 ft/min (152 m/min)
Payload: see text

Bell built two prototype YAH-63 helicopters for the U.S. Army's AAH competition of
1973. It lost to the Hughes YAH-64. Like virtually all Bell helicopters, the YAH-63 had a
two-bladed rotor but differed significantly from other Bell helicopter designs. The tail fin
had a T design with a small horizontal guard for the anti-torque tail rotor at its base. (Bell)

A YAH-63 AAH prototype simultaneously fires four pods of 2.75-inch rockets mounted on
the stub wings. Alternative AAH payloads were 16 antitank missiles. (Bell)

# Bell

301                                    V-15

The XV-15 tilt-rotor VSTOL aircraft was developed under the aegis of the U.S. Army and National Aeronautics and Space Administration (NASA) to demonstrate the potential role of this concept for military aircraft. Research began in 1951, resulting in the Bell-produced XV-3 convertiplane (*q.v.*). Design work on the XV-15 began in 1973 with the first of two prototype aircraft flying four years later. The U.S. Navy subsequently supported the program with the XV-15 becoming the leading candidate for a Navy-Marine Corps VSTOL aircraft for deployment in the early 1990s. Potential Navy roles are Airborne Early Warning (AEW) and Antisubmarine Warfare (ASW), as successor to the E-2 Hawkeye, S-3 Viking, and SH-3 Sea King; the Marine Corps is interested primarily in a medium-lift assault helicopter to replace the CH-46 Sea Knight and CH-53A/D Sea Stallion. In the latter role the XV-15 derivative would have a 23-troop capacity. Antihelicopter gunship and other roles have also been proposed. The Navy derivatives described above would have a loaded weight of approximately 30,000 pounds.

The XV-15 has two three-bladed rotors in twin nacelles that rotate to a horizontal position for conventional flight. Drive shafts are interconnected for emergency single-engine flight. The large rotor diameters necessitate that the aircraft takes off and lands with the nacelles angled upward. STOL operation is possible to obtain maximum payload. The nacelles are mounted on a short, high wing. The semi-monocoque fuselage is of conventional design with endplate tail fins. The tricycle landing gear is fully retractable. Wingspan over engine nacelles is 35 1/6 feet, and maximum width over rotor blades is 57 1/6 feet.

The second XV-15, which first flew on 23 April 1979, was the first to fully convert from helicopter to aircraft flight, doing so on 24 July 1979. A speed of 346 mph was reached in level flight on 17 June 1980. The technology demonstrators have civil registrations N702NA and N703NA.

First flight: 3 May 1977     Service introduction: not operational

A Bell XV-15 technology-demonstration aircraft flies in a conventional aircraft configuration with its engine/rotor nacelles in the horizontal position. Although the two prototypes have civil registrations, N 702NA and N703NA, they are funded by NASA and the Army (whose names are indicated on the tail fin) as well as by the U.S. Navy. (Bell)

## Characteristics

Crew: 1 pilot, 1 copilot

Engines: 2 Avco Lycoming LTC1K-4K turboshaft 1,800 shp each (for 2 minutes contingency; 1,550 shp each continuous)

Dimensions: length 42 ft 1 in (12.83 m); height 15 ft 4 in (4.67 m)*; rotor diameter 25 ft (7.62 m)

Weight: empty 9,670 lbs (4,390 kg); loaded 13,000 lbs (5,902 kg); maximum STOL takeoff 15,000 lbs (6,810 kg)

Speed: cruise 230-350 mph (370-564 km/h); maximum 382 mph (615 km/h)

Range: 512 miles (825 km)

Ceiling: hover OGE 8,650 ft (2,635 m); service with 1 engine 15,000 ft (4,570 m); service 29,000 ft (8,840 m)

Climb: 3000 ft/min (914 m/min)

*Height on rotor hubs when nacelles are in vertical position, tail height is 12 feet 8 inches

An XV-15 in flight with engine/rotor nacelles in the vertical position. The fully retracting landing gear is extended. Note the two-fin tail arrangement compared to the earlier XV-3 design, which was similar in concept. (Bell)

A head-on view of an XV-15 in landing/takeoff configuration. Operational tilt-rotor aircraft would be scaled up in size. Folding wing designs have been worked out for potential naval variants to permit their use aboard aircraft carriers or other surface warships. (Bell)

# Bell
D 292

The U.S. Army is funding the development by Bell of a composite-materials airframe helicopter under the Advanced Composite Aircraft Program (ACAP). The Army's goal is to achieve a weight savings of 22 percent in airframe structure over a baseline helicopter design. Bell's entry in the competition is a new airframe built around the firm's commercial Model 222's engines, transmission, and rotor system. The Bell effort is in competition with an ACAP design based on Sikorsky's S-76 design (formerly given the firm name Spirit).

The Bell 222, which first flew on 13 August 1976, is a light 8-10 seat commercial helicopter with a semi-monocoque fuselage, a highly streamlined design, and fully retracting tricycle landing gear. In the ACAP configuration, the D 292 will have a fixed, tail-sitting landing gear and other changes in addition to the use of advanced composite fuselage materials. Army specifications for the helicopter include rigid crash survival requirements, protection of vital systems to survive direct hits from 23-mm gunfire, and the use of laser-resistant structures and radar-absorbing materials to enhance "stealth" characteristics.

Model 222 helicopters are in wide commercial use, especially in support of offshore oil rigs. The helicopter was one of the two finalists in the U.S. Coast Guard's competition for a Short Range Rescue (SRR) aircraft, losing to the Aérospatiale SA 365. Under ACAP the Army will procure three helicopters from Bell and three from Sikorsky, with test flights to begin by September 1984. The helicopters will be considered technology demonstrators vice production prototypes. The following data are Army design specifications.

The Bell entry in the Army's Advanced Composite Aircraft Program, shown in this artist's sketch, will be only slightly smaller than the standard commercial Bell 222 helicopter which has a maximum takeoff weight of 7,850 pounds. The D 292 will have the traditional Bell two-bladed main rotor and a two-bladed anti-torque tail rotor on the left side of the vertical tail fin. (Bell)

**Characteristics**

Crew: 1 pilot, 1 crewman
Engines: 2 Avco Lycoming LTS 101-650C-2 turboshaft 675 shp each
Dimensions: rotor diameter 39 ft 9 in (12.12 m)
Weight: loaded approximately 7,500 lbs (3,405 kg)
Speed:
Range:
Ceiling:
Climb:
Payload: 2 troops

# Berliner

Between 1909 and 1925, Emile Berliner and his son Henry experimented with a variety of rotary-wing aircraft concepts and successfully flew a form of helicopter as early as 1919. The senior Berliner was a competitor with Edison in the development of the telephone and the gramophone.

There was some sponsorship of the Berliner efforts by the U.S. Army during the 1920s, when they modified a number of aircraft with monoplane, biplane and triplane configurations, powered by Le Rhône rotary engines, and usually with side-by-side, two-bladed wooden rotors mounted above the wings. The rotors were enlarged airscrews, with various systems of vanes in the rotor downwash for lateral control, and other devices being fitted in some experiments.

The Berliner helicopter flies over a flowered field at College Park, Maryland, a suburb of Washington, D.C. This was Berliner's first successful flight in 1922 with his aircraft in a monoplane configuration. College Park is credited with being the nation's first airport. (U.S. Air Force)

In this view of the Berliner helicopter, its wing is removed, and the main rotors and small tail rotor (atop fuselage) are clearly visible. (U.S. Air Force)

The Berliner helicopter in flight as a triplane. (U.S. Air Force)

The Berliner helicopter as a biplane. (U.S. Air Force)

# Boeing Vertol

| 107 | HC-1A | CH-113 { Labrador |
| | HRB } Sea Knight | Voyageur |
| | H-46 } | HKP-4 |
| | | KV-107 |

The Model 107 was developed in the late 1950s by Boeing Vertol for evaluation by the U.S. Army as a medium-lift troop transport. Ten 107s were ordered by the U.S. Army in 1958 as the YHC-1A, but this order was cut back to three when Boeing Vertol produced its Model 114 the next year. Five Model 114s were purchased as YHC-1Bs, although they were basically different aircraft from the Model 107s. The Army selected the YHC-1B for development, while the U.S. Marine Corps decided to procure the YHC-1A in quantity as the HRB-1. (In 1962 the YHC-lA/HRB-1 was redesignated CH-46A, while the YHC-1B became the CH-47A.)

The tandem rotor design is configured to take maximum advantage of the small, lightweight turboshaft engines. Two power plants are at the upper rear of the fuselage to facilitate the loading of vehicles or troops directly into the cabin. The 107s are powered by two General Electric turboshafts which drive two tandem, three-bladed, contra-rotating rotors. The blades installed at Boeing Vertol and Kawasaki plants are of steel and aluminum with 275 U.S. Navy and Marine Corps aircraft being refitted from 1980 onward with fiberglass blades. The fuselage, which is watertight for emergency water landings, is a semi-monocoque structure with the cockpit at the forward end of the main cabin. A non-retractable tricycle landing gear is provided, with the main wheels projecting from small sponsons on the after end of the fuselage. While the CH-46 Sea Knight is similar to the CH-47 Chinook design, the two aircraft are easily distinguishable from one another by their different sponsons (the CH-46 has small after sponsons while the CH-47 has full length fuselage sponsons) as well as by their different landing gear configurations.

Originally ordered for the U.S. Navy and Marine Corps with the designation HRB, the H-46 serves as the Marines' medium assault helicopter, with 12 active squadrons flying the aircraft. The Navy uses the H-46 primarily as a Vertical On-board Delivery (VOD) aircraft to transport munitions and supplies from auxiliary ships to warships, especially aircraft carriers. The Marine Corps began upgrading 275 aircraft to the CH-46E configuration in the early 1980s to provide medium lift capabilities through the decade. Model 107s serve in a number of foreign services, with Kawasaki producing the helicopter for Japanese Self-Defense Forces. (Boeing Vertol production ended in 1971 after 666 machines were produced for military and civilian customers.)

First flight: 22 April 1958     Service introduction: 1962
Users: Burma, Canada, Japan, Saudi Arabia, Sweden, United States

## Variants

| | |
|---|---|
| YHC-1A | prototype for U.S. Army and Marine Corps evaluation; 3 built; changed to CH-46C in 1962. |
| HRB-1 | production model for Marine Corps; 50 built; 46 changed to CH-46A in 1962 and 4 to UH-46A for Navy replenishment operations. |
| CH-46A | production helicopter for Marine Corps; 114 built. |
| HH-46A | SAR modification of CH-46A; doppler radar, modified hull for water operation, rescue hoist. |

| | |
|---|---|
| UH-46A | replenishment production model for Navy; 20 built. |
| RH-46A | CH-46A modified for minesweeping evaluation; 1 converted. |
| CH-46D | similar to CH-46A with 2 General Electric T58-GE-10 turboshafts 1,400 shp each; for Marine Corps; 266 built. |
| UH-46D | replenishment version of CH-46D for Navy; 10 built. |
| CH-46E | modernized CH-46A/D with two GE 1,870-shp T58-GE-16 turboshafts; fiberglass rotor blades; 275 planned for delivery through late 1983. |
| CH-46F | similar to CH-46D; improved avionics; 174 built. |
| CH-113 | Labrador; similar to CH-46A for SAR; 6 built for Canada. |
| CH-113A | Voyageur; similar to CH-46A for troop transport; 12 built for Canada. |
| HKP-4 | similar to CH-46A for Swedish Navy (4 ASW) and Air Force (10 SAR) with Bristol-Siddeley Gnome H 1200 turboshafts; 14 built. |
| KV-107/II-3 | Kawasaki license-built with 2 1,250-shp Ishikawajima-Harima CT58-IHI-110-1 turboshafts; mine countermeasure variant; 9 built for the Japanese Maritime Self-Defense Force (JMSDF). |
| KV-107/II-4 | troop transport for the Japanese Ground Self-Defense Force (JGSDF); 59 built. |
| KV-107/II-5 | SAR variant for the Japanese Air Self-Defense Force (JASDF); 8 to Swedish Navy as HKP-4C; production continuing with 30 built for JASDF by 1980. |
| KV-107/IIA-SM-1 | fire-fighting variant for Saudi Arabia; 4 built. |
| KV-107/IIA-SM-2 | SAR/aeromedical evacuation variant for Saudi Arabia; 2 built. |

**Characteristics (CH-46F)**

Crew: 1 pilot, 1 copilot, 1 crew chief
Engines: 2 General Electric T58-GE-10 turboshafts 1,400 shp each
Dimensions: length 84 ft 4 in (25.7 m); height 16 ft 8½ in (5.09 m); rotor diameter 51 ft (15.54 m)
Weight: empty 13,342 lbs (6,057 kg); loaded 23,000 lbs (10,442 kg)
Speed: cruise 154 mph (248 km/h); maximum 166 mph (267 km/h)
Range: 237 miles (381 km)
Ceiling: hover OGE 5,750 ft (1,753 m); hover IGE 9,500 ft (2,895 m); service 14,000 ft (4,265 m)
Climb: 1,715 ft/min (523 m/min)      Payload: 26 troops

A U.S Marine Corps CH-46F from Marine Medium Helicopter Squadron (HMM) 365 hovers over a helicopter carrier during exercises in the Atlantic. YM is the squadron identification code; 157678 is the bureau number; and 9 is the aircraft's number within the squadron. (U.S. Navy)

A U.S. Marine Corps CH-46A Sea Knight maneuvers to land aboard a helicopter carrier in the Western Pacific. The CH-46 serves mainly as the Marines' medium-lift helicopter and in the SAR and replenishment roles for the U.S. Navy. (U.S. Navy)

A KV-107 of the Japanese Maritime Self-Defense Force in flight. (*Ships of the World*)

Marines board a CH-46F from HMM-261 aboard a helicopter carrier; the Sea Knight has low-visibility markings. (U.S. Navy)

# Boeing Vertol

114

HC-1B
H-47          } Chinook
CH-147

The Chinook is a twin-turbine, tandem-rotor transport helicopter which was selected by the U.S. Army in 1959 as its medium-lift transport over a competing design from the same company. First evaluated as the YHC-1B, the production version was designated CH-47A. Over 1,000 Chinooks had been ordered as of 1980 by a number of military air arms and commercial operators. Production has been shared by Boeing Vertol and its Italian licensee, Meridionali, a division of Agusta.

The CH-47's fuselage is almost a rectangular box; it has a square cross section and is of all-metal, semi-monocoque construction. A large ramp permits the loading of light vehicles and troops into the cabin from the tail. Like the YHC-1A/CH-46A, the dual turboshaft power plants are mounted on the sides of the rear rotor pylon. The two contra-rotating, three-bladed tandem rotors are powered by two 3,750-shp Lycoming turboshafts, giving the helicopter a generous lift capability of almost 30,000 pounds for externally slung cargo. The Chinook was credited with recovering hundreds of downed aircraft during the Vietnam War. The landing gear is a non-retractable, wheeled quadricycle type. In addition to the three-man crew, 44 troops or 24 stretchers can be transported. Four Chinooks were modified to heavy helicopter gunships (ACH-47A) with over 2,000 pounds of armor, a 40-mm grenade launcher, five 7.62-mm machine guns, and two 20-mm multi-barrel Gatling guns. Dubbed "Go-Go Birds," they were evaluated in Vietnam, with two being lost.

The H-47 has become the Western world's standard for a medium-lift helicopter. It is flown by several air forces, and the U.S. Army continues to update and rely upon its Chinook fleet. The RAF had planned to acquire the Chinook as early as March 1967, but that plan finally died with the defense cutbacks in August 1971. Subsequently, the program has been resurrected because of the lack of an adequate medium-lift helicopter, and in 1978 the Chinook was ordered, with 33 being delivered from 1980 onward. Iran, Libya, Morocco, and Italy fly the BV 219 (CH-47C); Australia the BV 165; Canada the BV 173 (CH-147); Spain the BV 176/414; Argentina the BV 308/309; and Great Britain the BV 352 models.

First flight: 21 September 1961     Service introduction: April 1962
Users: Argentina, Australia, Canada, Great Britain, Iran, Italy, Japan, Libya, Morocco, Spain, Thailand, United States, Vietnam

**Variants**

YHC-1B    prototype evaluated by U.S. Army; 5 built, with 1 converted to CH-47B; others changed to YCH-47A in 1962.
CH-47A    production variant with 2 2,850-shp Lycoming T55-L-5 engines; 351 built for U.S. Army.
ACH-47A   gunship version ("Go-Go Bird"); 4 built.
CH-47B    production variant with 2 2,850-shp T55-L-7C turboshafts; redesigned rotor blades; 108 built for U.S. Army.
CH-47C    production variant with 2 3,750-shp T55-L-11A turboshafts; increased fuel, improved transmission, other changes; 270 built for U.S. Army; others for Iran, Italy.
CH-47D    modernized CH-47A/B/C models with 2 T55-L-712 turboshafts; lengthened

fuselage, improved transmissions, fiberglass rotor blades; loaded weight 50,000 lbs; 436 being modernized for U.S. Army; deliveries begin early 1982.

CH-147    CH-47C with 2 T55-L-11C turboshafts; 9 built for Canada.

Chinook    CH-47C with 2 T55-L-11E turboshafts; loaded weight 55,000 lbs; up to 28,000
HC 1    lbs cargo; 33 built for RAF.

## Characteristics

Crew: 1 pilot, 1 copilot, 1 crew chief
Engines: 2 Lycoming T55-L-11A turboshaft 3,750 shp each
Dimensions: length 99 ft (30.18 m); height 18 ft 7⅘ in (5.68 m); rotor diameter
    60 ft (18.29 m)
Weight: empty 21,464 lbs (9,745 kg); loaded 33,000 lbs (14,982 kg)
Speed: cruise 158 mph (254 km/h); maximum 189 mph (304 km/h)
Range: 230 miles (370 km)
Ceiling: hover OGE 13,600 ft (4,145 m); service 15,000 ft (4,570 m)
Climb: 2,880 ft/min (878 m/min)
Payload: 44 troops or 24 stretchers + 2 attendants or 28,000 lbs (12,712 kg) external
    slung cargo

Troops from the Army's 1st Cavalry Division (Air Mobile) climb down from a hovering CH-47 Chinook during the Vietnam War, demonstrating that helicopters could unload troops in an area where they could not hover near the ground or land. (Boeing Vertol)

A U.S. Army CH-47A Chinook lifts a T-33 jet trainer for transfer to a museum. During the Vietnam War the Chinook and other large helicopters recovered several hundred damaged aircraft that would otherwise have been lost. Like the somewhat similar Navy-Marine Corps CH-46, the Chinook has a rear loading ramp, tandem rotors atop streamlined housings, and fixed undercarriage. (Boeing Vertol)

This Canadian Armed Forces CH-147 is configured for long-range rescue operations, with a power winch located above the starboard door opening. Note the broad, flat underside and the Canadian roundel on the bottom of the fuselage as well as on the sides with the Canadian flag on the rear rotor pylon. (Boeing Vertol)

Two of the four ACH-47A "Go-Go Bird" gunships are shown in this photograph. They have a grenade launcher in a chin turret; machine guns and Gatling guns are fitted in fuselage openings, and the in-flight ACH-47A has rocket pods attached to hard points above the forward landing gear. The concept of a medium helicopter gunship was evaluated in Vietnam but was not successful. (Boeing Vertol)

# Boeing Vertol

237                          H-61

The Boeing Vertol YUH-61A was one of two helicopters that competed for the U.S. Army's Utility Tactical Transport Aircraft System (UTTAS) program. Both Boeing Vertol and Sikorsky were awarded contracts on 30 August 1972 to design, build, and test UTTAS prototypes. The first YUH-61A flew in November 1974, and the three prototypes were delivered to the Army in March 1976. After eight months of evaluations, on 23 December 1976, the Army selected the Sikorsky design (S-70/UH-60). The YUH-61A program was terminated at that time. Despite this setback, Boeing Vertol entered a modification of the YUH-61A in the Navy's LAMPS III competition against a Sikorsky modification of its UH-60A UTTAS and a Westland/Aérospatiale modification of their Lynx. Designated Model 237, it competed only on paper against the other two entrants, although a YUH-61A prototype was flown on board a Navy frigate to demonstrate its compatibility with the restricted operating environment on a ship at sea. Like the YUH-61A, the Model 237 also lost the competition to the Sikorsky navalized entrant (SH-60B), the latter being declared the winner of the LAMPS III contract

on 1 September 1977. The YUH-61A/Model 237 design was developed no
further.

Both UTTAS entries shared many characteristics by virtue of the Army specifications that both were designed to meet. Both had wheeled undercarriages and
were powered by two General Electric T700-GE-700 turboshafts; they were
delivered with minimal avionics but duplicate critical components and were
designed to be highly survivable in a combat environment. The first prototype
YUH-61A survived a 4,000-foot out-of-control crash into a stand of oak trees with
no casualties and was repaired to fly again. The YUH-61A differed from the
winning Sikorsky entry in having tricycle landing gear and a hingeless four-
bladed main rotor constructed of composite materials, as well as in being slightly
smaller and lighter. The rotor system design was adapted from that of the
Messerschmitt-Bölkow-Blohm Bö-105, for which Boeing Vertol holds the American license.

First flight: 29 November 1974
Service introduction: not operational

**Variants**

YUH-61A  UTTAS prototype for U.S. Army; 3 built.
Model 237  LAMPS III design offered to U.S. Navy; only mock-up built.

**Characteristics**

Crew: 1 pilot, 1 copilot, 1 crew chief
Engines: 2 General Electric T700-GE-700 turboshafts 1,500 shp each
Dimensions: length 60 ft 8.4 in (18.5 m); height 9 ft 7 in (2.92 m); rotor diameter 49
    ft (14.94 m)
Weight: empty 9,750 lbs (4,422 kg); loaded 19,700 lbs (8,944 kg)
Speed: cruise 167 mph (268 km/h); maximum 178 mph (286 km/h)
Range: 370 miles (595 km)
Ceiling: hover OGE 6,450 ft (1,966 m)
Climb: 664 ft/min (202 m/min)
Payload: 11 troops or 5,924 lbs (2,686 kg) internal cargo

The YUH-61A was Boeing Vertol's entry in the U.S. Army's competition of the early 1970s
for a Utility Tactical Transport Aircraft System (UTTAS), with orders planned for more
than 1,000 of the aircraft. The Boeing Vertol design lost to Sikorsky's UH-60A helicopter.
(Boeing Vertol)

One of three prototypes of the Boeing Vertol entry in the UTTAS competition demonstrates a low-level, high-speed maneuver during flight tests. (Boeing Vertol)

# Boeing Vertol
301                                    H-62

The Heavy Lift Helicopter (HLH) requirement that resulted in the CH-62 design was developed by the U.S. Army during the Vietnam War, although interest in an HLH that could lift most Army equipment dates back to the 1950s. Not until November 1970 was the Army able to formally request industry proposals for the advanced technology components necessary for the HLH concept. The HLH would be required to carry a maximum payload of 20 tons for a radius of 20 nautical miles. Loads up to 16 tons were to be slung under the helicopter, including tanks, bulldozers, artillery, containerized field hospitals, and power generating stations. Up to 20 tons of palletized cargo was to be straddled and lifted by the HLH with maximum pallet size being 40 x 12 x 12 feet. This capability would permit the HLH to lift 100 percent of an airborne division's weapons and equipment, including 16-ton Sheridan tanks, and 60 to 70 percent of the equipment of other Army divisions. Also, with the removal of its rotor blades and undercarriage, the HLH was to be air transportable in a C-5A transport. Boeing Vertol was selected to develop HLH technology, and, as a result, the firm built the Model 347 helicopter, based on the Model 107/CH-47 design. On 29 January 1973 Boeing Vertol was awarded a contract to build a single XCH-62 prototype, with a first flight scheduled for August 1975. However, on 1 October 1974, the Army was forced to cancel the HLH program because of higher-than-expected costs and because the Navy and Marine Corps had decided to pursue the Sikorsky CH-53E for their heavy-lift requirements.

The CH-62 was to have been a tandem-rotor helicopter, with the after four-bladed rotor mounted on a swept-back pylon, a refinement of the H-46/H-47 designs. The cargo operator was to have been seated in a rear-facing station behind the cockpit. Three turboshaft engines were to have been housed in the rear of the fuselage with power to have been transmitted to a combiner transmission, thus providing a single power source to the two rotor shafts. The planned hoist system was to have been able to lift up to 16 tons while the helicopter would have been capable of straddling palletized cargo up to 20 tons, which would be attached to fuselage hard points. Internal seating was planned for 35 troops, with high-density seating possible for 55. The fixed tricyle landing gear (with rear wheel) was to have been removable for air transport of the HLH, and it was intended that the helicopter could "kneel" on its landing gear to permit stowage on an aircraft carrier's hangar deck with a 19½-foot overhead. The rotor blades could also have been folded for carrier operation.

The U.S. Army planned at one point to procure approximately 150 of these helicopters. Navy and Marine Corps requirements for an HLH at that time totaled some 75 to 150 for an aggregate U.S. military requirement of some 300 helicopters. The prototype was not completed. A civil version to carry up to 110 passengers for short distances was under consideration, but was not pursued after cancellation of the military project.

First flight: not flown

### Characteristics

Crew: 1 pilot, 1 copilot, 1 flight engineer, 1 crew chief, 1 cargo operator
Engines: 3 Allison T701-AD-700 turboshaft 8,079 shp each with combining transmission to have an output rating of 17,700 shp
Dimensions: length 89 ft 3 in (27.2 m); height to after rotor hub 28 ft 7½ in (8.7 m); rotor diameter 92 ft (28.0 m)
Weight: empty 58,929 lbs (26,754 kg); loaded 118,000 lbs (53,572 kg)
Speed:
Range: 23-mile (37-km) radius with 40,000 lbs (18,160 kg) cargo; 1,000-mile (1,610-km) radius with 10,000 lbs (4,540 kg) cargo
Ceiling:
Climb:
Payload: 55 troops + 40,000 lbs (18,160 kg) external cargo

This is the unfinished Boeing Vertol XCH-62 (serial 72-2012), the planned prototype of the Army's HLH program. Note the rear-facing position for the cargo operator and the overall similarity to the Boeing Vertol 107/114 designs for tandem-rotor helicopters. (Boeing Vertol)

This is Boeing Vertol's 347, built to test HLH systems and concepts. A retractable cargo-operator's cockpit facing rearwards was fitted just in front of the forward landing gear. (Boeing Vertol)

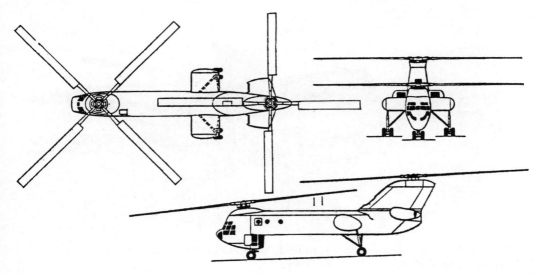

# Bothezat

The first U.S. Government-sponsored rotary-wing aircraft was developed by Dr. George A. de Bothezat, a former professor of the Petrograd Technical Institute. Beginning work in the United States in 1921, he designed and constructed a four-rotor, single-engine machine for the U.S. Army Air Service. The Bothezat machine's first flight, in late 1922, took it to a height of about 6 feet and it drifted with the wind to land some 500 feet away. During a two-year period the helicopter reached a height of about 30 feet. On one flight on 17 April 1923, it flew with three and then four men clinging to the outriggers to demonstrate stability in unbalanced and overload conditions.

The Bothezat machine had a large frame structure with four large, widely separated rotors to provide lift. Each six-bladed rotor had an individual collective pitch mechanism, with the pilot controlling the angle of the rotors. The rotors and two small vertical propellers were turned by a single 180-hp engine (later replaced by a 220-hp engine).

After extensive trials over a two-year period, with an Army investment of the then-considerable sum of $200,000, the helicopter was abandoned as being too complex. It also failed to meet the Army's requirement to go up 300 feet and return to the point of takeoff. Only one machine was built.

First flight: 18 December 1922        Service introduction: not operational

### Characteristics

Crew: 1 pilot
Engine: 1 Le Rhône radial 180 hp (later replaced with a similar 220-hp engine)
Dimensions: rotor diameter 26 ft 6 in (8.1 m)
Weight: loaded 3,748 lbs (1,700 kg)
Speed:
Range: maximum flight endurance approximately 2 minutes
Ceiling: hover 30 ft (9.0 m)
Climb:

The de Bothezat helicopter on the ground. "de Bothezat Helicopter" is printed on the tail (right) of the helicopter. (U.S. Air Force)

Three men hold onto the outriggers and tail (left) of the de Bothezat helicopter in a demonstration of the aircraft's stability during tests at McCook Field in Dayton, Ohio, in 1922-1923. (U.S. Army)

# Brantly

B-2                                    HO-3

The Brantly B-2 was a light, two-place commercial helicopter with an unusual blade arrangement including hinges at the hub and mid-blade which created a double articulation. Five examples of the B-2 were procured for evaluation by the U.S. Army in 1959 as the YHO-3, but no production orders resulted.

The B-2's fuselage was a stressed-skin structure with a monocoque, conical tailboom. The three-bladed main and two-bladed tail rotors were of all-metal construction and powered by a 180-hp Lycoming flat-four cyclinder engine. Tested originally with a wheeled undercarriage, the landing gear was changed to a skid type before the Army prototypes were delivered.

First flight: B-2 21 February 1953
Service introduction: not operational

**Characteristics**

Crew: 1 pilot, 1 copilot/observer
Engine: 1 Lycoming VO-360-A1A piston 180 hp
Dimensions: length 21 ft 9 in (6.62 m); height 6 ft 11¾ in (2.13 m); rotor diameter 23 ft 8⅞ in (7.24 m)
Weight: empty 980 lbs (445 kg); loaded 1,600 lbs (726 kg)
Speed: cruise 90 mph (145 km/h); maximum 100 mph (161 km/h)
Range: 300 miles (480 km)
Ceiling: hover 4,700 ft (1,430 m)
Climb: 1,580 ft/min (480 m/min)

This is one of the five YHO-3 light helicopters evaluated by the U.S. Army (serials 58-1492/496). Note the wheels that can be lowered below the skids to facilitate ground handling, the low-slung cockpit with bubble domes for the two crewmen, and the tapering fuselage shape. Besides the one-man, strap-on devices, the YHO-3 was one of the smallest helicopters evaluated by the U.S. Army. (U.S. Army)

# Cessna

CH-1                                                    H-41 Seneca

Cessna entered the helicopter market with the acquisition of the Seibel Helicopter Company in 1952. The CH-1 commercial helicopter series soon followed, the first CH-1 Skyhook flying in 1954. This four-seat utility helicopter had a cabin layout very similar to that of the Cessna series of light, private airplanes. Continued development of the commercial version resulted in the Model CH-1B, which was evaluated by the U.S. Army under the designation YH-41 Seneca. No military production resulted. Commercial production of the CH-1 Skyhook was terminated in December 1962 after Cessna determined that the helicopter market had not yet matured to the point at which continued investment would be profitable.

As evaluated by the U.S. Army, the YH-41 Seneca was a four-place, light observation helicopter with two-bladed main and anti-torque tail rotors, powered by a 260-hp six-cylinder Continental piston engine. The fuselage was an all-metal pod-and-boom type with skids for landing gear. Ten YH-41s were built for Army high altitude tests and evaluation. Some of these were subsequently redesignated NH-41A in 1962 to reflect their research role. Four were built for service with Ecuador's armed services.

First flight: CH-1 July 1954     Service introduction:          Users: Ecuador

**Characteristics**

Crew: 1 pilot, 1 copilot/observer
Engine: 1 Continental FSO-526 6-cylinder piston 260 hp
Dimensions: length 42 ft 8 in (13 m); height 8 ft 5 in (2.56 m); rotor diameter 35 ft (10.67 m)
Weight: empty 2,080 lbs (943 kg); loaded 3,100 lbs (1,406 kg)
Speed: cruise 95 mph (153 km/h); maximum 122 mph (196 km/h)
Range: 310 miles (500 km)
Ceiling: hover OGE 6,500 ft (1,980 m); hover IGE 9,600 ft (2,925 m); service 12,200 ft (3,720 m)
Climb: 1,030 ft/min (314 m/min)
Payload: 2 troops

Another light helicopter evaluated by the U.S. Army in the 1950s was the Cessna YH-41. The engine was in the nose with the rotor shaft between the two crewmen. The YH-41 Seneca had a distinctive cockpit shape and flat nose. (U.S. Army)

# Consolidated/Pennsylvania Aircraft Syndicate

## OZ

The U.S. Navy's single XOZ-1 autogiro was a Consolidated N2Y-1 tandem-seat, biplane trainer (Navy BuNo. A8602) rebuilt in the mid-1930s as an autogiro. Six of the basic N2Y-1 aircraft were purchased after evaluation of an XN2Y-1, originally a civilian Fleet I. These planes were used as familiarization trainers for the Navy "skyhook" pilots who flew fighters from the large Navy airships *Akron* and *Macon*.

The XOZ-1 was modified to an autogiro configuration by the Pennsylvania Aircraft Syndicate, with a four-bladed autogiro rotor, held aloft over the forward cockpit by four steel struts, replacing the upper wing. The lower wing was retained and supports added, and the wheeled undercarriage was replaced by twin floats. The two-bladed wooden air screw was retained, as were the two open, tandem cockpits. Wingspan was 27 ft 4 in.

The aircraft was tested by the National Advisory Committee for Aeronautics (predecessor to NASA).

First flight: 1937    Service introduction: not operational

### Characteristics

Crew: 1 pilot, 1 observer
Engine: 1 Kinner K-5 radial piston 155 hp
Dimensions: length 21 ft 4 in (6.5 m); height 10 ft (3.05 m); rotor diameter 32 ft (9.77 m)
Weight: empty 1,455 lbs (660 kg); loaded 1,985 lbs (900 kg)
Speed: cruise 90 mph (145 km/h); maximum 107 mph (172 km/h)
Range:            Ceiling:            Climb:

This is the lone Navy XOZ-1, a biplane conversion intended to demonstrate autogiro concepts. Note the four-legged pylon supporting the four-bladed rotor and the absence of a drive shaft to the rotor, which is necessary in a helicopter. (U.S. Navy)

# Curtiss-Wright
200                                    X-19

The X-19 was a U.S. military-sponsored development of the Curtiss-Wright "radical lift force" propeller concept. Although the aircraft had propellers vice rotors, they functioned in the same manner as the tilt-rotor concept tested by Bell in the XV-3 and XV-15 aircraft. Four propeller pods could be rotated from a forward position 90 degrees to the vertical position for VTOL and STOL operation. The propellers produced lift when in the forward-flight position as well as in the upward-angle configurations. Curtiss-Wright had earlier built the X-100 as a private venture to test the concept, with that aircraft having made its first STOL flight in March 1960. The U.S. Air Force ordered two prototypes of the Curtiss-Wright 200 on 17 July 1962 (serial 62-12197/198) with the designation X-19A. Subsequently, their evaluation became a tri-service Army-Navy-Air Force program. Interest was expressed in using the possible derivatives of the X-19A in the SAR, reconnaissance, transport, close air support, and armed escort and attack (i.e., "gunship") roles.

The X-19 prototypes had a conventional, semi-monocoque fuselage and fin-tail structure; two sets of high wings were fitted, one forward and one aft, with four wing-tip propeller pods fitted that could swivel upward 90 degrees. The span over the fiberglass propellers was 34 feet 6 inches. Two turboshaft engines were installed in the rear fuselage, with single-engine flight being possible in emergency situations. The nose-wheel tricycle landing gear was fully retractable into the fuselage. The prototypes had cabin seating for six.

The first prototype X-19A was delivered in 1963 and was used in flight tests until it crashed in August 1965. The second aircraft did not fly and the program was terminated in 1966. This was apparently the last aircraft to be built by the Curtiss-Wright firm.

First flight:                Service introduction: not operational

The first X-19 prototype hovering at low altitude. The after propeller pods are inclined slightly forward in this view taken at the firm's airport in Caldwell, N.J. (Curtiss-Wright)

**Characteristics**

Crew: 1 pilot, 1 copilot
Engines: 2 Lycoming T55-L-5 turboshaft 2,200 shp each
Dimensions: length 43 ft 5 in (13.23 m); height 16 ft (4.88 m)
Weight: loaded 12,300 lbs (5,580 kg)
Speed:
Range:
Ceiling:
Climb:
Payload: 4 troops

The X-19 is believed to have been the last aircraft produced by the Curtiss-Wright organization and the only rotary-wing aircraft formally attempted by that firm. The tilting propeller pods were similar to an extent to the Bell tilt-rotor concept. The X-19 was a "tri-service" program, funded by the U.S. Army, Navy, and Air Force. (Curtiss-Wright)

# Doman

LZ-5                                          H-31

The Doman LZ-5 was an eight-place utility helicopter evaluated by the U.S. Army as the YH-31. The YH-31 was unique for its time, having a completely sealed, rigid, non-articulated main rotor system, with four plastic-bonded laminated birch rotor blades that were covered with a plastic-bonded mahogany ply. The tail rotor had three blades of similar construction. The rotors were driven by a 400-hp Lycoming eight-cylinder piston engine that enabled the LZ-5 to travel at speeds in excess of 100 mph. The fuselage was a welded steel-tube framework covered with aluminum and magnesium skin. The landing gear was a wheeled quadricycle type with an unusual wheelbase of 7 feet 9 inches and a track of 7 feet 2 inches.

The commercial LZ-5 was relatively successful; American production was centered at the Doman plant in Danbury, Connecticut, and Canadian production in Ontario. However, the two YH-31s evaluated by the U.S. Army constituted the only military procurement of the Doman machine.

First flight: 27 April 1953
Service introduction: not operational

**Characteristics**

Crew: 1 pilot, 1 copilot
Engine: 1 Lycoming SO-580-A1A piston 400 hp
Dimensions: length 38 ft (11.57 m); height 10 ft 5 in (3.17 m); rotor diameter 48 ft (14.64 m)
Weight: empty 3,250 lbs (1,475 kg); loaded 5,200 lbs (2,360 kg)
Speed: cruise 99 mph (160 km/h); maximum 104 mph (166.4 km/h)
Range: 245 miles (392 km)
Ceiling: hover IGE 4,000 ft (1,216 m); service 11,500 ft (3,505 m)
Climb: 850 ft/min (259 m/min)
Payload: 1,950 lbs (885 kg) internal cargo

One of two prototype Doman YH-31 helicopters lifts off during flight tests. This odd-looking utility machine was not considered successful. The prototypes (52-5779/780) received minor modifications during their Army evaluation (e.g., the small horizontal stabilizers mounted on the tailboom here were removed). A Sikorsky H-19 sits in the background. (U.S. Army)

# Fairchild Hiller

FH1100                                    HO-5
                                          H-5

The Fairchild Hiller FH1100 is a light four- or five-place utility helicopter developed by Hiller (prior to its takeover by Fairchild Industries) for the U.S. Army's 1963-1964 Light Observation Helicopter (LOH) competition. Five prototype OH-5As were built for evaluation by the Army in competition with the Bell OH-4A and the Hughes OH-6A. (Prior to 1962 these helicopters were designated the Army's HO series.) The Hughes entry won this competition, and, like Bell, Hiller further developed its entry into a viable commercial helicopter. Unlike Bell, however, no derivatives of the FH1100 commercial version were purchased by the U.S. Government, although several foreign governments procured a few FH1100s as utility helicopters for their air arms.

The FH1100's fuselage is composed of two sections, a semi-monocoque cabin area and a tailboom. The two-bladed, semi-rigid main rotor and two-bladed aluminum tail rotor are driven by a 317-shp Allison 250-C18 turboshaft engine. Equipped with twin skid landing gear, both the prototype OH-5As and the commercial FH1100s could be armed with 7.62-mm machine-gun packs, grenade launchers, or antisubmarine weapons.

Although rejected by the U.S. Government, the FH1100 found military purchasers in a variety of Third World nations. A total of 246 OH-5As and FH1100s were produced for civilian and military users before Fairchild closed down the line in 1973. In 1980 an independent Hiller Aviation, Inc., bought the rights and tooling to produce the FH1100 with the intention of reopening the production line in 1981. Whether additional military orders will follow remains uncertain.

First flight: 26 January 1963
Service introduction: 1963
Users: Argentina, Ecuador, El Salvador, Philippines, Thailand

**Variants**

OH-5A    FH1100 evaluated by U.S. Army for the Light Observation Helicopter competition of 1963-1964; originally designated HO-5; 5 built.

FH1100    commercial version sold in Third World to military as well as to civilian customers; 241 built

**Characteristics**

Crew: 1 pilot
Engine: 1 Allison 250-C18 turboshaft 317 shp
Dimensions: length 39 ft 9½ in (12.13 m); height 9 ft 3½ in (2.83 m); rotor diameter 35 ft 5 in (10.8 m)
Weight: empty 1,396 lbs (633 kg); loaded 2,750 lbs (1,247 kg)
Speed: cruise 122 mph (196 km/h); maximum 127 mph (204 km/h)
Range: 348 miles (560 km)
Ceiling: service 14,200 ft (4,325 m)
Climb: 1,600 ft/min (488 m/min)
Payload: 3 or 4 troops

The Fairchild Hiller FH1100 in flight during the U.S. Army's LOH evaluation. Marked "experimental," this OH-5A has the civil registration N 81006 (the N prefix for U.S. civil aircraft). While not selected for Army use, the FH1100 was further developed for commercial operation. (Fairchild Hiller)

# Firestone
45                                    R-9

Intended for battlefield liaison, the R-9 was a small helicopter bearing a superficial resemblance to the contemporary Sikorsky machines. It had a small plexiglass-enclosed cockpit forward of the engine, a three-bladed main rotor, a narrow tailboom supporting a small anti-torque rotor, and a light tricycle landing gear. The fuselage had a metal alloy skin.

Neither of the two R-9 prototypes ordered in 1944 was completed, although a modified XR-9B was delivered in March 1946.

First flight:
Service introduction: not operational

**Variants**

XR-9    prototype model 45B with Lycoming XO-290-5 126-hp engine; 3-bladed rotor; 1,387 lbs loaded; not completed.

XR-9A   prototype model 45C with same engine; 2-bladed rotor; 1,380 lbs loaded; not
        completed.
XR-9B   prototype; modified model 45C; 1 built (serial 46-001).

**Characteristics**

Crew: 1 pilot
Engine: 1 Lycoming O-290-7 piston 135 hp
Dimensions: length 27 ft 7 in (8.4 m); height 8 ft 6½ in (2.6 m); rotor diameter 28 ft
    (8.5 m)
Weight: loaded 1,750 lbs (795 kg)
Speed: cruise 80 mph (128 km/h)
Range: 250 miles (400 km)
Ceiling: service 10,000 ft (3,050 m)
Climb: 1,000 ft/min (305 m/min)
Payload: 1 passenger

The single XR-9B was the only aircraft of this type to be completed. The serial 6001 on the
tailboom identifies it as the first U.S. Army aircraft ordered in 1946—the first of the
postwar period. Note that the national insignia lacks red bars on the white panel on either
side of the star; these were added on U.S. aircraft in 1947. The panel borders and star
background are blue. (U.S. Army)

This rear view of the XR-9B shows the narrow cross section of this light helicopter. There is
no tail control surface, only a skid to protect the anti-torque rotor, which is on the right side
of the tailboom. (U.S. Army)

# Firestone

## R-14

The U.S. Army planned to procure three lightweight R-14 helicopters from Firestone in 1946 to compete with the Bell 54 (R-15/H-15). However, the project was cancelled. The R-14 was to have had a three-bladed main rotor and a fan-cooled engine. A pilot and observer were to have been seated in tandem.

First flight: not flown

**Characteristics**

Crew: 1 pilot, 1 observer
Engine: 1 XO-470-1 piston

# Gyrodyne

GCA-41                              RON Rotorcycle
GCA-59                              DSN ⎤
                                    H-50 ⎦ DASH

The Gyrodyne Rotorcycle was built to compete for a U.S. Navy contract for a small, portable helicopter capable of carrying one man and his equipment over a short distance. Like the Hiller ROE, the RON could be folded into a small package that could be air-dropped and assembled by one man under combat conditions. The RON differed from its contemporary, the ROE, by using a pair of contra-rotating coaxial main rotors, alleviating the need for anti-torque tail rotors. The program terminated after some 15 XRON and YRON test helicopters were built and evaluated by the Navy and Marine Corps. However, a derivative of the RON was produced in quantity for the Navy in the Drone Antisubmarine Helicopter (DASH) program. The unmanned DASH was designed to give surface warships standoff ASW attack capabilities through the use of a drone ASW torpedo delivery platform.

The fuselage of both the RON and DSN/QH-50 was an aluminum tubular structure to which were attached the engine, landing gear, and all necessary equipment. Both the RON and most models of the drone version had inverted-V tail surfaces to provide directional and longitudinal stability, but these were deleted in the QH-50D version. The RON had wheeled tricycle landing gear while the QH-50 was fitted with skids.

During a DASH mission the QH-50 drone was "piloted" during takeoff and landing by the destroyer's DASH officer from a central console adjacent to the destroyer's flight deck. Control would be transferred after takeoff to an officer in the ship's Combat Information Center, who would "fly" the QH-50 by radar to the suspected location of the enemy submarine, as indicated by the destroyer's sonar, and drop its payload of one Mk-46 or two Mk-44 torpedoes. Effective range was thus limited to the destroyer's radar horizon. Ideally, the drone would then be flown back and recovered aboard the destroyer, but many of the QH-50s were lost during this phase of the mission. This was generally due either to the sudden change in the configuration of the helicopter after the payload was dropped, or simply to the inexperience of the DASH officer. Most QH-50s were withdrawn from service long before their destroyer platforms, although some were used as unmanned reconnaissance drones in the Vietnam War, and a few were used into the early 1980s as target drones for programs such as the U.S. Navy's Submarine Air Defense (SUBAD) missile. Over 500 QH-50s in four different variants were built for the U.S. Navy with several being delivered for service with the Japanese Maritime Self-Defense Force. A few QH-50C drones were still used in the United States as targets in the early 1980s.

First flight: RON 1956, DSN 1958
Service introduction: DSN/QH-50 7 January 1963
Users: Japan, United States

**Variants**

XRON-1  prototype rotorcycle with 40-hp Nelson H-59 piston engine; 15-ft rotors; 2 built with 1 later converted to 62-shp Solar T62 turboshaft with 17-ft rotors.
YRON-1  evaluation helicopter for Marine Corps with 62-hp Porsche YO-95-2 piston engine; 17-ft rotor; 3 built; some converted to 72-hp Porsche YO-95-6 engine with 20-ft rotor.
DSN-1   initial DASH version similar to YRON-1 with 72-hp Porsche engine; provision for safety pilot; first shipboard landing with pilot aboard on 1 July 1960; first drone shipboard flight on 7 December 1960; 9 built; changed to QH-50A in 1962.
DSN-2   similar to DSN-1 with 2 86-shp Porsche engines; piloted version only; tested equipment for production version; 3 built; changed to QH-50B in 1962.
DSN-3   production version with 270-shp Boeing T50-BO-4 turboshaft; changed to QH-50C in 1962.
QH-50D  final production version with 365-shp Boeing T50-BO-12 turboshaft; fiberglass rotor blades.

**Characteristics**

Crew: RON 1 pilot
      DSN unmanned
Engines: RON 1 Porsche YO YO-9 piston 62 hp
        QH-50D 1 Boeing T50-BO-15 turboshaft 365 shp

|  |  | YRON-1 | QH-50D |
|---|---|---|---|
| Dimensions: | length | 11 ft ½ in (3.36 m) | 7 ft 3½ in (2.22 m) |
|  | height | 8 ft (2.44 m) | 9 ft 8½ in (2.96 m) |
|  | rotor | 17 ft (5.18 m) | 20 ft (6.1 m) |
| Weight: | empty | 430 lbs (195 kg) | 1,035 lbs (470 kg) |
|  | loaded | 700 lbs (318 kg) | 2,328 lbs (1,056 kg) |
| Speed: | cruise |  | 63 mph (101 km/h) |
|  | maximum | 68 mph (109 km/h) | 92 mph (148 km/h) |
| Range: |  | 59 miles (95 km) | 141 miles (227 km) |
| Ceiling: | hover OGE |  | 11,300 ft (3,445 m) |
|  | hover IGE |  | 16,300 ft (4,965 m) |
|  | service |  | 16,000 ft (4,875 m) |
| Climb: |  | 410 ft/min (125 m/min) | 2,815 ft/min (856 m/min) |
| Payload: |  | nil | 2 Mk-44 or 1 Mk-46 ASW homing torpedo |

A QH-50D radio-controlled drone in flight. The contra-rotating propellers alleviated the need for an anti-torque tail rotor and thus minimized size to facilitate operations from small ASW ships. A single Mk-46 or two Mk-44 torpedoes could be attached between the skids. The device projecting from the left skid is a retracting sensor to detect the deck as the helicopter lands. A small two-fin tail was experimentally fitted in some units. (U.S. Navy)

The one-man XRON-1 had the dynamic components of the unmanned DSN/QH-50 but with a different frame and small inverted-V tail surface. There is a tricycle landing gear and the pilot's control stick extends down from the rotor head. During flight tests the DSN/QH-50C could be modified to carry a pilot just forward of the engine. (U.S. Navy)

A trio of YRON-1 one-man Rotorcycles in flight at the Marine Corps Schools, Quantico, Va. The RON was an effort to develop an aircraft that could move troops rapidly on the battlefield, but the cost and maintenance requirements made the concept impractical. More feasible was a single, larger helicopter carrying a squad or platoon of troops. (U.S. Marine Corps)

This RON has been modified to test a tilt-float concept for operations from the water as well as warships. The floats were rotated to a horizontal position during forward flight and to this vertical position for landing and takeoff. The concept, developed by naval engineer Eugene Handler, was also evaluated for larger fixed-wing aircraft. (Gyrodyne)

# Hiller
UH-12                              H-23 Raven
360                               HTE
                                  CH-112 Nomad

The Hiller 360 was a commercial helicopter that served as the predecessor of the long-lived Army H-23 Raven series and the Navy HTE series of three-place utility and training helicopters. Originally given the company designation UH-12 (for United Helicopters), the commercial H-12 was evaluated by the U.S. Army and Navy in 1950, leading to production orders from both services. Over 2,000 helicopters were built before production ceased in the mid-1960s.

The Raven's fuselage is composed of a semi-monocoque cabin floor which supports a plexiglass bubble cockpit enclosure, the power plant, and landing gear. The long, narrow tailboom is a sheet-metal monocoque structure, with no internal bracing. The two-bladed main and tail rotors are powered by a 232-hp Lycoming piston engine. Landing gear in the Army's H-23 series is composed of wide-track skids, while the Navy's HTE series is equipped with a wheeled undercarriage.

The Army's H-23 Ravens were used extensively during the Korean War for observation, casualty evacuation, and general utility. The Navy's HTE-1 and -2 variants were used almost exclusively in the training role, as were the later models of the Army series. Several hundred H-23s have been exported to the military forces of a variety of Third World nations as well as to Japan, the Netherlands, and Great Britain.

First flight: 1948        Service introduction: 1950
Users: Argentina, Canada, Chile, Colombia, Dominican Republic, Great Britain, Guatemala, Japan, Mexico, Morocco, Netherlands, Peru, United States, Uruguay

**Variants**

H-23A      production helicopter for U.S. Army with 178-hp Franklin 6V4-178-B33 engine; used for battlefield evacuation.
H-23B      similar to H-23A with 200-hp Franklin 6V4-200-C33; fitted with skids; 35 to the Netherlands; changed to OH-23B in 1962.
H-23C      redesigned dynamic components with bubble canopy; 145 built; changed to OH-23C in 1962.
H-23D      production helicopter with 250-hp Lycoming VO-435-23B; first flight 3 April 1956; 483 built; changed to OH-23D in 1962.
OH-23F     production helicopter with 305-hp Lycoming VO-540-9; used for geodetic survey work in Central and South America; 22 built.
TH-23F     private venture trainer; 3-seat cabin, IFR equipped; 1 built.
OH-23G     modification of H-23D production run; 21 to Britain (for Navy use).
CH-112     Canadian version of OH-23G; 24 built.
HTE-1      production 2-seat trainer for Navy with tricycle gear.
HTE-2      similar to HTE-1 with 200-hp Franklin 6V4-200-C33; quadricycle landing gear; 20 to Great Britain (for Navy use).

**Characteristics**

Crew: 1 pilot, 1 copilot/student, 1 observer
Engine: 1 Lycoming VO-540-A1B piston 323 hp derated to 305 hp
Dimensions: length 40 ft 8 in (12.4 m); height 9 ft 9½ in (2.98 m); rotor diameter 35 ft 5 in (10.8 m)
Weight: empty 1,755 lbs (796 kg); loaded 2,800 lbs (1,270 kg)
Speed: cruise 82 mph (132 km/h); maximum 96 mph (154 km/h)

Range: 225 miles (362 km)
Ceiling: hover OGE 7,200 ft (2,195 m); hover IGE 10,800 ft (3,290 m); service 16,200
    ft (4,940 m)
Climb: 1,290 ft/min (393 m/min)
Payload: 1 passenger or 2 litters (with pilot only)

A U.S. Navy HTE-2 from the Naval Air Station, Oakland, Calif., hovers over an *Essex*-class
carrier in the early 1950s. On the flight deck are several types of AD Skyraider attack
aircraft and an F9F Panther fighter (with wing-tip tanks). These helicopters were too small
for effective use aboard ships but were widely used by the U.S. Army in the Korean War.
(Hiller)

The U.S. Army's H-23 Ravens had skid-type landing gear while the Navy's HTE versions of
this light helicopter had wheels, which were more useful aboard ship and at air bases. This
H-23B was used by engineers at Fort Belvoir, Va., for observation, reconnaissance, wire-
laying, and other roles. (U.S. Army)

# Hiller

HJ-1                                         H-32 Hornet
                                             HOE

The Hiller HJ-1 was a development of the earlier HJ-2 Hornet, which was the first ramjet-powered rotorcraft built by Hiller, first flying in 1950. Evaluated by the U.S. Army as the YH-32 and by the Navy as the HOE-1, this later Hiller design was conceived as a light observation helicopter with a crew of two and a very short range. No production resulted from the evaluation.

The Hornet's fuselage was composed of a steel tube framework and a fiberglass and plastic laminate skin which could be detached and re-installed in a few minutes. Main and tail rotors both had two blades and were of all-metal construction. The main rotor had one Hiller 8RJ2B ramjet at the tip of each blade for the main propulsion system, and an auxiliary gasoline engine could spin the rotor up to 50 rpm to enable the ramjet engine to function. The tail had two small horizontal stabilizers in an inverted-V configuration, and the landing gear consisted of twin skids. Ordered in 1952, all 12 prototypes were delivered to the Army in 1956.

First flight:
Service introduction: not operational

**Variants**

YH-32   prototype evaluated by U.S. Army (serial 4963/974); 12 built.
HOE-1   prototype for U.S. Navy; not accepted (BuNo. 138651/653).

A line of YH-32s awaits delivery to the U.S. Army at the Hiller plant in Palo Alto, Calif. Note the rotor-tip jets and shallow inverted-V tail surfaces. These helicopters were not produced in large numbers, and the Navy version (HOE) was not successful. (Hiller)

**Characteristics**

Crew: 1 pilot, 1 copilot-observer
Engines: 2 Hiller 8RJ2B ramjets 40 lbst each
Dimensions: height 8 ft (2.44 m); rotor diameter 23 ft (7.0 m)
Weight: empty 544 lbs (246 kg); loaded 1,080 lbs (489 kg)
Speed: cruise 69 mph (111 km/h); maximum 80.5 mph (129.5 km/h)
Range: 28 miles (45 km)
Ceiling: service 6,900 ft (2,103 m)
Climb: 700 ft/min (213 m/min)

A U.S. Army YH-32 in flight. (U.S. Army)

# Hiller

## ROE Rotorcycle

The Hiller ROE-1 Rotorcycle was designed to a U.S. Navy specification for a one-man, portable helicopter which was to give Marine infantrymen a degree of mobility previously undreamed of in infantry combat. It could be folded into a small, transportable package by one man, para-dropped to troops in the field, reassembled in a few minutes, and flown away. Thirteen quick-release pins held the aircraft together. A Hiller-sponsored demonstration tour was so successful that Saunders-Roe of Great Britain entered into a licensing agreement with Hiller for British production of the helicopter.

The fuselage was a simple pylon composed of aluminum sheet that housed the vertically mounted 43-hp, four-cylinder air-cooled engine. The pilot's seat protruded from one side of the structure, immediately over one of the three landing struts that doubled as the pilot's footrest. Two additional struts completed the landing gear structure. The rotor system was composed of two-bladed main and tail rotors, the latter mounted at the end of a very narrow tailboom. The entire aircraft closely resembled what could be called a "strap-on" rotorcycle.

Seven rotorcycles were built by Hiller before the Navy terminated the program, with five similar to the YROE-1 being built for commercial marketing.

First flight: 10 January 1957
Service introduction: not operational

**Variants**

XROE-1  prototype helicopter evaluated by Navy from January to July 1957; 1 built.
YROE-1  service evaluation rotorcycles built for Marine Corps; 6 built.

**Characteristics**

Crew: 1 pilot-infantryman
Engine: 1 Nelson H-63B piston 43 hp
Dimensions: height 6 ft 11 in (2.1 m); rotor diameter 18 ft 6 in (5.63 m)
Weight: empty 300 lbs (136 kg); loaded 556 lbs (252 kg)
Speed: cruise 49 mph (79 km/h); maximum 66 mph (106 km/h)
Range: 166 miles (267 km)
Ceiling: hover OGE 2,600 ft (790 m); service 12,000 ft (3,660 m)
Climb: 920 ft/min (280 m/min)

The XROE-1 in flight over the Naval Air Station, Anacostia, Washington, D.C., during its evaluation by the Marine Corps. The helicopter's mini tailboom, with "Marines," national insignia, and other markings on it, supports the anti-torque rotor. (U.S. Marine Corps)

# Hughes

H-17 Flying Crane
H-28

In keeping with the late Howard Hughes's penchant for enormous aircraft (his 1947 "Spruce Goose" flying boat was the largest aircraft ever built), the XH-17 flying test bed he built for the U.S. Air Force in 1949 had a main rotor diameter of 130 feet! The primary distinction of this XH-17 was not its size, however. It was powered by two General Electric turbojets that supplied compressed air through ducts that led up to the rotor shaft and out four nozzles on the tips of the two rotor blades. This air was combined at the nozzles with fuel and burned to generate thrust. An anti-torque tail rotor was driven by linkages from the main rotor. No further production resulted, and the pressure jet concept for rotor propulsion was abandoned.

The XH-28 was intended as a refined XH-17. With an empty weight of 52,000 pounds and a maximum loaded weight of 105,000 pounds, it was to have been the first helicopter with a gross weight exceeding twice its empty weight. The XH-28's turbine engines were to have been housed in the fuselage, behind the cockpit, and the huge quadricycle landing gear was to have had "knees" bent outward to give the helicopter a wider track for lifting large trucks. A full-scale working mock-up of the XH-28 was built, but cutbacks in Air Force research and development during the Korean War led to cancellation of the project.

First flight: October 1952
Service introduction: not operational

**Characteristics**

Crew: 1 pilot, 1 copilot
Engines: 2 General Electric 7E-TG-180-XR-17-A (j 35) turbojets
Dimensions: length 53 ft 4 in (16.25 m); height 30 ft 1½ in (9.17 m); rotor diameter 130 ft (39.62 m)
Weight: empty 28,562 lbs (12,967 kg); loaded 43,500 lbs (19,749 kg)
Speed: cruise 60 mph (96 km/h); maximum cruise 83 mph (133 km/h)
Range: 40 miles (64 km)
Ceiling: service 13,100 ft (3,993 m); hover IGE 12,000 ft (3,658 m)
Climb: 865 ft/min (264 m/min)
Payload: 10,284 lbs (4,665 kg) external load

The Hughes XH-17 demonstrating its size by straddling two automobiles. (Hughes)

The lone Hughes XH-17 giant heavy-lift helicopter in flight with U.S. Air Force markings (serial 50-1842) in flight over its birthplace of Culver City, California. The high quadricycle landing gear was intended to permit carrying out-size cargo. Note the externally mounted engines, ladders to reach cockpit, and lattice tailboom to carry anti-torque rotor and horizontal stabilizer. (U.S. Air Force)

Another view of the Hughes XH-17 in flight. (U.S. Air Force)

# Hughes

| | |
|---|---|
| 200 | HO-2 |
| 269 | H-55 Osage |
| 300 | |

The Hughes 269 originated as a light, two-place commercial helicopter, flying for the first time in October 1956. The simplicity and ruggedness of its design interested the U.S. Army, which placed an order for five pre-production machines. These were designated YHO-2 and were delivered in 1958. Their evaluation program was very successful, but the Army did not place an immediate order for production machines. In the meantime, Hughes decided to market the 269 commercially in two versions: the two-seat 269A and the three-seat 269B. In mid-1964 the Army selected the Hughes 269A (later changed by Hughes to Model 200) as its basic training helicopter. Several other nations also selected the Hughes 200 and 300 (the new designation for the 269B) for their light training and utility duties. In U.S. Army service the Hughes design is known as the TH-55A Osage.

The Osage is a small, simply designed, two-seat training helicopter. Its fuselage is constructed of welded steel tubes with an aluminum skin for the non-plexiglass portions of the cabin. A three-bladed articulated main rotor of aluminum and a two-bladed steel-and-fiberglass tail rotor are powered by a 180-hp Lycoming flat-four engine located below the cabin seats. The tailboom is a simple monocoque tube, and the landing gear is composed of skids mounted on shock absorbers.

Over 850 of these units have been delivered to military operators worldwide, 792 of them to the U.S. Army. The Model 200/300 remains in production for commercial customers.

First flight: YHO-2 1958
Service introduction: November 1964
Users: Algeria, Brazil, Colombia, Ghana, Haiti, India, Japan, Kenya, Nicaragua, Sierra Leone, Spain, Sweden, United States

**Variants**

YHO-2   prototype model 269A for U.S. Army evaluation; delivered in 1958; 5 built.
TH-55A  production model for U.S. Army; 792 built.

**Characteristics**

Crew: 1 pilot, 1 student
Engine: 1 Lycoming HIO-360-B1A piston 180 hp
Dimensions: length 28 ft 10¾ in (8.8 m); height 8 ft 2¾ in (2.5 m); rotor diameter 25 ft 3½ in (7.71 m)
Weight: empty 1,008 lbs (457 kg); loaded 1,850 lbs (839 kg)
Speed: cruise 66 mph (106 km/h); maximum 86 mph (138 km/h)
Range: 204 miles (328 km)
Ceiling: hover OGE 3,750 ft (1,145 m); hover IGE 5,500 ft (1,675 m); service 11,900 ft (3,625 m)
Climb: 1,140 ft/min (347 m/min)

A Hughes YHO-2 prepares to take off from a field at Heidelberg, West Germany, during its evaluation by the U.S. Army in 1959. Not until 1964 did the Army order these helicopters in large numbers, as the H-55 Osage. (U.S. Army)

The Hughes TH-55 Osage was selected by the U.S. Army in 1964 as its basic training helicopter, with 235 being ordered that year (shown is 84-18126). A total of almost 800 were built for the Army. The differences between the YHO-2 (58-1328) and this TH-55A were minimal. (Hughes)

# Hughes

| | | |
|---|---|---|
| 369 | HO-6 | ⎫ |
| 500 | H-6 | ⎬ Cayuse |
| | | ⎭ |

Defender

The Hughes Model 369 was one of three helicopters evaluated in the U.S. Army's Light Observation Helicopter (LOH) competition of 1962-1963. Its design was based on the earlier Hughes 269, that company's first successful commercial helicopter. The Model 369, competing as the HO-6 against the Bell HO-4 and the Fairchild Hiller HO-5, was offered as a replacement for the Bell H-13, the Hiller H-23, and the Cessna O-1 fixed-wing observation aircraft, at the ridiculously low unit price of $29,415 for each bare airframe. This was 32% below its nearest competitor, and the HO-6—redesignated OH-6A in 1962—won the LOH competition. Hughes anticipated a total Army requirement for 4,000 helicopters, although the first production order totalled only 714 over a three-year period. The Army reopened the competition a few years later, and Bell won with its OH-58A variant of the Model 206, which was derived from its earlier LOH competitor, the HO-4.

The OH-6A was a light observation helicopter that sat four or could accommodate a crew of two and four soldiers seated on the floor. The fuselage was a pod-and-boom structure with clamshell doors at the rear of the pod, giving access to the dynamic components and engine. A 317-shp Allison turboshaft drove a four-bladed main rotor and two-bladed anti-torque tail rotor. Landing gear was composed of tubular skids, and an XM-27 7.62-mm machine gun or XM-75 grenade launcher could be fitted.

When Hughes won the LOH competition it simultaneously developed a commercial version of the OH-6A which it designated Model 500. The Model 500M was an export equivalent of the OH-6A and found customers in a variety of Third World nations and Japan. When a 420-shp version of the Allison engine became available, Hughes began marketing an upgraded version of the 500M, the 500M-D, which the company has named Defender. The Defender has been particularly successful as an export, lightweight, visual antiarmor attack helicopter, and as a lightweight, low-cost ASW helicopter. License arrangements covering the manufacture of the 500M-D have been concluded by Hughes with firms in South Korea and Italy, with the probability of more nations following. The Defender differs from the earlier OH-6A in having the more powerful Allison engine, a five-bladed main rotor, and a greater variety of optional equipment including TOW antitank missiles, armor, and self-sealing fuel tanks. None of the 1,434 OH-6As built for the U.S. Army remain in service.

First flight: 27 February 1963
Service introduction: 1966
Users: Argentina, Bolivia, Brazil, Colombia, Denmark, Dominican Republic, Israel, Japan, Kenya, South Korea, Mexico, Morocco, Nicaragua, Philippines, Spain, Taiwan, United States

**Variants**

| | |
|---|---|
| YHO-6 | original designation for prototypes competing in LOH; 5 built. |
| OH-6A | production version for U.S. Army; 1,434 built. |
| OH-6C | OH-6A modification to test 400-shp Allison turboshaft. |

| | |
|---|---|
| OH-6D | proposed Advanced Scout Helicopter (ASH) for U.S. Army. |
| 500M | commercially produced military export version of OH-6A; license-built in Italy, Argentina, Japan, and South Korea. |
| 500MD<br>Defender<br>Scout | Modification with 420-shp Allison 250-C2OB turboshaft; 5-bladed main rotor; optional armament includes 14 2.75-in rockets, 7.62-mm minigun, 40-mm grenade launcher, 30-mm chain gun. |
| 500MD<br>TOW | Antitank Defender armed with 4 TOW antitank missiles. |
| 500MD<br>Quiet<br>Advanced<br>Defender | Defender with quieting kit, including slow-turning, 4-bladed tail rotor and other features; mast-mounted optical sight. |
| 500MD<br>ASW | Defender with low-cost ASW package; 2 crew, search radar, MAD, 2 Mk-44 or Mk-46 torpedoes; can be armed with TOW or rockets for antiship attack; license-built by BredaNardi in Italy. |

**Characteristics (OH-6A)**

Crew: 1 pilot, 1 copilot
Engine: 1 Allison T63-A-5A turboshaft 317 shp
Dimensions: length 30 ft 3¾ in (9.24 m); height 8 ft 1½ in (2.48 m); rotor diameter 26 ft 4 in (8.03 m)
Weight: empty 1,229 lbs (557 kg); loaded 2,400 lbs (1,090 kg)
Speed: cruise 134 mph (216 km/h); maximum 150 mph (241 km/h)
Range: 380 miles (611 km)
Ceiling: hover OGE 7,300 ft (2,225 m); hover IGE 11,800 ft (3,595 m); service 15,800 ft (4,815 m)
Climb: 1,840 ft/min (560 m/min)
Payload: 2 troops

A Hughes 500M produced for Japan. The Japanese Ground Self-Defense Force procured 165 of these helicopters and the Japanese Maritime Self-Defense Force an additional 12. These are informally (and incorrectly) referred to as the OH-6J (for Japan). Note the streamlined shape of the fuselage and the rotor housing atop it. (*Ships of the World*)

This close-up of a Hughes 500MD Defender shows the craft's rotor-head periscope and 30-mm chain gun installed under the fuselage. The periscope enables the helicopter to hover out of sight behind trees and pop up to fire at the proper moment. The XM-230E1 can fire 750 rounds per minute, with a bicycle-type chain used to operate the moving parts of the gun. The rectangular shape on the side of the helicopter contains two Stinger antiaircraft missiles. (Hughes)

This Hughes 500MD in antisubmarine configuration is carrying a towed MAD device on the right side of the cockpit and two ASW homing torpedoes between the skids. In an ASW operation the helicopter would be guided to the submarine after initial detection by shipboard sonar. The ASW variant has a T-tail configuration. (Hughes)

# Hughes
385                                    V-9

The single XV-9A was built to evaluate hot-cycle propulsion, in which hot exhaust gases from the twin engines are ducted to the tips of the rotor blades. The gases are then deflected through nozzles and accelerated to near-sonic velocity. The aircraft successfully demonstrated the feasibility of the propulsion system, but the XV-9A—built only as a test bed—had poor handling and stability characteristics.

The XV-9A was built partly with components of existing helicopters to reduce costs. An OH-6A cockpit, existing Navy T64 engines, and an H-34 fixed undercarriage were used. The engines were fitted in pods on the side of the fuselage, with a V-tail having two movable rudders. The three-bladed rotor had conventional pitch change and flapping hinges, but was without drag hinges. No antitorque rotor was required because of the engine (gas generator) exhausts.

The XV-9A (serial 64-15107) was completed in 1964, and the test program was completed in August 1965 after 19 hours of flight test.

First flight: 5 November 1964
Service introduction: not operational

**Characteristics**

Crew: 1 pilot, 1 copilot
Engines: 2 General Electric YT64-GE-6 gas generators 2,850 shp each
Dimensions: length 45 ft (13.72 m); height 12 ft (3.66 m); rotor diameter 55 ft (16.76 m)
Weight: empty 8,600 lbs (3,904 kg); loaded 15,300 lbs (6,946 kg)
Speed: cruise 92 mph (148 km/h); maximum 138 mph (222 km/h)
Range:
Ceiling: hover OGE 13,200 ft (4,023 m); service 17,300 ft (5,273 m)
Climb: 2,000 ft/min (610 m/min)

The lone XV-9A during a test flight shows its unusual configuration which includes several helicopter components. "Hot Cycle Research" is written on the engine nacelle. (Hughes)

# Hughes
77                              H-64

The Hughes YAH-64 is a twin-engine, two-place attack helicopter that was the firm's entry in the 1973-1976 U.S. Army Advanced Attack Helicopter (AAH) competition. This program was initiated to develop an attack helicopter for antiarmor operations in day, night, and adverse weather conditions with emphasis on the helicopter's ability to be based with the troops on the front lines. Both competitors for the AAH award, the Bell YAH-63 and the Hughes YAH-64, first flew in September 1975, and two flying prototypes of each were delivered to the U.S. Army for evaluation in May 1976. The Army selected the Hughes design on 10 December 1976. Hughes was awarded a contract to begin a full-scale engineering development program which commenced in 1977. This Phase 2 of the AAH program included the construction of three more prototypes with installation of avionics and a fire-control system in all five aircraft.

The AH-64 has a four-bladed stainless steel, fully articulated main rotor and a four-bladed tail rotor with the blades set at a 60-degree/120-degree angle to each other for maximum quieting. Two General Electric 1,536-shp turboshafts are mounted on either side of the upper fuselage just aft of the main rotor. The fuselage is a two-place, narrow cross-section, semi-monocoque aluminum structure, with the copilot/gunner in the forward seat and the pilot aft. The tail was redesigned during the Phase 2 development process and consists of a low-set, fully movable horizontal stabilizer (stabilator) and vertical stabilizer in lieu of the original T-tail. The landing gear is fixed with two main wheels and a tail wheel. Sophisticated avionics include a Martin-Marietta Target Acquisition Designation System/Pilots Night Vision System (TADS/PNVS), which uses optics, forward-looking infrared, television, and a laser designation, tracking, and range-finding system. The last was used in conjunction with the new laser-guided Hellfire antitank missile, which has been tested successfully from the AH-64. A 30-mm chain gun is mounted between the main landing gear beneath the cockpit, and four hard points are located under the stub 16-foot, 4-inch wing for a variety of ordnance including 16 Hellfire missiles or 76 2.75-inch rockets in four pods.

Current plans call for production of 537 AH-64s by 1989 at the rate of 8 per month. The U.S. Army requires at least 574 units, and the U.S. Marine Corps will have a need for a new attack helicopter in the late 1980s.

First flight: 30 September 1975
Service introduction: December 1983 (est.)
Users: United States

**Characteristics**

Crew: 1 pilot, 1 copilot/gunner
Engines: 2 General Electric T700-GE-700 turboshafts 1,536 shp each
Dimensions: length 57 ft 9 in (17.6 m); height 12 ft 6⅞ in (3.83 m); rotor diameter 48 ft (14.63 m)
Weight: empty 10,268 lbs (4,662 kg); loaded 17,650 lbs (8,013 kg)
Speed: cruise 182 mph (293 km/h); maximum 235 mph (378 km/h)
Range: 380 miles (611 km)
Ceiling: hover OGE 12,400 ft (3,780 m); hover IGE 15,200 ft (4,633 m); service 20,500 ft (6,248 m)
Climb: 2,880 ft/min (878 m/min)        Payload: see text

A YAH-64 attack helicopter for the U.S. Army has a sinister look as it hovers near the ground. TOW antitank missiles are carried on the stub wings and a laser range finder/target designator is fitted in the nose of the helicopter. A 30-mm chain gun is suspended under the fuselage, between the main landing gear. (Hughes)

A YAH-64 prototype in flight carrying TOW missiles and a 30-mm chain gun under the fuselage. This is a Phase 2 helicopter, with the horizontal stabilizer mounted at the bottom of the tail fin and the anti-torque rotor mounted near the top. The landing gear is fixed.

This is the first Hughes YAH-64 prototype (73-22248) with its T-design tail configuration. Note the TOW missiles on stub wings, and the laser nose configuration. The 30-mm chain gun is under the fuselage, in the shadow of the helicopter. (Martin Marietta)

# Kaman

| K-225 | HTK |
|---|---|
| K-240 | H-22 |
| | TH-43E |

The Kaman HTK-1 was a three-seat training helicopter built for the U.S. Navy and Marine Corps, the first Kaman helicopter evaluated by those services. Its secondary missions included general utility and casualty evacuation, and it was occasionally used for submarine spotting. True to the standard Kaman configuration, the HTK-1's rotor system was a twin intermeshing and contra-rotating type, controlled by servo flaps for both cyclic pitch and collective pitch changes. One Navy HTK-1 was evaluated by the U.S. Army as the H-22, but no production resulted.

The HTK-1's structure was a pod-and-boom design, with sliding doors on either side of the pod and two elliptical tail fins at the end of the boom. In the HTK, two main rotors, each composed of two wooden blades, were driven by a 240-hp, six-cylinder engine. A wheeled quadricycle landing gear was fitted.

Kaman installed a Boeing 502-2 gas turbine engine in a K-225 which made its first flight in December 1951. Following evaluation of this configuration two similar Boeing XT50 turboshaft engines were fitted in an HTK-1, with that aircraft flying for the first time in March 1954. In the latter configuration both engines were used for takeoff and hovering with heavy loads, but one was shut down during cruise flight.

First flight: HTK-1 26 April 1951
Service introduction: September 1952
Users: United States

**Variants**

K-225      prototype evaluated by the U.S. Navy; 2 purchased 1950 plus one by the U.S. Coast Guard.
HTK-1      production trainer for Navy; 29 built; changed to TH-43E in 1962.
HTK-1K   helicopter modified for unmanned (drone) tests; first flight 30 July 1957; 1 built.

**Characteristics (HTK-1)**

Crew: 1 pilot, 1 copilot/student
Engine: 1 Lycoming O-435-4 piston engine 240 hp
Dimensions: length 41 ft (12.5 m); height 17 ft (5.18 m); rotor diameter 41 ft (12.5 m)
Weight: empty 2,273 lbs (1,032 kg); loaded 3,000 lbs (1,362 kg)
Speed: cruise 63 mph (101 km/h); maximum 81 mph (130 km/h)
Range: 132 miles (212 km)
Ceiling: hover IGE 6,700 ft (2,042 m); service 17,000 ft (5,182 m)
Climb: 1,300 ft/min (396 m/min)
Payload: 1 passenger or 1 stretcher

One of two Kaman K-225 helicopters which served as prototypes for the U.S. Navy's HTK and the later HOK/HUK/H-43 series. This is BuNo. 125447 after being fitted with a turboshaft engine. The letters FT near the rotor shafts indicate Navy Flight Test. No military designation was assigned to the K-225s although they did have bureau numbers. (U.S. Navy)

A Kaman HTK-1 on a demonstration flight in 1951 at Washington, D.C. (U.S. Navy)

The HTK-1K drone in flight under radio control. Developed under a joint Navy-Army program (noted on the helicopter's tail fin), a remote-control helicopter was to be used in a combat situation for reconnaissance, delivery of explosives, rescuing personnel, and other dangerous missions. On this flight there is a safety pilot (with hands raised off of controls in this view). (Kaman)

# Kaman

K-600                                    HOK
                                         HUK
                                         H-43 Huskie

The Kaman K-600 was essentially an enlarged Kaman HTK-1 which had been supplied to the U.S. Navy as a training helicopter in the early 1950s. The first K-600 was a four- or five-place general purpose helicopter that won a 1950 U.S. Navy design competition for a liaison helicopter. It was put into production as the HOK-1 for the U.S. Marine Corps and a few units were also procured for Navy use as the HUK-1. The U.S. Air Force selected a variant of the K-600 for local airbase crash and rescue duties, this being designated H-43A.

The HOK/HUK/H-43A helicopters were each powered by a Pratt & Whitney 600-hp radial piston engine. The next version of this Kaman design, the K-600-3, was procured by the USAF as the H-43B with a 825-shp Lycoming T53-L-1A/B turboshaft in place of the radial engine. This modification permitted the installation of the small turboshaft on the fuselage roof, rather than within the cabin itself, thus enlarging the usable cabin space. All versions of the K-600 shared the same rotor system, a set of twin intermeshing and contra-rotating rotors set at an angle to one another on the cabin roof. Each rotor had two blades. The cabin of the radial-engined versions could accommodate four or five, while the cabin of the H-43B could seat up to ten. The landing gear on all versions was quadricycle, with special devices that could be fitted to permit operation from soft or muddy terrain.

The H-43B was the most popular version of the K-600, some 193 being built for U.S. Air Force and foreign use. Most of these U.S. Air Force machines were upgraded to the HH-43F standard with a more powerful turboshaft. An attempt by Kaman to market the K-600 in the civilian sector was unsuccessful, and production was terminated in 1965.

First flight: 27 September 1956
Service introduction: April 1958
Users: Burma, Colombia, Iran, Morocco, Pakistan, Thailand, United States

**Variants**

XHOK-1  prototype Model K-600 for U.S. Navy-Marine Corps; 2 built.
HOK-1   production version for U.S. Marine Corps; 81 built; changed to OH-43D in 1962.
HUK-1   production version for U.S. Navy; 24 built; changed to UH-43C in 1962.
H-43A   production piston-engined version for USAF; 18 built; changed to HH-43A in 1962.
H-43B   production turboshaft-powered version for USAF and foreign sales; 193 built; changed to HH-43B in 1962.
HH-43F  similar to H-43B with 1,150-shp Lycoming T53-L-11 turboshaft.
QH-43G  radio-controlled drone for U.S. Navy; converted from HOK/HUK series.

**Characteristics**

Crew: 1 pilot, 1 copilot, 2 firefighters
Engine: 1 Lycoming T53-L-1B turboshaft 825 shp
Dimensions: length (fuselage) 25 ft 2 in (7.67 m); height 15 ft 6½ in (4.73 m); rotor diameter 47 ft (14.33 m)

Weight: empty 4,469 lbs (2,029 kg); loaded 9,150 lbs (4,154 kg)

Speed: cruise 109 mph (175 km/h); maximum 130 mph (209 km/h)

Range: 235 miles (378 km)

Ceiling: hover IGE 21,000 ft (6,400 m); hover OGE 18,000 ft (5,486 m); service
    25,000 ft (7,620 m)

Climb: 2,000 ft/min (610 m/min)

Payload: 3,880 lbs (1,762 kg) external slung cargo

A Navy HOK-1 (later OH-43D) leads a flight of Kaman helicopters—an HTK-1 fitted with floats, the turboshaft-powered K-225, and the second K-225 prototype.

A U.S. Air Force HH-43B Huskie practices rescue operations at an air base in South Vietnam during 1966. Note the exhaust pipe projecting over the tail assembly, four tail fins, wheel skids for operation in swamps or marshes, and two men coming aboard via the rescue hoist. The HH-43s were used mainly for base operations and rarely for combat rescues in Vietnam. (U.S. Air Force)

# Kaman

K-20                                      HU2K ⎫
                                          H-2   ⎬ Seasprite

                                          H-2 Tomahawk

The Kaman K-20 was developed to fulfill a 1956 U.S. Navy requirement for a long-range utility helicopter capable of operating from small ships. The Kaman design was originally designated as the HU2K-1 Seasprite and first flew in the summer of 1959. One hundred ninety of these 13-place helicopters were built for the U.S. Navy in 1961–1966. Three of the aircraft were later transferred from the Navy to the U.S. Army, where they were designated H-2 Tomahawk. From 1962 on, the Navy's shipboard utility and rescue aircraft were designated UH-2. In the early 1970s, in an effort to rapidly provide U.S. surface warships with ASW helicopters, the 105 surviving Seasprites were converted to an antisubmarine configuration and redesignated SH-2. This program was known as LAMPS I for Light Airborne Multipurpose System. Although the SH-60B Seahawk was developed as a successor, the Navy plans to procure additional SH-2F helicopters.

As built, these helicopters had one General Electric T58 turboshaft engine; from 1967 to 1970 the UH-2A and UH-2B variants were converted to a twin-engine configuration and redesignated -2C and -D, respectively, with the prefixes HH indicating armored combat rescue helicopter and UH the unarmored configuration. The SH-2 conversions were drawn almost exclusively from HH-2D helicopters. The H-2 has an all-metal, semi-monocoque, watertight structure, with retractable main landing gear and a fixed tail wheel. The four-bladed main rotor and tail rotor in the twin-engine configuration are driven by two General Electric turboshafts rated at 1,350 shp each. In the main ASW variants, the SH-2F can be distinguished from the SH-2D by the former having the tail wheel six feet farther forward to facilitate maneuvering aboard small warships. All surviving SH-2Ds were thus modified (along with other changes) in the late 1970s.

The HU2K-1 was deployed in the utility-rescue role aboard aircraft carriers and some large surface warships after its debut in the fleet. Of the few U.S. Army Tomahawks, one was evaluated as a ground support/attack helicopter with an M-60 four-gun turret and pylons for additional machine guns and rockets or air-to-surface missiles. Another was tested as a compound helicopter with a 2,500-lbst GE turbojet engine in J85 pods being fitted to the right side of the fuselage and small wings fitted to off-load the rotor during forward flight. Thus configured, the compound H-2 reached a maximum speed in excess of 225 mph during the 1965 test program that was sponsored by the Army and Navy. The LAMPS I conversion gave the U.S. Navy its first manned ASW helicopter capable of operating from cruisers, destroyers, and frigates. The first SH-2D deployed in December 1971. The SH-2 was the successor to the ill-fated unmanned ASW helicopter program (see Gyrodyne DSN/H-50 listing). The U.S. Navy plans the procurement of 90 additional SH-2F helicopters during the latter 1980s to insure an adequate number of ASW helicopters for those U.S. warships that cannot accommodate the SH-60B LAMPS III helicopter. In the ASW configuration the SH-2 is fitted with surface-search radar, a towed Magnetic Anomaly Detector (MAD), and expendable sonobuoys. No dipping sonar is provided. Submarines can be attacked with two externally carried Mk-46 ASW homing torpedoes (replacing the earlier Mk-44s). Three UH-2A/Bs evaluated AN/AQS-10 dipping sonar in 1963.

First flight: 2 July 1959
Service introduction: 18 December 1962
Users: United States

**Variants**

HU2K-1   prototype and original designation of production aircraft with 1 1,025-shp General Electric T58-GE-6 turboshaft; 4 built.

HU2K-1   production aircraft with 1 1,250-shp T58-GE-8 turboshaft; 2 crew plus 2 passengers; 84 built; changed to UH-2A in 1962.

HU2K-1U  similar to UH-2A with less instrumentation; 102 built; changed to UH-2B in 1962; survivors later modified to UH-2A avionics.

H-2      U.S. Army designation for BuNo. 147978 (high-speed research), 149785 (gunship).

UH-2C    conversion of UH-2A/B to twin T58-GE-8F turboshafts; all earlier models upgraded.

HH-2C    similar to UH-2C with additional instrumentation, lightweight armor, self-sealing fuel tanks, 7.62-mm machine guns in chin turret for armed SAR; 6 converted.

NUH-2C   Fitted with stub wings to carry Sparrow III or Sidewinder missiles; nose extended for fire control radar; one modified (BuNo. 147981).

HH-2D    similar to HH-2C with less armament and armor; 67 converted.

NHH-2D   HH-2D modified under the circulation control rotor program.

SH-2D    HH-2D converted to interim LAMPS I ASW configuration; 20 converted.

YSH-2E   SH-2D improved with special radar, ASW sensors; 2 converted; later changed to SH-2F.

SH-2F    final LAMPS I upgrade; new rotor system, sensors, avionics EW systems; 104 converted; 90 new aircraft planned.

XH-2     Navy conversion of UH-2 to circulation control rotor configuration to serve as test bed for simplified rotor head and other improvements; first flight September 1979; 1 converted (BuNo. 147981).

A Navy HU2K-1U sprays fire-fighting chemicals during an exercise at the Naval Air Station, Miramar, Calif. The Kaman helicopter, developed for utility, rescue, and fire-fighting activities, subsequently served in the combat rescue role. In the early 1970s, the surviving units were converted to the ASW role. (U.S. Navy)

**Characteristics (SH-2F)**

Crew: 1 pilot, 1 copilot, 1 sensor operator
Engines: 2 General Electric T58-GE-8F turboshafts 1,350 shp each
Dimensions: length 52 ft 7 in (16.03 m); height 15 ft 6 in (4.72 m); rotor diameter 44 ft (13.41 m)
Weight: empty 7,040 lbs (3,196 kg); loaded 12,800 lbs (5,811 kg)
Speed: cruise 150 mph (241 km/h); maximum 165 mph (265 km/h)
Range: 422 miles (679 km)
Ceiling: service 22,500 ft (6,858 m)
Climb: 2,440 ft/min (744 m/min)
Payload: 2 Mk-44 or Mk-46 ASW homing torpedoes

A Kaman UH-2A Seasprite helicopter from the carrier *Oriskany* (CVA-34) is about to land on the deck of the carrier *Forrestal* (CVA-59). The main landing gear is lowered and the fire-fighting boom is in the raised position. The tail code UP and HC-1 indicate Helicopter Combat Support Squadron (HC) 1, which provides utility, SAR, and replenishment helicopters to Pacific Fleet ships. (U.S. Navy)

This U.S. Army H-2 Tomahawk was fitted with turbojet pods on both sides of the fuselage and stub wings for high-speed helicopter research. However, it retained its original Navy bureau number (147978). The retractable landing gear, unusual in a utility-type helicopter, helped increase performance. (Kaman)

In an effort to provide ASW helicopters to U.S. Navy surface ships after the DASH program ended, in the early 1970s the 105 available H-2 helicopters were converted to the SH-2 ASW configuration. This SH-2D, with wheels tucked in, carries an ASW torpedo and is towing a MAD device. Above the torpedo is a rectangular opening for the sonobuoy dispenser. There is a radome under the nose. This SH-2D is from Light ASW Helicopter Squadron (HSL) 32 and is based aboard the cruiser William H. Standley (CG 32). (U.S. Navy)

# Kellett

KD-1                                         G-1        R-3
KH-17A                                       R-2        O-60

The U.S. Army Air Corps operated a total of 16 Kellett autogiros (in addition to the one Pitcairn autogiro) from 1936 onward. Except for the experimental de Bothezat and Berliner machines, these were the Army's first rotary-wing aircraft. They were improvements of the Kellett KD-1, the world's first rotorcraft to enter commercial service. Nine Kellett autogiros were acquired for tests before World War II (designated YG-1), and seven additional machines were procured by the Army for the observation role during the war (designated O-60).

These autogiros followed the basic La Cierva design but were superior in performance to the British-built C 30 design. The KD-1 did not have wings or rudders, but small elliptical fins were fitted on the lower side of the horizontal tail surfaces. The military versions were two-seat aircraft with a pylon forward of the cockpits supporting the three-bladed rotor. The YG-1 had an open cockpit; the XO-60 had a bubble which covered both pilot and observer in the style of pre-war observation planes. The rotor blades of the YG-1Bs could be folded back to facilitate ground handling.

The U.S. Army's initial two Kellett autogiros, acquired in 1936, were designated YG-1 and YG-1A. Both were destroyed in crashes. Seven additional aircraft were then ordered to permit simultaneous testing by the Air Corps and other Army branches. Differing from the earlier aircraft in minor respects, these were designated YG-1B and delivered to Wright Field in Ohio in 1938. One YG-1B was transferred to the National Advisory Committee for Aeronautics (NACA) for evaluation; one was provided with a Jacobs R-915-1 engine and redesignated YG-1C. Subsequently, one YG-1B became the XR-3 in the Army's new rotary-wing series while the lone YG-1C was changed to XR-2. A non-military Kellett autogiro was taken on the Antarctic expedition of 1934 by Rear Admiral Richard E. Byrd, and the following year Kellett autogiros began carrying mail for the U.S. Post Office Department. One aircraft was bought by Japan in 1939, leading to the Kayaba autogiro program.

In 1953 the U.S. Navy acquired a modified KD-1B, designated KH-17A, for modification to a rotor research aircraft. As built, the KH-17A had a 275-hp Jacobs radial engine; the Navy planned to add stub wings carrying two 140-hp Lycoming engines (giving a loaded weight of approximately 3,400 pounds). However, lack of funds prevented the modification, and the KH-17A was flown only in its original configuration, fitted with a four-bladed rotor. Although accepted by the Navy, it did not have a military designation or bureau number. It was the last true autogiro believed to have been flown by a military service.

First flight: 1936 (military version)
Service introduction: 1936
Users: United States (Japanese Ka-1 similar)

### Variants

YG-1    commercial KD-1 delivered to Army in 1936; Jacobs YR-755-1 225-hp engine; 1
        built (serial 34-278).
YG-1A   as YG-1 with high-frequency radio; delivered to Army in 1937; 1 built (serial
        36-352).

YG-1B improved aircraft with Jacobs R-755-3 engine; dual controls; 7 built (serial 37-377/382); delivered in 1938; 1 to YG-1C (37-378), 1 to XR-3 (37-380).

YG-1C YG-1B fitted with constant speed rotor in 1938; subsequently converted to XR-2.

XO-60 production aircraft based on XR-2 with Jacobs R-915-3 300-hp engine; 7 built (42-13604/13610); 6 redesignated YO-60.

**Characteristics (YG-1B/C)**

Crew: 1 pilot, 1 observer

Engine: 1 Jacobs R-755-3 radial piston 225 hp

Dimensions: length 28 ft 10 in (8.8 m); height 10 ft 3 in (3.1 m); rotor diameter 40 ft (12.2 m)

Weight: empty 1,352 lbs (614 kg); loaded 2,250 lbs (1,022 kg)

Speed: cruise 103 mph (166 km/h); maximum 125 mph (200 km/h)

Range: 360 miles (579 km)

Ceiling: service 14,000 ft (4,267 m)

Climb: 1,060 ft/min (323 m/min)

The Kellett YG-1 was the U.S. Army's first practical rotary-wing aircraft. The G-1 series had open, tandom cockpit seating compared to the enclosed, bubble-cockpit O-60 series produced during World War II. (U.S. Air Force)

The improved YG-1A in flight. The pilot is seated in the rear cockpit. Note the absence of wings, the streamlined rotor pylon, and the stripes (red and white) on the center rudder (partially hidden by the left-side tail fin). (U.S. Air Force)

A YO-60 makes a "jump start" with the rotor blades enabling a very short takeoff run. (U.S. Air Force)

Probably the world's last autogiro to fly in military markings was a KH-17A acquired by the U.S. Navy in 1953 (not given a Navy aircraft designation). This drawing shows how the Navy planned to modify the aircraft with wing-mounted engines for use as a test aircraft. It flew only in the original single-engine, wingless configuration. (U.S. Navy)

# Kellett

## R-8

The R-8 Synchropter was Kellett's first attempt at a military helicopter (the previous Kellett XR-2 and XR-3 being modified autogiros). Kellett's R-8 and R-10 helicopters introduced side-by-side, intermeshing rotor blades to U.S. helicopter design.

The R-8 was a relatively large helicopter with a bubble-shaped fuselage. The intermeshing rotor hubs carrying the three-bladed rotors were 4 feet apart, with a total rotor span of only 40 feet. Small tail fins were mounted forward of the craft's rudder. The cockpit was a plexiglass section forward of the engine. A tricycle landing gear was fitted.

Two prototypes were ordered in 1943 and 1944.

First flight: 7 August 1944
Service introduction: not operational

**Variants**

XR-8     prototype with 3-bladed rotors (serial 43-44714).
XR-8A   prototype with 3-bladed rotors (serial 44-21908).

**Characteristics**

Crew: 1 pilot, 1 observer
Engine: 1 Franklin O-405-9 piston 245 hp
Dimensions: length 22 ft 7 in (6.9 m); height 11 ft (3.4 m); rotor diameter 36 ft (11.0 m)
Weight: empty 2,320 lbs (1,053 kg); loaded 2,975 lbs (1,351 kg)
Speed: cruise 85 mph (137 km/h); maximum 100 mph (160 km/h)
Range:
Ceiling: service 7,000 ft (2,134 m)
Climb:

A Kellett XR-8 in flight. The intermeshing, contra-rotating rotors are clearly visible in this view as are the helicopter's tail fins. (U.S. Air Force)

The odd-looking Kellett XR-8 introduced side-by-side, intermeshing rotors to U.S. helicopter design. The Kaman firm subsequently developed a series of helicopters based on the same concept, which had been used earlier by German helicopter designers. The XR-8 also had an unusual tail configuration, with twin fin plates extending out from the after fuselage. (U.S. Air Force)

# Kellett

R-10
H-10

The R-10 was the first U.S. effort at developing a twin-engine helicopter, being significantly larger than existing American rotary-wing aircraft when ordered in 1945.

To some extent a scaled-up version of the R-8, the R-10 was intended to be an aerial ambulance. It had contra-rotating, intermeshing three-bladed rotors, and its engine nacelles were mounted on either side of the fuselage to allow maximum internal volume for stretchers or cargo. The R-10 was able to fly on one engine in a loaded condition up to about 4,600 feet.

Two prototype XR-10s were completed (redesignated XH-10 in 1948; serials 45-22793 and - 22795). Plans for an initial production run of ten similar helicopters designated H-10A were cancelled. A civil version was designated KH-2.

First flight: April 1947
Service introduction: not operational

**Characteristics**

Crew: 1 pilot, 1 copilot
Engines: 2 Continental R-975-15 piston 525 hp each
Dimensions: length 28 ft 8 in (8.7 m); rotor diameter 65 ft (19.8 m)
Weight: empty 6,640 lbs (3,001 kg); loaded 11,000 lbs (4,994 kg)

Speed: maximum 115 mph (185 km/h); cruise 90 mph (145 km/h)
Range: 160 miles (257 km)
Ceiling: service 15,000 ft (4,572 m)
Climb:
Payload: 10 troops or 6 stretchers or 3,550 lbs (1,612 kg) internal cargo

The Kellett XR-10 is believed to have been the first all-metal helicopter to be built. As an aerial ambulance it was to carry six stretchers in addition to a crew of two. To accommodate the stretchers, the XR-10 had its engines externally mounted. Note the intermeshing rotors and triple-fin tail configuration. (U.S. Air Force)

The Kellett XR-10 during its first flight at Kellett's plant in North Wales, Pa., in 1947. At the time it was the largest rotary-wing aircraft in the USAAF. (U.S. Air Force)

# Lockheed
186                              H-51

The Lockheed XH-51 was ordered as an experimental high-speed, low-drag helicopter for evaluation by the U.S. Army and Navy. The XH-51 had a rigid rotor system that provided extraordinary stability, high maneuverability, and an almost airplane-like performance. Two examples were ordered in 1962, and the first prototype flew in the fall of that year.

Extensive efforts were made to ensure the lowest possible drag coefficient for the XH-51's fuselage. The skin was flush-riveted to the stringers, the skid landing gear was fully retractable, and many of the rotor components were enclosed in a streamlined fairing. Also extremely streamlined, the fuselage was an aluminum alloy semi-monocoque structure which gracefully faired into the tailboom. The rigid rotor system was composed of a four-bladed stainless-steel main rotor and a two-bladed anti-torque tail rotor driven by a 500-shp United Aircraft turboshaft. There were accommodations in the two prototypes evaluated by the U.S. Army and Navy for a pilot and copilot only, but Lockheed built two five-seat commerical Model 286s that were otherwise identical to the XH-51s. (No commercial sales resulted from this venture.) The Navy evaluated one XH-51 with a dipping sonar for the ASW role.

One XH-51 was modified after delivery for research as a compound helicopter, a single 2,600-lbst turbojet being installed in the port wing root of a newly added main wing. To balance this structural addition, the horizontal stabilizer was dramatically increased in size. With a wingspan of almost 17 feet, this modified aircraft reached a speed of 302.6 mph. NASA also ordered a modified XH-51 which was delivered in 1964 in a five-seat configuration very similar to that of the commercial Model 286.

First flight: 2 November 1962
Service introduction: not operational

**Variants**

XH-51A          prototypes for U.S. Army/Navy evaluation; 2 built.
XH-51A          modified XH-51A for U.S. Army research of high-speed aircraft; 2,600-
Compound        lbst Pratt & Whitney J60-P-2 turbojet in port wing root; fitted with 16-ft
                11-in wing; first flight September 1964 without turbojet; first compound
                flight in early 1965; 1 converted.
XH-51N          prototype ordered for NASA for advanced flight study; 1 built.

**Characteristics (XH-51A)**

Crew: 1 pilot, 1 copilot
Engine: 1 United Aircraft of Canada T74 (PT6) turboshaft 500 shp
Dimensions: length 32 ft 4 in (9.85 m); height 8 ft 2½ in (2.5 m); rotor diameter 35 ft
    (10.67 m)
Weight: empty 2,640 lbs (1,199 kg); loaded 4,000 lbs (1,816 kg)
Speed: cruise 160 mph (257 km/h); maximum 174 mph (280 km/h)
Range: 241 miles (388 km)
Ceiling: hover OGE 5,000 ft (1,525 m); hover IGE 10,000 ft (3,050 m)
Climb: 1,800 ft/min (549 m/min)
Payload: 600 lbs (272 kg) flight test instrumentation

The first of the two Army-Navy XH-51A research helicopters produced by Lockheed. Both had Navy bureau numbers (151262/263) although Army was listed first in their markings. Note the streamlined shape and anti-torque rotor mounted on the left side of the tail fin; small horizontal stabilizers are mounted on the tailboom. (Lockheed)

The XH-51A as a compound helicopter under the aegis of the U.S. Army's Aviation Material Laboratories during a high-speed run off Oxnard, Calif. Stub wings and a turbojet engine pod have been fitted and the tail configuration has been modified. (Lockheed)

# Lockheed

## H-56 Cheyenne

The Lockheed AH-56 Cheyenne was a development of the earlier rigid-rotor, experimental Model 186, designated XH-51 for Army evaluation. The Cheyenne was the winner of a 1966 Advanced Aerial Fire Support System (AAFSS) competition and was a two-seat compound attack helicopter with a rigid rotor system and a pusher propeller in the tail. The original procurement contract called for the production of ten AH-56 Cheyennes for evaluation, all of which were delivered to the U.S. Army by July 1968. Weapon firing tests were conducted with a variety of armaments, including the new TOW antitank missile. The Army ordered 375 AH-56s on 7 January 1968. Initial deployment to Vietnam was then anticipated to occur no later than 1970.

The Cheyenne's fuselage was of conventional semi-monocoque construction and composed of a standard pod and boom. The main rotor was rigid with four blades; the four-bladed anti-torque tail rotor was mounted on the port side of the tail, and a Hamilton Standard three-bladed, variable-pitch pusher propeller was mounted in the tail. During forward flight the single 3,435-shp General Electric turboshaft provided approximately 2,700 shp to the pusher propeller and 700 shp to the main rotor to reduce the drag caused by the windmilling effect of the rotor if it were left totally unpowered. During vertical takeoffs and landings all power was fed to the main and tail rotors. The AH-56's crew was seated in tandem with a gunner forward of the pilot. The gunner controlled the nose turret which housed either a 7.62-mm minigun or a 40-mm grenade launcher. Additionally, a 30-mm antitank cannon was mounted below the rear fuselage and could be traversed through a full 360-degree field of fire. Four hard points were located on the aircraft's fuselage and stub wings to accommodate TOW missiles or 2.75-inch rocket pods.

In March 1969, six months before production was scheduled to start on the 375 ordered Cheyennes, significant cost overruns on the AH-56 program were reported. Unit costs skyrocketed from $1.2 million to over $2 million. Several technical problems in the Cheyenne's design also became apparent at the same time, which eventually resulted in the fatal crash of a preproduction test aircraft. These factors, as well as pressure from the Air Force, which felt that the Army was preempting Air Force missions by acquiring so capable an aircraft as the AH-56, caused the Army to cancel the Cheyenne's production contract on 19 May 1969 and send the Cheyenne back into research and development. Combat experience in Vietnam brought about a reorientation in Army thinking in the early 1970s, and the service decided that they did not need a deep interdiction attack helicopter but rather a less expensive attack helicopter that could operate over the battle area. The entire AH-56 program was therefore cancelled on 9 August 1972, and a new competition begun for an Advanced Attack Helicopter (AAH).

First flight: September 1967        Service introduction: not operational

**Characteristics**

Crew: 1 pilot, 1 copilot/gunner
Engine: 1 General Electric T64-GE-16 turboshaft of 3,435 shp
Dimensions: length 60 ft 1 in (18.31 m); height 13 ft 8½ in (4.18 m); rotor diameter
    50 ft 4⅘ in (15.36 m); wingspan 26 ft 8½ in (8.14 m)

Weight: empty 11,725 lbs (5,323 kg); loaded (VTOL) 22,000 lbs (9,988 kg)
Speed: maximum 242 mph (389 km/h)
Range: 875 miles (1,408 km)
Ceiling: hover OGE 10,600 ft (3,230 m); service 26,000 ft (7,925 m)
Climb: 3,420 ft/min (1,042 m/min)
Payload: rockets, missiles, ammunition (see text)

The Lockheed AH-56A Cheyenne was winner of the U.S. Army's AAFSS competition but
was not produced in numbers. A rigid-rotor helicopter (like Lockheed's XH-51A), the
Cheyenne had an elongated fuselage, with the anti-torque tail rotor mounted on the
horizontal tail surface and a ventral tail fin and wheel housing. Note the high-visibility
cockpit. (Lockheed)

An AH-56A with underwing stores and a 30-mm antitank cannon in a turret under the
fuselage. Note the camouflage paint scheme of this aircraft, en route to tests in the Army's
Yuma Proving Ground in Arizona. The only visible markings are "68831" on the tail fin
(USAF serial 66-8831). (Lockheed)

# McCulloch
MC-4                           H-30
                               HUM

The McCulloch Model MC-4 was a small, tandem-rotor utility helicopter which was evaluated by both the U.S. Army and Navy. It was a development of the earlier JOV-3, an even smaller, tandem-rotor helicopter designed in 1946. The Model MC-4C, five of which were tested by the Army as the YH-30 and by the Navy as the HUM-1, had a welded steel-tube framework covered with a light metal skin, supported on the ground by a tricycle undercarriage. The two inter-meshing tandem rotors each had three rivetless blades and were driven by a Franklin six-cylinder piston engine mounted horizontally in the middle of the airframe. The helicopter had accommodations for a pilot and a copilot in an enclosed cockpit in the nose and room for a 600-pound disposable load in the fuselage.

No production orders resulted from either the Army or Navy evaluation and attempts to market the MC-4 commercially were also unsuccessful. The designer of the MC-4, D. K. Jovanovich, eventually left McCulloch to form his own helicopter firm, Jovair, and had limited success in marketing a commercial adaptation of the MC-4 design in the mid-1960s.

First flight: 20 March 1951          Service introduction: not operational

**Variants**

YH-30   evaluation helicopter for U.S. Army; 3 built.
HUM-1  evaluation helicopter for U.S. Navy; 2 built.

**Characteristics**

Crew: 1 pilot, 1 copilot
Engine: 1 Franklin 6A4-200-C6 piston 200 hp
Dimensions: length 32 ft 5 in (9.88 m); height 9 ft 1 in (2.75 m); rotor diameter 22 ft (6.71 m)
Weight: empty 1,200 lbs (545 kg); loaded 2,000 lbs (908 kg)
Speed: cruise 85 mph (137 km/h); maximum 100 mph (161 km/h)
Range: 260 miles (418 km)
Ceiling: hover OGE 6,000 ft (1,828 m); service 16,000 ft (4,877 m)
Climb: 675 ft/min (206 m/min)
Payload: 600 lbs (272 kg) including pilot

The McCulloch MC-4 which was evaluated by the U.S. Army as YH-30 and by the Navy as HUM-1. The helicopter had the civil registration N 4071K and was not assigned a military serial number. (McCulloch)

# McDonnell

M-38

R-20 ⎫
H-20 ⎬ Little Henry
H-29 ⎭

The McDonnell's M-38 Little Henry was a one-man flying test bed for a ramjet-powered, two-bladed rotor system. Because the vehicle was capable of vertical free flight, it was assigned a helicopter designation, although it was simply a welded-tube test stand with the two-bladed rotor attached. Small ramjets, weighing only ten pounds each, were secured to the rotor tips and accelerated by an auxiliary starter that rotated the rotor blades to the high speeds necessary for the ramjets to function.

The Little Henry's fuselage was merely an open steel-tube tripod framework, within which were the pilot, fuel tanks, and controls. The ramjets propelled the rotor tips at a speed of 600 feet per second, generating enough lift to carry a load of 500 pounds. Various rotors were tested with diameters up to 20 feet.

The helicopter was flight tested by the U.S. Air Force with two being ordered as XR-20 and changed to XH-20 in 1948 (serial 46-689/690). The proposed production model was designated M-83. The McDonnell M-79 derived from the XH-20 was a private venture intended for crop spraying. The H-29 was to have been a two-seat development of the H-20; the project was cancelled.

First flight: 5 May 1948
Service introduction: not operational

An XH-20 Little Henry; note the rotor-tip ramjets. (U.S. Air Force)

**Characteristics**

Crew: 1 pilot

Engines: 2 rotor-tip mounted ramjets

Dimensions: structure length 12 ft 6 in (3.81 m); height 7 ft (2.13 m); rotor diameter
    18.5 ft (5.64 m)

Weight: empty 280 lbs (127 kg); loaded 780 lbs (354 kg)

Speed: maximum 50 mph (80 km/h)

Range:

Ceiling:

Climb:

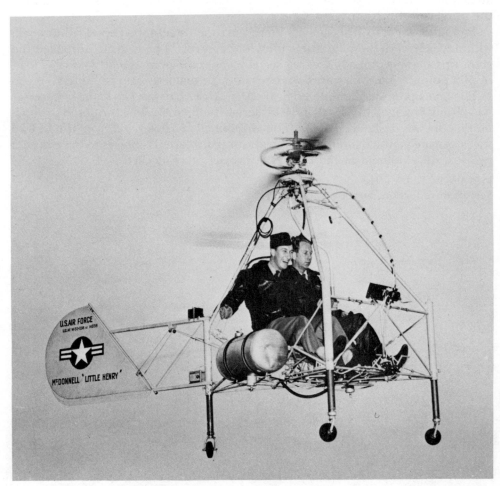

An XH-20 Little Henry in flight. The craft was developed to test ramjet concepts and was
fitted with simple controls and other features for short test flights. (U.S. Air Force)

# McDonnell

65                            HJD
                              HJH

The HJD was originally conceived as an ASW helicopter but was actually built as a flying laboratory to confirm theories on various helicopter rotor parameters. The lone helicopter built to this design (Navy BuNo. 44318) was ordered as the XHJD-1 in 1945, with the designation being changed to XHJH-1 in 1946.

The helicopter had side-by-side rotors mounted on outriggers extending from the engines which were themselves mounted on stub wings. In cruise flight the wings could support about ten percent of the aircraft's weight. The span of the aircraft was 41 feet from the center of the rotor hubs; the total span over the three-bladed rotors was 91 feet. The rotor blades and direction of the rotation as well as other aerodynamic features of the aircraft were varied during the flight test program. The original tail fin was subsequently supplemented with an externally braced horizontal control surface. The XHJH-1's main landing gear extended down from the engine nacelles and was externally braced; a tail wheel was also fitted. Extensive instrumentation was provided.

The lone XHJH-1 was engaged in test and evaluation from 1946 until 1951. The McDonnell company name for the aircraft was Whirlaway.

First flight: 27 April 1946
Service introduction: not operational

The first U.S. twin-engine helicopter, the Navy's XHJD-1 became the XHJH-1 shortly after its first flight in 1946 when the Navy changed the McDonnell code letter from D to H. It flew with the outer panels of the outriggers both covered and uncovered. Intended from the outset for research and development, the aircraft did not have an operational role.

**Characteristics**

Crew: 1 pilot, 1 crewman

Engines: 2 Pratt & Whitney R-985-AN-14B Wasp Junior radial piston 450 hp each
     T/O; normal 400 hp

Dimensions: length 32 ft 2 in (9.8 m); height 12 ft 3 in (3.7 m); rotor diameter 46 ft
     (14.0 m), later increased to 50 ft (15.2 m)

Weight: empty 7,386 lbs (3,353 kg); loaded 11,000 lbs (4,994 kg)

Speed: cruise 90 mph (145 km/h); maximum 120 mph (193 km/h)

Range: 300 miles (483 km)

Ceiling: hover 50 ft (15 m); service 12,900 ft (3,932 m)

Climb: 1,300 ft/min (396 m/min)

The XHJH-1, shown here hovering over the McDonnell plant at Lambert Field, St. Louis, was flown from April 1946 until June 1951 for rotary-wing research and evaluation. This photo is believed to have been taken in November 1949 and shows horizontal tail surfaces fitted. Rotor blades of various diameters were also fitted during the Whirlaway's career. (McDonnell Douglas)

# McDonnell

78                              HRH

This was to have been a heavy assault helicopter. Three aircraft were ordered in 1951 with the designation XHRH-1, but the project was terminated in 1953. The Navy BuNos. were 133736/738.

The HRH was to have had a single main rotor and rotor-tip jets, stub wings to unload the rotor at high forward speeds, and tractor propellers mounted on the wings, in effect making it a compound aircraft. For vertical and low-speed flight, the engines were to have been coupled through clutches to a pair of compressors which supplied high-pressure air to the rotor-tip jets. Wingspan was to have been 45 feet.

The HRH was co-winner with the Sikorsky HR2S (later H-37) for the Marine Corps's heavy assault requirement.

First flight: not flown

**Characteristics**

Crew: 1 pilot, 1 copilot
Engines: 2 Allison T56 turboshaft 3,790 hp each
Dimensions: length 65 ft 11 in (20.1 m); rotor diameter 66 ft (20.1 m)
Weight: loaded 30,412 lbs (13,807 kg)
Speed: maximum 276 mph (444 km/h)
Range: 230 miles (370 km)
Ceiling: hover OGE 10,000 ft (3,048 m)
Climb: 2,300 ft/min (701 m/min) vertical
        1,850 ft/min (564 m/min) propeller-driven flight
Payload: 30 troops

A full-scale mock-up of the McDonnell XHRH-1 showing the nose unloading ramp for troops and light vehicles. Note the conventional engine nacelles with three-bladed propellers. (McDonnell Douglas)

# McDonnell

86                            HCH

This helicopter was proposed in 1951 as a ship-to-shore flying crane. A contract was awarded to McDonnell in 1952 for three XHCH-1 prototypes (Navy BuNos. 138654/656), but the project was terminated in January 1959.

The single three-bladed rotor was to have had rotor-tip jets. The power plants and rotor system were to have been essentially identical to the HRH. When the HRH was cancelled, rotor development was transferred to this project and some rotor testing was accomplished.

First flight: not flown

**Characteristics**

Crew: 1 pilot, 1 copilot
Engines: 2 Allison T56-A-2 turboshaft 3,790 hp each
Dimensions: rotor diameter 65 ft (19.8 m)
Weight: loaded 35,000 lbs (15,890 kg)
Speed: cruise 103.5 mph (166.6 km/h) with slung cargo
Range: 92 miles (148 km)
Ceiling: hover OGE 7,500 ft (2,286 m)
Climb: 2,900 ft/min (884 m/min)

Mock-up of the McDonnell XHCH-1. The helicopter was to have a plexiglass cockpit, two externally mounted turbine engines, and a three-fin tail design. (McDonnell Douglas)

# McDonnell

L-25
H-33
V-1

This rotary-wing liaison aircraft was a joint effort of McDonnell, the U.S. Army, and the U.S. Air Force. Designed by Friedrich Doblhoff, Austrian helicopter pioneer who had developed the Wn 342 in Germany during World War II, the McDonnell aircraft used a jet-driven rotor for vertical flight. A pusher propeller driven by a piston engine and conventional wings to off-load the rotor were used for forward flight. The aircraft was initially designated L-25 as a liaison machine but soon changed to H-35 in the Army/USAF helicopter series. After the converti-plane designation (V) was established in 1952 the aircraft was changed to XV-1.

The fuselage had a cabin in its forward end with extensive plexiglass to facilitate observation and a seven-cylinder Continental radial engine in its after end. For vertical flight the engine drove two compressors that fed air through the three rotor blades to small pressure jets at the tips. For forward flight a two-bladed propeller was mounted at the after end of the fuselage. The rotor blades autorotated during forward flight. After tests a small rotor for directional control was installed at the after end of each boom. The straight wing (span 26 feet) supported twin booms, which had twin tail fins and were connected by a horizontal tail surface. The cabin could accommodate a pilot and copilot in tandem, or a pilot with three seated passengers or two stretchers. The under-fuselage landing gear consisted of two simple skids.

The first of two prototypes (serial 53-4016/017) was completed in early 1954, and tethered hover tests began on 15 February 1954. Problems with the pressure-jet system delayed free flights until that summer. The first successful conversion from helicopter to conventional flight took place on 29 April 1955. Various minor improvements were made in the second aircraft, which made its first flight on 14 July 1954. The XV-1 on 10 October 1956 became the world's first rotary-wing aircraft to reach a speed of 200 mph. The performance of the XV-1, however, did not justify developing it to operational status, especially in comparison with advanced helicopter designs, and the program was terminated in 1957.

First flight: 14 July 1954
Service introduction: not operational

### Characteristics

Crew: 1 pilot + 1 student in trainer configuration
Engine: 1 Continental R-975-19 radial piston 550 hp; McDonnell rotor-tip pressure jets
Dimensions: length (over tailbooms) 50 ft 5 in (15.37 m); height 10 ft 9 in (3.28 m); rotor diameter 31 ft (9.45 m)
Weight: empty 4,277 lbs (1,942 kg); loaded 5,505 lbs (2,499 kg)
Speed: cruise 138 mph (222 km/h); maximum 203 mph (327 km/h)
Range: 593 miles (955 km)
Ceiling: hover OGE 5,900 ft (1,798 m); service 19,800 ft (6,035 m)
Climb: maximum 1,300 ft/min (396 m/min); vertical 308 ft/min (94 m/min)
Payload: 3 troops or 2 stretchers

The first XV-1 (53-4016) convertiplane had an unusual design, reminiscent of some German war-era designs for utility and liaison aircraft. The pusher propeller was mounted at the after end of the fuselage, between the twin tailbooms. (U.S. Air Force)

This is the same aircraft in flight after modifications that included the installation of small anti-torque rotors at the end of the tailbooms. (McDonnell)

# Piasecki

PV-3                                                                    HRP-1 Rescuer

The tandem-rotor HRP, generally referred to in the Fleet as the "flying banana," was ordered by the U.S. Navy on 1 February 1944. The PV-3 was the second helicopter developed by Frank N. Piasecki's P.V. Engineering Forum, the first being the single-seat, single-main rotor PV-2. The subsequent PV-3 was the world's first practical tandem-rotor helicopter and at the time of its appearance also the world's largest. As the HRP Rescuer, the helicopter was evaluated in a number of roles by the Navy, Marine Corps, and Coast Guard. Fuselage seating was provided for up to ten passengers or six stretchers. A privately built demonstration helicopter (designated XHRP-X) flew on 7 March 1945, powered by a Wright R-975 piston engine. As a result, the Navy ordered two XHRP-1 prototypes for service trials, followed by an order in June 1946 for ten production HRP-1s with an additional ten being ordered later.

The HRP had the tandem rotors favored by Piasecki, with the three-bladed rotors at the extremities of the fuselage, which was "bent" at mid-point, giving it a distinctive appearance. The tubular frameworks of the prototypes were not covered with fabric. In service some of the production HRP-1s operated with the fabric covering removed to reduce weight. (The few HRP-2s had metal skin.) A twin-fin assembly was fitted, as well as a tricycle landing gear with the nose wheel behind the plexiglass cockpit. The HRP originally had a large door that hinged at the forward end, making it impossible to open in forward flight and difficult in a hover; it was replaced by a sliding door, and doughnut-type floats were included in some aircraft. During ASW evaluation an AN/AQS-4 dipping sonar was fitted.

Two XHRP-1 prototypes (BuNos. 37968/969) were followed by 20 HRP-1s and four helicopters built to the improved HRP-2 configuration (listed separately).

Three of the XHRP-1s served with the U.S. Coast Guard 1948-1952 and 12 with the U.S. Marine Corps 1948-1950 (being the second helicopter type to be assigned to the Marines, the Sikorsky HO3S-1 also entering service in 1948). The Marines used their HRP-1s to help develop vertical assault tactics during operations from the light carrier *Saipan* (CVL 48) and escort carrier *Palau* (CVE 122). Navy squadrons flew the HRP-1 into 1953. Some were later used for civilian operations.

First flight: HRP-1 15 August 1947
Service introduction: June 1947
Users: United States

**Variants**

XHRP-1  prototype with Wright R-975; 2 built, 1 for flight test and 1 for static test.
HRP-1  production aircraft; first flight 15 August 1947; 20 built.

**Characteristics (HRP-1)**

Crew: 1 pilot, 1 copilot
Engine: 1 Pratt & Whitney R-1340-AN-1 radial piston 600 hp T/O; 550 hp continuous
Dimensions: length 54 ft 9½ in (16.7 m); height 14 ft 11 in (4.55 m); rotor diameter 41 ft (12.5 m)
Weight: empty 5,193 lbs (2,358 kg); loaded 6,900 lbs (3,133 kg)
Speed: cruise 73.5 mph (118 km/h); maximum 99 mph (159 km/h)
Range: 265 miles (427 km)
Ceiling: hover OGE 5,400 ft (1,646 m); hover IGE 6,900 ft (2,103 m); service 8,500 ft (2,591 m)
Climb: 650 ft/min (198 m/min)
Payload: 8 troops or 6 stretchers

A U.S. Navy HRP-1 in flight displays the shape that led to its nickname "Flying Banana." Note the lack of unit/service markings, the large side door, forward cockpit, and close spacing of the nose wheel and main landing gear. Despite its odd appearance, the HRP-1 represented a significant step forward in the development of U.S. naval helicopters. (Piasecki)

# Piasecki

| | |
|---|---|
| PV-17 | HRP-2 Rescuer |
| PD-22 | |
| PD-42 | H-21 $\begin{cases} \text{Workhorse} \\ \text{Shawnee} \end{cases}$ |
| PD-43 | |
| PD-44 | HPK-1 |
| PD-47 | |

The HRP-2 was an improved version of the U.S. Navy's HRP-1 Rescuer (listed separately), with a streamlined, all-metal fuselage skin increasing its performance. Although the Navy procured only four HRP-2s, preferring instead the smaller but more capable Piasecki HJP/HUP, the U.S. Air Force purchased 214 H-21s with the name Workhorse and the U.S. Army acquired another 334 H-21s which were assigned the name Shawnee. From December 1961 until late 1963 the H-21 was the Army's workhorse of the Vietnam War, being replaced by the HU-1/UH-1 Huey. Production of the H-21 was started by the Piasecki Helicopter Corporation, as the firm was known from 1949, but was continued from 1955 by the successor Vertol Aircraft Corporation.* The 40-series designations were assigned by Vertol. Production totaled 557 HRP-2/H-21s for U.S. service plus almost 150 for foreign use. A U.S. Army H-21 made the first nonstop transcontinental helicopter flight across the United States on 24 August 1956, traveling 2,610 miles in 37 hours.

The HRP-2/H-21 design was a single-engine, tandem-rotor helicopter with three-bladed rotors mounted at the extremities of the fuselage. There was a plexiglass cabin in the nose, behind which was the cargo compartment, with the engine mounted in the rear of the fuselage. The HRP-2 was configured for 8 passengers or 6 stretchers, while the H-21A could carry 14 troops or 12 stretchers, and the H-21B/C could lift 20 troops. The Navy aircraft had a 600-hp Pratt & Whitney R-1340-AN-1; the Army/Air Force helicopters had a Wright R-1820 piston radial providing more than twice that power. Two H-21Cs had their single radials replaced by two General Electric T58 turboshaft engines. These were redesignated H-21D. There was no procurement of this configuration. The H-21s retained the Navy's close-set tricycle landing gear with fixed undercarriage. However, helicopters assigned to SAR functions often had doughnut-shaped floats fitted instead of wheels. Twin vertical fins were usually fitted at the tail. Several experimental weapon suites were fitted to Army H-21s, with one Army H-21C being armed with two .30-caliber and two .50-caliber forward-firing machine guns, a rocket pack with 24 2.75-inch folding-fin rockets, and two .30-caliber flexible MGs fitted at the side doors.

Three of the Navy's HRP-2s were flown by the Marine Corps. The Air Force H-21 program began with 18 YH-21s, the first tandem-rotor helicopter flown by

---

*Vertol was an acronym of Vertical Takeoff and Landing; Piasecki in 1955 formed the Piasecki Aircraft Corporation. See Appendix A.

that service. Subsequently, 33 H-21A models were ordered for USAF SAR operations, mainly in the Arctic, and another five went to Canada. These were followed by 334 H-21C variants for U.S. Army and foreign use. Of the latter, 26 went to the West German Army, 98 to the French Army, 10 to the French Navy, and 6 to the Japanese Air Self-Defense Force. Vertol also produced 11 Model 44A helicopters for use by the Swedish Navy, designated HPK-1 by that service.

First flight: HRP-2 10 November 1949, YH-21 11 April 1952
Service introduction: 1950
Users: Canada, France, West Germany, Japan, Sweden, United States

**Variants**

HRP-2 Navy variant with 600-hp Pratt & Whitney R-1340-AN-1 engine (as HRP-1); weight empty 5,205 lbs, loaded 7,500 lbs; 41-ft rotor diameter; 4 built (factory designation PV-17).

YH-21 USAF pre-production aircraft; 18 built (factory PD-22).

H-21A USAF production SAR helicopter with 1,250-hp Wright R-1820-103 engine de-rated to 1,150 hp; loaded 11,500 lbs; first flight October 1953; 38 built including 5 for Canada (factory 42); changed to CH-21A in 1962.

H-21B USAF production assault transport with 1,425-hp R-1820-103; loaded 15,000 lbs; auto-pilot, external fuel tanks, armor; first flight November 1955; 163 built for USAF (factory 421); some employed in SAR role designated SH-21B; changed to CH-21B and then to HH-21B in 1962.

H-21C U.S. Army production cargo/transport helicopter; similar to H-21B; first flight June 1953; 334 built for U.S. Army and foreign service (factory 43); changed to CH-21C in 1962.

H-21D H-21C fitted with 2 General Electric T58 turboshaft engines; first flight September 1957; 2 converted.

HPK-1 Swedish naval variant with 1,425-hp Wright 977C9HD1 Cyclone engine; 11 built (factory 44A).

**Characteristics**

Crew: 1 pilot, 1 copilot + crewmen in some roles
Engine: HRP-2 1 Pratt & Whitney R-1340-AN-1 radial piston 600 hp T/O; 550 hp continuous
H-21B/C 1 Wright R-1820-103 radial piston 1,425 hp

| | | HRP-2 | H-21B/C |
|---|---|---|---|
| Dimensions: | length | | |
| | height | 14 ft 10½ in (4.54 m) | 15 ft 5 in (4.7 m) |
| | rotor | 41 ft (12.5 m) | 44 ft 6 in (13.56 m) |
| Weight: | empty | 5,205 lbs (2,363 kg) | 8,000 lbs (3,632 kg) |
| | loaded | 7,500 lbs (3,405 kg) | 15,000 lbs (6,810 kg) |
| Speed: | cruise | (as maximum) | 98 mph (158 km/h) |
| | maximum | 100 mph (161 km/h) | 131 mph (211 km/h) |
| Range: | | | |
| Ceiling: | hover OGE | 4,600 ft (1,402 m) | |
| | hover IGE | 6,000 ft (1,829 m) | |
| | service | 9,800 ft (2,987 m) | 9,450 ft (2,880 m) |
| Climb: | | 780 ft/min (238 m/min) | 1,080 ft/min (329 m/min) |
| Payload: | | 8 troops or 6 stretchers | 20 troops |

This H-21 of the U.S. Air Force's 516th Troop Carrier Group is flying cargo to a radar station in the Arctic. These helicopters were used extensively and effectively by the USAAF and Army from the Arctic ice to the jungles of Vietnam before they were discarded in the mid-1960s. (The U.S. Army used them in Vietnam until June 1964.) (U.S. Air Force)

Soldiers secure an Army H-21C assigned to the 509th Transportation Company. Note the attitude of the H-21 when at rest; in flight the cabin is level, increasing crew comfort. The aircraft resembles only superficially its HRP predecessor. The naval version of the H-21, the HRP-2 Rescuer, was not produced in significant numbers. (U.S. Army)

An Army H-21C blasts away with rockets and machine guns during tests of armed helicopter configurations. Although such helicopters were used extensively by the French Army in Algeria (after some experiments in Indochina), the first true helicopter gunships to be employed in combat were the U.S. Army UH-1B Hueys of the Utility Tactical Transport Helicopter Company, which arrived in South Vietnam in mid-1962. (U.S. Army)

U.S. Army CH-21 Shawnee helicopters on Banchee Field, Fort Rucker, Ala., in 1963. A short time later many were in Vietnam. (U.S. Army)

# Piasecki

PV-14                                    HJP  } Retriever
PV-18                                    HUP

H-25 Army Mule

Following the relatively successful U.S. Navy trials with the HRP, the Navy ordered the improved HJP for shipboard utility and rescue duties, especially "plane guard" for pilots who crashed into the sea during carrier landings or takeoffs. The HJP designation was changed to HUP in 1949 when U was substituted for J in aircraft and squadron designations. In the fleet the HUP was known as the "hup-mobile" or "shoe" (because of its shape). The U.S. Army procured 70 of these helicopters as H-25s but subsequently transferred 50 to the Navy. Nineteen were procured for foreign use, mostly by the French and Canadian navies.

The HUP/H-25 had the Piasecki tandem-rotor design, with a smaller and more streamlined fuselage than the HRP/H-21 design. The two three-bladed rotors overlapped, thus reducing the size of the helicopter to facilitate shipboard operation. The HUP could fit on aircraft carrier elevators without folding its blades, and on most cruiser elevators with blades folded. The pilot and copilot sat in the nose, below the forward rotor, as in the HRP/H-21. Behind the cockpit the cabin could accommodate four passengers or three stretchers, with the single Continental engine mounted aft. The tubular, metal-covered fuselage rested on a fixed undercarriage. The HUP-1s had vertical tail fins on the after rotor pylon. They were deleted in later helicopters (which had auto-pilots fitted). The Navy variants had all-weather instrumentation, and some had AN/AQS-4 dipping sonar fitted for ASW operations (designated HUP-2S). A hatch in the bottom of the fuselage permitted personnel to be hoisted directly up into the cabin.

After trials with two XHJP-1s (BuNo. 37976/977), the Navy ordered 32 HUP-1 variants for shipboard operation. These were followed by 165 HUP-2s, some fitted with dipping sonar. The Marines flew 13 of the Navy HUPs. The Army procured 70 helicopters similar to the HUP-2, designated H-25A. These were too small for Army requirements and 50 were transferred to the Navy as HUP-3s. The Navy HUP-2/3 survivors were redesignated UH-25B/C, respectively, in 1962. Another 15 HUP-2s went to the French Navy and 3 HUP-3s went to the Canadian Navy.

First flight:
Service introduction: February 1949
Users: Canada, France, United States

**Variants**

XHJP-1  prototype helicopter; 2 built (factory designation PV-14).
HUP-1   production helicopter with 525-hp Continental R-975-34 engine; loaded 5,355 lbs; 32 built (factory designation PV-18).
HUP-2   production helicopter with 550-hp Continental R-975-42; some modified for ASW as HUP-2S; 165 built; changed to H-25B in 1962.
HUP-3   former U.S. Army H-25A transferred to Navy; 50 transferred; changed to H-25C in 1962.
HUP-4   modified HUP-2S; 1 modified (BuNo. 129978).
H-25A   production helicopter for U.S. Army with 525-hp Continental R-975-42; 70 built, with 50 transferred to U.S. Navy as HUP-3.

**Characteristics**

Crew: 1 pilot, 1 copilot plus crewmen in some roles

Engines: HUP-1 1 Continental R-975-34 radial piston 525 hp T/O; 500 hp continuous;
  H-25A same horsepower with R-975-42 engine

Dimensions: length 31 ft 10 in (9.7 m); height 12 ft 6 in (3.8 m); rotor diameter 35 ft
  (10.67 m)

| | | HUP-1 | H-25A |
|---|---|---|---|
| Weight: | empty | 4,214 lbs (1,913 kg) | |
| | loaded | 6,000 lbs (2,724 kg) | |
| Speed: | cruise | 75 mph (121 km/h) | 92 mph (148 km/h) |
| | maximum | 119.5 mph (192.5 km/h) | 115 mph (185 km/h) |
| Range: | | 275 miles (443 km) | 357 miles (574 km) |
| Ceiling: | hover OGE | 9,000 ft (2,743 m) | |
| | hover IGE | 10,200 ft (3,109 m) | |
| | service | | 12,700 ft (3,871 m) |
| Climb: | | 1,220 ft/min (372 m/min) | |
| Payload: | 4 troops or 2 stretchers + 1 attendant | | |

An HUP-2 from HU-2 hovers over the cruiser *Salem* (CA-139) while lowering it messages.
In the background the carrier *Lake Champlain* (CVA-39) and a destroyer refuel from a fleet
oiler during U.S. Sixth Fleet operations in the Mediterranean in 1957. (U.S. Navy)

An HUP-2 "Hupmobile" prepares to land on the carrier *Kitty Hawk* (CVA-63) behind another HUP-2 from Helicopter Utility Squadron (HU)1. Note the open circular doorway on the left side. The dark rectangular object below the helicopter is a raised jet blast deflector. During the 1960s, when this photograph was taken, U.S. carriers were assigned two utility/SAR helicopters. (U.S. Navy)

# Piasecki

| | |
|---|---|
| PV-15 | R-16 |
| PV-45 | H-16 Transporter |
| | H-16A ⎫ |
| | H-27 ⎬ Turbo Transporter |
| | ⎭ |

This large, graceful-looking helicopter was developed in response to a U.S. Air Force requirement for a long-range rescue helicopter. Initially designated XR-16, the two prototypes became XH-16 from June 1948 onward.* The XH-16 design included two radial engines, which were installed in the first prototype (serial 50-1269). The second (50-1270) had two turboshafts and was redesignated XH-27 on 3 October 1952. They were then changed to XH-16 and YH-16A, respectively. Like the previous Piasecki helicopters for military service, the H-16 design had three-bladed tandem rotors and, at the time of development, the H-16 was the world's largest helicopter. Subsequently, the YH-16A/XH-27 was also credited with being the world's first twin-turbine helicopter (renamed Turbo Transporter).

The H-16 design had a very large fuselage, almost the size of that of the four-engined C-54 (civil DC-6) transport. The all-metal helicopter had one engine forward, just behind the nose cockpit, and the second engine aft, in the upper section of the fuselage, providing clearance for vehicles and troops to enter the helicopter up a rear loading ramp. The after rotor was fitted to a large tail pylon that placed the after rotor hub almost 15 feet above the fuselage. The interchangeable landing gears could be increased in length to permit cargo pods to be

---

*The designation XR-16 was subsequently assigned to a large reconnaissance aircraft for the Strategic Air Command, but that project was cancelled.

slung under the helicopter. The amidships wheels were on faired outriggers with the tail wheel just forward of the ramp. At various times the two prototypes had horizontal tail surfaces fitted to the forward edge of the after rotor pylon, and the YH-16A was at one point fitted with large endplates mounted on struts attached to the rotor pylon. Although designed as a long-range rescue helicopter, the H-16 was evaluated largely in the troop/cargo-carrying role, having a fuselage cargo cabin 38 feet long, 9 feet wide, and 6 feet high, with 348 square feet of floor space. Normal cargo capacity was three jeep-type vehicles or 25 troops or 24 stretchers; however, maximum density loading could increase this significantly (see Payload, below).

Both prototypes were flight tested, with the XH-16 eventually being taken over by the Army for evaluation. The YH-16A established an unofficial helicopter speed record, reaching 166 mph at the beginning of 1956, but was destroyed in a crash on 5 January 1956. The H-16 project was ended that summer. A growth version YH-16B (PV-59) was planned.

First flight: XH-16 23 October 1953, YH-16A 1955
Service introduction: not operational

### Characteristics (XH-16 except where indicated)

Crew: 1 pilot, 1 copilot, 1 crewman
Engines: YH-16A 2 Allison YT38-A-10 turboshaft 1,800 hp each
        XH-16 2 Pratt & Whitney R-2180-11 radial piston 1,650 hp each (T/O; 1,300 hp sustained)
Dimensions: length 77 ft 7 in (23.65 m); height 25 ft (7.62 m); rotor diameter 82 ft (24.99 m)

|          |         | YH-16A                   | XH-16                    |
|----------|---------|--------------------------|--------------------------|
| Weight:  | empty   | 22,506 lbs (10,218 kg)   | 22,033 lbs (10,003 kg)   |
|          | loaded  | 33,577 lbs (15,244 kg)   | 37,600 lbs (17,070 kg)   |
| Speed:   | cruise  | 100 mph (161 km/h)       | 100 mph (161 km/h)       |
|          | maximum | 146 mph (235 km/h)       | 127 mph (204 km/h)       |

Range: 244 miles (393 km); rescue mission 1,432 miles (2,304 km)
Ceiling: hover 15,750 ft (4,801 m); service 22,900 ft (6,980 m)
Climb: 2,455 ft/min (748 m/min)
Payload: maximum 40 troops or 32 stretchers + 2 attendants or 3 light trucks

The first prototype H-16 Transporter in flight. This aircraft was perhaps the most graceful and the largest of the Piasecki tandem-rotor designs. In this view a small horizontal tail surface is fitted at the top of the after rotor pylon. The helicopter's nickname—Transporter—is on a black panel painted on the fuselage behind the cockpit. (Piasecki)

The second prototype—as the H-16A—in flight. No tail surfaces are fitted and an engine exhaust is visible under the forward fuselage. Note the widely spaced main landing gear and flat fuselage floor for handling jeep-type vehicles loaded through the rear ramp. (Piasecki)

# Piasecki

16H-1                                    Pathfinder II

The original Pathfinder was a high-speed compound helicopter developed as a private venture for research into high-speed rotary-wing aircraft. After two years of flight tests, in 1964 the U.S. Army and Navy sponsored modifications to the aircraft with the goal of attaining speeds up to 230 mph. Redesignated Pathfinder II under military sponsorship, the aircraft reached a speed of 225 mph and demonstrated excellent maneuverability.

The aircraft had an all-metal, three-bladed rotor (fully articulated) with a ducted propeller in the rear (known as a ring-tail) to provide forward thrust after takeoff. The ring-tail had vertical vanes in the duct to give directional and anti-torque control. The aircraft's small wing off-loaded the rotor during cruise. The rotor was mounted on a streamlined pylon above the semi-monocoque, all-metal fuselage. A fixed tail wheel was attached to the ring-tail while the main landing gear retracted into the wings.

Piasecki proposed the development of a series of military and civilian twin-turbine compound helicopters based on this design.

First flight: 16H-1 21 February 1962
Service introduction: not operational

**Variants**

16H-1    original configuration with Pratt & Whitney PT6B-2 turboshaft 550-shp engine;
         41-ft rotor; 2 crew + 3 passengers; reached speed of 170 mph; 1 built.

16H-1A modified aircraft for Army-Navy research; fitted with General Electric T58 turboshaft engine; new drive system, longer fuselage; reached 225 mph; renamed Pathfinder II; first flight 15 November 1965.

16H-1C additional modifications to aircraft.

### Characteristics (16H-1A)

Crew: 1 pilot, 1 copilot

Engine: 1 General Electric T-58-GE-5 turboshaft 1,250 shp

Dimensions: length 37 ft 3 in (11.4 m); height 11 ft 4 in (3.5 m); rotor diameter 44 ft (13.4 m)

Weight: empty 4,800 lbs (2,179 kg); maximum T/O weight in VTOL mode 8,150 lbs (3,700 kg); maximum T/O weight in STOL mode 10,800 lbs (4,903 kg)

Speed: cruise 175 mph (282 km/h); maximum 225 mph (362 km/h)

Range: VTOL mode 450 miles (724 km); STOL mode 970 miles (1,561 km)

Ceiling: hover OGE 7,800 ft (2,377 m); hover IGE 10,700 ft (3,260 m); service 18,700 ft (5,700 m)

Climb:

Payload: 6 troops

The Piasecki 16H-1A Pathfinder II was originally a rotary-wing research aircraft developed as a private venture. It was rebuilt into the configuration shown here under a joint Army-Navy contract. The ducted propeller at the extreme tail has vertical vanes which provided directional and anti-torque control. The main landing gear fully retracted to further streamline the aircraft's shape. (Piasecki)

# Pitcairn

| | |
|---|---|
| PA 33 | OP |
| PA 34 | G-2 |

Pitcairn autogiros were evaluated by the U.S. Navy, Marine Corps, and Army Air Corps in the 1930s to determine the value of short takeoff and landing aircraft.

The Pitcairn autogiros were based on the La Cierva designs, using conventional aircraft fuselages and engines, with standard tail surfaces, and stub wings that angled up at their extremities. The three-bladed rotor was mounted on a rigid tripod above the forward, open cockpit. One Navy aircraft (BuNo. A8977) was experimentally fitted with floats. In 1935 the Navy had Pitcairn remove the wings from aircraft A8850 and relied entirely on the unpowered rotor for lift. The XOP-1 was also flight tested by the Navy in a radio-controlled ("Robot") configuration. Take-off run was approximately 280 feet.

The Navy acquired three machines designated XOP-1 in 1931: one (A8850) was tested aboard the experimental aircraft carrier *Langley* (CV-1) on 23 September 1931; another (A8987) was used by the Marines in Nicaragua during 1932, where it was evaluated in the field against a Vought 02U-1 biplane during counterguerrilla operations. The conventional aircraft was superior in almost all respects, except that the autogiro could land at a precise location and stop with a roll of less than 50 feet. The Army's lone YG-2 was acquired in 1936 to determine its value for observation and artillery spotting in competition with the Kellett YG-1. The Army aircraft was destroyed during tests. The RAF acquired seven similar PA 39s in the United States during World War II (serial BW 828/834); three were lost at sea in January 1942 while being shipped to England.

The U.S. Navy's first rotary-wing aircraft, a Pitcairn autogiro assigned bureau number A8850, at the Naval Air Station Anacostia in Washington, D.C., in 1931. The aircraft is fitted with wings having upturned end panels. (U.S. Navy)

First flight: XOP-1 1931
Service introduction: 1931 (for test and evaluation)
Users: Great Britain, United States

**Variants**

XOP-1  commercial PA 34; 3 built for Navy.
XOP-2  XOP-1 with stub wings removed; 1 converted.
YG-2    commercial PA 33; Wright R957-9 400-hp engine; 1 built for Army.

**Characteristics (XOP-1)**

Crew: 1 pilot, 1 observer
Engine: 1 Wright R-975-E radial piston 420 hp
Dimensions: length 23 ft 1 in (7.0 m); rotor diameter 30 ft 3 in (9.2 m)
Weight: loaded 3,057 lbs (1,388 kg)
Speed: maximum 115 mph (185 km/h)
Range:
Ceiling:
Climb:

The U.S. Army's lone Pitcairn YG-2 at rest. No wings are fitted and the horizontal tail surfaces have upturned end panels. The undercarriage also differs from the Navy XOP-1 configuration. The red-and-white tail markings were used by U.S. military aircraft until 1942. (U.S. Air Force)

# Platt LePage

### R-1

This helicopter, the first aircraft to be designated in the U.S. Army's rotary-wing (R) series, was an experimental machine, one of several evaluated during the World War II period. The XR-1 and XR-1A were built under an Army contract awarded on 19 July 1940, the second such contract for a helicopter, the first having been given 19 years earlier to de Bothezat.

W. Lawrence LePage had visited Germany in the 1930s, and the XR-1 design was heavily influenced by the Fa 61 and other German rotary-wing concepts. The XR-1 had a conventional aircraft fuselage and tail assembly, but the engine was in the center of the aircraft and drove two rotors at the top of two streamlined pylons. The two-man crew sat in separate, tandem cockpits forward of the rotor pylons.

Flight tests of the XR-1 were satisfactory, but no additional machines were ordered for service. A second helicopter of this design, designated XR-1A, was built with more plexiglass paneling to improve visibility, and the observer was placed ahead of the pilot, an arrangement opposite to that of the XR-1.

The XR-1 was found to have a relatively weak airframe during static tests, and, despite repairs and modifications, flight tests proceeded slowly until the last flight on 21 June 1946. The second prototype (XR-1A) also flew until 1946, when it was transferred to a civilian user.

First flight: XR-1 May 1941        Service introduction: not operational

**Variants**

XR-1    experimental aircraft; 1 built (serial 41-001); damaged July 1943.

XR-1A   modified aircraft with R-985-AN-1 450-hp engine; 5,300 lbs loaded; first flight December 1943; 1 built (serial 42-6581); later flown as a civilian aircraft (registration NX 6950).

**Characteristics (XR-1)**

Crew: 1 pilot, 1 observer
Engine: 1 Pratt & Whitney R-985-2 radial piston 440 hp
Dimensions: length 29 ft 4 in (8.9 m); rotor diameter 30 ft 6 in (9.3 m)
Weight: XR-1 loaded 4,730 lbs (2,147 kg); XR-1A loaded 5,300 lbs (2,406 kg)
Speed: XR-1 maximum 110 mph (177 km/h); XR-1A 100 mph (161 km/h)
Range:
Ceiling:
Climb:

The Platt LePage XR-1A during flight tests, probably in 1944. This aircraft was the first U.S. helicopter with twin main rotors. (U.S. Air Force)

The XR-1A displays its ungraceful lines while on the ground. (U.S. Air Force)

# Rotor-Craft

## R-11

A single lightweight XR-11 was built for evaluation by the USAAF.

The helicopter had contra-rotating, intermeshing rotor blades with the hubs of the three-bladed rotors 12 feet 4 inches apart. It had a welded steel tubular construction with fabric covering.

Consideration was given to an enlarged helicopter of this type for commercial service, dubbed Rotorbus, that was to have carried 20 passengers.

First flight:          Service introduction: not operational

**Characteristics**

Crew: 1 pilot, 1 observer
Engine: 1 Continental A-100 piston 100 hp
Dimensions: length 15 ft (4.6 m); height 7 ft 6 in (2.3 m); rotor diameter 18 ft (5.5 m)
Weight: empty 900 lbs (409 kg); loaded 1,350 lbs (613 kg)
Speed:
Range:
Ceiling:
Climb:

The lone XR-11 (serial 45-9478), seen here with fabric covering removed, was a lightweight tandem-rotor helicopter that was evaluated briefly by the USAAF. (U.S. Air Force)

# Seibel
S-4A                                    H-24

The Seibel Sky-Hawk was a uniquely configured, light commercial design, two examples of which were procured for U.S. Army evaluation in 1951 as the YH-24. The craft was composed of a welded steel-tube framework, the forward section of which was completely open, the pilot sitting behind a windscreen and well forward of the power plant and rotor system. Aft of the pilot, and below the four-cylinder piston engine, was an enclosed compartment suitable for either a stretcher or seated passenger. Loading of this compartment was accomplished from the rear, below the tailboom.

The YH-24 was powered by a 125-hp Lycoming engine which drove two-bladed main and tail rotors constructed of laminated wood. The tail rotor was mounted on a tapered tubular monocoque tailboom, and the landing gear was the fixed, wheeled tricycle type. The Army was interested in the YH-24 primarily as a casualty evacuation helicopter. A later modification of the YH-24 shortened and widened the forward fuselage to permit side-by-side seating, while retaining the compartment beneath the engine. Skid-type landing gear was fitted to this variant, although no new designation was assigned. No production orders resulted from the Army evaluation.

First flight: 1951      Service introduction: not operational

**Characteristics**

Crew: 1 pilot
Engine: 1 Lycoming O-290-D piston 125 hp
Dimensions: length 35 ft 1 in (10.7 m); height 10 ft (3.05 m); rotor diameter 29 ft 1½ in (8.88 m)
Weight: empty 960 lbs (436 kg); loaded 1,500 lbs (681 kg)
Speed: cruise 60 mph (97 km/h); maximum 65 mph (105 km/h)
Range: 98 miles (158 km)
Ceiling: service 4,300 ft (1,311 m)
Climb: 700 ft/min (213 m/min)
Payload: 1 passenger

The unusual-looking Siebel YH-24 during low-level flight with the covering removed from the below-engine passenger space. A small anti-torque rotor was fitted at the end of the tailboom. There was no covering for the pilot's position. (U.S. Air Force)

# Sikorsky
VS-300

During 1939 Igor Sikorsky, while engineering manager of the Vought Sikorsky Division of United Aircraft Corporation, designed a rotary-wing aircraft. Designated VS-300,* the helicopter made its first free flight in May 1940. Initially, the aircraft could climb vertically, hover, fly sideways and backwards but could not fly forward. Modifications corrected this shortcoming, and on 15 April 1941 the VS-300 set an endurance record of 1 hour, 5 minutes, 15 seconds; on 6 May 1941 it set a world helicopter record of 1 hour, 32 minutes, 26 seconds. Although privately funded and developed, the VS-300 convinced American military officers of the feasibility of rotary-wing aircraft and provided a basis for the subsequent line of Sikorsky helicopters.

The VS-300 had a framework of welded steel tubes, with a three-bladed rotor on top and an engine and fuel tank inside. The single pilot (often Sikorsky wearing a homburg) sat in the small, open, non-instrumented cockpit in the nose. Originally the VS-300 had three airscrews on outriggers placed aft to give control and stability. Receiving several major and almost a score of minor modifications, the aircraft was redesignated the VS-300A by Sikorsky in early 1941. The final configuration saw the removal of the airscrews, the installation of a small, anti-torque rotor on the left side of the tail, and the replacement of the original 75-hp Lycoming with a larger engine. The VS-300A (registration NX 80998) flew with both wheels and twin floats. Compared to the earlier German machines, the Sikorsky helicopter was awkward, difficult to fly, and required extensive maintenance. Still, the design provided the basis for a long line of successful helicopters while Sikorsky-United Aircraft had the secure industrial base for a massive development and production effort.

The final version, which flew from December 1941 on, proved most impressive to those U.S. military officers who viewed it and led to immediate support for an improved helicopter (the R-4 series). The VS-300A flew until 1943 when it was relegated to a museum. Total flight time was 102 hours 35 minutes.

First flight: 14 September 1939 (tethered); first free flight 13 May 1940
Service introduction: not operational

**Characteristics (VS-300A)**

Crew: 1 pilot
Engine: 1 Franklin radial piston 90 hp and later 100 hp
Dimensions: length 27 ft 11 (8.5 m); height 10 ft (3.05 m); rotor diameter 30 ft
    (9.1 m)
Weight: loaded 1,150 lbs (522 kg)
Speed:
Range: 75 miles (121 km)
Ceiling:
Climb:

*VS for Vought Sikorsky; the 300 indicated Sikorsky's third helicopter design, the first two having been built in Russia prior to World War I.

Igor I. Sikorsky, age 52 and wearing his traditional homburg, at the controls of the VS-300 during an early tethered flight at Bridgeport, Conn. In this view there is a main rotor and two tail-mounted rotors. His VS-300, despite major problems, awakened U.S. military officials to the potential of helicopters. (Sikorsky Aircraft)

This is the first flight of the Sikorsky VS-300 helicopter with Igor I. Sikorsky at the controls. The helicopter was restrained from free flight by the weighted steel plate on the ground. In its various configurations the VS-300 flew a total of 102 hours and 35 minutes before retirement to a museum. (Sergei Sikorsky)

In still another configuration, the VS-300 in this view has a rounded nose, twin floats, and a bicycle basket mounted on the nose for carrying "cargo." This photo was taken during the summer of 1942. (Sergei Sikorsky)

# Sikorsky

VS-316A

R-4
HNS
Hoverfly I

This is believed to have been the world's first helicopter designed specifically for military use and was the first U.S. rotary-wing aircraft to be mass-produced. The U.S. Army Air Forces used a limited number operationally during World War II, mostly for rescue in Alaska, Burma, and other difficult-terrain areas. The U.S. Navy variant, designated HNS, was operated by the Coast Guard (which was a part of the Navy during the war). The R-4 was also the first helicopter operated by the British armed forces, being designated Hoverfly I. The Army flew tests with the XR-4 from a platform on the tanker *Bunker Hill* on 6-7 May 1943, and with the YR-4 from the Army transport *James Parker* on 6-7 July 1943. Subsequently, more rigorous trials were conducted at sea aboard the British merchant ship *Daghestan* and the U.S. Coast Guard cutter *Cobb* (WPG-181), during which the two R-4s took part in a trans-Atlantic crossing.

The R-4 was a refinement of Sikorsky's VS-300 design, with a faired, canvas-covered fuselage, side-by-side seating, and full dual controls. With a three-bladed main rotor and a tailboom supporting a smaller anti-torque rotor (on the left side), the R-4 set the design for future Sikorsky helicopters. The main landing gear was on outriggers with a small tail wheel, although many were fitted with twin pontoons for landing aboard ship or on water.

The U.S. Army ordered the prototype XR-4 in 1941, followed by orders for 30 helicopters for service trials. Several of the latter were transferred to Britain (the first on 2 July 1943) and the U.S. Navy/Coast Guard (first on 16 October 1943) for trials, although their pilots had earlier flown Army machines. Subsequently a production order for 100 of the R-4B variant was placed in 1943, with 22 of these going to the Coast Guard and 45 to Britain. One British machine (serial KL 110) was transferred to Canada. Six of the British machines were assigned to the King's Flight.

First flight: XR-4 13 January 1942
Service introduction: USAAF and USN/USCG 1943; RAF and RN 1945
Users: Canada, Great Britain, United States

**Variants**

XR-4        prototype with Warner R-500-3 165-hp engine; 36-ft rotor; 2,450 lbs loaded; 102 mph; 1 built (serial 41-18874).

YR-4A       service evaluation aircraft with Warner R-550-1 180-hp engine; 28-ft rotor; 2,900 lbs loaded; 75 mph; 3 built (42-107234/236).

YR-4B       evaluation aircraft similar to YR-4A; 27 built; 3 to USN/USCG, 7 to RAF.

R-4B        production aircraft; 100 built; 22 to USN/USCG, 45 to RAF/RN.

XR-4C       XR-4 reengined in 1943 with Warner R-550-1 engine; 38-ft rotor; 83 mph; 1 converted.

HNS-1       U.S. Navy designation for 23 YR-4B/R-4B; 21 survivors transferred from Coast Guard to Navy 1946-1947.

Hoverfly I  British designation for 52 YR-4B/R-4B helicopters transferred 1943-1945.

**Characteristics (R-4B)**

Crew: 1 pilot, 1 observer-passenger
Engine: 1 Warner R-550-3 Super Scarab radial piston 200 hp
Dimensions: length 35 ft 5 in (10.8 m); height 12 ft 5 in (3.8 m); rotor diameter 38 ft (11.6 m)
Weight: empty 2,020 lbs (917 kg); loaded 2,535 lbs (1,151 kg)
Speed: 75 mph (121 km/h)
Range: 130 miles (209 km)
Ceiling: service 8,000 ft (2,438 m)
Climb:

The classic Sikorsky: an R-4B in flight. The resemblance to the VS-300 can be seen in this view. Sikorsky R-4s were the only U.S. military helicopter to be used operationally during World War II. (U.S. Air Force)

A U.S. Navy HNS-1 being flown by the Coast Guard, which was given responsibility for Navy helicopter development and operations during World War II. This float-equipped HNS-1 is shown over the icebreaker *Northwind* (AG-89) during Rear Admiral Richard E. Byrd's 1947 expedition to the Antarctic. (U.S. Navy)

A Navy-Coast Guard HNS-1 is "stuffed" into a C-54 transport of the Air Transport Command at the Coast Guard air station in Brooklyn, N.Y. The helicopter was flown 1,000 miles on 29 April 1945, to Goose Bay, Labrador. It was then reassembled and rescued 11 Canadian airmen from two separate crashes in rugged territory, carrying them to safety one man per flight. (U.S. Coast Guard)

The first of a long line of Sikorsky military helicopters was the XR-4, shown here while assigned to the USAAF research and test facility at Wright Field in Ohio (now Wright-Patterson Air Force Base). (U.S. Air Force)

# Sikorsky
VS-316B                          R-6
                                 H-6
                                 R-7
                                 HOS
                                 Hoverfly II

A refinement of the basic Sikorsky R-4 design, the R-6 was developed in parallel with the R-5. The R-6 was flown by the USAAF and Navy/Coast Guard as well as the Royal Air Force and Royal Navy in the observation, utility, and rescue roles. Although the R-6/H-6 was produced in relatively large numbers (225 completed), the larger R-5/H-5 was considerably more popular.

The R-6 was similar in size and configuration to the R-4 but had a streamlined fuselage, smaller supports for the main landing gear, a nose wheel as well as a tail wheel, and a more powerful engine. The rotor system and transmission were the same. Some R-6 helicopters were fitted with twin pontoons for shipboard or water operation. During April 1945 a Navy HOS-1 was operated from the Coast Guard cutter *Cobb* (WPG 181), and the following year an XHOS-1 was fitted with the Hayes XCF dipping sonar.

Sikorsky built the XR-6 prototype and five XR-6A helicopters, after which Nash-Kelvinator built 26 similar YR-6A variants and then 193 R-6A production aircraft under USAAF contract. (Additional production of R-6A helicopters for U.S. Navy and British use was cancelled in favor of later aircraft.) The Navy/Coast Guard acquired three XR-6As for evaluation beginning in September 1944 (redesignated XHOS-1). Thirty-six Army R-6As (Navy HOS-1s) were later transferred to the USN/USCG, with 27 of these being flown by the Coast Guard (HOS-1G). Another 26 of the production aircraft went to Britain as the Hoverfly II in 1946—15 to the Royal Navy and 11 to the RAF.

First flight: XR-6 15 October 1943
Service introduction: USAAF and USN/USCG 1944; RAF and RN 1946
Users: Great Britain, United States

## Variants

XR-6      prototype with Lycoming 0-435-7 225-hp engine; 2,596 lbs loaded; 95 mph; 1 built (serial 43-47955).

XR-6A      prototype with Franklin 0-405-9 240-hp engine; 2,625 lbs loaded; 105 mph; 5 built (43-28240/244); 3 to U.S. Navy.

YR-6A      service evaluation aircraft similar to XR-6A; 26 built by Nash-Kelvinator.

R-6A      production aircraft; 193 built by Nash-Kelvinator; 36 to U.S. Navy and 26 to Great Britain (additional production cancelled).

R-6B      proposed variant with Lycoming 0-435-7 225-hp engine and other XR-6 features; cancelled.

XR-7      proposed XR-6A with Franklin 0-405-9 240-hp engine; cancelled.

XHOS-1      U.S. Navy designation for 3 XR-6A (Navy BuNo. 46446/448).

HOS-1      U.S. Navy designation for 36 R-6A; plans to transfer 64 additional aircraft were cancelled.

HOS-1G      designation for 27 HOS-1s flown by U.S. Coast Guard.

Hoverfly I      designation for 26 R-6A helicopters transferred to Great Britain; plans for the procurement of 124 additional aircraft were cancelled.

## Characteristics

Crew: 1 pilot, 1 observer-passenger
Engine: 1 Franklin O-405-9 radial piston 240 hp
Dimensions: length 38 ft 3 in (11.7 m); rotor diameter 38 ft (11.6 m)
Weight: loaded 2,590 lbs (1,176 kg)
Speed: cruise 70 mph (113 km/h); maximum 96 mph (154.5 km/h)
Range:
Ceiling: service 10,000 ft (3,048 m)
Climb: 800 ft/min (244 m/min)

The Sikorsky R-6 was developed parallel with the improved R-5 but was basically a refinement of the R-4 design. Note its four-wheel landing gear arrangement, streamlined structure, and improved frontal visibility. (U.S. Air Force)

An R-6A assigned to SAR operations, with Rescue painted on the top of the tailboom and high-visibility markings. Beginning with the R-6, helicopters flown by the U.S. Coast Guard had Navy designations with the suffix letter G (as HOS-1G) until the 1962 redesignation of U.S. military aircraft. (U.S. Air Force)

# Sikorsky

| | |
|---|---|
| VS-327 | R-5 |
| S-51 | H-5 |
| WS-51 | HO2S |
| | HO3S |
| | Dragonfly |

This helicopter was developed for the U.S. Army's observation role but was subsequently procured by the U.S. Navy and its component Marine Corps, being used extensively by those services in the Korean War (1950-1953). Like most Navy utility helicopters, it was also flown in the SAR role by the U.S. Coast Guard, and it was the first helicopter produced in Britain to be flown by the British armed services. (The basic USAAF R-5 designation was changed to H-5 in 1948).

The R-5 was an improvement on the previous R-4 design, having a streamlined configuration, a larger cabin, and accommodations for four persons in the later variants. Many of these aircraft were fitted to carry a stretcher pod on each side of the fuselage. Like its predecessor, the R-5 had the cabin forward with a plexiglass cockpit, a three-bladed main rotor, and an anti-torque rotor on the left side of the long tailboom. Most aircraft had a tricycle landing gear with "bent" nose wheel strut.

The USAAF ordered 4 XR-5 prototypes in early 1943, shortly after the first flight of the R-4. A fifth prototype was ordered later in the year. These were followed by 26 YR-5A helicopters for service trials and a production order for 100 R-5A aircraft, of which only 34 were completed. Later, 11 R-5F helicopters were ordered by the USAAF (based on the commercial S-51 helicopter). Another 45 H-5G/H helicopters were then ordered by the newly established U.S. Air Force for the SAR role. The U.S. Navy acquired 2 of the R-5A type in December 1945 for evaluation (HO2S-1) followed by a production run of 91 four-seat HO3S-1 variants, with deliveries starting in December 1946. The first 4 Navy helicopters accompanied Rear Admiral Richard E. Byrd's 1946-1947 expedition to the Antarctic (Operation High Jump). Of the Navy procurement, the Coast Guard flew 2 HO2S-1G and 9 HO3S-1G helicopters from 1946-1950. Nine of the HO3S-1 helicopters were used by the U.S. Marine Corps from 1948-1955, the first helicopters to be flown by that service. Westland in Britain produced 133 of the S-51 design under license for military and civil use. The RAF flew the helicopter as the Dragonfly in combat in Malaya from 1950-1956. (The S-51 was the first Sikorsky civil helicopter, with 58 being produced in the United States for non-military use; first flight 16 February 1946.)

First flight: XR-5 18 August 1943
Service introduction: USAAF 1943, USN HO2S-1 1946, HO3S-1 1947, RAF 1950
Users: Great Britain, United States

**Variants**

| | |
|---|---|
| XR-5 | prototype with Pratt & Whitney R-985-AN-5 450-hp engine; 2 crew in tandem seats; 4,850 lbs loaded; 5 built (serials 43-28236/239,47954). |
| XR-5A | prototypes refitted with British equipment; 2 XR-5 converted. |
| YR-5A/YH-5A | service trials aircraft; similar to XR-5; 26 built. |
| R-5A/H-5A | production aircraft; similar to YR-5A; able to carry stretcher on each side of fuselage; 34 built (66 additional helicopters cancelled); 2 to Navy. |
| R-5B | not used. |
| R-5C | not used. |
| R-5D/H-5D | SAR modifications of R-5A; Pratt & Whitney R-1340 600-hp engine; fitted with rescue hoist, external fuel tanks; 1 crew + 2 passengers; 21 converted. |
| YR-5E/YH-5E | YR-5A with dual controls; 5 converted. |
| R-5F/H-5F | SAR variant; modification of commercial S-51; 6,200 lbs loaded; 1 crew + 3 passengers; 11 built. |
| H-5G | SAR variant; similar to R-5F; 39 built. |
| H-5H | SAR variant with combination wheel/pontoon landing gear; 6,500 lbs loaded; 16 built. |
| HO2S-1 | YR-5A transferred to the Navy for evaluation in December 1945; 2 transferred (Navy BuNo. 75689/690); assigned to Coast Guard in 1946 as HO2S-1G. |
| HO3S-1 | Navy variant similar to USAF H-5F; 91 built with deliveries from December 1946; 9 assigned to USCG (as HO3S-1G) and 9 to USMC. |
| XHO3S-2 | improved design developed in 1950; not built. |
| XHO3S-3 | improved rotor system; 1 built. |
| Dragonfly | Westland-built rescue and cargo helicopter; Alvis Leonides 550-hp engine; 1 crew + 3 passengers; 5,374 lbs loaded; in addition to the helicopters listed here, several civil WS-51s were acquired for subsequent military use. |
| HR 1/3/4 | Royal Navy variant; 80 built; V 2966 was experimentally fitted with a 4-bladed main rotor. |
| HC 2/4 | RAF variant; 8 built. |

### Characteristics (HO3S-1)

Crew: 1 pilot
Engine: 1 Pratt & Whitney R-985-AN-5 Wasp Junior radial piston 450 hp
Dimensions: length 44 ft 11½ in (13.7 m); height 12 ft 6 in (3.8 m); rotor diameter 49
    ft (14.9 m)
Weight: empty 3,788 lbs (1,720 kg); loaded 4,985 lbs (2,263 kg)
Speed: cruise 75 mph (121.75 km/h); maximum 103 mph (166 km/h)
Range:
Ceiling:
Climb:
Payload: 3 passengers or 1 passenger + 2 stretcher pods or 950 lbs (431 kg)

A U.S. Marine Corps HO3S-1 lifts off from a hilltop with a wounded Navy hospital corpsman during the Korean War. The stretcher protrudes from the open window. Casualty evacuation was revolutionized by the helicopter during the Korean War. A rescue hoist is mounted on the left side of the cabin and an emergency landing light is installed on the nose. (U.S. Navy)

The Air Force H-5H fitted with both wheels and floats was configured specifically for the SAR role. The cabin blisters widen the fuselage so that three stretchers could be carried internally (two across the cabin in front of the engine and one behind the engine). A rescue winch was also fitted. (U.S. Air Force)

With their rotor blades secured, HO3S-1 helicopters of Marine Observation Squadron (VMO) 6 are snowed under during a November 1951 storm in Korea. (U.S. Navy)

# Sikorsky

S-52                                        H-18
S-59                                        H-39
                                            HO5S '

The Sikorsky S-52 was a four-place utility helicopter that was evaluated by the
U.S. Army as the YH-18 and saw service with the U.S. Navy as the HO5S-1. It was
the first American helicopter to have all-metal rotor blades and, in its earlier S-52
civilian version, set three international helicopter speed and height records.
These 1948 records were 129.6 mph over a 3-kilometer course, 122.75 mph over a
100-kilometer course, and 21,220 feet absolute height.

The semi-monocoque fuselage was a pod-and-boom type constructed of aluminum-magnesium alloy, with a three-bladed, all-metal main rotor and a two-bladed
anti-torque tail rotor driven by a six-piston, 245-hp air-cooled engine. A quadricycle fixed landing gear was fitted.

The U.S. Army evaluated four YH-18s in 1950 but did not procure any for
service use. The U.S. Navy purchased 89 S-52-3s as the HO5S-1 for general utility
duties, all of which were delivered by 1953.

First flight: July 1950     Service introduction: April 1951     Users: United States

### Variants

YH-18     prototype evaluated by U.S. Army for light utility role; 4 built.
HO5S-1  Navy production helicopters; 89 built.
XH-39     YH-18 design modified for Army evaluation with Turboméca Artouse II-XT-51-
              T3 turboshaft; four-bladed main rotor, three-bladed tail rotor; retractable land-
              ing gear; 1 built in 1954 (factory designation S-59).

### Characteristics

Crew: 1 pilot, 1 copilot/observer
Engine: 1 Franklin 0-425-1 air-cooled piston 245 hp
Dimensions: length 39 ft 2½ in (11.95 m); height 9 ft 9½ in (2.99 m); rotor diameter
     33 ft (10 m)
Weight: empty 1,650 lbs (749 kg); loaded 2,700 lbs (1,226 kg)
Speed: cruise 96 mph (154 km/h); maximum 110 mph (176 km/h)
Range: 415 miles (668 km)
Ceiling: hover OGE 5,900 ft (1,798 m); hover IGE 9,200 ft (2,804 m); service 15,500
     ft (4,724 m)
Climb: 1,300 ft/min (396 m/min)          Payload: 2 troops

One of four U.S. Army YH-18A helicopters after conversion to the XH-39 is shown in
flight over Bridgeport, Conn. The tricycle landing gear is retracted; note the structure
above the fuselage to house the turboshaft engine and four-bladed main rotor. (U.S. Air
Force)

A U.S. Marine Corps HO5S-1 with standard fixed quadricycle landing gear of the H-18/ HO5S design. The Marines flew the HO5S-1 for observation and scouting in Korea, but its use was overshadowed in that conflict by the more popular HO3S-1 and later HRS-1 as well as the smaller HTL. (U.S. Marine Corps)

# Sikorsky

S-53                                         HJS

The Sikorsky S-53 was a development of the very successful S-51 series and was designed specifically for utility, observation, and rescue duties aboard aircraft carriers, battleships, and cruisers. Three prototypes of this three- to five-place aircraft were procured in 1948 by the U.S. Navy as the XHJS-1, but no production contract resulted. Additional attempts to market the S-53 were unsuccessful, and the model was developed no further.

The S-53 featured a fuselage and rotor system very similar to that of the S-51, but with some modifications: the tail rotor was raised above head-height for safety, the landing gear was strengthened for operations from a pitching deck, and the three-bladed main rotor was fitted with a folding mechanism. Amphibious landing gear was optional. A trapdoor in the cabin floor permitted the installation of a camera or a hoist for the transfer of bulky cargo by means of a sling.

First flight: 1948
Service introduction: not operational

**Characteristics**

Crew: 1 pilot, 1 copilot
Engine: 1 Continental R-975-34 radial piston 500 hp
Dimensions: rotor diameter 49 ft (14.95 m)
Weight: loaded 4,750 lbs (2,157 kg)
Speed: cruise 90 mph (145 km/h); maximum 110 mph (177 km/h)
Range: 330 miles (531 km)
Ceiling: service 19,000 ft (5,791 m)
Climb: 1,000 ft/min (305 m/min)
Payload: 1-3 troops

An XHJS-1 in flight with U.S. Navy colors and small national insignias atop the engine housing and on the bottom of the tailboom. U.S. helicopter development was rapid in the late 1940s, and the XHJS-1 was one of many designs evaluated but not procured in quantity. (Edgar Deigan)

# Sikorsky

S-55

H-19 Chickasaw
HO4S
HRS
Whirlwind

The Sikorsky S-55 was used by the air arms of all U.S military services, the armed forces of Great Britain and France, as well as dozens of other nations. A 12-seat utility helicopter, the S-55 was adapted for ASW, troop transport, SAR, and a variety of other duties, both civil and military.

The S-55's fuselage was large and awkward-looking, with the crew's compartment above and forward of the cabin. A high-set tailboom extended aft from the upper fuselage and the boom. The construction of the fuselage was semi-monocoque, with an aluminum-magnesium skin. The rotor system consisted of a three-bladed main rotor and a two-bladed tail rotor, both of all-metal construction. A variety of power plants were used to power the S-55, and they are listed in the variants section below. The landing gear was normally of the wheeled quad-ricycle type, although SAR variants were sometimes equipped with floats. A total of 1,067 S-55s was built for military customers by Sikorsky in the ten-year production run of the aircraft, and an additional 547 were built by the S-55's foreign licensees: Westland in Great Britain, which designated the S-55 the Whirlwind, Sud-Est in France, and Mitsubishi in Japan. Designated the H-19 Chickasaw in U.S. Army and Air Force service, the HO4S in U.S. Navy and Coast Guard service, and the HRS in U.S. Marine Corps service, the Chickasaw first saw combat in Korea with the U.S. Army as a troop transport and medical evacuation helicopter. In the latter role, the H-19 could carry six stretchers and medical attendant. The H-19 also saw service in the early stages of the Vietnam War with U.S. and Vietnamese forces, in the Malaysian conflict as the Whirlwind with British forces, and around the globe with the French Foreign Legion.

First flight: 21 November 1949
Service introduction: 1950
Users: Argentina, Austria, Brazil, Canada, Chile, Cuba, Denmark, Dominican Republic, France, Ghana, Great Britain, Greece, Guatemala, Honduras, India, Israel, Italy, Japan, Jordan, South Korea, Kuwait, Netherlands, Nigeria, Norway, Pakistan, Philippines, Portugal, Qatar, South Africa, Spain, Taiwan, Thailand, United States, Venezuela, South Vietnam, Yugoslavia

## Variants

| | |
|---|---|
| YH-19 | prototype test aircraft for USAF with 600-hp Pratt & Whitney R-1340-S1H2 Wasp radial air-cooled piston engine; 5 built. |
| H-19A | production helicopter for USAF with 600-hp P&W R-1340-57; 56 built. |
| HO4S-1 | production helicopter for U.S. Navy; similar to H-19A; 10 built. |
| HRS-1 | production helicopter for U.S. Marine Corps; similar to HO4S-1; 60 built; some upgraded to HRS-3 standard. |
| H-19B | similar to H-19A for USAF with 700-hp Wright R-1300-3 radial; 266 built, some of which were for foreign transfer; changed to UH-19B in 1962 with SAR helicopters becoming HH-19B. |
| HO4S-3 | similar to H-19B for U.S. Navy; 81 built with 15 to the Royal Navy as Whirlwind HAS 22 and 3 to Netherlands. |
| HRS-2 | similar to H-19B for U.S. Marine Corps; 101 built with 10 to Royal Navy as Whirlwind HAR 21; changed to CH-19E in 1962 |
| HRS-3 | similar to HRS-2 with minor equipment differences; 109 built; 4 to USAF as H-19B and 20 to Spain; changed to UH-19F in 1962. |
| HO4S-3G | SAR helicopter similar to HO4S-3 for U.S. Coast Guard; 30 converted from HO4S-3; changed to HH-19G in 1962. |
| H-19C | production helicopter for U.S. Army; similar to H-19A; 72 built; changed to UH-19C in 1962. |
| H-19D | similar to H-19B for U.S. Army; 270 built; some to foreign transfer. |

### Whirlwind

| | |
|---|---|
| HAR 1 | Westland-built Whirlwind for Royal Navy; similar to H-19A with 600-hp P&W R-1340-40; 10 built. |
| HAR 2 | similar to HAR 1 for RAF; 10 built. |
| HAR 3 | similar to HAR 1 for Royal Navy with 700-hp Wright R-1300-3. |
| HAR 4 | similar to HAR 2 for RAF with 600-hp P&W R-1340-57. |
| HAR 5 | similar to HAR 3 for Royal Navy with 750-hp Alvis Leonides Major A.Le.M5 piston radial engine; drooped tailboom to give additional clearance to main rotor. |
| HAS 7 | similar to HAR 5 for Royal Navy; first ASW helicopter built in Great Britain; with radar, dipping sonar, homing torpedoes. |
| HCC 8 | VIP-configured HAS 7 for Queen's Flight; 2 built. |
| HAR 9 | converted HAS 7 with 1,050-shp Rolls Royce Gnome turboshaft, first flight 28 February 1959. |
| HAR 10 | production turboshaft-powered Whirlwinds for RAF; optional armament of 4 Nord SS 11 air-to-surface missiles. |
| HCC 12 | VIP-configured HAR 10 for Queen's Flight. |

### Characteristics (H-19A)

Crew: 1 pilot, 1 copilot
Engine: 1 Pratt & Whitney R-1340-57 Wasp radial piston 600 hp
Dimensions: length (fuselage) 42 ft 2 in (12.85 m); height 13 ft 4 in (94.07 m); rotor
    diameter 53 ft (16.16 m)
Weight: empty 4,795 lbs (2,177 kg); loaded 7,900 lbs (3,587 kg)
Speed: cruise 85 mph (137 km/h); maximum 101 mph (163 km/h)
Range: 405 miles (652 km)
Ceiling: hover OGE 2,000 ft (610 m); hover IGE 6,400 ft (1,951 m); service 10,500 ft
    (3,200 m)
Climb: 700 ft/min (213 m/min)
Payload: 10 troops or 8 stretchers or 2,855 lbs (1,296 kg) internal cargo

A U.S. Navy HO4S-3 from Air Development Squadron (VX) 6 shows the unusual lines of
the widely used Sikorsky S-55 design. The engine was mounted in the nose, providing a
large cabin area for cargo or troops, with the pilots seated above. The helicopters had a
small, inverted-V tail surface and a tail rotor protection skid. (U.S. Navy)

An S-55 of the Canadian Navy hovers while lowering its dipping sonar to seek out a
submarine. An ASW homing torpedo is mounted on the side of the fuselage. ASW has been
a prime helicopter mission, dating back to German operations in World War II. Modern
helicopters also use expendable sonobuoys, magnetic detectors, radar, and other devices to
seek out submarines. (Canadian Armed Forces)

A mechanic opens the clamshell doors to gain access to the engine of a U.S. Air Force YH-19. The engine is canted at about 45 degrees with the drive shaft passing at the same angle beneath the pilot to a universal joint which is attached to the rotor shaft. This arrangement required minimum space for the engine. Note the tail fin configuration. (U.S. Navy)

# Sikorsky

S-56  HR2S
H-37 Mojave

The Sikorsky S-56 was designed to fulfill a U.S. Marine Corps requirement for an assault transport helicopter that was capable of lifting 23 fully equipped troops. The prototype XHR2S-1 was ordered by the U.S. Navy in 1951 and underwent a short evaluation by that service in 1954. A production order for the heavy helicopter followed, and the first production machines were delivered in 1956. One preproduction example was tested by the U.S. Army as the YH-37 in 1954, and a large Army order to Sikorsky followed.

The S-56 was a large, twin-engine, single-rotor helicopter that was one of the first to have a retractable undercarriage. It was Sikorsky's first attempt at a multi-engine helicopter, although that firm decided to retain the standard main and anti-torque tail rotors rather than adopt the tandem rotor configuration used by other firms with twin-engined helicopters. The main rotor had five blades and the tail rotor had four blades. Two 2,100-hp radial engines were located in pods at the tips of a small stub wing. The main landing gear also retracted into these pods while the tail wheel was fixed. Clamshell doors in the nose of the fuselage permitted the loading of small vehicles as well as troops. The cockpit was above this door and forward of the cabin. In an effort to develop a helicopter radar surveillance capability, two aircraft were converted to the HR2S-1W configuration but were not successful.

A total of 154 S-56s was produced for the U.S. Army and Marine Corps. Some Army H-37As were later fitted with auto-stabilization equipment.

First flight: 18 December 1953
Service introduction: May 1956
Users: United States

**Variants**

XHR2S-1  prototype helicopters; 4 built.
HR2S-1  production version for U.S. Marine Corps; 55 built; changed to CH-37C in 1962.
HR2S-1W  helicopter fitted with AN/APS-20E search radar in radome under fuselage nose for airborne early warning; 2 converted.
YH-37A  XHR2S-1 evaluated by U.S. Army.
H-37A  production version for U.S. Army; 91 built; changed to CH-37A in 1962.
H-37B  H-37A upgraded with automatic stabilization equipment and modernized avionics; changed to CH-37B in 1962.

**Characteristics**

Crew: 1 pilot, 1 copilot, 1 crew chief
Engines: 2 Pratt & Whitney R-2800-54 radial piston 2,100 hp each
Dimensions: length 88 ft (26.8 m); height 22 ft (6.71 m); rotor diameter 72 ft (21.95 m)
Weight: empty 20,831 lbs (9,457 kg); loaded 31,000 lbs (14,074 kg)
Speed: cruise 115 mph (185 km/h); maximum 130 mph (209 km/h)
Range: 145 miles (233 km)
Ceiling: hover OGE 1,100 ft (335 m); service 8,700 ft (2,652 m)
Climb: 910 ft/min (277 m/min)
Payload: 23 troops or 24 stretchers

A U.S. Marine Corps HR2S-1 twin-engine helicopter lifts an experimental automatic artillery weapon weighing 3,000 pounds. Twin external drop tanks are also fitted. This was Sikorsky's first helicopter with twin engines, which, mounted externally, allowed for maximum internal cargo space. (U.S. Marine Corps)

This is one of two Navy HR2S-1W helicopters configured for the Airborne Early Warning (AEW) role. The aircraft was not successful in the radar surveillance role mainly because of the vibration inherent in rotary-wing aircraft. A horizontal tail surface was fitted to the right side with the anti-torque tail rotor on the left side. (U.S. Navy)

An Army H-37 sits in the Arizona desert with its clamshell nose doors open and a jeep 4 × 4 light truck driving out. The Marines were able to operate these relatively large aircraft from helicopter carriers as well as from shore bases and in the field. (U.S. Army)

# Sikorsky

S-57                                    V-2

The Sikorsky S-57 was a proposed convertiplane, assigned the U.S. military designation XV-2. However, this early 1950s project was cancelled after design studies.

# Sikorsky
S-58

| H-34 | Choctaw |
| HSS | Seabat |
| HUS | Seahorse |
| Wessex | |

A 1952 U.S. Navy requirement for an ASW helicopter to replace the Sikorsky S-55s then used in that role led to the Sikorsky S-58. The basic design was extremely successful, with over 2,300 S-58 helicopters being produced for civilian and military applications by Sikorsky, Westland, and Sud-Est in the aircraft's 25-year production run. The vast majority of the S-58 aircraft built by Sikorsky and Sud-Est were powered by piston engines while virtually all of the Westland-built machines were powered by British-built turboshafts.

Westland replaced the Wright radial engine of the Sikorsky-built series with a Napier Gazelle turoboshaft of 1,430 shp. The first prototype for this configuration flew on 17 May 1957, and the first production Wessex flew in April 1960. Westland further developed the power plant of the S-58 in 1962 when it flew its first Mk 2 with two coupled Bristol Siddeley Gnome turboshafts, each rated at 1,350 shp but limited to a total of 1,550 shp at the rotor head. The British Company produced some 400 helicopters of the Wessex series (the different variants of which are listed below). All variants of the S-58 series shared the same basic fuselage, a semi-monocoque structure similar in configuration to that of the S-55. The cockpit was above and slightly forward of the cabin, with the power plant housed in the nose. The S-58 differed from the S-55 primarily in the tailboom configuration, that of the S-58 reaching aft as a continuation of the fuselage and terminating in a vertical stabilizer with a four-bladed, all-metal tail rotor. The main rotor also had four blades and was powered by different versions of the Wright R-1820 radial engine in the Sikorsky-built versions, and by turboshaft in the Westland Wessex variants. The landing gear in all variants was a non-retractable, three-wheeled type with the tail wheel at the extreme rear of the fuselage. The cabin could seat 12 to 18 troops or 8 stretchers could be carried.

The first model S-58 was accepted by the U.S. Navy for evaluation as the XHSS-1 Seabat, an antisubmarine search-and-attack helicopter capable of operating from a cruiser or aircraft carrier. After Navy evaluation, an initial order was placed for the production HSS-1, which became operational in August 1955. One HSS-1 was supplied to the Royal Navy for evaluation and was the basis of the Westland Wessex series under license from Sikorsky. The U.S. Marine Corps also received some 500 S-58s in a utility version which they designated HUS-1 and -1A (the -1A equipped with pontoons). The U.S. Army evaluated one of the Marine HUS-1s, which resulted in a production order from the Army for S-58s designated H-34A. Several Marine and Army units were delivered in a VIP configuration for the President's Executive Flight Detachment, while others from the Army and Marine Corps orders were diverted to military assistance programs. The S-58 was used in a multitude of roles in a variety of air arms. One Marine HUS-1 was even tested for a close-support role with the Bullpup air-to-ground missile, with a successful firing taking place in June 1960. Surplus S-58s continue in civilian service, some re-engined with turboshaft power plants. Many are still in military service, although all have been retired from the active and reserve components of the U.S. armed forces.

First flight: 8 March 1954
Service introduction: August 1955
Users: Argentina, Australia, Belgium, Brazil, Brunei, Cambodia, Canada, Central African
Republic, France, West Germany, Ghana, Great Britain, Haiti, Indonesia, Iraq, Israel,
Italy, Japan, Laos, Netherlands, Nicaragua, Philippines, Taiwan, Thailand, United States,
Uruguay, South Vietnam

## Variants

| | |
|---|---|
| XHSS-1 | prototype S-58 for U.S. Navy evaluation; 3 built. |
| HSS-1 | Seabat; initial production variant for U.S. Navy ASW; crew of 4; 215 built; changed to SH-34G in 1962. |
| HSS-1N | Seabat; improved HSS-1 with automatic stabilization and night-flight equipment; 156 built; changed to SH-34J in 1962. |
| HUS-1 | Seahorse; initial production utility/troop transport for U.S. Marine Corps; 2 crew + 14 troops; 596 built; changed to UH-34D in 1962. |
| HUS-1A | Seahorse; modified HUS-1 with external fuel tanks and floats; changed to UH-34E in 1962. |
| HUS-1G | SAR variant for U.S. Coast Guard; 6 modified from HUS-1; changed to HH-34F in 1962. |
| HUS-1L | HUS-1A modified for Antarctic operation; 4 converted; changed to LH-34D in 1962. |
| HUS-1Z | VIP-configured HUS-1 for presidential use; 8 built; changed to VH-34D in 1962. |
| H-34A | Choctaw; initial production transport helicopter for U.S. Army; similar to HUS-1; 437 built plus 21 transferred from Marine HUS-1 order; some transferred to foreign military services; changed to CH-34A in 1962. |
| H-34C | H-34A with automatic stabilization equipment for U.S. Army and USAF; 21 built plus conversions from H-34As; changed to CH-34C in 1962. |
| VH-34C | H-34C with VIP interior for presidential use. |

Wessex

| | |
|---|---|
| HAS 1 | ASW helicopter similar to HSS-1 with 1 1,430-shp Napier Gazelle 161 turboshaft. |
| HC 2 | transport helicopter with 2 Rolls-Royce Gnome turboshaft for RAF; 3 crew + 16 troops. |
| HAS 3 | similar to HAS 1 with 1 1,850-shp Gazelle 165 turboshaft. |
| HCC 4 | VIP-configured HC 2 for Queen's Flight. |
| HU 5 | troop transport similar to HC 2 for Royal Marines. |
| HAS 31 | ASW helicopter similar to HAS 1 with 1 1,540-shp Gazelle 162 turboshaft; 27 built for Australia. |

## Characteristics (HSS-1/SH-34G)

Crew: 1 pilot, 1 copilot, 2 sensor systems operators
Engine: 1 Wright R-1820-84 nine-cylinder radial piston 1,525 hp
Dimensions: length 46 ft 9 in (14.25 m); height 15 ft 11 in (4.86 m); rotor diameter 56
    ft (17.07 m)
Weight: empty 8,400 lbs (3,814 kg); loaded 13,300 lbs (6,038 kg)
Speed: cruise 98 mph (158 km/h); maximum 123 mph (198 km/h)
Range: 182 miles (293 km)
Ceiling: hover OGE 2,400 ft (732 m); hover IGE 4,900 ft (1,494 m); service 9,500 ft
    (2,896 m)
Climb: 1,100 ft/min (335 m/min)
Payload: 2 Mk-44 ASW homing torpedoes

A squad of Royal Marines waits for their Wessex HU 5 to land and embark them. The right-side cabin door is closed. The letter A on the tail indicates that the helicopter is assigned to the carrier *Albion* and the E the aircraft's position within its squadron. The exhaust from the turboshaft engine is located above and forward of the landing gear. (Royal Navy)

A U.S. Coast Guard HUS-1G shortly after delivery to that service with an external fuel tank fitted on the left side. Note the small horizontal tail surface and streamlined fuselage. (U.S. Coast Guard)

A U.S. Navy HUS-1A from Air Development Squadron (VX) 6 in Antarctica while supporting the Navy-civilian Operation Deep Freeze 61. The helicopter is painted in high-visibility orange, with the aircraft's individual name "The Kitty Hawk" painted just forward of the open door. The JD on the tail is the VX-6's code. (U.S. Navy)

A French Navy HSS 1 hovers while raising a rescue basket during an SAR exercise. The H-34/HUS/HSS-1 series was produced in France by Sud-Est and in England by Westland. (French Armed Forces)

# Sikorsky

S-61

HSS-2 ⎫
H-3  ⎬ Sea King
   ⎭

HH-3E Jolly Green Giant
HH-3F Pelican
CH-124
Commando

Designed to fulfill a 1957 U.S. Navy requirement for an antisubmarine helicopter, the H-3 series of helicopters has come to serve in a variety of roles for a number of air arms. A relatively heavy helicopter for its time, the H-3 has a large fuel capacity giving it high endurance for antisubmarine warfare or long range for rescue missions. A U.S. Air Force variant was used extensively during the Vietnam War to rescue downed American flyers deep within North Vietnam. Originally designated the HSS-2—which was changed in 1962 to SH-3—the Sea King entered U.S. Navy service in 1961. The SH-3A served as the basis for a variety of other Sikorsky military and commercial models: the Canadians purchased several Sea Kings for ASW, designating them CHSS-2 and then CH-124; the VH-3A was built for U.S. Army and Marine Corps use as presidential helicopters; the Air Force operates a utility version of the Sea King; and several SH-3As were converted for search and rescue (HH-3A) and minesweeping (RH-3A). An extensively revised fuselage from the original Sikorsky S-61A and B models identifies the S-61R which was sold to the Air Force and Coast Guard as a search and rescue (HH-3E/F) and utility-cargo helicopter (CH-3C/E). The SH-3A broke a number of speed records shortly after its service introduction. In December 1961 it set records for 3, 100, 500 and 1,000 kilometers at 199, 182.8, 179.5 and 179.3 mph, respectively. In February 1962 it became the first helicopter to break the 200-mph barrrier by registering 210.6 mph over a 19-kilometer course. The current world's records exceed these only marginally. A USAF HH-3E made the first nonstop trans-Atlantic helicopter flight.

The early S-61A and B models have a boat-type hull of metal semi-monocoque construction and a folding tailboom to facilitate stowage. The S-61R variants have a pod-and-boom, non-watertight fuselage that is longer but narrower than the earlier Sea King versions, and which has a hydraulically operated rear ramp. All versions share the same five-bladed main rotor and five-bladed tail rotor system except that the blades on the S-61R series do not fold. The S-61A and B have retractable twin main and non-retractable single tail wheel landing gear, while the S-61R has a fully retractable tricycle undercarriage.

The Sea King's equipment for the ASW mission includes an active or passive dipping sonar, active and passive sonobuoys, MAD gear, surface search radar, and automatic stabilization equipment. Eight hundred forty pounds of weapons can be carried, including nuclear depth bombs or up to four Mk-46 torpedoes. The original SH-3A production series has been upgraded several times to the current SH-3H standard, as have later production SH-3D models.

Sikorsky has built 651 of the military S-61 helicopters while foreign licensees in Italy (Agusta), Japan (Mitsubishi) and Great Britain (Westland) have added 391 additional units to that total, as of the start of 1980; production continues in Italy and the United Kingdom. The S-61 serves as the principal ASW helicopter of several nations, being used by the U.S. Navy from ten large aircraft carriers.

First flight: 11 March 1959
Service introduction: September 1961
Users: Australia, Belgium, Brazil, Canada, Egypt, West Germany, Great Britain, India,
Iran, Italy, Japan, Malaysia, Norway, Pakistan, Qatar, Spain, United States

## Variants

| | |
|---|---|
| XHSS-2 | prototype with 2 1,050-shp T58-GE-6 turboshafts; 1 built. |
| YHSS-2 | service trials aircraft; 7 built. |
| HSS-2 | production Sea King with later helicopters having 2 1,250-shp T58-GE-8 turboshafts; 225 built for U.S. Navy, 41 for Canadian Navy (CHSS-2), 11 for Japanese Maritime Self-Defense Force; changed to SH-3A in 1962 (factory designation S-61B). |
| NH-3A | SH-3A modified as compound research helicopter; streamlined fuselage and swivelling tail rotor to provide thrust; 1 converted. |
| RH-3A | SH-3A converted for minesweeping; ASW gear removed, additional cargo door, bubble windows, rear-view mirrors, variety of towed minesweeping gear; 9 converted. |
| VH-3A | VIP transports for presidential use (originally HSS-2Z); 5 built operated for U.S. Army and Marine Corps, with 1 presented to Egyptian President Sadat by President Nixon. |
| HH-3A | SH-3A converted for search and rescue; ASW gear removed, 2 7.62-mm minigun turrets installed behind sponsons, extra fuel tanks, armor, rescue hoist; 12 converted. |
| CH-3B | amphibious transport, similar in configuration to SH-3B without ASW gear; 3 crew plus 26 troops or 15 litters or cargo; 3 built for USAF for missile site support and drone recovery; 8 built for Danish Air Force as S-61A; 10 built for Royal Malaysian Air Force as S-61A-4. |
| CH-3C | production helicopter with enlarged fuselage, rear loading ramp; 2 1,300-shp T58-GE-1 turboshafts; 41 built for USAF, 1 modified to JCH-3C for serial icing tests (factory S-61R). |
| SH-3D | upgraded variant of SH-3A with 2 1,400-shp T58-GE-10 turboshafts; 74 built for U.S. Navy; 4 built for Argentine Navy as S-61D-4. |
| VH-3D | upgraded variant of VH-3A; 11 built for U.S. Army and Marine Corps. |
| CH-3E | CH-3C with 1,500-shp T58-GE-5 turboshafts; 42 built. |
| HH-3E | search and rescue variant for USAF; with 2 7.62-mm minigun turrets on each sponson, in-flight refueling, self-sealing tanks, armor, rescue hoist; 50 built (named Jolly Green Giant). |
| HH-3F | similar to HH-3E for U.S. Coast Guard; combat equipment removed; 4 crew + 15 passengers; 40 built (named Pelican). |
| SH-3G | SH-3A converted to utility helicopter; ASW gear removed, floor strengthened; 105 converted (with 6 equipped with 7.62-mm minigun pods for armed SAR). |
| SH-3H | SH-3G converted to ASW and missile defense missions; fitted with dipping sonar, MAD, sonobuoys, radar, ESM; 11 converted by 1980. |
| YSH-3J | SH-3G modified as LAMPS III (Sikorsky SH-60B) test bed; 2 converted. |
| Sea King HAS 1 | Westland license-built SH-3D for Royal Navy with 1,500-shp Rolls Royce Gnome H.1400 turboshafts; 56 built. |
| Mk 41 | similar to HH-3A for West German Navy for SAR; 22 built. |
| Mk 42 | similar to HAS 1 for Indian Navy for ASW; 12 built. |
| Mk 43 | similar to Mk 41 for Norwegian Air Force for SAR; 10 built. |
| Mk 45 | similar to HAS Mk 1 for Pakistani Navy for ASW; 6 built. |
| Mk 48 | similar to Mk 41 for Belgian Air Force for SAR; 5 built. |
| Mk 50 | similar to HAS Mk 1 for Australian Navy for ASW; 10 built. |

Commando
  Mk 1       transport developed by Westland based on Sea King; 3 crew + 21 troops;
             first flight 12 September 1973; 5 built for Egypt.
  Mk 2       enlarged Mk 1; 28 troops; 25 built for Egypt, 4 built for Qatar.
  Mk 3       armed multi-role with pintle-mounted 7.62-mm MG in cabin; external
             fittings for gun pods, rockets, or missiles; reportedly produced for Qatar.
Sea King
  HAS 2      improved HAS 1 for Royal Navy for ASW/SAR; 21 built.
  HAR 3      similar to Mk 41 for RAF for SAR; 16 built.
  HC 4       similar to Commando Mk 2 for Royal Marines; 15 built.
  HAS 5      conversions of earlier British Sea Kings to improve ASW performance;
             Decca 71 radar; 17 delivered from October 1980.

## Characteristics (SH-3D)

Crew: 1 pilot, 1 copilot, 2 sonar operators
Engine: 2 General Electric T58-GE-10 turboshafts 1,400 shp each
Dimensions: length 72 ft 8 in (22.15 m); height 16 ft 10 in (5.13 m); rotor diameter 62
    ft (18.9 m)
Weight: empty 11,865 lbs (5,387 kg); loaded 21,000 lbs (9,534 kg)
Speed: cruise 136 mph (219 km/h); maximum 166 mph (267 km/h)
Range: 625 miles (1,006 km)
Ceiling: hover OGE 8,200 ft (2,499 m); hover IGE 10,500 ft (3,200 m); service 14,700
    ft (4,481 m)
Climb: 2,200 ft/min (671 m/min)
Payload: 840 lbs (381 kg) of depth bombs or torpedoes

A U.S. Navy SH-3D from HS-4 on the deck of the antisubmarine carrier *Yorktown*
(CVS-10). (U.S. Navy)

An SH-3D Sea King of U.S. Navy Helicopter Antisubmarine Squadron (HS) 4 from the aircraft carrier *Ranger* (CVA-61). A practice ASW torpedo is mounted under the sponson housing the main landing gear. There is a rescue hoist above the door. The Sikorsky S-61 rivals the Bell Model 204 and its many derivatives for versatility. (U.S. Navy)

A Sea King from the carrier *Ark Royal* carrying four Mk-44 ASW torpedoes. The dipping sonar dome retracts into the boat hull and a rescue hoist is installed. (Royal Navy)

An HH-3E Jolly Green Giant of the U.S. Air Force's 37th Aerospace Rescue and Recovery Squadron during a rescue operation over South Vietnam in 1967. The USAF variants of the H-3 had a rear ramp, shown here lowered while in flight, with a 7.62-mm machine gun fitted for covering fire during rescues; other guns were also fitted. This -3E does not have a refueling probe. (U.S. Air Force)

A U.S. Air Force HC-130P Hercules rescue-tanker aircraft refuels an HH-3E Jolly Green Giant over the Tonkin Gulf in preparation for a rescue mission into North Vietnam. The HC-130P has two refueling hoses with drogues streamed from wing-mounted fuel tanks. Both aircraft are camouflaged and have low-visibility markings and small national insignia. (U.S. Air Force)

An unusual Sea King: Officially listed as an HSS-2, the U.S. Navy's BuNo. 148033 was actually a Sikorsky S-61F compound research helicopter sponsored by the Army and Navy. The aircraft had two pod-mounted Pratt & Whitney J60-P-2 turbojets to complement the two General Electric T58-GE-8B turboshafts, a 32-ft wingspan, and the five-bladed rotor shown here was later replaced by a six-bladed rotor. First flight as a compound helicopter was on 21 May 1965. Engine ratings were 2,900 lbst each for the J60s and 1,200 shp each for the T58s. (Sikorsky)

# Sikorsky

S-62

HU2S
H-52 } Sea Guard

This was a commercial design that used the dynamic components of the piston-engined S-55/H-19 helicopter series and a single turboshaft engine. The Sikorsky S-62 was tested by the U.S. Coast Guard for the SAR role. An initial order for four HU2S-1Gs resulted in February 1962, with that designation changing a few months later to HH-52A. This helicopter replaced the HH-34 in Coast Guard service with a total of 99 being procured before production terminated in 1970.

The HH-52A has a watertight boat-hull fuselage of semi-monocoque construction. The three-bladed main rotor and two-bladed tail rotor are driven by a single 1,250-shp T58-GE-8 turboshaft mounted above the cabin and beneath the main rotor. In addition to the crew of three, the cabin can accommodate ten fully equipped troops. The main landing gear is semi-retractable into the flotation gear, while the tail wheel is fixed.

Of the 99 HH-52As procured for the U.S. Coast Guard, 79 were still operational in 1981. These will be replaced as the Aérospatiale HH-65A Dolphin enters Coast Guard service in the 1980s. No other U.S. service operated the HH-52, but some are in service with the Indian Air Force, Japanese Air Self-Defense Force, and the government of Thailand. These foreign military sales were negotiated by Mitsubishi, Japanese licensee for the S-62.

First flight: 14 May 1958
Service introduction: January 1963
Users: India, Japan, Thailand, United States

A Coast Guard HH-52A after a water landing. Note the single-engine configuration compared to the twin-engine configuration of the larger Sea King design (HH-3F Pelican in Coast Guard service). (Melvin Fredeen)

**Characteristics**

Crew: 1 pilot, 1 copilot, 1 crew chief
Engine: 1 General Electric T58-GE-8 turboshaft 1,250 shp
Dimensions: length 45 ft 5½ in (13.86 m); height 14 ft 2½ in (4.33 m); rotor diameter
    53 ft (16.15 m)
Weight: empty 5,083 lbs (2,308 kg); loaded 8,300 lbs (3,768 kg)
Speed: cruise 98 mph (158 km/h); maximum 109 mph (175 km/h)
Range: 474 miles (763 km)
Ceiling: hover OGE 1,700 ft (518 m); service 11,200 ft (3,414 m); hover IGE 12,200 ft
    (3,719 m)
Climb: 1,080 ft/min (329 m/min)
Payload: 3,017 lbs (1,370 kg) internal cargo or 6 passengers

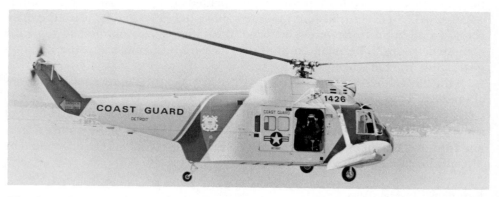

The Coast Guard is the only U.S. military service that flies the Sikorsky S-62, assigned the
military designation HU2S-1G and subsequently HH-52A from 1962 on. On the fuselage
of this HH-52A, based at Detroit, Mich., is the Coast Guard insignia: a small blue stripe and
a wide red stripe with the service's shield. (U.S. Coast Guard)

# Sikorsky

S-64                                                    H-54 Tarhe

The Sikorsky S-64 Skycrane was based upon the earlier Model S-60, developed
by Sikorsky as a company project with some assistance from the U.S. Navy. One
example of the S-60 was constructed using the piston engines and dynamic
components of the S-56/H-37 Mojave and a skeletal fuselage configured to accept
a pod under its back. This prototype first flew in March 1959 and was used to
demonstrate, among other things, a lightweight, heliborne minesweeping appa-
ratus (See Bell 61/HSL). The aircraft was lost in April 1961, but it had already
generated considerable interest in the U.S. Army. The next company-sponsored
flying crane, a turboshaft-powered version of the S-60 designated S-64, was tested
by the Army in 1963. Two additional prototypes were built by Sikorsky for
evaluation by the West German Army. As a result of these evaluations, the U.S.
Army ordered six S-64s as the YCH-54A Tarhe, the first of which was delivered in
late 1964. By 1965 CH-54A production models were in service in Vietnam.

The S-64 is a twin-turbine flying-crane helicopter capable of lifting a variety of
podded cargo, vans, and slung cargo weighing up to 12½ tons. Its main rotor is
composed of six aluminum, fully articulated blades, and its tail rotor has four
aluminum blades. These are powered by two Pratt & Whitney T73 turboshafts
mounted atop the shallow fuselage's ventral surface. An outrigger-shaped struc-

ture on either side of the aircraft houses the fixed main landing gear, which can be raised or lowered to permit the Tarhe to "squat" onto its cargo. The forward cabin houses the cockpit and a freight master's station for controlling the cargo handling equipment as well as flight controls for piloting the helicopter while hovering to pick up a slung load. U.S. Army production of the CH-54A/B variants totalled 95 machines. Commercial versions were the S-64E and S-64F; two of the CH-54A type were also sold commercially.

The CH-54B variant holds several international records. These are primarily payload-to-height and time-to-height records. Several commercial variants are operated by logging companies, but no foreign military forces procured any S-64s other than for evaluation.

First flight: 9 May 1962
Service introduction: 1965
Users: United States

**Variants**

S-64A       prototype evaluated by U.S. and West German armies; no military designation
            assigned; 3 built.
YCH-54A   pre-production prototypes for U.S. Army delivered in 1964-1965; 6 built.
CH-54A    production helicopter; 60 built.
CH-54B    upgraded CH-54A with 2 Pratt & Whitney JFTD-2-5A turboshafts 4,800 shp
            each; strengthened gearbox, rotor head, landing gear, 12½-ton lift capacity; 29
            built.

**Characteristics (CH-54A)**

Crew: 1 pilot, 1 copilot, 1 freight master
Engines: 2 Pratt & Whitney JFTD12-4A (T73-P-1) turboshafts 4,500 shp each
Dimensions: length 88 ft 6 in (26.97 m); height 25 ft 5 in (7.75 m); rotor diameter 72
     ft (21.95 m)
Weight: empty 19,234 lbs (8,732 kg); loaded 42,000 lbs (19,068 kg)
Speed: cruise 105 mph (169 km/h); maximum 126 mph (203 km/h)
Range: 230 miles (370 km)
Ceiling: hover OGE 6,900 ft (2,103 m); hover IGE 10,600 ft (3,231 m); service 9,000
     ft (2,743 m)
Climb: 1,330 ft/min (405 m/min)
Payload: 20,000 lbs (9,080 kg) external sling

The Sikorsky commercial S-60 was the progenitor of the military S-64/H-54 heavy-lift helicopters and was evaluated by the U.S. military services in several roles. Pictured here is an exercise with a section of a Bell HSL carrying towed minesweeping gear. There was extensive civilian use of the S-60. (Sikorsky)

One of three CH-54B Tarhe helicopters fitted with skis in 1971 for evaluation by the U.S. Army in Alaska. Two auxiliary fuel tanks are also fitted. Note the side windows for the rear-facing cockpit of the freight master. (Sikorsky)

Resembling giant grasshoppers, U.S. Army CH-54A Tarhe helicopters sit on a runway at Finthen in West Germany. Both the S-60 and S-64 models are generally referred to as flying cranes despite the Army's official assignment of the Indian name Tarhe to the military CH-54s. (U.S. Army)

An Army CH-54A from the 1st Cavalry Division (Air Mobile) takes off carrying a detachable pod that can be used as a command post, hospital, or for other purposes during operations near An Khe in South Vietnam in 1966. Neither the helicopter nor pod have the low-visibility markings that came into vogue about this time in an effort to reduce helicopter vulnerability. (Sikorsky)

# Sikorsky

S-65          H-53 $\begin{cases} \text{Sea Stallion} \\ \text{Super Jolly} \end{cases}$

   The Sikorsky S-65 is a hybrid helicopter, having an enlarged version of the S-61/H-3 fuselage coupled with the dynamic components of the S-64/H-54 flying crane. The result is a formidable-appearing heavy helicopter that can transport 37 fully equipped troops or 24 stretchers and four attendants. One U.S. Navy variant is equipped for minesweeping while one USAF version is an all-weather SAR helicopter. The original CH-53A was developed as a heavy assault helicopter for the U.S. Marine Corps. The first flight of this variant took place in 1964 and production machines became operational in 1966. USAF interest in the S-65 soon followed, and units were ordered to replace the HH-3s in the SAR role. The U.S. Navy adopted a variant of the H-53 for aerial mine countermeasure duties, and it was this aircraft that was used in the ill-fated American hostage rescue attempt in Iran in April 1980. Seven of the 30 RH-53Ds procured were lost as a result of that mission. Ironically, six RH-53Ds had been sold to the Government of Iran before the Shah's ouster, with Iran being the only country other than the United States to operate the minesweeping variant.

   The S-65's rotor system is composed of a folding, six-bladed main rotor and a four-bladed tail rotor. These are powered by two General Electric turboshafts mounted on either side of the upper fuselage. The fuselage is a box-like, semi-monocoque structure with a rear loading ramp and a folding tailboom. The twin-wheeled tricycle landing gear retracts into the rear of sponsons located on each side of the fuselage and forward into the nose. The HH-53s have a rescue hoist with 250 feet of cable and a tree-penetrator device for jungle rescue. The helicopter is capable of water operation, is armed with three 7.62-mm miniguns and fitted with armor plating, and has a special all-weather navigation system.

The CH-53A/D variants were the U.S. Marine Corps's heavy assault helicopter from the mid-1960s until 1980, when they were reclassified as medium helicopters (as were the CH-46 Sea Knights) in view of the greater capabilities of the three-engine CH-53E. The Air Force flies primarily SAR variants, which are informally called "Super Jollys," a reflection of the name assigned to the smaller HH-3E rescue helicopters. Production of the twin-engined S-65s has ended in the United States and at VFW-Fokker in West Germany. Current production centers on the CH-53E, described separately.

First flight: 14 October 1964
Service introduction: 1966
Users: Austria, West Germany, Iran, Israel, United States

**Variants**

CH-53A    Sea Stallion; production variant for U.S. Marine Corps with 2 T64-GE-6B turboshafts; 143 built.

HH-53B    Super Jolly; production for USAF SAR role with 2 T64-GE-3 turboshafts; refueling probe, 3 7.62-mm miniguns; 8 built.

CH-53B    similar to HH-53B with T64-GE-7 turboshafts.

HH-53C    similar to HH-53B/Ch-53B; 58 built.

CH-53D    similar to CH-53A for Marine Corps with 2 3,925-shp T64-GE-413 turboshafts; 126 built.

RH-53D    similar to CH-53D with advanced minesweeping gear; 30 built for U.S. Navy, 6 for Iranian Navy.

CH-53E    three-engined variant described separately.

VH-53F    VIP-configured variant; 6 ordered, but later cancelled.

CH-53G    CH-53D for West Germany.

HH-53H    HH-53Cs modified to improved all-weather capability including FLIR, terrain following/avoidance radar, inertial navigation system.

S-65-Oe   HH-53C for Austrian Air Force equipped for SAR in Alps; 2 built.

**Characteristics (CH-53D)**

Crew: 1 pilot, 1 copilot, 1 crew chief
Engines: 2 General Electric T64-GE-413 turboshafts 3,925 shp each
Dimensions: length 88 ft 3 in (26.9 m); height 24 ft 11 in (7.6 m); rotor diameter 72 ft 3 in (22.02 m)
Weight: empty 23,485 lbs (10,662 kg); loaded 42,000 lbs (19,068 kg)
Speed: cruise 173 mph (278 km/h); maximum 196 mph (315 km/h)
Range: 257 miles (414 km)
Ceiling: hover OGE 6,500 ft (1,981 m); hover IGE 13,400 ft (4,084 m); service 21,000 ft (6,401 m)
Climb: 2,180 ft/min (664 m/min)
Payload: 37 troops

The Sikorsky S-65/H-53 series is the largest operational helicopter in Western military service with the CH-53E variant (listed separately) being a specialized heavy-lift aircraft. This is a West German CH-53G, one of the first of more than 100 produced for the German Army. (Sikorsky)

A U.S. Navy RH-53D minesweeping Sea Stallion maneuvers on the deck of the helicopter carrier *Inchon* (LPH-12) off the northern coast of Egypt in 1975. This RH-53D is from Helicopter Mine Countermeasures Squadron (HM) 12, the first of three such U.S. units. The fully retractable tricycle landing gear puts the helicopter low to the deck to facilitate loading and unloading troops. (U.S. Navy)

A U.S.Navy CH-53A Sea Stallion prepares to lift an Mk-105 minesweeping sled from the amphibious ship *Raleigh* (LPD-1). The Y-shaped objects on the sled are foils that fold down when in the water to permit high-speed towing. The Navy used CH-53A helicopters for minesweeping in the early 1970s pending delivery of the improved RH-53D Sea Stallions. (U.S. Navy)

This is one of eight Sikorsky HH-53C rescue helicopters converted to the HH-53H configuration under the USAF Pave Low 3 program to provide a night/all-weather rescue capability. Shown here is the refueling boom, under which is mounted a Forward-Looking Infra-Red (FLIR) sensor, with a "thimble" dome on the left side of the nose housing a terrain following/avoidance radar. The HH-53Hs are informally called "Black Knights." (U.S. Navy)

The U.S. Air Force flies the HH-53B Super Jolly in the combat rescue role. The helicopter is fitted with an in-flight refueling probe, external fuel tanks on the side sponsons, armor, provisions for mounting guns, and a rescue hoist (just forward of the engine pod). (Sikorsky)

# Sikorsky

S-65A                                             H-53E Super Stallion

The CH-53E Super Stallion is the result of a U.S. Navy/Marine Corps requirement for a shipboard-compatible helicopter capable of lifting 16 tons. The Sikorsky CH-53 series was chosen by the U.S. Navy in 1973 as the basis for such an aircraft, as the original S-65 design had a provision for the addition of a third engine. Sikorsky was awarded a contract to develop the three-engined variant of their successful Sea Stallion and two prototype YCH-53Es were built for evaluation. The first of these flew in March 1974, less than a year after being ordered. This helicopter was later destroyed in a ground accident, but testing was resumed with the second prototype, which first flew in January 1975. Two pre-production prototypes were then built, and full-scale production was started early in 1978. The CH-53E is the most powerful helicopter ever produced outside the Soviet Union and can lift double the capacity of the smaller CH-53D with only a 50 percent increase in engine power.

The fuselage of the CH-53E is 6½ feet longer than that of the CH-53D and has the same cross-sectional dimensions. The primary differences between the two machines are in the power plants, rotors, and tail section, and, of course, performance. The Super Stallion's main rotor is composed of seven titanium blades rather than the six aluminum blades of its predecessor. The rotor transmission can absorb up to 13,500 shp for up to ten seconds, and 11,570 shp for 30 minutes. The three General Electric turboshafts, one mounted on the centerline aft of the rotor hub and one each on either side of the hub, each have a maximum power rating of 4,380 shp for ten minutes and 3,670 shp continuously. The CH-53E tail section consists of a large vertical stabilizer canted to port with a massive four-bladed tail rotor 20 feet in diameter positioned at its top on the left side, and a large gull-wing horizontal stabilizer on the right side.

The Navy and Marine Corps chose the S-65A for their Heavy Lift Helicopter (HLH) over the Army's proposed Boeing Vertol CH-62 design, contributing to that service's decision not to develop the CH-62. In the early 1970s the Navy and Marine Corps together required some 75 to 150 helicopters. However, only 33 of the CH-53E variants had been approved for Marine service and 16 for the Navy as of 1980. The latter will be used for Vertical On-board Delivery (VOD) of munitions and supplies from auxiliary ships to aircraft carriers, or, with special equipment installed, in the mine countermeasure role with the designation MH-53E.

First flight: YCH-53E, 1 March 1974, CH-53E 13 December 1980
Service introduction: 1980
Users: United States

**Characteristics**

Crew: 1 pilot, 1 copilot, 1 crew chief
Engines: 3 General Electric T64-GE-416 turboshaft 4,380 shp each T/O; 3,670 shp
each continuous (see text)
Dimensions: length 99 ft 1 in (30.2 m); height 27 ft 9 in (8.46 m); rotor diameter 79 ft
(24.08 m)
Weight: empty 32,048 lbs (14,550 kg); loaded 69,750 lbs (31,667 kg)
Speed: cruise 173 mph (278 km/h); maximum 196 mph (315 km/h)

Range: 306 miles (492 km)

Ceiling: hover OGE 7,480 ft (2,280 m); hover IGE 10,720 ft (3,267 m); service 12,400 ft (3,780 m)

Climb: 2,380 ft/min (725 m/min)

Payload: 55 troops or 30,000 lbs (13,620 kg) internally or 32,200 lbs (14,619 kg) external slung cargo

One of the two YCH-53E prototypes demonstrates its heavy-lift capability by carrying a 16-ton combat vehicle. The CH-53E is the largest heavy-lift helicopter in the West and is being supplied to the U.S. Navy and Marine Corps. Auxiliary fuel tanks are fitted in this view. (Sikorsky)

This head-on view of a CH-53E shows the helicopter's distinctive three-engine configuration. The only other three-engine helicopter in service use is the French Super Frelon while the Soviet Mi-12 Homer has four engines. (Sikorsky)

# Sikorsky

S-66

The Sikorsky S-66 was that firm's entry in the hotly contested U.S. Army competition for the Advanced Aerial Fire Support System (AAFSS). This was a design competition, with the winner receiving a contract for engineering development of an advanced gunship helicopter. Lockheed was named winner of the AAFSS effort in March 1966, leading to development of the AH-56 Cheyenne. Sikorsky subsequently applied many of its design concepts for the AAFSS to the privately developed S-67 Blackhawk.

# Sikorsky

S-67                                        Blackhawk

This high-speed helicopter gunship was developed by Sikorsky as a private venture in response to Vietnam combat experience. Some of the Blackhawk's features were based on the Sikorsky S-66 entry in the U.S. Army's 1965 competition for an Advanced Aerial Fire Support System (AAFSS) as well as on flight experience with the S-61F compound helicopter. Design of the S-67 began in August 1969, and the sole Blackhawk to be built flew for the first time exactly one year later. Although touted as a highly maneuverable gunship, the Blackhawk could be employed as a troop carrier as well, in the style of the later Soviet Mi-24 Hind.

Designed from the outset as a gunship, the Blackhawk had an all-metal, semi-monocoque fuselage with a narrow cross section. The pilot and copilot/gunner were seated in tandem forward, beneath a single plexiglass canopy. As a troop carrier the main fuselage cabin could be divided into two levels, the upper deck seating 15 troops and the lower section housing fuel and ammunition. The tail configuration consisted of a swept-back, vertical fin, which extended below the fuselage. The upper section of the fin housed the anti-torque rotor, the five-bladed rotor being fitted on the left side. A horizontal stabilizer, which could be set in a vertical position for hovering flight, was also provided. The main landing gear retracted into the fuselage with a fixed tail wheel on the vertical fin. Stub wings, which were easily detached, were fitted to help off-load the rotor during high-speed flight. In the gunship role, the Blackhawk used the wings to carry missiles or rockets on four stations plus wing-end stations for Sidewinder air-to-air missiles. Two 1,500-shp General Electric turboshaft engines fitted above the low-profile fuselage powered the five-bladed main rotor as well as the anti-torque rotor. The aircraft's dynamic components were modified from the S-61R helicopter. Wing-span was 27 feet 4 inches. Typical armament loads were 16 TOW antitank missiles or 8 19-round 2.75-inch rocket pods, plus Sidewinders. An under-fuselage turret, with essentially a 360-degree field of fire, could be fitted with a 20-mm or 30-mm cannon, or multi-barrel 20-mm cannon, or a 40-mm grenade launcher. Without external ordnance or troops, up to four tons of cargo could be carried by sling.

The Blackhawk (civil N671SA) was flight tested from 1970 to 1974. In its original configuration the helicopter reached a record speed of 216.844 mph on a 3-kilometer course in December 1970, and later that month reached 220.885 mph on a 15/25-kilometer course. Sikorsky then received Army funding to modify the tail configuration with a ducted fan system. Flight testing in this mode began in 1974 and speeds of 230 mph were achieved in a dive. The aircraft was recon-figured to its original tail later that year and crashed in September 1974. In addition to its payload and versatility, the Blackhawk demonstrated a very high degree of maneuverability.

First flight: 20 August 1970
Service introduction: not operational

**Characteristics**

Crew: 1 pilot, 1 copilot/gunner
Engines: 2 General Electric T58-GE-5 turboshaft 1,500 shp each
Dimensions: length 64 ft 9 in (19.74 m); height 15 ft (4.57 m); rotor diameter 62 ft (18.9 m)
Weight: empty 12,514 lbs (5,681 kg); combat as gunship 14,000 lbs (6,356 kg); loaded 22,050 lbs (10,011 kg)
Speed: cruise 138-187 mph (222-301 km/h); maximum 193 mph (311 km/h)
Range: as transport with 15 troops 220 miles (354 km) at 165 mph (265 km/h)
Ceiling: service with 1 engine 4,500 ft (1,372 m); service 17,000 ft (5,182 m)
Climb: 2,350 ft/min (716 m/min)
Payload: 15 troops or 8,000 lbs (3,632 kg) slung cargo or 16 TOW missiles + 2 Side-winder missiles*

*Maximum weapons load, including turret, ammunition, and external stores was 8,000 lbs.

The Sikorsky S-67 demonstrates its weapon-carrying ability with two dummy AIM-9 Sidewinder air-to-air missiles, 16 dummy wire-guided TOW antitank missiles, and a belly-mounted 20-mm cannon. The Blackhawk was designed to carry up to 24 TOW missiles in the AAFSS role. Note the camouflage paint scheme. (Sikorsky)

A head-on view of the Sikorsky S-67 Blackhawk, showing the aircraft's narrow cross section, tandem seating, twin engines, and stub wings that both unload the rotor in forward flight and provide hard points for weapons. (Sikorsky)

# Sikorsky

S-69                                    H-59 ABC

The Sikorsky S-69 was developed for the U.S. Army as a research aircraft to test the aerodynamic properties of the Advancing Blade Concept (ABC) as well as the flight envelope possible in an aircraft so configured for the U.S. Army. Two prototype S-69s were completed, one in 1973, the other in 1975, and were designated XH-59A. The first crashed early in its flight testing program, causing corrective changes to be made to the control system of the second aircraft. The first XH-59A was subsequently repaired and modified for use as a wind tunnel test vehicle.

The ABC uses two coaxial, three-bladed contra-rotating rigid rotors powered by a 1,825-shp PT6T-3 Turbo Twin Pac located within the fuselage. At high speeds, only the advancing blades of each of the contra-rotating rotors are generating lift, thereby off-loading the retreating blades and eliminating the penalties of blade stall inherent to standard helicopter designs. This dramatically improves maneuverability and stability and alleviates the need for a wing to supplement the rotor to achieve greater speed.

The Army's test program began in July 1975 with the XH-59A configured as a pure helicopter. In March 1977, two Pratt & Whitney J60 turbojets were installed, one on each side of the fuselage, to investigate the ABC design at higher forward speeds. The Army was joined in this phase of the program by both the Navy and NASA.

First flight: 26 July 1973       Service introduction: not operational

**Characteristics**

Crew: 1 pilot, 1 copilot
Engines: 1 Pratt & Whitney Aircraft of Canada PT6T-3 Turbo Twin Pac 1,825 shp
    plus 2 Pratt & Whitney J60-P-3A turbojets 3,000 lbst each
Dimensions: length 41 ft 5 in (12.62 m); height 12 ft 11 in (3.94 m); rotor diameter 36
    ft (10.97 m)
Weight: loaded 11,100 (5,039 kg)
Speed: maximum as helicopter 184 mph (296 km/h); maximum as compound 322
    mph (518 km/h)
Range:
Ceiling: compound 600 ft (183 m); hover IGE helicopter 6,700 ft (2,042 m)
Climb:

The Sikorsky XH-59A ABC research aircraft in flight. Note the contra-rotating rotors, streamlined configuration with fully retracting wheels, and twin tail fins. Fuselage markings denote its sponsors: Army, Navy, NASA, USAF. Military configurations of the ABC have been proposed. (Sikorsky)

A Sikorsky XH-59A ABC in a landing configuration with gear lowered. The ABC concept is that the lift load of the aircraft at high forward speeds is carried primarily by the advancing rotor blades. (Sikorsky)

# Sikorsky

S-70                                        H-60 Black Hawk

The Sikorsky S-70 was designed to fulfill the U.S. Army's requirement for a Utility Tactical Transport Aircraft System (UTTAS) to replace the Bell UH-1 Huey in assault helicopter companies, air cavalry, and aeromedical evacuation units. As specified by the Army, the UTTAS competition winner would have a crew of 3 and be capable of transporting 11 combat-equipped troops or an equivalent weight at a 4,000-foot altitude with a sustained cruise of 201 mph. External dimensions were to permit six UTTAS to be loaded in one C-5A transport, two in the C-141, and one in the C-130 Hercules. All contenders for the award were to use two General Electric T700 turboshafts, the same engine selected to power the contemporary Advanced Attack Helicopter (AAH). Other characteristics specified by the Army included wheeled landing gear, a minimal avionics package, an armament of two 7.62-mm machine guns, an alternative configuration for four to six litters, manual blade folding, and either duplicate critical components or armor protecting them. The Sikorsky entrant in the competition was designated YUH-60. Both Sikorsky and its competitor, Boeing Vertol, supplied the Army with three prototypes, a ground test vehicle, and a static airframe. The competition began in March 1976, and on 23 December 1976 the Sikorsky entrant was declared the winner.

The Black Hawk is designed to absorb a great deal of punishment to increase its survivability over that of its predecessor, the UH-1. Its rotor system is built so as to continue functioning for 30 minutes after a main spar has been severed by a 23-mm shell. Fuel tanks will survive a 12.7-mm shell hit, and a single 7.62-mm shell hit anywhere on the lower hemisphere of the aircraft will not bring it down for at least thirty minutes. The main gear will absorb a 9g landing, and the crew's seats a 14½g landing. Internal equipment requires a 25g stress for it to break away, and the dynamic components will remain in place under 20g sideways and 10g inverted stresses. The UH-60A is equipped with a four-bladed main rotor constructed of titanium spars inside a Nomex honeycomb core covered with an epoxy-fiberglass composite skin. The tip of each blade is swept back 20 degrees. The tail rotor has four blades constructed of a graphite-epoxy composite. The tail incorporates a stabilator at the base of the vertical stabilizer. Landing gear on the UH-60A is non-retractable, although the EH-60B main gear does swing aft to permit its radar a 360-degree field of rotation. Armament consists of one or two M-60 machine guns firing from the cabin doors; up to four mine dispensers can be carried with a capacity of 320 air-dropped antitank mines.

The first production model of the H-60, the UH-60A, was delivered to the U.S. Army in 1979. A second variant, the EH-60B SOTAS (Stand-Off Target Acquisition System) is currently under development. Using a Motorola avionics package consisting of a rotating under-fuselage radar and data links, the EH-60B will give Army commanders the updated status of enemy ground vehicle activity every 15 seconds. A third variant of the H-60, the Navy's SH-60B LAMPS III, is described separately. The Army plans to acquire 1,107 UH-60As plus 123 of the EH-60B variant. A production rate for both Army variants of 96 aircraft per year is planned for the early 1980s. The U.S. Marine Corps may acquire a modified UH-60 for the medium-lift requirement, to replace the CH-46 and CH-53A/D helicopters in the 1990s. Interest in the UH-60 has been expressed by several air forces, and Sikorsky anticipates a foreign sales potential of 500 to 600 units.

First flight: YUH-60 17 October 1974
Service introduction: June 1979
Users: United States

**Variants**

| | |
|---|---|
| YUH-60 | prototype helicopter in UTTAS competition; 3 built. |
| UH-60A | production version; first flight 17 October 1978; 1,107 planned through 1980s. |
| EH-60A | Quick Fix II; proposed variant equipped to intercept, locate, and jam enemy communications; to replace EH-1H Quick Fix. |
| YEH-60B | prototypes for Stand-Off Target Acquisition System (SOTAS); under-fuselage, rotating, side-looking radar antenna (19-ft long); data link; first flight 6 February 1981; 8 built. |
| EH-60B | production SOTAS helicopter; 123 planned. |
| SH-60B Sea Hawk | Navy LAMPS III described separately. |

**Characteristics**

Crew: 1 pilot, 1 copilot, 1 crew chief
Engines: 2 General Electric T700-GE-700 turboshafts 1,543 shp each
Dimensions: length 64 ft 10 in (19.76 m); height 16 ft 10 in (5.13 m); rotor diameter 53 ft 8 in (16.36 m)
Weight: empty 10,900 lbs (4,949 kg); loaded 16,450 lbs (7,468 kg)
Speed: cruise 167 mph (269 km/h); maximum 224 mph (360 km/h)
Range: 373 miles (600 km); up to 1,000 miles (1,069 km) with limited internal payload and external fuel tanks.
Ceiling: hover OGE 10,400 ft (3,170 m); service 19,000 ft (5,791 m)
Climb: 2,460 ft/min (750 m/min)
Payload: 11 troops or 2,640 lbs (1,199 kg) internal cargo

An Army UH-60A Black Hawk demonstrates its maneuverability by banking more than 90 degrees. (U.S. Army)

A YUH-60A Black Hawk prototype during U.S. Army evaluation. This squad-carrying helicopter is being procured in large numbers by the U.S. Army. (U.S. Army)

The prototype YEH-60B SOTAS—Stand-Off Target Acquisition System—helicopter lifts on its first flight 6 February 1981. The 19-foot radar antenna is stowed beneath the fuselage. During flight, the wheels swing back and the antenna is extended to rotate, giving battlefield commanders surveillance of enemy vehicle movements. (Sikorsky)

# Sikorsky
S-70L                                    SH-60 Seahawk

The SH-60B is an ASW helicopter that is integrated with a parent warship to form the LAMPS III (Light Airborne Multi-Purpose System). In a 1976-1977 U.S. Navy competition for the LAMPS III airframe, the Sikorsky S-70L, a derivative of that company's winner of the Army's UTTAS competitions, the UH-60A, was declared the winner over two competitors, a Boeing Vertol entry based on their YUH-61 and a modification of the Westland/Aérospatiale Lynx. The S-70L is designated SH-60B Seahawk in U.S. Navy service, and approximately 65 percent of its components are the same as those of the UH-60A. (The LAMPS I was the Kaman HU2K/UH-2 Seasprite modified to the SH-2 ASW configuration.)

The Navy's LAMPS III is unique in that it is the first aircraft program wherein the prime contractor has been the avionics manufacturer, the IBM Corporation. The complexity and sophistication of LAMPS virtually dictated this choice, since the prime contractor must integrate both airborne and shipboard electronics. Sikorsky is the subcontractor for the LAMPS III airframe. The SH-60B differs from the UH-60A primarily in its avionics suite, which contains search radar, doppler navigation radar, MAD, ECM, and sonobuoys. Structurally, the SH-60B has a considerably modified interior, as well as flotation, an electrically folding main rotor and a folding tail, and the tail wheel has been strengthened and moved forward. A storage-ejector panel for 25 sonobuoys is fitted on the port side and a MAD "bird" is stowed to starboard.

In its antisubmarine warfare mission, the LAMPS helicopter is launched from the parent ship upon detection of a suspected submarine contact by the ship's sensors or an outside source. Upon arrival in the vicinity of the datum (suspected submarine location), the SH-60B releases expendable sonobuoys to localize the target. The information derived from the sonobuoys is processed aboard the helicopter or transmitted via data link for processing and analysis aboard the parent ship. Final localization is accomplished by active or passive sonobuoys or MAD. The helicopter carries Mk-46 homing torpedoes for attack. On an antiship surveillance and targeting mission, the SH-60 uses radar and electronic equipment to detect, identify, and localize over-the-horizon surface ship threats to the parent ship. Using the data transmitted by link from the SH-60B, the parent ship can launch antiship missiles. A total of 204 aircraft are planned for operation from some 115 U.S. Navy cruisers, destroyers, and frigates. (Including training and pipeline requirements, this number will not be sufficient.) Australia, Spain, Japan, West Germany, Norway, Taiwan, the Netherlands, and Canada have expressed interest in the SH-60B LAMPS.

First flight: 12 December 1979   Service introduction: 1984 (est.)   Users: United States

**Characteristics**

Crew: 1 pilot, 1 copilot, 1 systems operator
Engines: 2 General Electric T700-GE-401 turboshafts 1,713 shp each
Dimensions: length 64 ft 10 in (19.76 m); height 17 ft 2 in (5.23 m); rotor diameter 53 ft 8 in (16.36 m)
Weight: empty 13,648 lbs (6,196 kg); loaded 19,377 lbs (8,797 kg)
Speed: cruise 155 mph (249 km/h)
Range:
Ceiling: service 10,000 ft (3,048 m)
Climb: 1,192 ft/min (363 m/min)        Payload: 2 Mk-46 ASW homing torpedoes

A prototype U.S. Navy SH-60B in flight with dummy ASW torpedo visible on left side of fuselage. Above the torpedo is a sonobuoy dispenser. A towed MAD device is fitted on the other side of the fuselage. No dipping sonar is provided in these ship-based LAMPS helicopters, which will rely upon shipboard sonar for initial submarine detection. (Sikorsky)

A prototype SH-60B (below) in flight with an SH-3 Sea King. The SH-60B has a different role than the Sea King, which operates only from aircraft carriers with dipping sonar. However, a similarly equipped variant of the SH-60 will probably replace the Sea King aboard carriers during the 1980s. (Sikorsky)

# Sikorsky
S-72                                    RSRA

The Rotor Systems Research Aircraft (RSRA) is a joint NASA and U.S. Army program in which a variety of rotor and propulsion systems are being evaluated. Chosen over a competing Bell design in October 1973, the Sikorsky S-72 is a flying test bed for the systems under study, giving the program a testing capability that could not be duplicated in a wind tunnel. The first S-72 has been engaged in government flight testing since February 1977 and the second S-72 since early 1979.

The S-72 can be flown in a variety of configurations. It has removable, low-mounted main wings, tail surfaces like those of an airplane, and removable TF34-GE-400A turbofan engines in S-3A Viking engine pods on the sides of the fuselage. Its permanent power is supplied by a pair of 1,400-shp T58-GE-5 turboshafts normally driving a five-bladed main rotor system from a Sikorsky S-61 and a five-bladed anti-torque tail rotor on the left side of the vertical stabilizer. The aircraft can be flown as a pure helicopter, a pure airplane, or a compound helicopter. Wingspan is 45 1/12 feet. This variety of options permits a number of rotor systems to be tested, even those that would not normally support a pure helicopter of this weight. An ejection system that jettisons the rotor blades and extracts the crew through an escape hatch in the top of the fuselage on rocket-assisted ejection seats provides an extra measure of crew safety. The S-72s are heavily instrumented and have an on-board digital computer that controls the aircraft during some research missions, allowing extremely precise duplication of preprogrammed maneuvers.

The RSRA research program is expected to continue through the 1980s to provide data for both military and civilian helicopter development.

First flight: as helicopter 12 October 1976; as compound helicopter 10 April 1978
Service introduction: not operational

The first of two Sikorsky RSRA research aircraft produced for the U.S. Army and NASA is shown here in flight prior to being fitted with external TF-34 turbofan engines. With the addition of wings and engines—as well as two roof-mounted turboshafts—the aircraft is considered a compound helicopter. (Sikorsky)

## Characteristics

Crew: 1 pilot, 1 copilot, 1 flight engineer

Engines: 2 General Electric T58-GE-5 turboshafts 1,400 shp each plus 2 removable General Electric TF34-GE-400A turbofans 9,275 lbst each

Dimensions: length 70 ft 7 in (21.51 m); height 14 ft 6 in (4.42 m); rotor diameter 62 ft (18.9 m)

Weight: empty helicopter configuration 14,490 lbs (6,578 kg); loaded 18,400 lbs (8,354 kg) empty in compound configuration 21,022 lbs (9,544 kg); loaded 26,200 lbs (11,895 kg)

Speed: helicopter maximum 184 mph (296 km/h); compound helicopter maximum 345 mph (555 km/h)

Range:

Ceiling:

Climb:

The first RSRA aircraft after being fitted with TF-34 turbofan engines on the sides of its fuselage and swept-back wings below the engines. (Sikorsky)

# Sikorsky

(S-76)

The U.S. Army is funding a helicopter with engines, transmission, and rotor systems of the Sikorsky S-76 as part of the Advanced Composite Aircraft Program (ACAP). Additional details of the program are provided under the Bell D292 listing, with that helicopter being the second design in the ACAP effort.

The Sikorsky S-76 is a large commercial helicopter capable of carrying 12 passengers plus a crew of 2. The fuselage is a composite structure, with a fiberglass nose, light alloy honeycomb cabin, and semi-monocoque tailboom. The tricycle landing gear is fully retracting, giving the aircraft a highly streamlined shape. The ACAP design provides for a fixed, tricycle gear and new fuselage.

Over 400 S-76s had been sold to commercial operators throughout the world by early 1981, used primarily in support of offshore oil rigs. Sikorsky initially submitted the S-76 in the Coast Guard's Short Range Rescue (SRR) aircraft competition but withdrew to exploit the commercial market. (See Bell D 292 and Aérospatiale SA 365 listings.) The commercial S-76 was originally named Spirit, but it was changed to simply S-76 in 1980 because of the religious implications of the name in some countries. The Army plans to procure three ACAP helicopters each from Sikorsky and Bell, with test flights to begin by September 1984. The helicopters will be considered technology demonstrators vice production prototypes. The following data are Army design specifications.

**Characteristics**

Crew: 1 pilot, 1 crewman
Engines: 2 Allison 250-C30 turboshaft 650 shp each
Dimensions: rotor diameter 44 ft (13.41 m)
Weight: loaded approximately 8,470 lbs (3,845 kg)
Speed: maximum 161 mph (259 km/h)
Range:
Ceiling:
Climb:
Payload: 6 troops

This is an artist's concept of the Sikorsky rebuilt S-76 commercial helicopter, configured to compete in a U.S. Army program to develop advanced helicopter components. (Sikorsky)

# APPENDIX A

# Rotary-Wing Aircraft Designers

## Aérospatiale

Formed by the 1 January 1970 merger of Nord Aviation, Sud Aviation, and SEREB (Société Pour L'Étude Et La Réalisation d'Engins Balistiques), Aérospatiale has continued the product line of each of its predecessors. As a result of a mid-1960s agreement negotiated by Sud Aviation, it coproduces several helicopters with Westland of Great Britain and manufactures others exclusively. Negotiations in 1980-1981 with MBB of West Germany for coproduction of the PAH-2 have been abortive. (Aérospatiale has an equally impressive fixed-wing list of products, including the Anglo-French Concorde and the A300 Airbus.) Like its predecessors, Aérospatiale is a state-owned company, comprising the whole of the French nationalized aircraft industry.

## Aerotecnica

A service company that specialized in crop spraying and aerial photography, Aerotecnica branched out in 1953 to experiment with helicopter design and production. The French designer Jean Cantinieau emigrated to Spain to direct the new helicopter division and produced several prototype helicopters in the next few years. These designs were neither commercially nor militarily successful, however, and Aerotecnica suspended operations in 1962.

## Agusta

Giovanni Agusta founded the company that bears his name in 1907 to build biplanes. Since the aircraft manufacturing business in Italy fluctuated violently between prosperity and depression, the Costruzioni Aeronautiche Giovanni Agusta turned to the manufacture of motorcycles as well, retaining a small plant to produce light, fixed-wing aircraft. Until 1954, Agusta achieved its greatest fame in the motorcycle manufacturing business. In that year, however, Agusta acquired a license from Bell Helicopter to manufacture the popular Bell 47/H-13 series, and the name Agusta, or Agusta-Bell, has now become synonymous with many helicopters. The majority of Agusta's work has been the adaptation and license manufacture of foreign helicopter designs. Agusta-built Bell designs include the following models: 47, 204, 205, 206, and 212. Versions of the Sikorsky SH-3D and Boeing Vertol H-47 have also been built by Agusta, the latter at the Meridionali factory. Indigenous designs have been few and, until the late 1970s, relatively unsuccessful. However, the Agusta A 109 Hirundo and the A 129 Mongoose have the potential to be particularly popular aircraft in the 1980s. The facilities manufacturing Bell, Boeing Vertol, and Sikorsky designs are separate and demonstrate a very high degree of management talent.

# American Helicopter

Formed in 1947 by C.D. Denney, the American Helicopter Company experimented with pulse-jet engines attached to the tips of rotors as a means of helicopter propulsion. Three military models were constructed under government contract: the Top Sergeant in 1949, the Buck Private in 1951, and the XH-26 Jet Jeep in 1952. (The first two carried the company designations XA5 and XA6.) In 1954 the company was acquired by Fairchild, which did not continue to market the pulse-jet concept.

# Autogiro Company of America

Formed by Harold F. Pitcairn as a subsidiary of his Pitcairn Autogiro Company, the Autogiro Company of America was the sole licensee for production of Cierva autogiros in the United States. Kellett Aircraft and the Buhl Company also entered into agreements with this Pitcairn subsidiary, enabling them to use Cierva patents. In 1940, the Autogiro Company of America, which had by that time changed its name to AGA Aviation, took over all Pitcairn's contracts. In 1943, it was absorbed by Firestone Tire and Rubber Company. (See Pitcairn.)

# Bell

Lawrence D. Bell began working as an aircraft mechanic in 1912, was later associated with the Glenn L. Martin and Consolidated Aircraft companies, and in 1935 he formed his own aircraft firm. Bell produced several thousand P-39 Airacobra and P-63 Kingcobra fighters; the first U.S. jet-propelled aircraft, the P-59 Airacomet; and the XS-1/X-1 rocket test aircraft, as well as several lesser designs. However, no fixed-wing aircraft were produced by Bell after World War II except for test and research aircraft. Helicopter development began at Bell in 1942, with the Bell 47 design (U.S. military H-13 Sioux) probably being the world's most widely used helicopter of the 1950s and the Bell 204 and its derivatives of the Huey and Cobra series being produced in greater numbers than any other helicopter in history. The firm continues as one of the three major U.S. helicopter producers, the others being Boeing Vertol and Sikorsky.

# Berliner

Shortly after the Wright brothers' first successful flight, Emile Berliner, an inventor of mechanical devices, decided to build a vertical flight machine. His first attempts in 1908 ended in failure but spurred him on to additional experimentation. Joined by his son Henry, Berliner completed the first successful flight of a "gyrocopter" in 1920. Experimentation by father and son continued through the mid-1920s, ending when Henry Berliner became more interested in fixed-wing aircraft.

# Boeing Vertol

Vertol was the name adopted by the Piasecki Helicopter Corporation in 1956. Boeing Aircraft purchased Vertol in 1960 and continued the work begun by

Piasecki. The H-46 and H-47 series have been highly successful Vertol designs, while Vertol's H-61 entry in the U.S. Army's UTTAS competition lost out to the Sikorsky entry. Boeing Vertol is the American licensee for production of the Messerschmitt-Bölkow-Blohm Bö 105. (See Piasecki.)

A U.S. Marine Corps CH-46D hovers during a demonstration flight, revealing the small after sponsons that support the main landing gear. The Boeing Vertol CH-47 series, with the same basic configuration, has sponson-like structures extending along the sides of the helicopter. (U.S. Navy)

# Brantly

Newby O. Brantly was vice president of the Pennsylvania Elastic Company which financed a prototype coaxial-rotor helicopter. Design of this prototype began in 1941 and the first flight of the aircraft, intended for commercial use, occurred in 1946. Subsequently, the Brantly Helicopter Corporation was formed and the YHO-3 observation helicopter was produced for evaluation by the U.S. Army.

# Bratukhin

Ivan Pavlovich Bratukhin directed the helicopter design brigade* at TsAGI during the 1930s. He replaced Yuryev as head of the special design bureau (OKB-3) at the Moscow Aviation Institute in early 1941. This organization produced the Omega and the B-series helicopters. However, following a re-evaluation of Soviet helicopter programs in the late 1940s, interest in these Bratukhin machines ended, and OKB-3 was ordered to develop a new helicopter design to compete with the single-rotor Yakovlev Yak-100 and Mil' Mi-1 helicopters. Bratukhin began work on the B-11 in 1947 and then a larger troop helicopter, to have been powered by two engines. Subsequently, a convertiplane design was begun, but in 1951 the OKB-3 was disbanded and work on Bratukhin designs halted.

# Brennan

Beginning in 1919, the Royal Aircraft Establishment at Farnborough built and tested a helicopter designed by Louis Brennan. Tethered flights within a Farnborough hangar began in 1924 and free flights commenced in 1925. The single prototype crashed, and no other Brennan designs were built under his name.

# Bristol

The Bristol Aeroplane Company originated before World War II as the British and Colonial Aeroplane Company, producing aircraft and operating a flying school. The firm produced primarily fighter aircraft in both World Wars and from 1920 on was a leading manufacturer of aero engines. In 1944 the Bristol company absorbed the Hafner Gyroplane organization with Raoul Hafner being appointed chief engineer of Bristol's new helicopter department. Bristol produced the first helicopter to receive a certificate of airworthiness in Britain (1949). The firm became Bristol Aircraft in 1951 and part of the Westland group of the British Aircraft Corporation in 1960.

---

*From the 1920s on until around World War II, the Soviets used the term "brigade" to indicate a subdivision of the design organization. By the late 1930s and early 1940s, the term bureau had come into common use.

# Central Bohemian Machine Works

The Central Bohemian Machine Works is a part of the Czechoslovak State Aeronautical and Automobile consortium, Czechoslovenska Zovody Automobilove A Letecke, Narodni Podnick, formed in the early 1950s. It produced a series of light, experimental helicopters from 1955 into the early 1960s. This HC series of aircraft entered limited production as the HC-2 but received no large military orders. The few examples built are no longer airworthy, and the Central Bohemian Machine Works closed down its helicopter facilities in the mid-1960s.

# Cicaré Aeronautica

An Argentine mechanic, Augusto Ulderico Cicaré, designed and built two prototype helicopters using his own and borrowed funds. In 1972, these two aircraft, the Cicaré No. 1 and No. 2, provided the basis for the establishment of the Cicaré Aeronautica Company, which was awarded an Argentine government contract to produce a light helicopter suitable for training and agricultural operations. Development of a series of prototypes and a subsequent flight test program for the resulting Colibri helicopter has occupied the company since its formation.

# Cierva

Juan de la Cierva completed his engineering studies in Madrid in 1918 when he built his first aircraft, a three-engine biplane. His research into alleviating aircraft stall led to his development of the autogiro concept. After three unsuccessful models built in 1920-1922, he built a scale model of a machine with non-rigid blades that could flap as they rotated. This led to his successful C 4 design, which made the first successful rotary-wing flight near Madrid on 9 January 1923. This design was the basis for the approximately 500 autogiros built during the latter 1930s and early 1940s (except for some Soviet designs). Cierva went to England in 1925 where he started the Cierva Autogiro Company, Ltd. He subsequently licensed manufactures in Britain, France, Germany, Japan, and the United States. Cierva died in an airline crash in England in December 1936. The Cierva firm became the Helicopter Division of Saunders-Roe in 1950, with Saunders-Roe being subsequently acquired by Westland in 1959.

# Curtiss-Wright

Formed in 1908 by Glenn Curtiss as Curtiss Aircraft, Curtiss-Wright was an early American pioneer in the production of general purpose and racing biplanes. The Curtiss "Jenny" was world-renowned as a World War I trainer and postwar barnstorming aircraft, and Curtiss flying boats were the first aircraft to cross the Atlantic. Subsequently, Curtiss produced successful lines of fighters and cargo planes. The sole Curtiss entry in the rotorcraft field was a design by M. B. Bleecker that was produced in the early 1960s as the X-19A.

# Doblhoff

Friedrich von Doblhoff was an Austrian engineer at the Weiner Neustädter Flugzeugwerke in Vienna during World War II. He is credited with being the first person to experiment with jet propulsion for helicopters, beginning in 1942. His designs used a piston engine driving an air compressor. The compressed air was mixed with fuel before being piped to chambers at the tips of the rotor blades, at which point the mixture was ignited some 280 times per second. The first prototype of this design (Wn 342) flew in 1943, the first helicopter to fly by jet propulsion. At the end of World War II, Doblhoff emigrated to the United States where he worked for McDonnell on that firm's compound helicopter designs.

# Doman Helicopters

Glidden Doman, a former Sikorsky engineer, formed the company that bore his name in August 1945. Doman had patented a new rotor system, and the U.S. Army Air Forces were interested in investigating its applications. Prototype orders only were received from the U.S. military, although a civilian version of the Doman helicopter entered production in both the United States and Canada. Several variants were produced through the late 1950s and early 1960s.

# Fairchild Hiller

The result of the 1964 acquisition of Hiller Aircraft Company by Fairchild Engine and Aeroplane Corporation, Fairchild Hiller's primary product has been the FH1100, designated the OH-5 in U.S. Army service. (See Hiller Aircraft.)

# Fairey

Charles Richard Fairey was the first engineer at Short Brothers until 1915 when he founded the Fairey Aviation Company. The firm concentrated on the production of naval and military aircraft with only one major civilian project, the four-engine FC 1 airliner, which was abandoned in September 1939 before first flight. Fairey's interest in helicopters began in June 1945 when a special branch was set up with J.A.J. Bennett as chief technician. About that time the firm acquired rights to the jet helicopter designs of von Doblhoff of Austria. The Gyrodyne was the first helicopter built by Fairey, with that design later being refined into the Jet Gyrodyne. Several additional helicopter designs followed, none of which entered series production. The firm was absorbed by Westland Aircraft in 1960. (Sir Richard Fairey died in 1956.)

# Firestone Tire and Rubber

Firestone entered the rotorcraft market for the first time in 1943 when it acquired G and A Aircraft, formerly AGA Aviation Corporation, a subsidiary of Pitcairn. It continued work on the earlier companies' contracts for a glider, an autogiro, and a helicopter but terminated its rotorcraft work shortly after the war ended. (See Pitcairn.)

# Flettner

From 1905 onward, Anton Flettner designed control systems for zeppelins and developed a highly successful remote-control mechanism during World War I. In the 1920s he invented a system of vertical rotating cylinders for marine propulsion which was fitted in two ships. Flettner began rotary-wing aircraft experiments in 1922, leading to a helicopter that flew in tethered flight in 1933. He also experimented with autogiro designs. His helicopters were the first to feature intermeshing, contra-rotating synchronized rotors (subsequently adopted by Kamov and Kaman). Flettner's Fl 265, which flew in May 1939, was superior to the earlier Fa 61 and flew several months before Sikorsky's VS-300 began its tethered tests. He emigrated to the United States in 1947 and served as a consultant to the U.S. Navy until 1949 when he founded the Flettner Aircraft Corporation.

# Focke-Achgelis

Henrich Karl Johann Focke participated in aircraft design and construction from 1909 onward, becoming chief of design for Focke-Wulf Flugzeugbau AG when that firm was founded in 1924. He established his own research organization in 1931 which became Focke-Achgelis GmbH. After building Cierva autogiros under license, he built a scale-model helicopter in 1934 followed by his Fa 61, which made its first successful free flight on 26 June 1936 (exactly one year after the less-publicized flight of the Bréguet-Dorand helicopter). Focke was considered politically unreliable by the Nazis and participated in no aircraft design during World War II. After the war he worked in the French aviation industry and later emigrated to South America where he continued his helicopter efforts.

# Gyrodyne

Peter J. Papadakos founded the Gyrodyne Company of America in 1946 to develop a rotorcraft that had the qualities of both a rotary- and fixed-wing aircraft. Most GCA designs were characterized by contra-rotating rotors, a configuration used in both GCA's gyrodyne experiments and their conventional helicopter production. The company's most successful product in terms of duration of production run and units produced was the U.S. Navy's DSN/QH-50 antisubmarine drone.

# Hafner

Raoul Hafner completed his initial helicopter design about 1928 while at the Technische Hochschule in Vienna. In collaboration with Bruno Nagler, and financed by Major Coats, the cotton millionaire, Hafner began construction of his R I helicopter in 1929. The helicopter had a wire-braced, rigid rotor with torque offset by large vanes but could achieve only short hops. Hafner's R V, built in 1931, was similar but with a more powerful engine. It also, however, had severe flight limitations. Hafner moved to England in 1932 where, influenced by Cierva, he turned to autogiro development. In 1944 he joined the Bristol Aeroplane Company to set up a helicopter division and supervised design of the Sycamore and their Belvedere as well as several lesser helicopter efforts. In 1960 Bristol was taken over by Westland, where Hafner served as technical director of research until his retirement in 1970.

# Hiller

Stanley Hiller, Jr., founded the Hiller Aircraft Company in 1942 and flew his first airplane design only two years later. Hiller's early work was primarily with coaxial rotors in partnership with the Kaiser Corporation, but shortly after the war Hiller abandoned both Kaiser and the coaxial rotor concept and renamed his company United Helicopters. It was under the aegis of this firm that Hiller designed and built his model UH-12, known in U.S. Army service as the H-23. This aircraft enjoyed almost 15 years of production and kept Hiller and United Helicopters in the forefront of the helicopter production business. United Helicopters reverted to Hiller Aircraft Company in the late 1950s when it became a division of Electric Autolite Corporation. In 1964 Hiller's company was bought by Fairchild Engine and Aeroplane Corporation, primarily a fixed-wing aircraft manufacturing firm that had acquired American Helicopter Company in 1954 and would take over Republic Aviation in 1965. This 1964 acquisition resulted in the formation of the Fairchild Hiller Corporation.

# Hughes

The Hughes Aircraft Company was established in 1936 as a subsidiary of the Hughes Tool Company. Under the direction of Howard Hughes, Hughes Aircraft constructed several unusual planes including the world's largest airplane, the "Spruce Goose" flying boat, and the world's largest helicopter, the XH-17 Flying Crane, originally designed by Kellett. (The only flight of the former took place in 1947, while the first flight of the latter occurred in 1952.) Hughes Aircraft concentrated on the helicopter market from the mid-1950s on and produced several commercially and militarily successful light helicopters. The Hughes 500M is currently the company's major export, while the Hughes Army AH-64 is the firm's major U.S. program.

# Kaman

Charles H. Kaman was head aerodynamicist in the rotor section of United Aircraft Corporation's Hamilton Standard propeller division from 1940 to 1945. In 1945 he set up the Kaman Aircraft Corporation and began designing helicopters with intermeshing, contra-rotating rotors. His first helicopter, designated K-125, flew in January 1947, leading to development of the U.S. Navy's HU2K/H-2 series and the U.S. Air Force's H-43 series. A modification of Kaman's K-225 was the first turbine-powered helicopter to fly in the United States. During the 1980s, the firm's major helicopter effort will be production of the SH-2F antisubmarine helicopter for the U.S. Navy. Previously the firm converted its UH-2 variants to the ASW configuration, thus the 1980's aircraft will be the first "new" SH-2F helicopters.

# Kamov

Nikolai Ilich Kamov began work with the TsAGI autogiro construction team in 1929 where he joined N.K. Skrzhinsky in producing rotary-wing aircraft and led one of the TsAGI autogiro brigades. In 1940, Kamov established a new factory for the production of gyroplanes. He participated in various rotary-wing aircraft projects at TsAGI until about 1945 when the Kamov design bureau (OKB) was established. The Kamov team concentrated on contra-rotating rotor systems, developing a series of highly successful military helicopters. Kamov died in 1973. Under the direction of S. Mikhéev, however, the Kamov bureau continues to function as one of the two major Soviet helicopter organizations.

Although this Ka-20 Harp appeared with two air-to-surface missiles in the Moscow Aviation Day display on 9 July 1961, no operational helicopters have been observed with these weapons. The Ka-20 was further developed for shipboard use as the Ka-25, given the NATO code name Hormone.

# Kármán

Dr. Theodore von Kármán became interested in aeronautics while studying in Paris and in 1912 became director of the Aeronautical Institute at Aachen, Germany. During World War I he served as director of the research group at the Flieger Arsenal at Fischamend where, during 1917-1918, he participated in helicopter development with Petróczy and Zurovec, primarily of the PKZ 1 and possibly of the PKZ 2. He later came to the United States and became a citizen in 1936. Associated with several aeronautical research institutes, from 1941 onward he was involved in work on rocket and jet propulsion and served as a scientific advisor to the U.S. Army Air Forces during the war. (See Petróczy and Zurovec.)

# Kayaba

The K.K. Kayaba Seisakusho (Kayaba Industrial Company) was engaged in autogiro research in the 1930s. After the crash of a Kellett KD-1A autogiro during 1939 trials in Japan, the Kayaba firm was asked to develop an autogiro based on the Kellett aircraft. This led to the production of the Ka-1 at the firm's plant in Sendai (Miyagi Prefecture).

# Kellett

W. Wallace Kellett founded the Kellett Autogiro Corporation in 1929 and began building Cierva autogiros under license in the United States. In July 1939 he commenced the first scheduled air mail service by rotary-wing aircraft in the United States with flights between the Philadelphia post office and Camden airport in New Jersey. One of his autogiros was taken to Antarctica by Rear Admiral Richard E. Byrd in the U.S. Navy's 1934 expedition. During World War II, Kellett built a helicopter for the U.S. Army with intermeshing rotors, the first American machine to use this configuration. A small number of Kellett autogiros (O-60) series were also built for the Army during the war. In 1949 the Kellett plans and patents were sold to the Hughes Aircraft Company, including the design for the giant XH-17 Flying Crane. When Kellett died, the firm had serious financial difficulties but did become solvent again. However, no additional military aircraft were built.

# Lockheed

The Lockheed Corporation, with two major aircraft divisions, Lockheed-California and Lockheed-Georgia, is one of the oldest, most prolific, and most imaginative firms in aviation history. Originally founded in 1916 as the Lockheed Aircraft Company by brothers Allen and Malcolm Loughhead, the firm's more famous aircraft include the Vega civil transport; Harpoon, Hudson, and Ventura bombers and P-38 Lightning fighter of World War II; postwar Neptune and Orion maritime patrol planes; Constellation and L 1011 transports; P-80 and F-104 jet fighters; and the U-2 and SR-71/YF-12 "spy" planes. In the late 1950s, Lockheed began development of an advanced, rigid-rotor helicopter design which flew under U.S. Army and Navy sponsorship as the XH-51 in late 1962. This aircraft was further developed into the AH-56 Cheyenne helicopter gunship, which won a 1966 U.S. Army competition. However, changes in the Army's view of gunships, based on the Vietnam War, higher-than-expected costs, and technical problems, led to cancellation of the AH-56 program in 1972.

# MBB (Messerschmitt-Bölkow-Blohm GmbH)

Willi Messerschmitt, designer of the famed Me 109 fighter and Me 262 jet-propelled fighter of World War II, reformed the Messerschmitt Company after the war. Following an initial period during which it produced only "bubble" mini-cars, the firm reentered the aviation field. During the 1960s the firm amalgamated with Bölkow, and in 1969 it merged with the Hamburger Flugzeugbau GmbH, becoming known as MBB. Subsequently, such firms as Junkers and Siebel were incorporated into MBB. The firm has produced the HFB 320 series of transport, cargo, and business aircraft, as well as the Bö 105 helicopter, and has participated in several other German and multi-national aircraft programs.

## McCulloch

In 1949 D. K. Jovanovich and Frank Kozloski disbanded their own small helicopter design firm, Helicopter Engineering and Research Corporation, and joined the newly formed Helicopter Division of McCulloch Motors Corporation. They brought with them a design of a small, tandem-rotor helicopter, the MC-4, which was an enlargement of a similar helicopter they had built and tested in 1948, the JOV-3. This design met with very little success, despite being flight tested by the military, and the McCulloch Helicopter Division was closed in the late 1950s. Jovanovich then formed his own firm, the JOVAIR Corporation, to market the designs he had produced while at McCulloch. The updated version of the MC-4 achieved some commercial success, entering limited production in 1965. No military orders ensued, however, and the company has since ceased operations.

## McDonnell

During the 1930s, James S. McDonnell, an aeronautical engineer, worked for a number of American aviation-related firms, including the Glenn L. Martin Company as chief engineer on several bombers. He left Martin in 1938 and founded the McDonnell Aircraft Corporation in 1939. McDonnell produced components for other aircraft companies during the war and developed only a single major original design, the XP-67 twin-engine fighter. However, with the advent of jet aircraft, McDonnell took its place as a major manufacturer, beginning with the U.S. Navy's FD-1 (later FH-1) Phantom, ordered in 1943. The following year McDonnell was awarded a Navy contract for the world's first twin-engine, twin-rotor helicopter, the XHJD-1 (later XHJH-1). In addition, that same year McDonnell acquired control of the Platt LePage Aircraft Company of Eddystone, Pa., which had received a U.S. Army contract in July 1940 to build the XR-1 helicopter. The efforts of Platt LePage and McDonnell failed to establish a major helicopter program, however, and Platt LePage ceased operation in 1946. Neither McDonnell designs nor a convertiplane developed with the help of Austrian helicopter pioneer Doblhoff were successful. McDonnell, however, has been most successful in the jet era with such aircraft as the F-4 Phantom and the F-101 Voodo. In 1967 the firm absorbed Douglas Aircraft, forming the McDonnell Douglas Corporation.

# Mil'

Mikhail Leont'yevich Mil' joined TsAGI in 1931 after completing his studies at the Novocheakassy Aviation Institute. He worked on a number of autogiro and helicopter designs, and from January 1933 onward directed research on gyroplanes. During World War II he was chief of TsAGI's scientific research laboratory for rotorcraft and a professor of the Kazan Aero-Technical Institute. In December 1947 the Mil' helicopter design bureau (OKB) was established and produced a succession of major Soviet helicopter designs, the Mil' GM-1/Mi-1 being the first rotary-wing aircraft of Russian design to be manufactured in large numbers. Mil' died in 1970. The Mil' design bureau continues as the principal Soviet helicopter organization under the direction of Mirat N. Tishchenko.

Soviet troops disembark from an Mi-4 Hip helicopter. Although more advanced helicopters have emerged from Soviet factories, the Hip continues in Soviet and foreign service in large numbers. There is a gondola under the fuselage for an observer. (Courtesy J.W.R. Taylor)

# Petróczy

Stefan Petróczy, an aviator, was a lieutenant in the Austro-Hungarian Army engaged in training balloon crews in 1916 when he became involved in helicopter development. He worked with Kármán and Zurovec on early military helicopters and by the end of World War I was commandant of the Flieger Arsenal at Fischamend, some 12 miles from Wein on the western side of the Danube. Although principally a repair facility for aircraft engines, Fischamend became involved in a number of aviation projects and even constructed training aircraft, thus providing a substantial base for the early Austro-Hungarian helicopter efforts. (See Kármán and Zurovec).

# Piasecki

Frank N. Piasecki worked as a mechanic for Kellett Autogiro, then as a mechanical designer at the National Machine Company, and finally with Platt LePage Aircraft Corporation before founding his own company in 1943, the P.V. Engineering Forum (the firm's title was changed to Piasecki Helicopter Corporation in 1947). In 1943 Piasecki built the second helicopter to be flown in the United States, largely using automobile and outboard motor components. He then perfected the tandem twin-rotor design resulting in the U.S. Navy's XHRP-1, which first flew in March 1945 and led to the highly successful HUP/H-21 series. In 1955 Piasecki was removed from board chairmanship of the company, and he formed a new firm, the Piasecki Aircraft Corporation. The Piasecki Helicopter Corporation then became the Vertol Aircraft Corporation (subsequently Boeing Vertol). The Piasecki Aircraft Corporation has continued to work on vertical-lift aircraft concepts.

Piasecki's Pathfinder II leaves the ground during early flight tests in 1965. Sponsored by the Army and Navy, the aircraft had a novel ring-tail or propeller-in-shroud configuration, one of many designs intended to alleviate the need for an anti-torque tail rotor. The retractable main landing gear is extended beneath the stub wings; part of the covering of the rotor pylon is removed; and the cockpit has a side panel missing. (Piasecki)

# Pitcairn

The founder of Eastern Airways (later Eastern Air Lines), Harold F. Pitcairn, also founded Pitcairn Aircraft, which he used to design and build mail-carrying biplanes for his airline. In 1928 Pitcairn became interested in gyroplanes and brought a Cierva autogiro to the United States from England. He subsequently divested himself of Eastern Airways and changed the name of his other company to Pitcairn Autogiro Company. Several different autogiros were built and tested by Pitcairn's company, exploiting Cierva licenses which were obtained by Autogiro Company of America, a Pitcairn subsidiary. The last such design was built in 1941, one year after all Pitcairn work had been taken over by AGA Aviation Corporation, formerly a Pitcairn subsidiary, the Autogiro Company of America. AGA soon changed its name to G and A Aircraft, and in 1943 was taken over by Firestone, which continued the autogiro work initiated by Pitcairn.

# Platt LePage

Haviland H. Platt and W. Laurence LePage founded this firm in July 1940 to design tandem-rotor helicopters. That same month, the U.S. Army Air Corps awarded the firm a contract to design and construct the XR-1 helicopter. A second, modified prototype, the XR-1A, was ordered the next year, but no production orders followed. McDonnell Aircraft Corporation took control of the firm in 1944, but, unable to obtain any contracts, the firm ceased operation in 1946.

# Rotor-Craft

Rotor-Craft was formed by Gilbert W. Magill in the mid-1940s to apply rigid-rotor techniques to helicopters. In 1953 Magill acquired the patents of another firm specializing in rigid-rotor applications, the Landgraf Helicopter Company. Despite having designed and built some prototypes for U.S. Navy flight testing, Rotor-Craft had no design that entered production, and the company ceased operations in the late 1950s. Lockheed benefitted from Rotor-Craft and Landgraf research, however, and began investigating rigid-rotor technology in 1958. (See Lockheed.)

# Saunders-Roe

Saunders-Roe took over the Cierva Company on 22 January 1951, and, with it, a helicopter development capability. Previous to this acquisition, the firm had designed and manufactured seaplanes almost exclusively since its formation in 1912. In 1960 Saunders-Roe was acquired by Westland which then produced the Scout, designed by Saunders-Roe.

# Seibel

Formed in 1948 to investigate a novel method of lateral and longitudinal control in helicopters, Seibel developed and built several prototype platforms, one of which was tested by the U.S. military. No production orders ensued, however, and in the late 1950s Seibel was acquired by Cessna Aircraft, which attempted to market a conventional, four-place helicopter designed by the Seibel team. This effort was unsuccessful and the Seibel Division of Cessna was abolished in December 1962.

# Sikorsky

In 1909, at the age of 19, Igor Sikorsky built his first helicopter in his native Russia. Although that design failed, by the end of the next year he had built a rotorcraft that could take off but could carry no pilot. Frustrated, he turned to conventional aircraft and built large bombers for the Tsar's army during World War I. He fled the Bolsheviks in 1917, settling in the United States some two years later where he founded the Sikorsky Aero Engineering Corporation. This firm similarly produced fixed-wing aircraft, primarily flying boats and amphibians, and in 1929 was taken over by United Aircraft Corporation, parent company of Chance Vought and Pratt and Whitney. In the late 1930s Sikorsky returned to helicopter design and built the VS-300, America's first successful helicopter. With the gradual decrease in demand for flying boats from the airlines, Sikorsky Aircraft gave more and more attention to its helicopter programs, and a series of extremely successful designs followed. The VS-300 evolved into the Sikorsky S-51, and the highly successful SS-55, S-58, and S-61 followed over the next 15 years. Igor Sikorsky himself participated in the development of these designs until his death in 1972. Sikorsky Aircraft has continued a very healthy helicopter product line and continues to produce examples of the S-61 as well as the new S-70, the Army UH-60A and Navy SH-60B, plus the commercial S-76 (initially named Spirit). Sikorsky's son Sergei continues with Sikorsky Aircraft (a division of United Technologies).

A U.S. Coast Guard HH-52A Sea Guard taxis on the water near the Coast Guard Air Station at Miami, Florida. Although a military service, the Coast Guard is not a part of the U.S. Department of Defense. However, in wartime it is under the direction of or actually merged with the Navy. This single-engine helicopter is being replaced by the Aérospatiale SA 366G, designated HH-65A Dolphin in U.S. service. (U.S. Coast Guard)

A Sikorsky HO3S-1 from Navy Helicopter Utility Squadron (HU) 2 returns the commander of the U.S. Sixth Task Fleet to his flagship, the heavy cruiser *Albany*, in the eastern Mediterranean. Subsequently, most types of surface warships and many auxiliaries were fitted with landing areas on their sterns. (U.S. Navy)

A VH-3A Sea King helicopter of Marine Experimental Squadron 1 flies over Washington, D.C., with the 555-foot Washington Monument in the background. (HMX)1 operates helicopters for the White House; with the President embarked a helicopter is designated *Marine One*. The squadron currently flies the VH-3D variant. (U.S. Navy)

A U.S. Marine Corps CH-53A Sea Stallion is maintained aboard the helicopter carrier *Tripoli* (LPH-10) during operations in the South China Sea. With delivery of the first three-engine CH-53E Super Stallions in 1981, the Marine Corps redesignated the CH-53A/D as medium helicopters. (U.S. Navy)

# Skrzhinsky

Nikolai Kirilovich Skrzhinsky joined TsAGI in the 1920s and in 1929, with Kamov, built the first Soviet autogiro, the KaSkr-1. Subsequently he directed one of the TsAGI autogiro brigades.

# Sud Aviation

Sud Aviation was the result of a 1 March 1957 merger between Sud-Est and Sud-Ouest, two firms established in the nationalization of the French aviation industry before World War II. Both had been engaged in helicopter development and production prior to the amalgamation, giving Sud Aviation a strong base in the rotary-wing field. Helicopters subsequently produced by Sud Aviation included the Alouette series, designed by Sud-Est, the Djinn, designed by Sud-Ouest, and the Sud Aviation-designed Super Frelon, Puma, and Gazelle. In 1970 Sud Aviation, Nord Aviation, and SEREB were combined to form Aérospatiale, which continues as the French aerospace industry's design and production agent for helicopters.

# Sud-Est

The Société Nationale de Constructions Aeronautiques du Sud Est (SNCASE) was established in 1936 as a result of the nationalization of the French aircraft industry. Early French manufacturers consolidated within SNCASE included CAMS, Lioré, Olivier, Potez, SPCA, and Romano. Helicopter work began soon after the merger, a continuation of autogiro work initiated in the early 1930s by Lioré and Olivier. Several autogiros were developed and built during World War II, and Sud-Est's first true helicopter, a derivation of the Focke Fa 223, made its first flight in 1948. Sud-Est's leading position in the helicopter industry stemmed from its series of Alouette helicopters, development of which began in the late 1940s with the Alouette I. When Sud-Est and Sud-Ouest merged in 1957 to form Sud Aviation, the new company continued to market the then-new Alouette II. Aérospatiale subsumed Sud Aviation in 1970.

# Sud-Ouest

A product of the nationalization of the French aircraft industry before World War II, Sud-Ouest was formally known as Société Nationale de Constructions Aeronautiques du Sud Ouest (SNCASO) from its formation in 1936 until its merger with Sud-Est in 1957 to form Sud Aviation. Sud-Ouest's helicopter work began shortly after World War II and centered on applications of rotor-tip jet propulsion. Early experiments used a piston engine to drive a compressor which propelled air through the rotor tips. The first successful design adapted a gas-turbine engine and was marketed as the SO 1220 Djinn.

# Swidnik

This firm was established in 1951-1952 as the Swidnik WSK (Wytwornia Sprze-tu Komunikacyjnego or Transport Equipment Manufacturing Center) and initially produced components for the Polish-built LiM-1 variant of the MiG-15 fighter aircraft. In 1955 the firm began production of the SM-1, the license production version of the Mi-1 helicopter, with more than 1,700 being built in Poland. The firm was named for Polish aircraft designer Zygmunt Pulawski and given the additional designation PLZ (Zygmunta Pulawskiego) in 1957. Subsequently, Swidnik, which it is generally known as, has produced the Mi-2 helicopter and several non-military aircraft variants, some in collaboration with the Detroit Allison Divison of the General Motors Corporation.

# TsAGI

The Central Aero-Hydrodynamic Institute (TsAGI) was created in 1918 to direct Soviet aviation development. The leader of the experimental aerodynamic section of TsAGI, B.N. Yuryev, had a major interest in helicopter development, and by 1925 formal rotary-wing programs were initiated. Although Yuryev was assigned to other work, at the end of 1930 his group produced the first TsAGI helicopter, designated 1-Э A. Parallel with this effort, another TsAGI group, including I.P. Bratukhin, developed an autogiro designated 2-Э A, which was based on a Cierva design. Further work continued on both projects, with N.I. Kamov and M.L. Mil' joining the TsAGI rotary-wing efforts in 1931. By 1933,

TsAGI's special division contained a helicopter brigade under I.P. Bratukhin and three autogiro brigades under V.A. Kuznetsov, N.I. Kamov, and N.K. Skrzhinsky. These brigades produced a number of experimental machines. In January 1940 part of the group under Bratukhin was transferred to the Moscow Aviation Institute (MAI) where a new helicopter branch was established. Autogiro work was continued at TsAGI under Kamov as late as 1943 when all further efforts in that field were cancelled. At MAI Bratukhin directed the development of helicopters from 1945 to 1947, and A.S. Yakovlev worked there on helicopters from the end of 1944 onward. However, no Soviet helicopter was considered suitable for production after the war, and, in response to this situation, in 1947-1948 three helicopter design bureaus (OKB) were established under Bratukhin, Yakovlev, and Mil'.

# United Helicopters

See Kaman and Hiller Aircraft Company.

# Westland

Westland Aircraft was formed in 1935 from the aeronautical division of Petters, Ltd., an engine manufacturing firm. Until 1946 the main output of the firm was

A Westland Wessex HU 5 (left) and HAS 1 practice in-flight refueling during a 1964 demonstration over Farnborough, England. Helicopter-to-helicopter refueling has demonstrated little utility; however, in-flight refueling of helicopters from fixed-wing aircraft proved valuable during the U.S. participation in the Vietnam War and several rescue operations. (Royal Air Force)

fixed-wing aircraft, but in that year Westland acquired a license from Sikorsky to manufacture the S-51 for British use. In two years Westland became the leading European manufacturer of helicopters, producing its version of the S-51, the Dragonfly. Later Sikorsky licenses have included the SS-55, S-56, and S-58 (which in British service became the Wessex). Indigenous helicopter designs were not produced until Westland acquired both Saunders-Roe and Bristol Helicopter in 1960. These companies led to the Skeeter/Scout/Wasp series of light helicopters and the Bristol Sycamore and Belvedere designs. Westland concluded a coproduction agreement in the mid-1960s with Sud-Aviation, now Aérospatiale of France, that covered a variety of new helicopter designs, one of them by Westland: the Lynx. Consequently, production now centers on the Sikorsky S-61 and derivatives thereof, the Aérospatiale Puma and Gazelle, and the Westland Lynx.

A Royal Navy Sea King HAS 2 lifts a Royal Marine Gazelle from the deck of the helicopter carrier *Hermes* in preparation for transporting the smaller helicopter ashore in Northern Norway. The Sea King was from No. 812 Naval Air Squadron and the Gazelle from the 3rd Commando Brigade Air Squadron, both participating in NATO exercises when this photo was taken in 1979. (Royal Navy)

# WNF (Weiner Neustädter Flugzeugwerke)

See Doblhoff.

# Yakovlev

Russia's Alexandr Sergeyevich Yakovlev began his aviation career with model aircraft, with several of his designs winning prizes. He worked in an airfield workshop and in 1926 entered the aero-motor section of the Zhukovsky Air Force Engineering Academy. He designed his first aircraft while there, a light sports plane. Yakovlev graduated from the Air Academy in 1931 and entered the aviation industry at GAZ (factory) No. 39. He won a major prize for his UT-2 basic trainer and sports plane. One of his aircraft had a mishap in 1933 and he was found guilty of faulty design work. Yakovlev was rescued from obscurity when his successful UT-1 and UT-2 came to Stalin's attention, and in 1934 he was made a chief designer. His first military aircraft, the I-26 or Yak-1 fighter, flew in 1941. A variety of aircraft types were developed by the prolific designer. In late 1944 he began work on helicopters at the Moscow Aviation Institute (MAI). Yakovlev produced two major helicopter designs, the Yak-24 Horse and Yak-100. However, the design bureau (OKB) that carries his name has concentrated on large fighter-type aircraft, commercial transports, and fixed-wing VTOL aircraft. His Yak-15, which passed service tests in May 1947, became the first turbojet fighter to enter Soviet service. His son Sergei is now associated with the Yakovlev OKB.

# Yuryev

Boris Nikolayevich Yuryev demonstrated an interest in rotary-wing aircraft from 1907 on. In 1910 he was named chairman of the commission for helicopters at the Moscow Higher Technical School. By 1912 he had sufficient financial backing to produce a primitive helicopter which was exhibited at the 1912 International Aeronautical and Automobile Exhibition in Moscow. Although Yuryev was awarded a gold medal for the project, only ground tests were made after the exhibition, and the failure of a rotor shaft and then lack of financial backing ended his efforts. After the Russian Revolution, Yuryev joined TsAGI which began serious work on helicopters in 1925 under his leadership. A special helicopter group was created in TsAGI later in 1926. Yuryev remained at TsAGI until 1928, by which time work on the 1-Э A helicopter was well along. In January 1940 an experimental helicopter design bureau (OKB-3) was formed in the Moscow Aviation Institute under Yuryev, but within three months he was replaced in that position by Bratukhin.

# Zurovec

Wilhelm Zurovec was an engineer at the Flieger Arsenal at Fischamend during World War I. In collaboration with Petróczy and Kármán, he constructed the PKZ 1 helicopter in 1917 and subsequently the PKZ 2 in 1917-1918. (See Kármán and Petróczy.)

# APPENDIX B

# Rotary-Wing Aircraft Designations

The following describes the basic military autogiro and helicopter designations used by the major armed forces who have operated rotary-wing aircraft and the designers and design institutions. There are variations on most of these schemes.

**France**

Aérospatiale has absorbed all of the primary helicopter manufacturing firms in France and has continued the manufacturer's designation series begun by its predecessors. These series consisted of a two-letter firm designation followed by a sequential number. Sud-Ouest helicopters were designated by the prefix SO while Sud-Est designs were prefixed with SE. All designs initiated after the Aérospatiale merger were prefixed with SA. Thus, the Alouette II series of helicopters ran from model numbers SE 3130 to SA 313B to SA 318C, while the Alouette III was first the SE 3160, then the SA 316B and when re-engined the SA 319B. French helicopters used by other nations' military services tend to retain the designation and name given by the manufacturer although the Aérospatiale SA 366 Dauphine has become HH-65A Dolphin in U.S. Coast Guard service.

**Germany (Third Reich)**

German aircraft manufacturers designated their helicopters by two-letter abbreviations of the designer's name, followed by a sequential number (encompassing all German aircraft types). The autogiro and helicopter design designations were:

Wn  Wiener-Neustädter-Flugzeugwerke (WNF)
Fl  Flettner
Fa  Focke-Achgelis
Fw  Focke-Wulf

**West Germany**

The single postwar German helicopter producer, Messerschmitt-Bölkow-Blohm, follows the basic two-letter and number designation scheme. Thus, the Bö 105 is the 105th design from the Bölkow design bureau.

**Great Britain**

The British helicopter designation system used the helicopter's name, such as Sea King, plus an alphanumeric designation noting the aircraft type (i.e., H for helicopter) plus its mission, followed by a sequential number for the specific helicopter. Thus, Sea King HAS 2 is the second model of the Sea King configured for antisubmarine warfare. Mark numbers are used to indicate manufacturer variants (e.g., Sea King Mk 41) and are not generally used by the British armed forces.

The type-mission letters used for British helicopters are:

AH   Army Helicopter
HAR  Helicopter Air Rescue

HAS  Helicopter Antisubmarine
HC   Helicopter Cargo
HCC  VIP Configuration
HR   Helicopter Rescue
HT   Helicopter Trainer
HU   Helicopter Utility

## Italy

The primary producer of helicopters in Italy is the Agusta firm which has two distinct systems for designating its helicopters. License-built examples of foreign-designed helicopters normally add the prefix A to the original manufacturer's model number, as AB 206 for the Bell model 206 JetRanger. The second system consecutively numbers Agusta's own designs, as A 101 or A 109. Some air forces operate both Agusta license-built and original manufacturer helicopters with the different designations applied to the same basic aircraft, as Agusta AB 206 and Bell OH-58.

## Japan

The Japanese armed forces used several designation systems for aircraft from 1927 to 1945 which are generally well known in the West (e.g., A6M Type 00, assigned Allied code name Zeke). However, aircraft which did not originate with the Army Air Force's headquarters (Koku Hombu) were assigned the manufacturer's designation. Thus, the Kayaba Ka-1 and Ka-2 autogiro projects.

## Union of Soviet Socialist Republics

The earliest Soviet aircraft were identified by the names of their designers or design institutions. During the 1930s a system of letter-number designations were introduced with the letter A in various combinations indicating Autogiro (Avtozhir). In both of these schemes the Cyrillic alphabet caused some transliteration difficulties. For example, Yakovlev in the Russian style is two letters while in the Roman alphabet it becomes three letters (Yak).

By the 1930s, a scheme for having each designer or design bureau (OKB for Opytno-Konstruktorskoye Byuro [experimental design bureau]) number its aircraft designs sequentially was well-established. However, there have been instances of confusion when a single aircraft has both an internal designer and military designation such as Tu-95 and Tu-20 for the Bear bomber-type aircraft.

The designer/design bureau designations that apply to autogiros and helicopters are:

B       Bratukhin
Ka      Kamov
KaSkr   Kamov-Skrzhinsky
Mi      Mil'
TsAGI   Central Aero-Hydrodynamic Institute (Tsentral'ny Aerogirrodina-
        micheski Institut)
Yak     Yakovlev

Suffix letters (as Ka-15M) are used to indicate variations of basic aircraft designs:

A       Aeroflotsky (configured for commercial Aeroflot use)
*bis*   Variant

| F  | Forsazh (engine boosted)        |
|----|---------------------------------|
| K  | Kupe (VIP configuration)        |
| M  | Modifikatsirovanny (modified)   |
| N  | Nochnoi (night)                 |
| P  | Passazhersky (passenger version)|
| PV | (Propulsion variant)            |
| U  | Usilenny (trainer)              |

After World War II, Western intelligence developed a scheme of type numbers which were indiscriminately assigned to all Soviet aircraft with no effort being made to identify designer, type, or sequence. Thus, type 32 was the Mi-1 helicopter and Type 36 the Mi-4. A new designation scheme was derived by NATO in 1954 that allocated specific names to different Soviet aircraft with the initial letter indicating the type with H naturally assigned to helicopters. Under this concept, the Mi-1 became the Hare and Mi-4 the Hound.

## United States

Prior to 1962 the U.S. armed services used separate aircraft designation systems, with the Navy and Marine Corps (both under the Navy Department) using the same one. In general, the Army and (from 1947) the Air Force used similar alphanumeric systems with an initial letter indicating the type and the number the sequence within the type. The following letters were in use between 1924 and 1962; unless indicated as U.S. Army, they were used by the Air Force and its predecessor organizations which were part of the U.S. Army.

| G  | Giroplane (1935-1939)                          |
|----|------------------------------------------------|
| H  | Helicopter (1948-1962)                         |
| HC | Cargo Helicopter (U.S. Army, 1959-1962)        |
| HO | Observation Helicopter (U.S. Army, 1959-1962)  |
| HU | Utility Helicopter (U.S. Army, 1959-1962)      |
| L  | Liaison                                        |
| O  | Observation (1924-1942)                        |
| R  | Rotary-wing (1941-1948)                        |
| X  | Special Research (1948-1962)                   |
| V  | Convertiplane (1954-1962)                      |

The two principal prefixes for the above designations were X for experimental and Y for prototype or pre-production aircraft.

The U.S. Navy designation scheme in use from 1922 to 1962 used a more detailed method of indicating (1) aircraft mission, (2) manufacturer, (3) manufacturer's aircraft sequence, (4) variant, and (5) modification of that variant. Thus, in HR2S-1W the H indicated helicopter, the R transport, the S Sikorsky, the 2 the second transport helicopter by Sikorsky, the 1 the first variant, and W that the helicopter was radar-equipped (for warning).

Prefixes under this scheme included X for experimental and Y for trials aircraft; suffixes were A for amphibious, G for Coast Guard use, L for arctic operation, N for night/all-weather, and Z for VIP configuration.

The basic mission designations for naval aircraft were:

| DS | Drone Antisubmarine   |
|----|-----------------------|
| HC | Cargo Helicopter      |
| HJ | Utility Helicopter    |
| HN | Training Helicopter   |

HO   Observation Helicopter
HR   Transport Helicopter
HS   Antisubmarine Helicopter
HT   Training Helicopter
HU   Utility Helicopter
RO   Rotorcycle

In addition, two rotary-wing aircraft were designated in the observation series by the Navy (the OP and OZ).

Manufacturer designations used in this system were:

B   Boeing Vertol
D   McDonnell (later H)
E   Hiller
G   Gyrodyne (later N)
H   McDonnell
K   Kaman
L   Bell
M   McCulloch
N   Gyrodyne
P   Piasecki
P   Pitcairn
S   Sikorsky
Z   Consolidated-Pennsylvania

In 1962 all U.S. military helicopters were redesignated within a single Air Force-type system with the letter H followed by a consecutive numbering system. Some numbers were repeated from the Air Force 1948-1962 series (H-1 through H-6). Prefix designations indicated aircraft status or mission configurations in accordance with the following:

A   Attack
C   Cargo
E   Electronic Warfare
H   Search and Rescue
J   Temporary Special Test
L   Cold Weather
N   Permanent Special Test
O   Observation
Q   Drone
R   Reconnaissance
R   Mine Countermeasures
S   Antisubmarine
T   Trainer
U   Utility
V   VIP
X   Experimental
Y   Prototype

In addition, in 1962 the designation V was established for VSTOL or STOL aircraft with some rotary-wing aircraft subsequently being assigned this designation in conjunction with the experimental prefix (forming the series designation XV).

# APPENDIX C

# Rotary-Wing Aircraft Armament

During World War II the German Air Force flew ASW helicopters armed with depth charges and the Japanese Air Force operated autogiros with depth charges in the antisubmarine role, while some German helicopters and Soviet autogiros were armed with light machine guns. The U.S. Army Air Forces experimented in carrying small, 25-pound practice bombs in R-4 helicopters, first with the observer holding them in his lap and pitching them out, and then with under-fuselage racks.

By 1950 the French Air Force armed some of its few helicopters in Indochina, a prelude to the extensive French use of armed helicopters in the subsequent Algerian war. Similarly, during the Korean War the U.S. Army and Marine Corps fitted .30-caliber M-60 machine guns in helicopter door openings, while more elaborate weapons were experimentally fitted to helicopters by Marine Experimental Squadron (HMX) 1 at Quantico, Virginia, during this period. The U.S. Army later conducted tests in conjunction with the development of air mobile and sky cavalry tactics at the Army Aviation School at Fort Rucker, Alabama.

The massive U.S. helicopter operations in the Vietnam War of the 1960s led to the development of extensive weapon systems specifically for use on helicopters. These weapons and other major weapons employed on Western military helicopters are described in this appendix as are two identified Soviet missiles.

### Gun/Rocket Systems

XM-3 weapons system with two 2.75-inch rocket pods (48 total); for UH-1A/B Huey helicopters.

M-5 ball turret containing M-75 40-mm grenade launcher with provision for 150 or 315 grenades; for UH-1B/C Huey helicopters.

XMB-8 turret containing XM-129 40-mm grenade launcher with 156 grenades; for OH-6A Cayuse helicopter.

M-16 armament system consisting of two 7.62-mm M-60C machine guns and two fixed 2.75-inch M-158 rocket pods. The flexible MGs have 3,000 rounds, belt fed; the rocket pods are fixed to fire straight ahead. For UH-1B/C Huey helicopters.

XM-18 fixed gun pod with 7.62-mm M-134 cannon with 1,500 rounds, linkless fed; for AH-1G HueyCobra.

M-21 weapon system with two 7.62-mm M-134 cannon with 4,800 rounds and two 2.75-inch M-158 rocket pods; for UH-1B/C helicopters.

M-23 manually aimed gun system for use from helicopter doors with one 7.62-mm M-60D with 400-round belt for each door; for UH-1D Huey.

M-24 as M-23 with 200-round belt box, for CH-47 Chinook.

M-27 Minigun with 7.62-mm M-134 machine gun in fuselage pod with 2,000 rounds ammunition; for OH-58A Kiowa (Hughes).

XM-28 chin turret with two 7.62-mm M-134 cannon with 8,000 rounds or two 40-mm XM-129 grenade launchers with 600 grenades, or combination of one gun and one grenade launcher (4,000/300 rounds); for AH-1 HueyCobra (Emerson).

XM-35 fixed six-barrel 20-mm barrel XM-195 cannon mounted on sponson; link fed with 950 rounds; for AH-1G HueyCobra (General Electric).

M-60 series of flexible 7.62-mm machine guns; belt fed.

M-61A1 six-barrel, 20-mm Vulcan cannon with linked or linkless ammunition (General Electric).

M-75 rapid-fire launcher for 40-mm grenades with flexible magazine chute.

M-78 grenade launcher; modification of M-75.

XM-93 flexible gun system for helicopter doors with single 7.62-mm GAU-2B/A (similar to M-134); for UH-1N Huey.

XM-94 flexible 40-mm XM-129 grenade launcher for helicopter doors; for UH-1N Huey.

M-97 universal weapons turret for M-197, XM-230, XM-188, and other gun systems; developed for AH-1T SeaCobra (General Electric).

TAT-101 Tactical Armament Turret with two 7.62-mm M-60C machine guns with 1,200 rounds link-belt fed; for Sioux Scout (Emerson).

TAT-102 turret similar to TAT-101 with two 7.62-mm M-134 machine guns with 8,000 rounds belt fed; for AH-1G HueyCobra (Emerson).

XM-129 40-mm grenade launcher (Aeronutronic Ford).

M-134 six barrel 7.62-mm with linkless feed (General Electric).

XM-140 lightweight 30-mm cannon mounted in turret or sponson (Emerson).

TAT-140 turret with 30-mm XM-140 gun (Aeronutronic Ford).

TAT-141 turret with 7.62-mm M-134 gun and XM-129 grenade launcher (Emerson).

XM-156 multiple armament mount; for UH-1B/C Huey.

XM-157 rocket pod for seven 2.75-inch rockets.

XM-159C rocket pod for 19 2.75-inch rockets.

TAT-161 turret for Vulcan-type rotary or Gatling cannon, including M-61A1, XM-197; turret similar to TAT-101 (Emerson).

XM-188 three-barrel, lightweight, rotary 20-mm cannon; available with link belt or linkless ammunition (General Electric).

XM-188E1 three-barrel, lightweight, rotary 30-mm cannon for use in AH-1S turret; link-fed ammunition.

XM-195 six-barrel, lightweight, rotary 20-mm cannon with short barrel and blast deflectors; link-fed ammunition (General Electric).

XM-197 three-barrel, lightweight, rotary 20-mm cannon with link or belt or linkless ammunition; fitted to AH-1J SeaCobra (General Electric).

XM-214 six-barrel, rotary 5.62-mm Minigun for pintel or turret mounting; linked-belt ammunition (General Electric). XM-218 .50-cal. machine gun (pintel).

XM-230 E1 chain gun 30-mm rapid-fire cannon (single barrel).

GAU-2B/A six-barrel, rotary 7.62-mm machine gun for M-21 or M-28 turrets, or pintel mountings; linked-belt ammunition; for HH-53, UH-1H/N, SH-3A (pintel); UH-1B/D; AH-1G (turret) helicopters (General Electric).

GAU-12/U five-barrel, lightweight, 25-mm rotary cannon for turret on AH-1T HueyCobra; linkless feed (General Electric).

Minigun multi-barrel 5.56-mm machine gun (using same ammunition as M-16 automatic rifle) (General Electric).

MiniTAT turret for 5.56-mm or 7.62-mm Minigun for installation in small helicopters (Emerson).

A U.S. Navy airman loads 600-round ammunition boxes for a 7.62-mm M-60 machine gun on a UH-1B Huey helicopter in Vietnam. At left are boxes of 40-mm grenades for the gunship's grenade launcher. Once airborne, the sailor will man the right-door gun. (U.S. Navy)

A gunner readies a 7.62-mm multi-barrel XM-93 machine gun in the doorway of a U.S. Air Force UH-1H helicopter during a training mission. Note the overhead feed of ammunition. Multi-barrel Gatling guns of this type were first used in combat in the Vietnam War. (*Airman*)

A cluster of 2.75-inch rocket tubes are readied on a U.S. Navy UH-1B Huey gunship aboard the landing ship *Harnett County* (LST-821) at anchor in the Mekong Delta during the Vietnam War. There are M-60 machine guns mounted outboard of the rocket tubes with their ammunition belts seen in the upper left of this photograph. (U.S. Navy)

One of five Hughes YAH-64 helicopters maneuvers over a desert area during flight/ordnance tests of the U.S. Army's Advanced Attack Helicopter (AAH). The nose is fitted with laser and night-vision sensors and range finders; a 30-mm chain gun is mounted under the forward fuselage; and 2.75-inch rocket pods are on the stub wings. This view of the second YAH-64 was taken shortly after it achieved its 1,000th flight hour early in 1981. (Hughes)

## Guided Missiles

AM-38 Exocet antiship missile (air-launched version of M-38); length: 17 ft (5.2 m), diameter 1 ft 1 in (330 mm), span 3 ft 3 in (1 m); weight 1,543 lbs (701 kg); propulsion two-stage solid propellant; range 24+ miles (39+ km); guidance inertial cruise, active radar homing; warhead 220 lbs (100 kg) high explosive (Aérospatiale).

AM-39 lightweight version of AM-38 (air-launched version of MM-39).

AS 11 antitank missile (air-launched version of SS 11; designated AGM 22A in U.S. service) length 3 ft 11 in (1.2 m), diameter 6½ in (165 mm), span 1 ft 7 in (480 mm); weight 66 lbs (30 kg); propulsion two-stage solid propellant; range 9,800 ft (2,987 m); wire guidance; warhead high explosive (Aérospatiale).

AS 12 antitank and antiship missile (air-launched version of SS 12); length 6 ft 2 in (1.87 m), diameter 8 in (200 mm), span 2 ft 1⅓ in (633 m); weight 165 lbs (75 kg); propulsion two-stage solid propellant; range 5 miles (8 km); wire guidance; warhead 66 lbs (30 kg) high explosive (Aérospatiale).

Bullpup-A (AGM-12B) air-to-surface missile; length 10 ft 6 in (3.2 m), diameter 1 ft (305 mm), span 3 ft 4 in (1 m); weight 571 lbs (259 kg); propulsion storable liquid 12,000 lbst (5,448 kg static thrust); range 7 miles (11 km); guidance radio command; warhead 250 lbs (114 kg) high explosive; experimental only—fired from U.S. Marine Corps HUS-1 (Martin).

Hellfire antitank missile (Hellfire = Helicopter-Launched Fire-and-forget); weight approximately 90 lbs (41 kg); propulsion solid propellant; guidance laser and infrared; warhead high explosive; being developed for U.S. Army AH-64 (Rockwell International).

HOT antitank missile (HOT = Haut subsonique Optiquement Teleguide); length 4 ft 2½ in (1.28 m), diameter 5½ in (140 mm), span 12¼ in (310 mm); weight 46 lbs (21 kg); propulsion two-stage solid propellant; range 2½ miles (4 km); wire guidance with optical aiming and infrared tracking; warhead high-explosive (hollow charge) (Euromissile).

Marte antiship missile; (modified Sea Killer surface-to-surface missile); length 4 ft 3¼ in (1.29 m), diameter 8 in (203 mm); propulsion solid propellant; range 6 miles (10 km) as Mk1 or 12 miles (19 km) as Mk 2; guidance radio command or radar beam-riding; warhead 77 lbs (35 kg) Mk 1 or 154 lbs (70 kg) Mk 2 (Sistel).

Martel antiship missile; length AS 37 13 ft 9 in (4.2 m) or AJ 168 12 ft 9½ in (3.9 m), diameter 1 ft ¾ in (398 mm), span 3 ft 11¼ in (1.2 m); weight AS 37 1,210 lbs (549 kg) or AJ 168 1,150 lbs (522 kg); propulsion solid propellant; guidance AS 37 radar homing or AJ 168 television (optical) radio command; warhead 330 lbs (150 kg) high explosive (Hawker Siddeley Dynamics and Engins Matra).

Sagger antitank missile (Soviet designation PUR-64); length 2 ft 10 in (860 mm), diameter 4¾ in (120 mm), span 1 ft 6 in (455 mm); propulsion solid propellant; wire guidance; warhead high-explosive (USSR).

Sea Skua antiship missile; length 9 ft 3½ in (2.82 m), diameter 8 in (203 mm), span 1 ft 11½ in (595 mm); weight 540 lbs (245 kg); propulsion solid propellant; guidance semi-active radar homing; warhead 44 lbs (20 kg) high explosive (British Aircraft Corp.).

Sparrow (AIM-9F) air-to-surface missile (originally air-to-air missile); length 12 ft (3.66 m); diameter 8 in (203 mm), span 3 ft 4 in (102 mm); weight 440 lbs (200 kg); propulsion solid propellant; guidance semi-active radar homing; warhead high explosive; experimental only—fired from U.S. Navy UH-2 (Raytheon).

A U.S. Marine Corps HUS-1 helicopter fires a Bullpup air-to-surface missile during a 1960's evaluation of the feasibility of arming helicopters with such weapons. (U.S. Marine Corps)

Swatter antitank missile; length 3 ft 8 in (1.12 m), diameter 6 in (152 mm), span 2 ft 2 in (611 mm); propulsion solid propellant; wire guidance possibly with terminal homing; warhead high-explosive armor piercing (USSR).

TOW (BGM-71A) antitank missile (TOW = Tube-launched, Optically tracked, Wire-guided); length 3 ft 10 in (1.17 m), diameter 6 in (152 mm); weight 40 lbs (18 kg); propulsion two-stage solid propellant; range 1½ miles (2.4 km); wire guidance with line-of-sight automatic optical tracking; warhead high-explosive armor piercing (Hughes).

**Torpedoes**

Mk-44 antisubmarine torpedo; length 8 ft 6 in (2.6 m); diameter 12¾ in (324 mm); weight 514 lbs (233 kg); propulsion electric battery; guidance active-passive acoustic; warhead 88 lbs (40 kg) high explosive. Replaced in U.S. and British service with Mk-46.

Mk-46 antisubmarine torpedo; length 8 ft 6 in (2.6 m), diameter 12¾ in (324 mm); weight 586 lbs (266 kg); propulsion solid propellant; guidance active-passive acoustic; warhead high explosive.

Even aircraft as small as this Royal Navy Wasp, shown firing an AS-12 air-to-surface missile, have been fitted with antiship as well as antisubmarine weapons. In general, however, in missile strike operations these helicopters are more valuable for over-the-horizon targeting of enemy ships for ship-launched missiles. (Royal Navy)

A U.S. Navy UH-2C Seasprite is armed with Sparrow III missiles for evaluation during the 1960s. Neither the Bullpup nor Sparrow were carried operationally by helicopters. (U.S. Navy)

A Soviet Mi-8 Hip gunship carrying six 32-round pods for 57-mm rockets with rails for AT-2 Swatter antitank missiles. A 12.7-mm machine gun can be fitted in the nose. Other Hips have been seen carrying six antitank missiles. In this gunship role, the helicopters can carry troops.

# APPENDIX D

# Rotary-Wing Aircraft Serials

The British and U.S. military services assign sequential serial numbers to virtually all of their aircraft. Some British aircraft additionally have civil registration numbers (G series) while U.S. military-sponsored research aircraft that operate only in the United States may have only civil registration numbers (N series).

The current British military serial scheme began in 1916 with one letter initially and from 1940 on two letters plus up to three numbers. Thus, XD 798 was a Westland Whirlwind HAR 2. RAF and Royal Navy aircraft are numbered in the same series. A principal reference is *British Military Aircraft Serials* by Bruce Robertson.

The U.S. Army and (from 1947) U.S. Air Force have used a basic serial scheme that began in 1921 with a new series of numbers beginning each fiscal year with the prefix for that year. Accordingly, 51-2446 was a Bell H-13D, the 2,446th aircraft order in fiscal 1951. (When painted on the aircraft the serial would be given as 12246.) Most Army/Air Force series are listed in *United States Military Aircraft Since 1909* by F.G. Swanborough, and *United States Air Force Serials 1946 to 1977*, published by the Merseyside Aviation Society.

The U.S. Navy has assigned serial numbers to aircraft from 1914 onward, beginning with A51 and going to A9206 (including the XOP-1 autogiros). Subsequently, all-number serials were assigned. For example, serial 125528 was a Kaman HOK-1 (changed to OH-43D in 1962). These serials are referred to as bureau numbers for the Bureau of Aeronautics which controlled naval aircraft design and procurement from 1921 to 1959 (when changed to Bureau of Naval Weapons and, from 1966, the Naval Air Systems Command). A complete list of bureau numbers through 1970 is found in *United States Naval Aviation 1910-1970*, by Messrs. A.O. Van Wyen, Clarke Van Fleet, and Lee M. Pearson. Also see *United States Naval Aircraft Since 1911* by Gordon Swanborough and Peter M. Bowers, and *United States Navy Serials 1941-1976*, published by the Merseyside Aviation Society.

Helicopters from the U.S. Army's 101st Aviation Battalion fly past the Egyptian pyramids on the outskirts of Cairo during exercises of the U.S. Rapid Deployment Force in November 1980. Two OH–58 Kiowa scouts are followed by four UH–60 Black Hawk troop carriers and two AH–1S Cobra gunships. All were flown from the United States to Egypt in cargo aircraft. (U.S. Army)

A Super Frelon of the Chinese armed forces lands aboard an auxiliary ship during operations in the Western Pacific. The Chinese government has expressed considerable interest in replacing its Soviet-designed helicopter fleet with American and French machines, with 50 Aérospatiale Dauphin 2 helicopters reported to have been placed under contract in 1980. (*Ships of the World*)

# Index

*Military designations are indexed; commercial names and numbers are used only when no military designations were given.*